The theory of the kingdom

A unified model of human agency

Andrew Allen Root
Independent Researcher

Series in Philosophy of Religion

VERNON PRESS

www.vernonpress.com

In the Americas:
Vernon Press
1000 N West Street, Suite 1200
Wilmington, Delaware, 19801
United States

In the rest of the world:
Vernon Press
C/Sancti Espiritu 17,
Malaga, 29006
Spain

Series in Philosophy of Religion

Library of Congress Control Number: 2023946576

ISBN: 978-1-64889-757-3

Cover designed by Vernon Press. Logo designed for Oppositeville Holdings by David Fritch of Thinkable Solutions.

Table of contents

List of figures

Abstract

This original monograph presents a theory of the economy of the kingdom of God. The theory implies a model of human agency integrating known essentials of the real economy with the eternal kingdom economy. The kingdom economy is characterized by life, peace and growth. The model shows effective agents produce kingdom economy outputs by being salt and light, arresting corruption and revealing truth. Individual and organizational practices that arrest corruption and reveal truth can resolve longstanding real economy shortcomings. God is the owner in the model. God is holy, loving, sovereign and unlimited. The owner is the monopolist source of spiritual credence goods necessary for productive agency. The quantity of goods supplied is in proportion to an agent's relationship and offering of time and money. The owner relates to agents through an internally inscribed behavioral contract. The owner intervenes in the real economy by communication rather than by restricting individual freedom.

Practical implications of the model include: 1) Group bias may be resolved by the privileged surrendering oversight of disputed resources to a small group of mature aggrieved individuals. 2) Testing is required to promote agents to new levels of authority and productivity. Testing tends to benefit all stakeholders. 3) In the kingdom economy the primary method of lowering agency costs is bonding. Bonding means increased time spent in activities such as continuing education, apprenticeship and community building.

Introduction

This original monograph presents a new model of human agency in the context of the economy of God. Humankind does not yet observe the full benefits of the kingdom economy. Bad human behavior means suffering remains part of life in the real economy. Jesus did not ask God to take his followers out of the world. Rather, kingdom agents are to work to reduce suffering and increase life and peace. Kingdom agents are meant to preserve, and to illuminate truth. The theory of the kingdom accounts for the current overlap of the real economy and the kingdom economy. The study "draws upon the whole bible"[1] and is a bibliology "dependent on the work and insights"[2] of exegetical scholars and social scientists. The result is an inductive arrival at the theory of the kingdom.[3]

An owner-agency relationship is the setup of the eternal economy[4] described in the Christian bible. Similarly, agency theory motivates most economic and finance literature.[5] The bible vividly defines agency and displays it as the vehicle for meeting the kingdom of God's economic objectives. The study considers agency issues such as monitoring and bonding, testing, risk aversion, investment, equity, governance, information asymmetry, and owner communication.[6]

All political economies have an objective function. For example, the objective function of the central bank of the United States is maximum employment and stable prices. At a firm level, Edmans[7] envisions a social welfare objective function. Similar to economies with non-monetary objectives,[8] the kingdom economy is not intended to maximize tangible wealth. Rather the kingdom economy is designed to maximize peace, growth, and life.[9]

In the real economy, resources are limited and must be rationed. Rationing is accomplished by price or, time or force. An eternal, biblically defined economy has unlimited resources. Resource allocation is based on an exchange of intangible heart labor for credence goods.[10] This book advances a substantial but disconnected stream of literature. Practicing the King's Economy,[11] Capital and Ideology,[12] Doing Virtuous Business,[13] and Bulls, Bears & Golden Calves[14] each provide motivation for *The Theory of the Kingdom.*

The most common theoretical motivation for academic agency-oriented studies is a 1976 finance paper by Jensen & Meckling.[15] It is by no means the last word on agency nor the only viable motivating theory.[16] However, Jensen & Meckling have come to define agency theory for businesses. Owners of modern businesses use agents to manage day-to-day operations. Using agents enables a firm to grow very large and simultaneously maximize the value of the firm. The owner-agent setup is familiar to almost any employee or business owner.

Using agents has its problems. Agents are motivated by self-interest. Agents will stretch their expense accounts. Agents will extract private benefits with no benefit to the owner. Agents will trade on the owner's good name for their own benefit. For example, I may take a job thinking about how it will help me get a better job in the future. Agents are risk averse. Much of the net worth and prospects of an agent depends on the success of the owner's business. God is the owner in the theory of the kingdom. Despite the costs, he chooses to accomplish his economic mission with human agents. God makes this choice because of his love for humankind.[17] Love for each person is the owner's *why*. The owner engages me in the kingdom economy for my benefit.

This book is unique because it does not apply a biblical worldview to existing economic and finance theories. I present *The Theory of the Kingdom* as the true model of agency, based on an inductive study of the entire bible. I use prior literature of all types to test the model. Said another way, I assume the Bible is true and as such *The Theory of the Kingdom* should be testable with prior academic literature and human experience. In each chapter, I tend to follow an outline of considering the real economy, the kingdom economy and practical implications for living according to the model.

To make substantial progress with this study, readers should agree, at least temporarily, to assume two things: 1) God is the creator, and 2) His attributes are as defined in the Bible. In the Bible, the owner-agent construct is visible from the first book to the last. Businesses use contracts and incentives to maximize the benefits of using agents while minimizing costs. God is the ultimate owner of all things. God created people in his image to accomplish his will on earth. God chooses to work through people. God activates his agents through the indwelling Holy Spirit and the living sacrifice of a surrendered heart. God is committed to human agency. Agency applied to his own son. More than once, the Bible records Jesus saying he was on earth to do the will of the father and to fulfill all the required acts of righteousness.[18] Agents are to live today according to the example of Jesus.

The Bible is full of instructions on how I can operate to bring life into the real economy here and now. Finance and business literature is also full of insights and proof regarding biblical agency and its practical effect on economies, businesses, and people. My research shows agency is everywhere in almost every important biblical interaction. For example, the study shows how stories as unusual as God coming to kill an uncircumcised Moses are examples of agency.[19]

Real economy models begin with an assumption of scarce resources and diminishing marginal returns. Resources are land, labor (including entrepreneurship), and capital. Capital can be money, equipment, or other intangible items such as the value of a brand, intellectual property, or organizational capital. Resources are scarce in the real economy. Resources have to be rationed. Rationing may be done by price, by time, or by some violent means such as a mugging or war. The fact religious individuals make choices given the dual reality of real economy shortages and a future hope of unlimited resources led scholars Azzi & Ehrenberg to develop a two-period consumption model.[20] In the model, agents choose to save for eternity and defer consumption into the afterlife. Laurence Iannaccone has a different view.[21] Iannaccone assumes individuals maximize enjoyment in the present by trading secular consumption for temporal religious consumption. There is a large body of social science research providing evidence for a biblically defined model of human agency.

The model of human agency is also unique due to the biblical teaching of an owner with unlimited resources and unlimited time. Returns are measured based on the Christian doctrine of an already arrived, but not yet fully realized, kingdom economy. The real economy constructs of limited resources, efficient markets, and the negative effects of sin are still in force. At the same time, the messianic era began with the arrival of Jesus. This is a hopeful fact. Because of Jesus, I can live according to *The Theory of the Kingdom* now simply by a choice of my own free will.

This book is written to a cross-over audience. The book will be useful for teaching finance and business to graduate students at faith-based institutions. The book is also useful for business practitioners working to make money and deliver results while at the same time living for an eternal purpose. Readers will encounter a new integrated model of human agency. The model results in several new avenues for future research. At the end of chapters and sections, readers will find practical applications to be productive in both the real economy and the eternal kingdom economy.

The study has four purposes. First, the content is for teaching about God's plan of human agency. Second, the model results in several testable propositions for new research by academics, practitioners, and pastors. Third, I provide practical applications for living an eternally productive life. Finally, the most important reason to read this book is to live a peaceful, fulfilling, live-giving existence now. Communities around the world desperately need kingdom agents to arrest corruption, to preserve, to illuminate truth and to contribute to growth and peace.

Notes

[1] Erickson, M. J. (1998). *Christian theology* (p. 21) Baker Academic.
[2] Erickson, M. J. (1998). *Christian theology* (p. 23) Baker Academic.
[3] In seeking to address "what the whole bible says" about the dual realities of a tangible real economy and permanent kingdom economy this manuscript does address several elements of a systematic theology (Erickson, 1998)(Grudem, 2009). The manuscript addresses: a) Theology proper - placing God as the owner of all, b) Bibliology - a complete review of Genesis through Revelation, c) Christology - Christ as both owner and model agent, d) Pneumatology - the present messianic era can also called the age of the Holy Spirit, and the Holy Spirit is a source of heart capital. e) Eschatology - The model of human agency is relevant in the present day. The small circle of the real economy will ultimately give way to the large circle of kingdom economy. This study does not discuss in detail a doctrine of anthropology (i.e. humanity and the natural world). I do agree with a peer review suggesting anthropology is a vital area. Topics such as ESG (environmental, social governance) and DEI (diversity, equity and inclusion) require the full treatment of a separate future study. For example, economist Thomas Piketty has devoted two large volumes to the study of capital and economic equity (Piketty, T., 2014) (Piketty, T., 2020). Soteriology is also less of a focus in this manuscript as I am writing in part for business practitioners and the general welfare rather than only for those who are practicing Christ-followers. Finally, for this manuscript and the introduction of a new model of human agency, the remaining elements of a systematic theology, including the doctrine of the church and of angels, were deprioritized. It is my hope that a theologian would extend this study into the remaining gaps. Prior studies of the intersection of theology and the real economy have focused on narrower parts of scripture. For example Moxnes' focus is the gospel of Luke (Moxnes, 2004), Blomberg's book is oriented to Matthew (Blomberg, 2001) and Baugus' (2019) to the Mosaic law.
[4] Azzi, C., & Ehrenberg, R. (1975). Household allocation of time and church attendance. *Journal of political Economy, 83*(1), 27-56. http://dx.doi.org/10.1086/260305.
[5] Jensen, M. C., & Meckling, W. H. (2019). Theory of the firm: Managerial behavior, agency costs and ownership structure. In *Corporate Governance* (pp. 77-132). Gower.
[6] Levit, D. (2020). Words speak louder without actions. *The Journal of Finance, 75*(1), 91-131. http://dx.doi.org/10.1111/jofi.12834.
[7] Edmans, A. (2020). *Grow the Pie: How Great Companies Deliver Both Purpose and Profit–Updated and Revised.* Cambridge University Press. http://dx.doi.org/10.1017/9781108860093.
[8] Williams, C. C. (1996). The new barter economy: an appraisal of Local Exchange and Trading Systems (LETS). *Journal of Public Policy, 16*(1), 85-101. http://dx.doi.org/10.1017/S0143814X0000787X.
[9] New American Standard Bible, 1971, Isaiah 9:7. New American Standard Bible, 1971, John 10:10. New American Standard Bible, 1971, Romans 8:6.
[10] Iannaccone, L. R. (1998). Introduction to the Economics of Religion. *Journal of economic literature, 36*(3), 1465-1495.
[11] Rhodes, M., Holt, R., & Fikkert, B. (2018). *Practicing the King's Economy: Honoring Jesus in how We Work, Earn, Spend, Save, and Give.* Baker Books.
[12] Piketty, T. (2020). *Capital and ideology.* Harvard University Press. http://dx.doi.org/10.4159/9780674245075.

[13] Malloch, T. R. (2011). *Doing virtuous business: The remarkable success of spiritual enterprise.* Thomas Nelson.
[14] Stapleford, J. E. (2015). *Bulls, bears and golden calves: Applying Christian ethics in economics.* InterVarsity Press.
[15] Jensen, M. C., & Meckling, W. H. (2019). Theory of the firm: Managerial behavior, agency costs and ownership structure. In *Corporate Governance* (pp. 77-132). Gower.
[16] Agency theory according to Jensen & Meckling (1976) as motivation is for the purpose of developing a detailed point of social science comparison for the new Theory of the Kingdom. Jensen & Meckling (1976) remains a leading theory in academic literature even though there are several well-entrenched alternatives. Alternatives include the Upper Echelon theory (Hambrick & Mason, 1984), stakeholder theory (Freeman, 2010), and the behavioral finance stream (Barberis & Thaler, 2003). Within agency theory Jensen & Meckling is also not the last word. The research of sociologist Kathleen Eisenhardt (1989) is important to later chapters in this book. There are future research opportunities in evaluating the kingdom economy relative to multiple theories and multiple methods.
[17] New American Standard Bible, 1971, John 3:16.
[18] New American Standard Bible, 1971, John 6:38. New American Standard Bible, 1971. New American Standard Bible, 1971, Matthew 3:15.
[19] New American Standard Bible, 1971, Exodus 4:24-26.
[20] Azzi, C., & Ehrenberg, R. (1975). Household allocation of time and church attendance. *Journal of political Economy, 83*(1), 27-56. http://dx.doi.org/10.1086/260305.
[21] Iannaccone, L. R. (1984). *Consumption Capital and Habit Formation with an Application to Religious Participation* (Publication No. T29220) [Doctoral dissertation, The University of Chicago]. ProQuest Dissertations & Theses Global.

Chapter 1

Introduction to the model of human agency

This study begins with a picture of the complete model of human agency, shown in Figure 1.1. The model is for the end of suggesting specific personal actions. God achieves his economic objectives through the actions of human agents. Humankind was created to live in a growing, just, and sustainable economic and financial system. The economy of the kingdom of God will grow forever.[1] Jesus oversees and sustains it[2] and all humankind is on equal footing in it.[3] The real economy I experience now, on a day-to-day basis, is a shadow of the perfect system. The perfect agency-oriented system is visible in part now. I can choose to live according to the perfect system now.[4] The remainder of this chapter includes an overview of the key elements of the model, motivating Bible passages, and prior academic articles and books. Following chapter one I consider each element of the model in more detail, develop agency issues such as testing and risk-taking, and present evidence found in academic literature and case examples.

Service, generosity and love versus cycles of greed and fear

The term *Kingdom of God* has a different tone and connotation as compared to usual terms of art, such as the real economy or free markets. The different tone is important for this study. Success and advancement in the economy of God requires me to act differently relative to the norms of the real economy. How wealth is accumulated today can be similar at times,[5] but it is much more often the opposite. Greed and fear drive economic and stock market cycles. Economists George Akerlof and Robert Shiller use the term "Animal Spirits" to describe the emotional attributes of the real economy.[6]

Service, generosity, and love drive the economy of God. Money and monetary systems are at the center of the real economy and all types of markets. God is at the center of the kingdom economy. This study enables me to put on decoder glasses. It focuses my attention on what can only be seen with the spiritual eyes of my heart.[7] The model of human agency is real, it is in force, and it helps me to make life-giving economic choices now.[8]

The model of human agency is developed based on a Christian bibliology. The model is well supported by evidence from the real economy. The owner-agent construct is common in both the visible real economy and the invisible kingdom economy. Land, labor, and capital are resources in both economies. Productive uses of resources are often different, however. For example, the yielded strength of meekness, to prefer a coworker, or to give to a charity, may each simultaneously reduce real economy wealth and increase eternal economy wealth.

Real economy wealth is important today. However, money cannot be directly deposited into eternity. Money must be transformed into a lasting asset. Two ways to transform money into a permanent asset are by giving it away or by yielding a monetary right to another. In following the economic system of the kingdom of God, I decide whether to pursue financial returns now or to receive rewards later.[9] By heart intent, with each action I choose, returns now or rewards later. Each action has a single intent. My intention cannot simultaneously be for consumption in the real economy and rewards in the kingdom economy. The transmutation of wealth to eternity requires an agent to serve God and not money.[10]

Figure 1.1. Model of human agency.

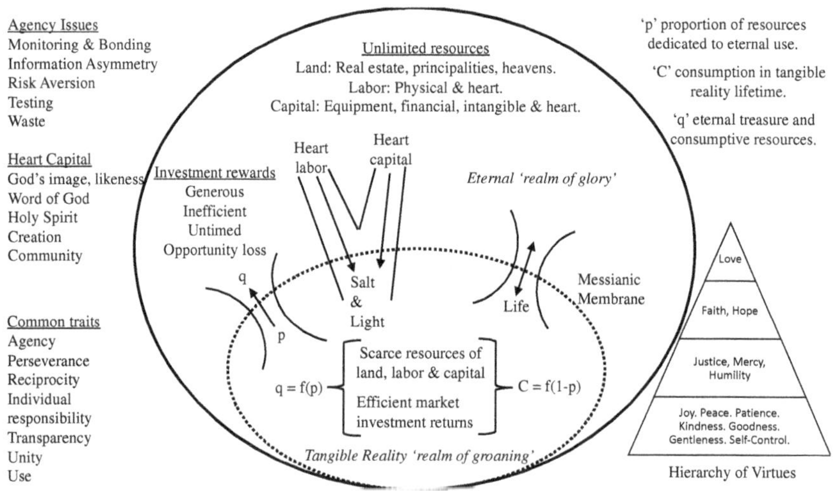

Figure 1.1 major message: The model of human agency is an integrated view of how to live in the small circle of the real economy while living for and producing the outputs of the large circle of the kingdom economy. The barrier between the visible real economy and the invisible kingdom economy is permeable and it is called the Messianic Membrane. Agency action works at the intersection of the two realms to bring kingdom economic resources into the real economy.

The small circle represents the real economy

The model of human agency is depicted as a small circle within a large circle. The small circle represents the real economy I live in now.[11] The economy of the Kingdom of God is the large circle. The large circle completely encompasses and rules over the small circle. The small circle present-day economy is characterized by scarce economic resources. Small circle markets vary in terms of efficiency and fairness. In the center of the small circle is a list of essential resources humankind uses to achieve socioeconomic objectives. Land, labor, and capital are required to produce goods and services. Resources are owned by individuals and households. Individuals and households exchange resources with businesses for income and rent. The circular flow of resources[12] is at the center of the real economy.

For example, consider the case of a small construction company. My friend Leroy runs a successful construction and remodeling firm. His firm is involved in a single specialized aspect of construction. For Leroy to generate a profit, he needs to own or rent a place to prepare his work. He needs a warehouse and a yard. Leroy needs land. Leroy needs a team to do the work as he directs. Leroy needs labor. Leroy needs capital in the form of equipment, money, experience, and know-how to deliver a product that makes his customers happy. Leroy needs financial capital and intangible intellectual capital. Individuals and households use their resources in the real economy to earn income, consume, and drive economic output and growth.

One difficulty with the small circle economy is there are not enough resources. Resources are scarce. Humankind has unlimited wants. Leroy will only have a team to work with inasmuch as he pays them well compared to other available jobs and compared to the cost of living. The resource scarcity problem is solved by rationing. Rationing is accomplished by price, time, or acts of violence. For example, if a public health crisis leads to a shortage of toilet paper, I may overcome the scarcity by one of several methods. I may pay more than normal for a roll of toilet paper. I may use less toilet paper per trip to the bathroom. I may choose to arrive early at a grocery store and stand in line to get in on the daily ration of toilet paper. I may also, and this is much less desirable, decide to threaten my neighbor and take their toilet paper. My ultimate choice could be to invest in an alternative to toilet paper. I may purchase a bidet, flushing the toilet paper problem altogether.

Rationing by price and time influences the allocation of financial capital in particular. In general, financial capital is allocated efficiently. The return I can reasonably expect to make is proportional to the risk I am willing to assume. Efficiency is sometimes confused with the human tendency towards manias and mispricing.[13,14] However, in general, the efficiency of financial markets works for both the owner of capital and the borrower of capital. As an owner, if I invest in a business, the return will be in proportion to my risk. If I borrow money, the interest rate will be in proportion to how risky I appear to the lender.[15] Consider the situation of borrowing money to buy a home. I borrow because I suffer from a current scarcity of cash. According to the circular flow model, this can be solved by exchanging my future cash flow for a lump sum of cash now from a bank. The bank has money for me to borrow because other individuals with savings have invested their money in the bank.

In the small circle, the terms of a home mortgage are based on a market for money and time, in the context of the riskiness of my credit. The first house I purchased was in Port Chester, New York. The price of the three-bedroom house was more than what I had in the bank. This scarcity was solved by signing a mortgage. I agreed to pay a U.S. bank more than I borrowed. I agreed to pay the bank equal amounts of money, each month for 30 years. Why do I even introduce something so banal as a home mortgage? Conflicts between borrowers and lenders are obvious to the human condition and resource scarcity in the small circle economy. I will later demonstrate the activities of borrowing, lending, interest, ownership, and market efficiency are all redeemed in the kingdom economy . God himself, as the loving owner of everything, puts himself in debt to me. The debt is owed based on simple, generous acts toward the poor.[16] The model of human agency shows the creator of the universe, with unlimited resources, makes each agent a generous and inefficient offer.

The basic real economy process of rationing occurs every day. Scarcity and rationing cause the general level of prices to rise (i.e., inflation). Scarcity causes men and women in less developed countries to stand in line for food, clean water, and medical care. Scarcity causes nations to go to war. Scarcity is exacerbated by greed, pride, and waste. Scarcity is not good. Indeed, scarcity is why the small circle economy is called the "realm of groaning".[17] Scarcity is a fact of life in the real economy. The Bible has much to say about how to invest and live in the real economy. I review the instructions and evidence later.

Individual offerings redeem scarcity to produce life

The good news is in the kingdom of God scarcity can be redeemed to produce life. Life is produced now by agents giving obedient, sacrificial, and generous offerings. Offerings can be very costly.[18] Yet the offering directly improves life in the small circle. Love and generosity influence areas of widespread concern, including economic fairness and environmental sustainability.

The scarce resources I control now can be redeemed by offering them back to God for his use. This can be conceptualized with the small circle variable called proportion. Proportion is represented by the small letter "*p*". Income I earn in the real economy can be consumed now, or it can be offered back to God for use in the kingdom economy. Proportion is defined as the ratio of resources I offer back to God, relative to my entire stock of resources. I naturally think of my resources in terms of money. Similarly, the most common specific type of proportion discussed in religious circles is the concept of the tithe.[19]

I may choose to obediently give 10% of my income to a local church.[20] Yet the model of human agency is not measured by a specific proportional offering of money. The terms of exchange in the kingdom of God are all-encompassing. I decide what proportion of all my land, labor, and capital to give to God in exchange for utility now and other eternal spiritual goods later. According to economist and religion scholar Laurence Iannaccone, spiritual goods are a type of credence good.[21] I will study credence goods in some detail in chapter 12, *The law of proportion.* Credence goods have qualities that make true value difficult to measure. Two examples of credence goods are car repair services and wine. The return on my proportional offering is based on the righteous judgment of God. The proportion concept was introduced in an article by scholars Corry Azzi & Ronald Ehrenberg.[22] Azzi & Ehrenberg model how people allocate their time based on an expectation of eternal life. Several of the notations in the small circle come from Azzi & Ehrenberg. Consumption today in the human agency model of Figure 1.1 is noted by an upper-case "*C*". Eternal consumption is noted by the lowercase "*q*". God has given me free will. It is up to me to choose how much of my present-day consumption to defer to the permanent economy. I choose my *q*. I decide each moment of each day how I will split consumption between the kingdom of God and the real economy. The ratio of my split is defined as my proportion. Increasing my proportion raises my ultimate eternal wealth and consumption. At each moment of each day, I choose which circle receives my resources. The agency investment objective of my life is to drive up my proportion as high as possible. When I look at my life through the law of proportion rather than through the law of supply and demand, a discussion regarding the right percentage of my income to give to my local church becomes less important.

Two-way resource transport across the permeable messianic membrane

The barrier between the small circle and the large circle is called the messianic membrane. In the biblical model, Jesus is the Messiah. The arrival of Jesus into the world was the moment a new model of economic interaction and resource exchange became possible. According to Burge, Cohick & Green,[23] the primary theme of Jesus' New Testament teaching is the arrival of the kingdom of God. The authors report about 80 separate sayings of Jesus regarding the kingdom of God. The kingdom of God has come to earth, and humankind now lives in an overlapping period of history where Jesus has already come, but both the real economy and the kingdom economy are each still in force. This is the essence of Christian eschatology. The two economies exchange resources across a permeable barrier.[24] The messianic membrane is also temporary. The membrane will eventually disintegrate and the kingdom economy will remain.[25]

The messianic membrane permits the transport of wealth into eternity and the acquisition of resources for use in the real economy now. I can use my agency authority to transport the resources of the kingdom of God across the membrane. The owner supports my use of resources to preserve, to arrest corruption, to sustain life and to illuminate truth. Wise agency actions produce peace, life, and growth. The membrane is also permeable in the direction of eternity. I can defer my current income and consumption. When I give away money, property or time as an act of worship to God I transport wealth into the permanent economy.[26] When I believe God, or when I labor for the life of another person in need, I receive credit in an eternal ledger.

An important innovation of the model of human agency is accounting for both economies and the concept of a permeable membrane across which I transport resources. The membrane permits the transport of spiritual virtue into the real economy. Agents are to be salt and light in the present day. The salt and light terminology was introduced by Jesus.[27] The obedient, virtuous human agent is salt and light, producing growth, peace, and life. It may also be present-day income and wealth are produced by virtuous action. It may be individuals coincidentally accumulate valuable territory, labor, or capital for use in the real economy. The fairly well-known miracle of Jesus turning water into wine at the marriage of Cana is an example of resource appropriation.[28] Wealth in the real economy is not the intent or main purpose of transport of resources across the messianic membrane. The purpose is growth, life, and peace. Chapter five develops this purpose in detail.

There is human suffering in the small circle. Addressing the problem of human pain[29] is not the goal of this book. For now, I simply state as a fact that suffering in all its forms comes from life in the small circle. Causes of human suffering include bad human behavior, scarce resources and a scarred environment. Jesus expressly came to enter into my suffering and give me the authority to receive comfort and give comfort by transporting resources across the messianic membrane. The permeable membrane permits the inter-economy flow of suffering for redemption.[30] Suffering is relevant for this book because the economy of God includes compensation for unjust suffering.[31] The permeable messianic membrane enables me to live according to the rules of the kingdom now, knowing that even my suffering is being accounted for by a fair owner.

The big circle is a benefit to all humankind

I define the economy of the kingdom of God according to Christian bibliology. Self-identifying Christ followers will recognize the governing principles of the big circle. If I am not a born-again Christian,[32] as Jesus described the status of His followers, I will still recognize many principles of the big circle, and benefit from its wisdom. All humankind benefits from the rules and values of the kingdom economy, whether or not it is acknowledged as real. Consider the actions of a refugee. Human refugees sometimes leave an oppressive home country for a better life. A person flees oppression for a new region whether or not they have legal status in the new region or even fully understand its laws. So it is with the economy of God and it benefits for all humankind.

The big circle in the model of human agency envelops and governs what happens in the small circle. The economy of today will eventually give way and be dissolved in favor of the eternal economy represented by the large circle.[33] For the time being, human agents work and produce in the real economy. It is a mandate of any born-again agent to invest in the real economy, producing life-giving economic products.[34] The more agents behave according to large circle principles the more humankind will experience its glory now.[35]

The large circle region of the model has a very different set of fundamentals. The first difference in economic fundamentals between the large and small circle regions is unlimited resources. All resources in the real economy were created. The mechanism of creation is not at all the subject of this book and it is not relevant given my starting assumption regarding the authority of scripture. Rather, I assume, based on the biblical record the earth and known universe were created by God through his son Jesus. God retains ownership rights and ultimate responsibility for maintenance and restoration.[36] The theological assumptions made to construct and defend the model of human agency are of the most basic sort. The innovation presented in the model is not one of depth regarding creation but rather of synthesis regarding economic interactions. Resources are unlimited in the big circle. An omnipotent, eternal God has an unlimited ability to create new resources as required. Common economic axioms that begin with an assumption of limited resources do not apply in the large circle.

Additional large circle resources of heart labor, heart capital and spiritual territory

The categories of economic resources in the large circle of the model of human agency are the same as in the small circle. The differences in the kingdom of God are additional dimensions to each resource and each type is unlimited. In addition to physical land, there is unseen territory. Human agents can acquire and use eternal real estate. Unseen real estate has a direct influence on life now.[37] The terminology used in the Bible for unseen realms includes principalities, heavens, heavenlies, the grave, and hell.

Labor in the big circle includes individual physical labor. However, the more important stock of labor is heart labor. This is not a surprise, as even in the real economy, intangible intellectual attributes are more highly valued than physical attributes. The economy of God grows primarily on the heart labor of individuals. When Jesus introduces his economy in the sermon on the mount he lists actions that are almost entirely heart-based. Humility, meekness, mourning, prayer, mercy, and peacemaking are entirely a function of the work I do in my heart.[38] Nowhere on the list is swinging a hammer as part of building a house, for example. Reading the Bible in the context of heart labor reveals an almost unending number of ways to work in the big circle. Some heart labor, such as peacemaking, sounds normal. Some of heart labors, such as dwelling together in unity, sounds more unusual. Some heart labor even sounds like hard labor. In this latter category, I put being thirsty for righteousness, patiently enduring unjust suffering and fasting.[39] My study of heart labor in later chapters includes considering the joint product nature of heart labor. Doing heart labor produces a direct benefit and also builds the capacity to do more heart labor in the future.

Capital in the real economy is physical, financial and intangible. Physical capital is equipment such as a farm tractor. Financial capital includes money that may be used to buy more equipment or to lend out to a borrower. Intangible capital includes investments in research, organizational know-how, and the consumer brands created by investments in marketing.

The most important type of capital in the kingdom economy is heart capital. A large stock of heart capital enables me to do and say what is right. A deficiency of good heart capital causes me to hurt others.[40] Heart capital is distributed to human agents without regard to ethnicity, gender, or age. Regardless of my abilities or relationships in the small circle of the real economy, I can acquire as much heart capital as I am willing to pursue. Some of the richest, most powerful, and most influential people in the kingdom economy have zero financial capital. The richest individuals in the large circle have a full stock of heart capital.[41]

Investment opportunity is plentiful, and rewards are generous

Returns in the large circle are completely different from the real economy. I assume unlimited resources in the eternal economy. It follows to ask *what is the owner's limit on payments for investment?* There is no limit to the resources and rewards an agent may receive. The large circle does not have a fixed bonus pool or limited money supply. Jesus was the model of human agency. Jesus received the heart capital of the Holy Spirit "without limit."[42] Jesus has given his own authority to agents to do the work of the kingdom.[43] The owner has already allocated to me all the heart capital and territory I will ever need to be productive in the large circle and in the small circle.[44]

The owner of the universe is fair and knows how to give good gifts.[45] The human agency model defines large circle returns as running over windfalls[46] and agents are encouraged to open their mouths wide for what may come to them.[47] I live in the real economy now and have real physical needs. Returns may be in the form of physical provision or financial capital now. However, the vast majority of large circle returns are in things agents truly crave. A short list includes peace of mind, repaired family relationships, a clear mind, hope for the future, and a rich eternal life.[48]

The returns in the large circle economy compare favorably against the real economy of today. Returns today are in some form of capital to be accumulated and then consumed now or else left behind when I die. Returns on lending, borrowing, and ownership are linked by risk-adjusted flows of financial capital in a resource-constrained reality. Thank God, in the permanent economy, returns look more like windfalls and gifts. Greedy investment manias don't blow up and ruin my future reward in the kingdom economy. Simple acts of kindness to another human in need are rewarded and securely held for all eternity.[49] For example, *The Theory of the Kingdom* says I can trade a bad loan to a poor person with bad credit for a risk-free return repaid by God himself.[50] The investment setup of the large circle is compelling.

I have an agency mandate. There are good works the owner has already prepared for me to do.[51] The translation of risk-adjusted returns from the present day into eternal windfalls happens by intentions and how I choose to live life. My day-to-day choices matter. In the model, there is a transformation of the variable p (my proportion), into q (my eternal treasure).

I can move my present-day capital into eternity. The model has conditions on the translation of wealth, however. If I choose to do good but advertise my good deeds for all to see I shouldn't expect any great reward.[52] For example, I may build a new community hospital. I may build the hospital to get my family's name on it and secure a public legacy of philanthropy. In that case, according to the model of human agency, it is unlikely much of the hospital investment will translate into eternity. However, if I build the hospital solely out of love for God and love for my neighbor, and I do my best to avoid any personal accolades for it, the investment will translate into future q. The objective is to increase the proportion of my resources offered back to God in love. I leave it solely in his hands to decide on the eternal benefits I will realize.[53] The wealth-building proposition of the model of human agency is uniquely attractive. The wealth-building proposition requires zero financial capital and it is open to everyone at all times.

A final feature of the windfall investment characteristic of the economy of God has to do with the concept of losses. In my investment account today, a large drop in the stock market can severely damage my real economy future. A period of high inflation can harm my expected consumption in retirement. Regardless of how carefully I have saved, a stock market crash, failure of a business or even being the victim of fraud can severely damage my real economy financial future. In the permanent economy, all past returns are safe.[54] Nothing will remove my credit for charitable acts or heart labors done on behalf of my neighbor. I may, of course, miss some opportunities to be generous. I may miss a chance to exhibit meekness with my own family. In that way, I experience opportunity loss. Further, interim accounting of returns is extremely difficult in the large circle. I may realize an actual real economy loss that the owner intends to make up in the future.[55] The overall return construct of the kingdom economy is biased to give me every opportunity to accumulate a lasting windfall.

Notes

[1] Isaiah 9:6-7.

[2] New American Standard Bible, 1971, Colossians 1:15-20. New American Standard Bible, 1971, Genesis 9:13-17. New American Standard Bible, 1971, Revelations 11:18.

[3] John 3:3. New American Standard Bible, 1971, 2 Peter 3:9. New American Standard Bible, 1971, Romans 3:10. Romans 3:23. New American Standard Bible, 1971, Isaiah 53:6.

[4] New American Standard Bible, 1971, John 17:14-23. New American Standard Bible, 1971, Galatians 5:16-25.

[5] Robertson, P., & Slosser, B. (1982). *The Secret Kingdom: A Promise of Hope and Freedom in a World of Turmoil.* T. Nelson.

[6] Akerlof, G. A., & Shiller, R. J. (2010). *Animal spirits: How human psychology drives the economy, and why it matters for global capitalism.* Princeton university press. http://dx.doi.org/10.2307/j.ctv36mk90z.

[7] New American Standard Bible, 1971, Matthew 13:9-16. New American Standard Bible, 1971, Ephesians 1:18. New American Standard Bible, 1971, 2 Corinthians 4:4.

[8] John 10:10. 2 Corinthians 4:18.

[9] New American Standard Bible, 1971, Matthew 6:19-21. Matthew 6:24. Matthew 6:33.

[10] Matthew 6:24.

[11] New American Standard Bible, 1971, Isaiah 40:22.

[12] Federal Reserve Bank of St. Louis. (2022, May 10). *Economic Lowdown Video Series* (Episode 6). The Federal Reserve, Federal Reserve Bank of St. Louis. https://www.stlouisfed.org/education/economic-lowdown-video-series/episode-6-circular-flow.
[13] Mackay, C. (2012). *Extraordinary popular delusions and the madness of crowds.* Simon and Schuster. http://dx.doi.org/10.1037/14716-000.
[14] My research as an academic and previously from a multi-decade career at global investment banks and hedge funds has cemented a personal bias in favor of market efficiency. It is true individuals are biased and self-interested. Individuals differentially value non-monetary benefits. Further, markets misprice assets all of the time. For example, I have observed the savings and loan crisis, ASEAN and Russian Ruble currency crises, the internet bubble, a global financial crisis, U.S. debt downgrade, COVID-19 pandemic and the regional banking crisis of 2023. It is easy to demonstrate market mispricing. Efficient markets do not mean the absence of regular asset mispricing. Rather, efficient markets mean the likelihood I will consistently identify mispricing in advance, and thereby earn an above risk adjusted return on the basis of that knowledge, is very close to zero. Market prices reflect the best current expectation of all known information, including the weighted average of irrational individual biases. Insiders may still earn abnormal returns (Augustin, Brenner & Subrahmanyam, 2019). However, there is scant evidence, using any number of multifactor models (multiple including Fama & French (2015), Carhart (1997), Hou, Xue & Zhang (2015)) that other forms of knowledge, rational or behavioral, earn abnormal returns.
[15] Friedman, M. (1975). *There's no such thing as a free lunch* (pp. 113-15). LaSalle, IL: Open Court.
[16] New American Standard Bible, 1971, Proverbs 19:7. New American Standard Bible, 1971, Matthew 10:42.
[17] New American Standard Bible, 1971, Ecclesiastes 1:8. Ecclesiastes 1:13. Ecclesiastes 1:15. New American Standard Bible, 1971, Ecclesiastes 2:11. New American Standard Bible, 1971, Ecclesiastes 5:10. New American Standard Bible, 1971, Ecclesiastes 6:7. Romans 8:19-23.
[18] New American Standard Bible, 1971, Matthew 19:21. New American Standard Bible, 1971, Luke 18:22. New American Standard Bible, 1971, Romans 12:1.
[19] New American Standard Bible, 1971, Genesis 14:17-24. New American Standard Bible, 1971, Malachi 3:10. New American Standard Bible, 1971, Hebrews 7. Romans 12:1.
[20] New American Standard Bible, 1971, Matthew 5:17 and New American Standard Bible, 1971, Mathew 22:40. New American Standard Bible, 1971, Matthew 17:1-3. New American Standard Bible, 1971, Malachi 3:8-12. The choice of giving 10% of income relates to Jesus' statements validating the law and the prophets. God validates the doctrinal link between Jesus and the law and prophets with the appearance of Moses (i.e. the law) and Elijah (i.e. the prophets) at the transfiguration. In the book immediately preceding Matthew, the Old Testament prophet Malachi declares a requirement to tithe and a reward for tithing.
[21] Iannaccone, L. R. (1998). Introduction to the Economics of Religion. *Journal of economic literature, 36*(3), 1465-1495.
[22] Azzi, C., & Ehrenberg, R. (1975). Household allocation of time and church attendance. *Journal of political Economy, 83*(1), 27-56. http://dx.doi.org/10.1086/260305.
[23] Burge, G. M., Cohick, L. H., & Green, G. L. (2010). *The New Testament in Antiquity: A Survey of the New Testament within Its Cultural Context.* Zondervan Academic.

[24] Isaiah 9:6. Isaiah 53. New American Standard Bible, 1971, Matthew 4:17. New American Standard Bible, 1971, New American Standard Bible, 1971, Matthew 16:13-20. New American Standard Bible, 1971, Matthew 27:51-54. New American Standard Bible, 1971, Mark 1:15. New American Standard Bible, 1971, Luke 17:20-21. New American Standard Bible, 1971, John 1:29-36. New American Standard Bible, 1971, John 14:6. Romans 8. Colossians 1:13. New American Standard Bible, 1971, Hebrews 4:14-16. New American Standard Bible, 1971, Hebrews 5:8-10.

[25] New American Standard Bible, 1971, Revelation 21:1-8. Revelation 21:22-27. Also see New American Standard Bible, 1971. New American Standard Bible, 1971, Daniel 2:44-45. New American Standard Bible, 1971, Daniel 7:26-28. New American Standard Bible, 1971, Zechariah 14:9. New American Standard Bible, 1971, Revelation 5:10. Revelation 11:15.

[26] Proverbs 19:7. Matthew 6:2. Matthew 6:6. Matthew 6:19-20. Matthew 12:41-44. New American Standard Bible, 1971, Mark 14:3. New American Standard Bible, 1971, Luke 21:1-4.

[27] Matthew 5:13-16.

[28] New American Standard Bible, 1971, John 2:1-12.

[29] Lewis, C. S. (2001). *The problem of pain.* Zondervan.

[30] Hebrews 4:14-16. New American Standard Bible, 1971, 1 Peter 3:18.

[31] New American Standard Bible, 1971, 1 Peter 2:19-25. 1 Peter 3:8-9. 1 Peter 3:14. New American Standard Bible, 1971, 1 Peter 4:12-19. New American Standard Bible, 1971, 1 Peter 5:1. 1 Peter 5:10.

[32] John 3:3-7.

[33] Revelation 21:4.

[34] New American Standard Bible, 1971, Genesis 1:26-28. New American Standard Bible, 1971, Genesis 9:1-10. New American Standard Bible, 1971, Luke 19:12-13. Matthew 5:13-16.

[35] New American Standard Bible, 1971, 1 Kings 10:4-9. Matthew 5:13-16.

[36] New American Standard Bible, 1971, Genesis 1:1. New American Standard Bible, 1971, Psalms 24:1-3. John 1:3. New American Standard Bible, 1971, Acts 3:21. Colossians 1:15-20.

[37] New American Standard Bible, 1971, Job 1:6-12. New American Standard Bible, 1971, Daniel 10:12-13. New American Standard Bible, 1971, Acts 1:9-12. New American Standard Bible, 1971, Ephesians 6:12. New American Standard Bible, 1971, 1 Peter 3:19. New American Standard Bible, 1971, Book of Revelation.

[38] New American Standard Bible, 1971, Matthew chapters 5, 6 and 7.

[39] New American Standard Bible, 1971, Isaiah 58. Matthew 6:16-18. 1 Peter 4:12-19.

[40] New American Standard Bible, 1971, Luke 6:45.

[41] New American Standard Bible, 1971, Luke 2:36-39. Luke 21:1-4. Acts 3:6.

[42] John 3:34.

[43] Matthew 18:18. New American Standard Bible, 1971, Matthew 28:18-20. John 14:12. New American Standard Bible, 1971, 2 Peter 1:3.

[44] Ephesians chapter 1. In this instance I focus on Ephesians 1:3 which reads "Blessed be the God and Father of our Lord Jesus Christ, who has blessed us with every spiritual blessing in the heavenly places in Christ."

[45] New American Standard Bible, 1971, Matthew 7:11. New American Standard Bible, 1971, Luke 11:13. New American Standard Bible, 1971, Psalm 89:14. Isaiah 9:7. New American Standard Bible, 1971, Acts 17:31. New American Standard Bible, 1971, 1 Peter 1:17.

[46] Luke 6:38. Luke 18:28-30.
[47] New American Standard Bible, 1971, Psalm 81:10.
[48] New American Standard Bible, 1971, Jeremiah 29:11. New American Standard Bible, 1971, Malachi 4:6. New American Standard Bible, 1971, Luke 15:11-32. Romans 12:2. New American Standard Bible, 1971, Romans 15:13. Galatians 5:22-23. New American Standard Bible, 1971, Ephesians 4:23. New American Standard Bible, 1971, Philippians 4:7. Luke 18:18-30.
[49] Matthew 10:42. New American Standard Bible, 1971, Mark 9:41.
[50] Proverbs 19:7.
[51] Ephesians 2:10.
[52] Matthew 6:1-8.
[53] Psalm 89:14. Matthew 7:11. Luke 11:13. 1 Peter 1:17. New American Standard Bible, 1971, Revelation 20:11-13.
[54] Matthew 6:19-21.
[55] New American Standard Bible, 1971, Joel 2:25.

Chapter 2

Human agency

Agency is a term describing the relationship between an owner and a person to whom the owner delegates authority. Agency relationships are created by the separation of ownership and control. In this chapter, I will begin with a brief overview of the real economy agency. I then discuss the biblical agency narrative. The many benefits of agency include scale and mutual enjoyment of success. The costs of agency are significant. Motivated by love, God, as owner of all, had a detailed plan to deal with the costs of agency. Included in the analysis of kingdom agency is a section on the unique nature of the owner. God is holy, loving, sovereign and unlimited. He is not like any real economy shareholder. I conclude the chapter by analyzing the implications of serving this particular owner and the pervasiveness of agency in the Christian bible.

Real economy agency

Agency drives growth in real economy organizations. Businesses separate ownership and control to grow and maximize risk-adjusted returns. The key paper in corporate finance is the *Theory of the Firm* by Jensen & Meckling.[1] The study defines agency theory. The paper has motivated tens of thousands of finance and management studies. By many measures, the article is one of the most cited of all time for any academic discipline and perhaps the most cited in academic business literature. Consider by comparison data from the London School of Economics Impact blog indicating that 32% of social science articles have zero citations.[2]

An article of similar stature to the *Theory of the firm* on a different topic of the efficiency of financial markets was written by Eugene Fama and published in the Journal of Finance (1970).[3] Fama's *Efficient Capital Markets* has been cited at less than half the rate of *Theory of the Firm*, and yet was still an important reason for Fama being awarded a share of a Nobel Prize in Economics (2013). Before Jensen & Meckling, in 1937, Ronald Coase published the *Nature of the firm*.[4] Coase's article published in Economica has been well cited at about half the rate of the Theory of the Firm. Four decades on the *Theory of the firm* remained the most downloaded article from the Journal of Financial Economics ("JFE").

In modern businesses, the flow of delegated authority is from owners to agents. Agents manage day-to-day operations. Owners benefit from the scale and value created by correct manager decisions. Owners suffer losses from poor investments and manager misbehavior. Agents realize monetary and non-monetary benefits from the terms of their employment. Agents voluntarily give up some personal freedom and privacy to fulfill the terms of their employment. Overall, using agents enables owners to grow a large firm, maximize the value of the firm, and diversify investments across many firms.

Agents are risk averse. In biblical parlance, it would be said agents are fearful. Risk aversion of agents causes or amplifies the costs of separating ownership and control. Agents are afraid of losing their jobs, their status, wealth and future prospects. Agents will at times, avoid risky but value-creating investments in favor of stability and safety.

The separation of ownership and control results in costs not incurred by owner-managed organizations. The costs of using agents include monitoring, testing, and waste. Waste includes excess expenses and self-serving investments that benefit the manager but not the owner. It is obvious agents benefit at the expense of owners from an upgrade to a business class flight, from the purchase of a favored brand of coffee in the break room, or an extra-long paid lunch break. Agency waste can be egregious. The former CEO of U.S. company General Electric was discovered to have taken two private jets on business trips.[5] The CEO flew in one jet. The other jet flew empty and came along as a backup.

Agents run the day-to-day operations of large modern organizations

Owners of the largest modern corporations are called shareholders. Shareholders do not generally run the day-to-day operations of the businesses they own. Shareholders elect a board of directors. The board of directors appoints a Chief Executive Officer ("CEO"). Daily management of the business is delegated to the CEO. The CEO subsequently delegates responsibility to a larger group of managers and workers. Agency enables organizations to grow very large. In the real economy agency relationships are governed by a combination of employment contracts, laws, and social customs. Large modern businesses are a nexus of written and implied contracts.

CEOs of modern businesses may avoid the risk of taking a good investment. On the other hand, a CEO may intentionally make a bad investment because it suits a selfish purpose. A CEO may even buy another firm to increase compensation and entrench her position, regardless of the value implications for the owner.[6] Despite the clear and predictable misbehavior of individual agents, agency models maximize the value and scale of organizations. Owners use agents because of the net benefits of size, diversity of investments, and increased total wealth potential. The framework of agency theory will be used throughout the book to analyze and test the components of *The Theory of the Kingdom.*

Biblical agency

The meta-narrative of Christian theology is unique among world religions and it can be stated simply. God created the heavens and the earth.[7] God gave humankind the mandate to relate to one another and the environment in such a way as to be fruitful and multiply,[8] filling the earth with life. Unfortunately, humans violated the terms of agency and surrendered their delegated authority to Satan.[9] The human and environmental toll of misbehavior is significant. God foresaw this agency problem. At just the right time, God sent his son Jesus as a human agent to die in my place and take back authority over all creation.[10] Jesus' obedience was perfect and he successfully instituted the present epoch.[11]

Figure 2.1. Meta narrative of the creation, fall and redemption of humankind and the earth.

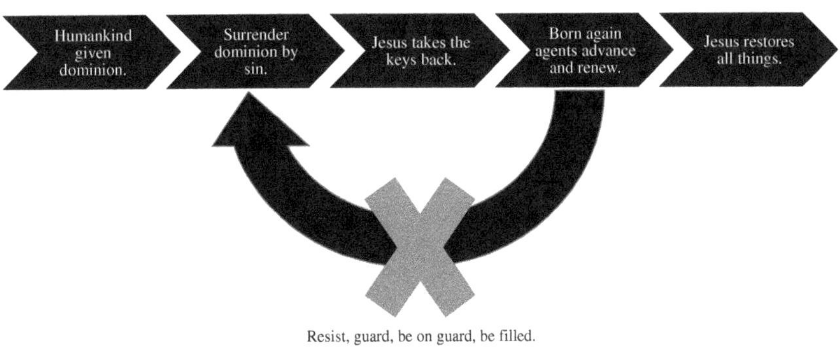

Figure 2.1 major message: The meta-narrative of the biblical account is all people are created in the image and likeness of God. However, humankind surrendered its agency authority over the earth due to sin. Jesus came to earth to redeem all people from sin, in a plan conceived before the world was made. Each person now has a choice to follow Jesus or to follow their own will. Those that choose Jesus participate in the present-day advance of the kingdom economy on earth. Ultimately, Jesus will return to make all things new. Humans retain their agency authority and identity by heart labor that holds territory and preserves and builds heart capital.

Jesus' motivation was love and the joy of offering each person the chance to be born again and to become partners in building the kingdom economy now and in the age to come.[12] In terms of the age to come, at some point in the future, Jesus will return to earth. Jesus' return will mark the end of the messianic age and the overlapping real economy.[13] At the point of Jesus' return, the model of human agency becomes less relevant, though my actions now will influence assignments in the future age. The small circle real economy will dissolve and only the kingdom of God will remain. This is the Christian meta-narrative of history. A picture of the meta-narrative is given in Figure 2.1. The practical connection is in the same way I might choose to work for a great company and obtain the benefits of employment, anyone can choose to call on the name of Jesus now and thereby take up the opportunity to participate in the kingdom economy, according to the terms of the model of human agency.

The theory of the kingdom is based on the agency set up defined at the beginning of human history and the present location in history as shown in Figure 2.2. God is the owner.[14] God designed a kingdom that would grow based on the activity of human agents. To be an agent is to act. I generally cannot physically see or hear God, Jesus, or the Holy Spirit. Kingdom agency action therefore requires faith. The most common source of kingdom agent faith is *hearing* instructions of the owner in the Bible and obeying its principles.[15]

Figure 2.2. Representation of Christian eschatology.

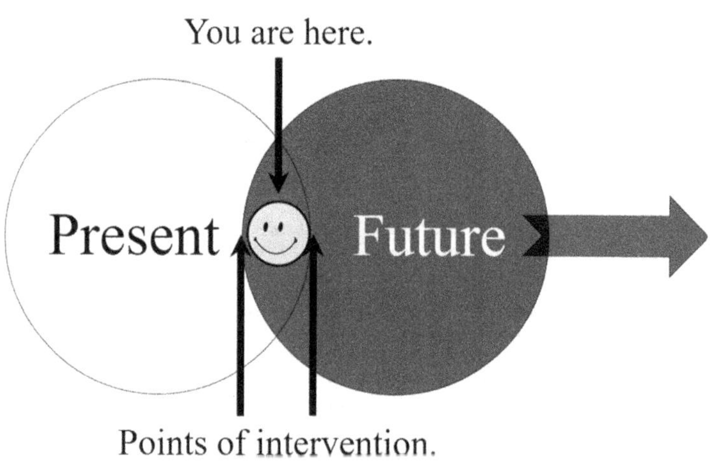

Figure 2.2 major message: The current era of human history began with the arrival of Jesus on earth. It is an overlapping period of the real economy and the kingdom economy. The model of human agency accounts for both economies, still in effect.

The owner-agent construct is recorded in the first book of the Bible, Genesis, as well as one of the oldest books, Job. God refers to Job as his faithful servant.[16] The owner-manager relationships described with Hebrew, Greek, and Aramaic words written down between 1200 BC and 100 AD are different from present-day English. However, the meaning of the terms for owners or agents is the same. The supreme owner in the owner-agent construct of the model of human agency is God. In the Old Testament, God chose his name, YHWH. It is pronounced Yah-Way and means Lord. YHWH appears 6828 times in the Old Testament and refers only to God.[17] The New Testament equivalent is the Greek noun *pantokrator* which may be translated as almighty or ruler of all.[18] YHWH is the ultimate owner in the model. There are other types of owners in the Bible. Property owners are used by Jesus to teach about the kingdom economy.[19] Vine's identifies principals and owners using terms translated into English as lord, owner, and master.

Moving down a level, the Bible records the activities of senior agents. The Hebrew word *Sar* is one such senior agent noun. Strong's concordance defines senior agent terms such as commander, captain, prince, or leader. Many CEOs and senior executives of modern corporations would likely think of themselves in such terms. Sar is used 420 times in the Old Testament. In the New Testament, three terms I may recognize for agent include the servants of the parable of the talents, disciples, and ambassadors.[20]

Joint-Heir Organizations

Unique in Christian theology and the model of human agency is a promise of friendship and partnership. Messianic era agency is influenced by Jesus' declaration I am not only a worker bee, rather I am a friend, informed about all the fundamentals of the kingdom economy.[21] The owner is willing to share the inner workings of the kingdom with me. I may not have the capacity for understanding it all, but it is available.[22] I am also a fully vested joint heir. Paul's statement in Romans indicates the agency engagement is inclusive.[23] The first part of the inheritance is a deposit of the Holy Spirit in my heart now. Inheritance connotes eternal riches. It can also mean my share in the owner himself. In either case, it is a unique element of the kingdom model that I am an immediate co-heir with Jesus. I will return to this point in the chapter on heart capital.

A joint-heir organization is well suited to God's purposes. It is well known that joint-ownership corporate structures, such as partnerships are critical to maintaining organizational integrity.[24] The more complete the separation of ownership and control, the less successful organizations are at maintaining a virtuous culture. The kingdom economy is unique. It is an inclusive organization of fully vested partners and friends working toward the ends of life and peace on the earth now.

Characteristics of the owner

God is a unique owner. To be a productive agent, I must consider relevant aspects of the owner's character. For brevity, I confine my analysis to a list of four characteristics. I trust the mode of analysis will spur additional research as each attribute of God's character bears upon the actions of his agents. For now, I consider the implications of the fact the owner of the kingdom realm is holy, loving, sovereign, and unlimited.

The owner is holy

The owner is holy. God gives a seemingly impossible command to "be holy because I am holy."[25] Holy is a noun, not an adjective. To be holy is to be sacred, eminent, blameless, or saintly. Holy is what the owner is. I find it helpful to understand what holy means by comparing it to opposites such as profane or common. In the opening of Luke's gospel, it is said God's name is holy.[26] Jesus, explaining how to approach God in prayer, instructs me to call God both father and holy.[27] John's revelation vision records the creatures closest to God in heaven, the ones seeing him most clearly, as crying out God is Holy, continuously. Theologian R.C. Sproul indicates understanding the implications of God's holiness must be at the very foundation of my objectives.[28]

I can think of at least three ways the owner's holiness should influence my real economy behavior. First, God's holiness engenders in me a healthy fear. I hope the fear is enough to overcome a fear of people that may otherwise so easily keep me from doing right. Second, since the owner is holy, I take my agency responsibilities most seriously. I will seek to perform excellently. I will try to seize on the thing for which God has made me his agent,[29] delivering uncommonly good results. Third, I will avoid the profane and wasteful activities that commonly consume people in large organizations. In modern business, owners bear the cost of employees wasting time or using company resources for personal gain. God is holy. I fear succumbing to the temptation to trade on the name of YHWH for my personal gain.

The owner is loving

The owner is loving. The Bible's claim of God's loving character is well known. The gospel of John and the letter 1 John contain well-known sentences indicating the love of God for humanity. John 3:16 says, "For God so loved the world he gave his only son". 1 John 4:8 says, "But anyone who does not love does not know God, for God is love".

In the context of agency, I think of God's love when doing chores with my children. When the children were young, I might engage them in washing the car, doing dishes, or changing light bulbs. Engaging with my junior agents resulted in a longer and less efficient process. I engaged the children in part for their benefit. To become healthy adults, children need to learn certain skills. The engagement, however was truly more for my benefit. I love my children. I loved having them with me. Their presence at my side brought me joy. It is the same with the kingdom economy. God doesn't need me to perform. He has no needs and requires no particular human effort.[30] He engages me in his organization because he loves me and wants me with him. Awareness of God's love gives me the freedom to engage in my kingdom economy work with the enthusiasm of a young child.

Professor D.A. Carson analyzes the 1 John 4:8 passage in detail.[31] The analysis of God as love and then Jesus' healing of a cripple on the Sabbath provides insight into the model of human agency. John chapter five records the healing of a paralytic at the pool of Bethesda in Jerusalem. Jesus' violation of the sabbath resulted in a charge by religious officials; he was breaking the law requiring all Jews to rest on the sabbath. Jesus replied by indicating he was only doing what his father taught him to do.[32] Further, Jesus indicated God shows the son all he is doing.

Carson beautifully describes the flow of logic relevant to work in the context of a model of agency. At this point in the history of John's writing, the vast majority of Jewish sons were trained in their father's vocation. It was a cultural assumption the son would follow in the father's business. God showed Jesus, his obedient son, who became a human agent for God's redemptive purpose, everything he was doing because he loved Jesus. The practical effect on my life is God loves me and I am therefore confident the Holy Spirit will show me what to do in my day-to-day work.

God is sovereign

God is sovereign. The unqualified sovereignty of the owner is unique to the model of human agency. Owners of modern businesses contract with agents according to laws and customs. First, thankfully, owners in most democratic countries are required to relate to their managers and laborers without regard to ethnicity or gender. Second, ownership transfer is governed by laws. The movement of fully owned assets across borders is often restricted by international treaties and trade agreements. In contrast, the owner of all, YHWH, has complete sovereignty. God is bound by his word and character[33] and he does not lie.[34] Yet, there are no external controls dictating terms of governance back to God.

In the oldest book of the Bible, God makes a clear statement of his sovereignty to Job. In chapter one, the Bible says Job suffered tremendous personal and financial loss. In the subsequent chapters, Job and his friends extensively, and almost entirely incorrectly, analyze the potential reasons for Job's sufferings. Toward the end of the book, in a withering criticism of Job's complaint, God asks a series of rhetorical questions regarding who is the designer, builder, and owner of all the heavens and the earth. God makes clear he is sovereign over everything in the universe.[35]

Job starts and ends his period of suffering in essentially the same place. Job starts by saying, "The Lord gave and the Lord has taken away. Blessed be the name of the Lord."[36] At the end of the book, in a series of confessional statements, Job affirms God is all-powerful and that his objectives will all be accomplished. The intimacy of encountering God in that way leads Job to repent of all his prior inaccurate conceptions of God and to accept God's purposes.[37]

In the new testament, defining the present messianic era, Jesus' words and actions make clear he, the son of God and messiah, is sovereign over all. Through the course of the four biblical gospels, Jesus' words and deeds demonstrate he is Lord over the weather, over food, over death, over all spiritual forces, and even Lord over the law of God, including the sabbath. Jesus is sovereign. Blomberg notes, for example, Matthew's account of Jesus' easter week entry into Jerusalem signifies he is Lord over even untamed animals and property. Jesus has a call option on all my resources at all times.[38] Generally, Jesus exercises his option according to my personal choice to yield and obey.

Productive kingdom agency requires humility

The sovereignty of the owner is an important point of emphasis for agents and brings into relief the fine balance of divine sovereignty and agent responsibility. The personal virtue that unlocks the power of God's sovereignty in my life is humility. According to Andrew Murray, humility is the key link to my own "journey toward holiness."[39] As I can observe with Job, full submission to the sovereignty of God is the correct posture for agents in the kingdom economy.

King David of Israel demonstrated humble submission when he was threatened by his son Absalom and forced to flee Jerusalem.[40] The scene of David's departure is compelling. David is leaving a powerful position under duress. He is forced out of his job and his home. David marches into exile. The Bible indicates David walked along barefoot, weeping, with his head covered. David did not try to rally a group of loyalists to mount a defense and maintain his position. David simply indicates it is up to God alone whether he will be restored to his position and return home to Jerusalem. "Let him (God) do to me as seems good to him."[41] David is an example of humility and submission to God's sovereignty in the face of humiliation. There are, of course, situations and circumstances for me to stand, compete and fight. However, there are situations where, in humility, I consciously rededicate every part of my future hope to the sovereign owner.

The owner is unlimited

The owner in the kingdom economy is unlimited. In the real economy, owners are limited, and therefore, investment resources are limited. Businesses must choose between investment projects. The mechanism of choosing is called capital budgeting. Businesses don't have enough cash flow to invest in every potential growth project. The selection of investment projects and allocation of money to a list of projects is called a capital budget.

Good managers use capital budgeting to make value-creating investments. Good managers deliver growth and value to their owners. Bad managers lose money. Bad managers eventually lose their jobs. The key to the model of human agency is to consider the difference an unlimited owner makes. God's resources are unlimited. He can invest in any and all projects. The return I deliver in the kingdom economy is important, but it isn't critical to the survival of God's organization. God can make up for my bad agency choices and apparent losses. In later chapters on economic resources and investing, I will have more to say about the unlimited nature of the owner. For now, I submit the character of God, including his unlimited nature and his love, gives me a sense of freedom and moves me to risk-taking action.

Agents are moved to timely action

Faith, hope, and love are the enduring virtues of Christian theology.[42] I have briefly discussed love in the context of God's character and working as an agent. The love of God for humankind is a key to answering the *why* question of the model of human agency. Faith is central to Christian theology and a key to understanding the relationship between God and humankind.[43] *Pistis*, the Greek term for faith, means belief. However, it has dimensions beyond intellectual conviction. Christian faith is faith in God for the salvation of humankind through the work of Jesus on the cross. Christian *pistis* was also seen during the era of the Roman empire to be at the intersection of "cognition, emotion, action, and relationship."[44] Evidence of my faith is not just my intellectual belief, it is action. My actions must evidence my faith.[45]

The model of human agency is only effective inasmuch as agents are active. I must take initiative to do what I feel inspired or directed to do. I find a large part of my actions on any given day are motivated by common Christian virtues. Most often, I am to be the salt and light of the beatitudes[46] by acting daily on my faith in very small ways. The bigger purpose of what I do is based on what I perceive the Holy Spirit has directed me to do as a vocation. As billions of Christ-followers act on what they feel directed to do, Jesus builds his kingdom on earth.

Tim Keller of Redeemer church in New York City previously taught on discerning agency calling. Keller noted in his pastoral experience, each person sees the needs of the same situation differently. Agents do well when they take note of the needs of people they "resonate" with.[47] For example, at a rural Virginia church where Keller once pastored, three individuals saw the same neighboring community rather differently. One saw a need for evangelism. One saw a need for a food pantry. The third church member saw a church in need of administrative restructuring before attempting to evangelize or feed anyone. The model of human agency would say yes to each of the three people. Act to meet the need you resonate with. I activate the model of human agency by acting quickly to fill the needs I resonate with. The integration of individual agency actions for a larger purpose is up to God. In my real economy experience, it is easy to guide an over-active employee and near impossible to motivate an under-active employee. Effective agents are active.

Actions are undertaken with urgency. Biblical imagery and stories indicate agents are to act without undue delay. Imagery includes running a race,[48] running at times like frightened prey, avoiding excessive sleep,[49] always being ready to answer questions,[50] or even being ready for the end of the Messianic age itself.[51] In more concrete and practical terms, the book of Acts chapter six records a report of the inequitable distribution of food between ethnic groups within the growing Christian church. Acts chapter six does not indicate they studied the accuracy of the complaints. Church leaders simply acted to resolve the problem.

The active posture of agents contrasts somewhat with a need for patience, particularly as it relates to speaking.[52] Patience is a fruit of the spirit[53] and I am admonished to be slow to speak. Perhaps the meaning is kingdom agents are intended to be more doers than speakers. The Franciscan tradition would say I should preach by my example, with a further admonishment that a "worldly spirit loves to talk a lot but do nothing."[54] A worldly spirit is a person living for the real economy rather than for the kingdom economy.

Of the three enduring Christian virtues, faith, hope, and love, hope has stood out to me as less relevant to the theory of the kingdom. I would rather have success than hope. My feeling is opposed by the fact of Jeremiah's prophecy, where God promises his people hope and a future.[55] I don't present success only. I also need hope for future success.

Dr. Charles Richard Snyder was a pioneer in the field of positive psychology. He wrote extensively on the topics of hope and forgiveness. He developed valid scales to measure hope and wrote several papers relevant to this study. Snyder defines hope as "the perceived capability to derive pathways to desired goals and motivate oneself via *agency thinking* [emphasis added] to use those pathways."[56] All people experience success and failure. When a hopeful person experiences failure or hits a roadblock, they are more likely to find an alternative path to success. Hope is an action-oriented agency process. The more hope I have, the more active and resilient I will be. Snyder has shown the wisdom of Jeremiah's prophecy. I need both hope and a future. I am more hopeful about my future, knowing God has promised both.

Agency is pervasive

Agency is the dominant organizational mode for real economy organizations, particularly large organizations with dispersed ownership. Agency is dominant in the biblical model as well. Biblical examples of human agency include: a) instructions to Ezekiel in the valley of dry bones,[57] b) a priestly blessing in Numbers chapter six, c) the effectiveness of the words of the prophet Samuel[58] and d) the ministry of Jesus.[59] A complete accounting of human agency in the Bible could take up an entire book on its own. For now, I review one example of biblical agency, because it sounds like a modern business meeting.

The example comes from the Book of Numbers, chapter six. To churchgoers, it may be a familiar benediction, hymn, or even a bedtime prayer over a child. It is the first line and third line of the passage that is pertinent to agency. The passage in the New Living Translation reads:[60]

> Line 1: The Lord said to Moses, tell Aaron and his sons to bless the people of Israel with this special blessing:
>
> Line 2: May the Lord bless you and protect you. May the Lord smile on you and be gracious to you. May the Lord show you his favor and give you his peace.
>
> Line 3: Whenever Aaron and his sons bless the people of Israel in my name, I myself will bless them.

This is an agency-oriented instruction. God, the owner, could have blessed each person directly. Alternatively, God could have instructed Moses to bless the people. Moses was the head of the human organization. Instead, God used his preferred economic model and engaged several levels of agents to achieve his socioeconomic objectives. I paraphrase the passage in modern business terms:

> God, the sole shareholder, said to Moses, his CEO, "tell your Senior Vice President of Operations, Aaron, and his senior managers to offer all employees the following benefits:
>
> The protection of the owner.
> The favor of the owner.
> The approval of the owner.
> The peace of the owner.
>
> When the senior vice president of operations and his senior managers do this, I will fully support them. I will stand behind their offer and provide the promised resources and benefits to all the employees."

The kingdom economy runs based on human agency.

Notes

[1] Jensen, M. C., & Meckling, W. H. (1976). Theory of the Firm: Managerial Behavior, Agency Costs and Ownership Structure. *Journal of Financial Economics, 3*(4), 305-360. http://dx.doi.org/10.1016/0304-405X(76)90026-X.

[2] Remler, Dahlia (2014, April 14). Are 90% of academic papers really never cited? Reviewing the literature on academic citations. *The London School of Economics and Political Science*. https://blogs.lse.ac.uk/impactofsocialsciences/2014/04/23/academic-papers-citation-rates-remler/.

[3] Fama, E. F. (1970). Efficient capital markets: A review of theory and empirical work. *The journal of Finance, 25*(2), 383-417. http://dx.doi.org/10.2307/2325486.

[4] Coase, R. H. (1937). The nature of the firm. *Economica, 4*(16), 386-405. http://dx.doi.org/10.1111/j.1468-0335.1937.tb00002.x.

[5] Gryta, T., Lublin, J. S. & Maremont, M. (2017, October 29). GE Board Kept in the Dark About CEO's Extra Plane. *The Wall Street Journal*. https://www.wsj.com/articles/ge-board-was-kept-in-the-dark-about-ceos-extra-plane-1509274805.

[6] Bertrand, M., & Mullainathan, S. (2003). Enjoying the quiet life? Corporate governance and managerial preferences. *Journal of political Economy, 111*(5), 1043-1075. http://dx.doi.org/10.1086/376950.

[7] Genesis 1:1.

[8] Genesis 1:28. Genesis 9:7.

[9] New American Standard Bible, 1971, Genesis 3:6. Romans 3:23.

[10] Romans 5:6-8.

[11] New American Standard Bible, 1971, Hebrews 2:5-9.

[12] New American Standard Bible, 1971, Hebrews 12:2. Romans 8:17.

[13] New American Standard Bible, 1971, Matthew chapter 24. New American Standard Bible, 1971, Hebrews 9:28. New American Standard Bible, 1971, Revelation 1:7. Revelation 21:5.
[14] New American Standard Bible, 1971, 1 Samuel 2:12. Psalms 24:1-2. New American Standard Bible, 1971, Psalm 50:10-12.
[15] New American Standard Bible, 1971, Romans 10:17.
[16] Job 1:8.
[17] Vine, W. E., & Unger, M. (1996). *Vine's complete expository dictionary of Old and New Testament words: with topical index.* Thomas Nelson. p140.
[18] Strong, J. (2009). *Strong's exhaustive concordance of the Bible.* Hendrickson Publishers.
[19] New American Standard Bible, 1971, Matthew 20:1-16.
[20] Luke 19:11-27, 2 Corinthians 5:20.
[21] New American Standard Bible, 1971, John 15:15.
[22] Bruce, F. F. (1994). *The Gospel of John: Introduction, Exposition, Notes.* (pp. 311-312) Wm. B. Eerdmans Publishing.
[23] Stott, J. (2014). *The message of Romans: God's good news for the world.* InterVarsity Press.
[24] Guiso, L., Sapienza, P., & Zingales, L. (2015). The value of corporate culture. *Journal of Financial Economics, 117*(1), 60-76. http://dx.doi.org/10.1016/j.jfineco.2014.05.010.
[25] New American Standard Bible, 1971, Leviticus 11:44.
[26] New American Standard Bible, 1971, Luke 1:49.
[27] Matthew 6:9-10.
[28] Sproul, R. C. (2013). *The holiness of God.* Tyndale House Publishers, Inc..
[29] New American Standard Bible, 1971, Philippians 3:12.
[30] New American Standard Bible, 1971, Acts 17:24-28.
[31] Carson, D. A. (1999). God Is Love. *Bibliotheca Sacra-Dallas-, 156,* 131-142.
[32] New American Standard Bible, 1971, John 5:19.
[33] New American Standard Bible, 1971, 2 Timothy 2:13.
[34] New American Standard Bible, 1971, Numbers 23:19.
[35] New American Standard Bible, 1971, Job chapters 38 to 41.
[36] Job 1:28.
[37] New American Standard Bible, 1971, Job 42:1-6.
[38] Blomberg, C. L. (1992). *Matthew: An exegetical and theological exposition of Holy Scripture* (Vol. 22, p. 312). B&H Publishing Group.
[39] Murray, A. (2017). *Humility.* B&H Publishing Group.
[40] New American Standard Bible, 1971, 2 Samuel 15:13
[41] 2 Samuel 15:26.
[42] New American Standard Bible, 1971, 1 Corinthians 13:13.
[43] Morgan, T. (2015). *Roman faith and Christian faith: Pistis and fides in the early roman empire and early Churches* (p. 1). OUP Oxford. http://dx.doi.org/10.1093/acprof:oso/9780198724148.001.0001.
[44] Morgan, T. (2015). *Roman faith and Christian faith: Pistis and fides in the early roman empire and early Churches* (p. 285). OUP Oxford. http://dx.doi.org/10.1093/acprof:oso/9780198724148.001.0001.
[45] New American Standard Bible, 1971, James 2:18.
[46] Matthew chapter 5.

[47] Keller, T. (2023, June 21). Vocation: Discerning Your Calling. *Redeemer City to City.* http://storage.cloversites.com/highpeakfellowship/documents/Vocation-Discerning_Your_Calling.pdf.
[48] New American Standard Bible, 1971, 1 Corinthians 9:24, Philippians 3:14.
[49] New American Standard Bible, 1971, Proverbs 6:1-11.
[50] 1 Peter 3:15.
[51] Matthew 25:1-13.
[52] New American Standard Bible, 1971, James 1:19.
[53] Galatians 5:22-23.
[54] Habig, M. A. (1973). St. Francis of Assisi: Omnibus of Sources (Rule of 1221, pp. 44-45). *London, SPCK.*
[55] Jeremiah 29:11.
[56] Snyder, C. R. (2002). Hope theory: Rainbows in the mind. *Psychological inquiry, 13*(4), 249-275.
[57] New American Standard Bible, 1971, Ezekiel chapter 37.
[58] New American Standard Bible, 1971, 1 Samuel 3:19.
[59] John 5:19. Philippians 2:8.
[60] New Living Translation Bible, 1996, Numbers 6:22-27.

Chapter 3

Circle within a circle

Management scholar Henry Mintzberg says more is better when it comes to theories. Mintzberg teaches the first place to start is with an interesting question.[1] One question that arises from the apparent contradiction of two prior books in this genre, *Christian Economics* and *Practicing the King's Economy*, is whether or not the Bible contains the essentials of an economic model to unify the real economy and eternal kingdom economy. This chapter studies what the bible says about the real economy and the kingdom economy. The chapter moves prior Christian economy theory forward by proposing a single model where the two realms interact via the messianic membrane. The shape of the model of human agency is circular. The prophet Isaiah records God looking down on a circular earth[2] and subsequent images from space showed a spherical earth. The chapter ends with an example of how living according to the model can improve real economy equity.

Four categories of Christian economic theory

A study of finance and economic theory in the context of a Christian worldview can result in a chicken-or-egg discussion. Many decades ago, a team led by John C. Bennett declared there is no "Christian Economics."[3] It was suggested that Christian ethics could bring an interesting perspective to the study of economics. Economic science was the antecedent. More recently, *Practicing the King's Economy* suggests that "every kingdom has an economic policy."[4] The apostle Paul declared God the father put everything under the authority of Jesus.[5] The causal force is God and the kingdom of God arrived long before the first award of the Nobel Prize for Economic Science. The bible presents a clear economic point of view. Jesus has a kingdom. It is present, growing, and coming. It is a realm called Peace. The realm of Peace has an economy.

Compassionate Christian economics

I organize the prior panoply of Christian economic theories into a rough four-part typology. The four categories are compassionate, complimentary, conflict, and cash. The first category I call compassionate theories. Compassionate theory authors and researchers are from a broad range of disciplines, including finance, economics, leadership, and especially theology. Excellent representative works in the compassion stream include *Neither Poverty nor Riches,*[6] *Practicing the King's Economy,*[7] and *The Economy of the Kingdom.*[8] Common themes include care for the poor, environmental responsibility, and restrained personal consumption.

Complimentary Christian economics

The second category is complementary theories. This bucket begins with technical finance or economic theories, investigating religion in a comparative and often neutral way. One definition of economic theory is rational choice theory. Individuals are expected to make rational choices to maximize wealth and happiness. Laurence Iannaccone notes studying religious choice as a type of rational choice can help understand important issues. Iannaccone gives examples such as how religious goods are different from real economy goods or whether high-cost religions grow less well than accommodating religions.[9] The complementary category includes works such as *Economics as Religion,*[10] *Economics in Christian Perspective,*[11] and *Faithful Economics.*[12] Iannaccone's paper *Introduction to the Economics of Religion* is the most cited in the complimentary stream.[13] Macroeconomic issues such as taxation and political economy are more prevalent in the complimentary stream than in the compassionate stream. Though, it is still common for complimentary studies to include the study of poverty and wealth inequality.

Christian conflict economics

The third category is conflict theories. Conflict theory and models include conspiracy theories about entrenched power structures of the real political economy manipulating economic outcomes for greater power or to even intentionally bring about an apocalypse and new world order.[14] In conflict theory models, rational agent thought processes may change to potentially irrational processes, including a prepper mentality.[15] This bucket includes conspiracy theories such as the clandestine ruling group, the Illuminati, or freemasons as socio-economic puppeteers. Conspiracy models may lead proponents to forecast the sabotage of a national currency or food supply. The *Routledge Handbook of Conspiracy Theories*[16] is a useful reference guide to conflict theories. For a quick trip into the quicksand, readers may also choose streaming video or the blogosphere.

I am not writing to support or refute any particular conflict theory. I would point out a few biblical facts relevant to conflict theories. First, at the very end of the messianic age, just before Jesus returns, the Bible tells of a political regime that will implement an individual financial embargo on Christ-followers.[17] The precise timing of the embargo is not forecastable.[18] Up until the final moment when Jesus returns, I am to continue investing in the kingdom economy.[19] Jesus also states every person chooses to serve either God or money.[20] It seems to me the best way to understand the real economy is with rational choice models. Jesus may have been leading in that direction when he said beware the leaven of Herod.[21] Herod the Great was above all, politically shrewd and ambitious, dying an extremely wealthy man.[22,23] Herodian leaven is best understood through a love of money.

Christian cash economics

The fourth group I term cash theories. The literature in this category uses biblical wisdom to achieve present-day success. The cash category has the most real economy popularity, at least based on book sales. Two representative studies in this stream are *The Blessed Life*[24] and *Financial Peace*.[25] The second book, Dave Ramsay's book, has solid advice on building real economy wealth. I have used the Ramsay book to teach classes on personal financial planning. The content of the cash theories stream is most relevant to the practicalities of building wealth in the real economy. A later chapter on individual investment discusses real economy principles of wealth building. Building wealth in the real economy is not at all the focus of *The Theory of the Kingdom*.

A new theory of the kingdom

Any useful attempt to integrate the real economy and the biblical kingdom economy must integrate three parts. First, a new theory must incorporate the real economy and its well-established financial and economic models. Agency theory[26] is the dominant theory across several business disciplines. Global capital markets are best understood in the context of Fama's efficient market hypothesis.[27] The Marshallian law of demand and supply is real.[28] Applied mathematics is indispensable to understanding the partial effect of economic inputs and testing any propositions that may arise out of *The Theory of the Kingdom*. Second, a new theory must survey the Bible for principles and stories that fill in the economic model of the invisible kingdom realm. Third, a new theory must propose how the real economy and the invisible economy interact. If the two economies do not interact, the four-part typology of prior Christian economic thought would be sufficient.

The simplified diagram of *The Theory of the Kingdom* is shown in Figure 3.1. The real economy is represented by a small circle. The kingdom economy is represented by the large circle that fully envelops the small circle. The point of interaction between the two economies is called the messianic membrane. The membrane is permeable. The terms of exchange across this permeable barrier are detailed in the Bible. Resources are moved back and forth as agents act, with the Holy Spirit alongside, according to the model. The model is, of course, not exactly correct. As statistician E.P. Box said, "all models are wrong, but some are useful." The purpose of *The Theory of the Kingdom* it that it may be useful in moving readers toward a new revelation of Jesus and his growing kingdom of peace and life.

Figure 3.1. Simplified model of human agency.

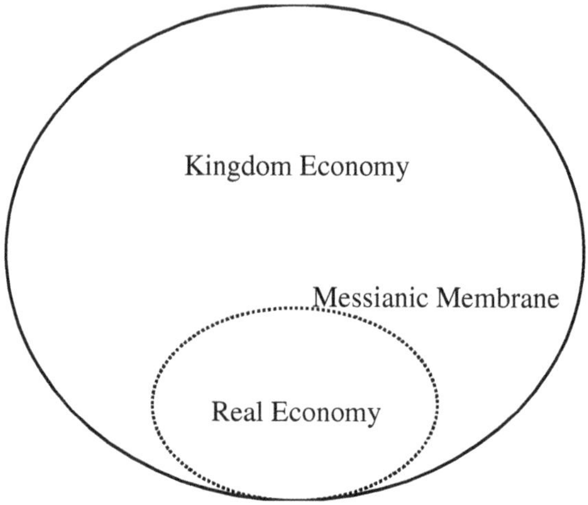

Figure 3.1 major message: Jesus instituted the kingdom of God on earth. At the same time, the real economy continues to function. The interaction of the two realms is governed by Jesus and the personal work of the Holy Spirit, sent as a guide for life and peace. The messianic membrane represents the permeable barrier that mediates the interactions of the temporary real economy and the permanent kingdom economy.

Messianic membrane

A membrane is a thin layer of separating material. Membranes can separate human organs from other parts of the human body. The purpose of the membrane in the model of human agency is to assist in visualizing the all-encompassing role of Jesus, mediating the relationship between my life in the real economy and kingdom economy. Jesus is a full mediator. There is no entry into the kingdom economy except by Jesus. The apostle Paul wrote to Timothy, "For there is one God, and one mediator also between God and mankind, the man Christ Jesus."[29]

One mediator

Emil Brunner's explanation of Jesus as the mediator suggests a membrane. My account in heaven without Jesus registers as unfaithful. Without a messianic mediator, I am not permitted to cross into the kingdom of heaven.[30] However, the death of Jesus on the cross allowed humanity an opportunity to be righteous before God.[31] D.R. de Lacey argues Jesus as a mediator is an essential tenet of the apostle Paul's theology.[32]

The first disciple to properly identify Jesus is Peter. He uses the word *Christos* in Luke 9:20. *Christos* is translated as Christ or Messiah and means anointed one. In antiquity, the title anointed one is given to a king.[33] An extensive discussion of the context of messianic belief is found in *Rebecca's Children: Judaism and Christianity in the Roman World.*[34] Segal's analysis draws on the messianic prophecy of Isaiah 53. At the time of the Apostle Paul's writing, the Judean community was waiting for a Messiah but did not expect the actual one to be crucified. According to Segal, the success and longevity of Christianity are in part due to novel doctrinal elements of individual faith, non-violence, and an apolitical messianic vision of the "Kingdom of God."[35] Jesus is the true messiah that reigns over a kingdom that will never end.[36] The messianic membrane represents the permeable barrier that mediates the interactions of the temporary real economy and the permanent kingdom economy.

Agency choice and kingdom come now

In my agency role, I am told to pray and ask God for his kingdom to come, and for his will to be done now as it is in heaven.[37] I believe the objective of the kingdom economy is for life, peace, and growth.[38] How does this happen? How do I make rational choices to bring the reality of the kingdom of God into the real economy?

Jesus' sermon, recorded in Matthew chapters five, six, and seven, provides direction. The opening of Matthew five is a list of kingdom of heaven virtues. The list of virtuous behaviors and attitudes includes humility, mourning, meekness, a desire to do right, mercy, guilelessness, peacemaking, and even being persecuted for living right. Stott reflects the sentiment of anyone hearing the list for the first time. Everything about Jesus' kingdom is different.[39] Following the list of virtues, I am introduced to the metaphor of salt and light.

If I live according to the instructions, I will be salt and light. Salt, in this context, was a preservative.[40] If I act as a peacemaker, I keep the real economy from rotting, or at least in the communities where I have influence. In contrast, if I seek real economy conflict and am a ready brawler, I am worthless in the kingdom economy. Light has a purpose and an association. Light reveals. A substantial part of my purpose in writing this book is to bring to light how it is individuals can act as rational kingdom agents and not just rational real economy agents. Jesus' reference to light associates directly with

John's statement Jesus' life is the light for all humankind.[41] Light also connects with Jesus' statement, "I am the light of the world; he who follows me will not walk in darkness but will have the light of life."[42] Any light that comes off me to reveal truth in my community is a function of being *in Christ.*[43]

To be salty is to act with wisdom

By being salt and light, I am engaged in bringing the resources and products of the kingdom economy into the real economy now. The meaning of being salt and light is identity and action. Salt is a noun. I am salt. The second word, to lose saltiness, can be translated as savor or tasteless and is a verb. The Greek word *moraino* means to become foolish, insipid, or tasteless. If I act foolishly, and not according to the virtues of Jesus' teaching, even though I am salt, I am no longer a producer in the kingdom economy. Said positively, to act with wisdom is to be salty. Wisdom comes from the guidance of the Holy Spirit, whose mind is life and peace.[44] Further, at any point I need wisdom, I simply ask, and it will be given.[45]

To visualize how the model of human agency works, I think about how salt influences the flow of water across membranes. Osmosis is the process of water moving across a membrane from a low salt concentration area to a high salt concentration area. A salty kingdom agent living in the real economy should create a flow of water from the kingdom economy to the real economy. Imagine I work at a firm struggling to treat its workers fairly. If I enter the committee room where worker treatment is being discussed, the room instantly becomes saltier. My presence and actions should cause water to flow from the kingdom economy into the real economy. Water is an essential sustaining resource. Water cleanses, and it represents God's power in general. My presence and wise, salty actions should produce a better corporate culture and better outcomes for all workers. As I become saltier over time, and the number of Christians in the real economy grows, more water will flow from the kingdom economy into the real economy.

A ruptured membrane between the two economies

Jesus equates the process of being born again with being born of the spirit and water.[46] The Holy Spirit is the agent of spiritual rebirth.[47] Carson's comments on the meaning of water suggest a link to Ezekiel 36:25-27, rather than to water baptism. Carson writes the messianic era is characterized "by spectacular cleansing symbolized by water that washes away all impurities and idols, and the powerful gift of the Spirit that transforms the hearts of people."[48] Editor comments included as a footnote to Pamment's article bring up several ancient cultural considerations about water and birth. Most interesting is the phrase "to give birth" in ancient Akkadic and Hebrew languages. It is associated with the ***rupture of the membrane*** [emphasis added] and a release of water. The messianic membrane is a dotted line because the work of Jesus on the cross ruptured it. I envision salty agents attracting a flow of cleansing water from the kingdom economy into the real economy now.

Inter-economy essentials

There are important general essentials given in scripture regarding kingdom agency in the real economy. I introduce two essentials here and address the remaining ones in the chapters following. High-order essentials include the work of the Holy Spirit and real economy engagement.

Age of the Holy Spirit

The messianic era is also called the age of the Holy Spirit.[49] The most important general essential is the work of the Holy Spirit in effective human agency, which is to live and act to bring kingdom life, peace, and growth here now. One major message of Lee's *God's New Testament Economy* is the most important variable for effective kingdom agency is the work of the Holy Spirit.[50] Lee uses the phrase the Holy Spirit is "on us economically."[51] The term economy is a translation of the Greek word *oikonomia*. The word is more often translated as stewardship or dispensation. The Holy Spirit is dispensed in me for the administration and stewardship of the kingdom economy. FF Bruce indicates the sending of the Holy Spirit fulfilled the Old Testament prophecy of Joel.[52] The Holy Spirit is the owner alongside me in the real economy to comfort, advocate and help.[53] The Holy Spirit is specifically given for power[54] and insight[55] required to exercise my agency authority.[56] In the age of the Holy Spirit, I can accomplish any assignment through Messiah Jesus.[57]

An answer before the question

To bring the business application of the Holy Spirit essential into sharper focus, I use the personal anecdote of my first successful interview at an investment bank. In the final year of my MBA program, I interviewed for many different jobs. My first choice was to work at an investment bank. Wall Street firms did not recruit at my school. I was turned down by several banks, often without an interview. In fact, I was turned down in many industries. I was turned down for junior managerial jobs at a small hotel and even for an assistant store manager role at the now-defunct consumer electronics chain Radio Shack.

Being from Canada, my number one choice was to work for Dominion Securities ("DS"). DS was the clear Canadian industry leader. I received an interview at DS, in large part from a personal connection with one senior partner. While waiting in the lobby for my first interview, I picked up a copy of the Globe and Mail newspaper. The lead business story was regarding the appointment of a new Bank of Canada governor. Gordon Thiessen was taking over leadership from John Crow. I read the story and then was called to my first meeting.

The first meeting was with the head of capital markets. After some small talk, my interviewer asked what I thought of the new Bank of Canada governor. I remembered the entire Globe and Mail story. I didn't just remember a quote or two. Even now, I remember the major message of the story and the entire situation like it was yesterday. All of the nuances of the story came alive in my mind at a moment in time. I answered the question. I could tell from the expression on the interviewer's face he was surprised I had such a well-considered answer. I was surprised. Up until 10 minutes before he asked the question, I hadn't heard the name Gordon Thiessen. At that moment, I knew for certain the Holy Spirit had given me an answer to a question I didn't know was coming. The first meeting set up a successful day of interviews. I received a job offer and, a few months later, started my investment banking career at DS.

Every working day, the Holy Spirit has been my guide. On interview day at DS it was to my benefit. The benefit was not just for me. It benefited my wife. Hopefully, it benefited DS and its clients. I expect it was a benefit to our church the rest of our community. I concur with Lee that, "The Christian Life must be a life in the Spirit, by the Spirit, and with the Spirit."[58]

Engagement

Jesus taught in parables.[59] One of Jesus' stories was told in response to a misconception Christ-followers had about when the kingdom of God will have fully come and what to do while waiting. I don't know when the messianic era will end, but I do know what I am to do in the waiting. I am to continue doing business in the real economy. The setup of the Luke 19 parable included a rich noble leaving for a long trip. Before leaving, the noble's three agents were given capital to invest. The noble gave the key instruction "do business until I come."[60] Matthew's gospel similarly records the story.[61] The message is to engage in real economy business every day. Accumulation of money is, of course, not the goal of kingdom agency. God does not need money. Rather, I invest all my resources to bring a return of life, peace, and growth. Money may or may not accumulate through my actions. Kingdom life, peace, and growth must accumulate through my actions.

A further survey of scripture makes clear that Christ-followers should be highly engaged in the real economy. I must make every effort to avoid the tragedy of being "paralyzed with fear."[62] and not investing my resources. The emphasis on remaining engaged in the real economy can be taken from Jesus' final moments in prayer. Jesus did not ask the Father to take his agents out of the world.[63] It would set up an unusual model if, at the moment I was born again, I was whisked up into the clouds. The absence of engaged kingdom agents being salt and light would make for a bleak real economy. The latter sentiment in Jesus' prayer of *being sent* is an "appointment for a specific task and the equipment to do it."[64] Kingdom agents have an assignment and all the necessary tools to engage in business and bring life, peace, and growth to the world now.

Real economy engagement is not unique to the New Testament. Engagement is the message of the entire bible. The prophet Jeremiah delivered a message to a group of exiles living in Babylon. The message was a command to build houses, build families, pray for the community, and to work for the common good of the community. There is a self-interest component to always engaging in the local economy. The community also has a share in the real economy benefit.

The biblical pattern is to engage. Through my engagement, the conditions of my family and community should improve. Engagement in the messianic age brings the resources and effects of the realm of peace across the messianic membrane into the real economy now.

Application

Inequity and conflict in real economy businesses arise in part due to the lack of Holy Spirit insight. Holy Spirit insight brings life and peace.[65] Consider the early twenty-first-century case of Wells Fargo Bank. The very large and troubled bank hired CEO Charles Sharf to improve its fortunes. Wells Fargo's owners hired Sharf to make money in the same way he had for the owners of Visa. Part of Mr. Sharf's mandate was to meet ethnic-minority recruiting and promotion goals. The goals were not met. Reuters news agency reported Mr. Sharf as saying, "While it might sound like an excuse, the unfortunate reality is that there is a very limited pool of black talent to recruit from."[66] This statement did not bring peace and life to Wells Fargo. The statement is also wrong.

Mr. Sharf's statement is wrong because all people are created in the image of God[67] and thus have heart capital and latent capabilities beyond what a resume may say. Second, before I point an accusing finger, the Wells Fargo CEO was simply repeating the mistake of the bible prophet Samuel. The mistake is judging people by what I can see with my eyes. In selecting a King for Israel, Samuel judged based on what he could see. Samuel looked at each candidate's size and stature. God corrected Samuel by saying, "Do not look at his appearance or at the height of his stature....for God does not see as man sees, since man looks at the outward appearance, but the LORD looks at the heart."[68]

How do I follow God's instruction to Samuel and avoid the mistake of Mr. Sharf? I use the guidance of the Holy Spirit. The owner sees the heart of each person and will guide me in evaluating people from the inside out. Over the years, I have been able to hire some wonderful candidates who have been passed over solely based on their appearance or resume. When making business decisions, if I ask, the Holy Spirit will help me produce life and peace in the real economy now.

Notes

[1] Mintzberg, H. (2017). Developing theory about the development of theory. In S.W. Floyd & B. Wooldridge (Eds.), *Handbook of middle management strategy process research* (pp. 177-196). Edward Elgar Publishing. http://dx.doi.org/10.4337/9781783473250.

[2] Isaiah 40:22.

[3] Bennett, J. C. (1954). *Christian values and economic life* (p. 210). Harper.

[4] Rhodes, M., Holt, R., & Fikkert, B. (2018). *Practicing the King's Economy: Honoring Jesus in how We Work, Earn, Spend, Save, and Give* (p. 39). Baker Books.

[5] New American Standard Bible, 1971, 1 Corinthians 15:27.

[6] Blomberg, C. L. (1999). *Neither Poverty Nor Riches. New Studies in Biblical Theology.* Grand Rapids/Cambridge: William B. Eerdman's Publishing Co.

[7] Rhodes, M., Holt, R., & Fikkert, B. (2018). *Practicing the King's Economy: Honoring Jesus in how We Work, Earn, Spend, Save, and Give.* Baker Books.

[8] Moxnes, H. (2004). *The economy of the kingdom: Social conflict and economic relations in Luke's Gospel* (Vol. 23). Wipf and Stock Publishers.

[9] Iannaccone, L. R. (1992). Religious markets and the economics of religion. *Social compass, 39*(1), 123-131. http://dx.doi.org/10.1177/003776892039001012.

[10] Nelson, R. H. (2015). *Economics as religion: From Samuelson to Chicago and beyond.* Penn State Press. http://dx.doi.org/10.5325/j.ctv1rnpjqb.

[11] Claar, V. V., & Klay, R. J. (2015). *Economics in Christian Perspective: Theory, Policy and Life Choices.* InterVarsity Press.

[12] Henderson, J. W., Pisciotta, J. O., & Pisciotta, J. L. (Eds.). (2005). *Faithful economics: the moral worlds of a neutral science.* Baylor University Press.

[13] Iannaccone, L. R. (1998). Introduction to the Economics of Religion. *Journal of economic literature, 36*(3), 1465-1495.

[14] Dein, S. (2021). Covid-19 and the apocalypse: Religious and secular perspectives. *Journal of religion and health, 60*(1), 5-15. http://dx.doi.org/10.1007/s10943-020-01100-w.

[15] Kabel, A., & Chmidling, C. (2014). Disaster prepper: Health, identity, and American survivalist culture. *Human organization, 73*(3), 258-266. http://dx.doi.org/10.17730/humo.73.3.l34252tg03428527.

[16] Butter, M., & Knight, P. (Eds.). (2020). *Routledge handbook of conspiracy theories.* Routledge. http://dx.doi.org/10.4324/9780429452734.
[17] New American Standard Bible, 1971, Revelation 13:17.
[18] Matthew 24:36.
[19] Luke 19:13.
[20] Matthew 6:24.
[21] Mark 8:15.
[22] Grant, F. C. (1926). *The Economic background of the Gospels.* Oxford University Press, H. Milford.
[23] Marshak, A. K. (2015). *The many faces of Herod the Great* (p. xiii), Wm. B. Eerdmans Publishing.
[24]Morris, R. (2016). *The Blessed Life: Unlocking the Rewards of Generous Living.* Baker Books.
[25] Ramsey, D., & Ramsey, S. (1997). *Financial peace.* Viking.
[26] Jensen, M. C., & Meckling, W. H. (2019). Theory of the firm: Managerial behavior, agency costs and ownership structure. In *Corporate Governance* (pp. 77-132). Gower.
[27] Fama, E. F. (1970). Efficient capital markets: A review of theory and empirical work. *The journal of Finance, 25*(2), 383-417. http://dx.doi.org/10.2307/2325486.
[28] Marshall, A. (2009). *Principles of economics: unabridged eighth edition.* Cosimo, Inc. http://dx.doi.org/10.1057/9781137375261.
[29] New American Standard Bible, 1971, 1 Timothy 2:5.
[30] Brunner, E. (1934). *The mediator: A study of the central doctrine of the Christian faith* (Vol. 3, Chapter 18, paragraph 2), James Clarke & Co..
[31] 2 Corinthians 5:21.
[32] De Lacey, D. R. (1987). Jesus as mediator. *Journal for the Study of the New Testament,* 9(29), 101-121. http://dx.doi.org/10.1177/0142064X8700902906.
[33] Burge, G. M., & Green, G. L. (2020). *The New Testament in Antiquity: A Survey of the New Testament Within Its Cultural Contexts* (p. 258), Zondervan Academic.
[34] Segal, A. F. (1986). *Rebecca's children: Judaism and Christianity in the Roman world* (pp. 93-94), Harvard University Press.
[35] Segal, A. F. (1986). *Rebecca's children: Judaism and Christianity in the Roman world* (pp. 93-94), Harvard University Press.
[36] Williams, J. J. (2021). *Redemptive Kingdom Diversity: A Biblical Theology of the People of God* (p. 48) Baker Academic.
[37] Matthew 6:10.
[38] Isaiah 9:6-7. John 10:10. Romans 8:6.
[39] Stott, J. (2014). *The Message of the Sermon on the Mount.* InterVarsity Press.
[40] Blomberg, C. L. (1992). *Matthew: An exegetical and theological exposition of Holy Scripture* (Vol. 22, p. 102). B&H Publishing Group.
[41] John 1:4.
[42] New American Standard Bible, 1971, John 8:12.
[43] 2 Corinthians 5:17.
[44] Romans 8:6.
[45] James 1:5-6.
[46] John 3:3-5.
[47] Pamment, M. (1983). John 3: 5:'Unless one is born of water and the Spirit, he cannot enter the kingdom of God.' *Novum Testamentum, 25*(2), 189-190.

[48] Carson, D. (2019, July 29). What Does 'Born of Water and the Spirit' Mean in John 3:5? *The Gospel Coalition.* https://www.thegospelcoalition.org/article/born-water-spirit- mean/
[49] Bruce, F. F. (1973). The Holy Spirit in the Acts of the Apostles. *Interpretation, 27*(2), 166-183. http://dx.doi.org/10.1177/002096437302700203.
[50] Lee, W. (1986). *God's New Testament Economy* (p. 451). Living Stream Ministry.
[51] Lee, W. (1986). *God's New Testament Economy* (p. 67). Living Stream Ministry.
[52] Joel 2:28-32.
[53] John 14:16. In the verse referenced here the Holy Spirit is an advocate or in Greek the paraclete. In addition to advocate, sometimes consoler, or in the New King James Version a helper.
[54] New American Standard Bible, 1971, Luke 24:49. Acts 1:8. The Greek word for power in the Acts verse is dunamis.
[55] Matthew 10:19. James 1:9. New American Standard Bible, 1971, Luke 12:12. Luke 21:15. New American Standard Bible, 1971, Mark 13:11.
[56] New American Standard Bible, 1971, Luke 9:1-2. Greek word for authority is exousia.
[57] Philippians 4:13.
[58] Lee, W. (1986). *God's New Testament Economy* (p. 451) Living Stream Ministry.
[59] Blomberg, C. L. (1992). *Matthew: An exegetical and theological exposition of Holy Scripture* (Vol. 22, pp. 216-217). B&H Publishing Group. Blomberg's comment can be summarized as indicating parables were stories with a spiritual dimension. Parables had the effect of bringing revelation to some and concealing revelation to others. I might be physically capable of hearing the parable. Yet only if I open my heart in the hearing, as an act of my will, will I understand and receive the message.
[60] Luke 19:13.
[61] Matthew 25:14-30.
[62] Blomberg, C. L. (1992). *Matthew: An exegetical and theological exposition of Holy Scripture* (Vol. 22, p. 374). B&H Publishing Group.
[63] John 17:15.
[64] Tenney, M. C. (1997). *John: the gospel of belief* (p. 248) Wm. B. Eerdmans Publishing.
[65] Romans 8:6.
[66] Helander, K. (2020, September 22). Wells Fargo's CEO comments about diverse talent anger some employees. *CNBC.* https://www.cnbc.com/2020/09/22/wells-fargo-ceo-ruffles -feathers-with-comments-about-diverse-talent.html.
[67] Genesis 1:26-28.
[68] New American Standard Bible, 1971, 1 Samuel 16:7.

Chapter 4

Communication over intervention

In this chapter I study the ways in which an owner may guide the actions of agents. Modes of owner intervention include physical intrusion, tight supervision and communication. Owners may change the mode of intervention over time. In the theory of the kingdom, it is important to understand how owner-agent communication has changed in the present messianic era and how it is different compared to the real economy. I finish the chapter with a simple daily application.

The issue of how God intervenes in the affairs of human agents is as relevant as ever. Fallible human agents sometimes cause and sometimes experience pain. C.S. Lewis' the *Problem of Pain* deals with the costs of human agency.[1] A synopsis of the problem is humans are not all morally good and often suffer. Therefore, God cannot be good, all-powerful, or perhaps even real. The question of human suffering will remain relevant until the end of the messianic age.[2] Almost 60 years after Lewis, Blomberg's New Testament-based answers to current challenges regarding belief in God begins with the issue of human suffering.[3] One proposed reason is because of our location in history, the messianic era, humanity still experiences suffering and the law of sowing and reaping still applies.[4]

Tragic collapse of two towers

An example of human pain pertinent to the study of business is the story of the ancient tower of Siloam. The tower of Siloam collapsed and 18 people died. Jesus stated the people who died in the collapse were not at fault.[5] The 18 were simply in the wrong place at the wrong time. In twenty-first century London, UK, the families of 72 people killed in the Grenfell Tower fire know the same grief as the families of the ancient tower of Siloam. The Grenfell Tower victims died because of bad business. The deaths were caused by the design, regulatory and fire-fighting failures of human agents.[6] In a later chapter on individual investment returns, I address how the model of human agency includes lasting compensation for some types of human suffering.[7]

God could choose to intervene directly before I make a serious business or personal mistake. He could have intervened to evacuate the Grenfell Tower before the fire, for example. He appears to selectively intervene. The opposite of intervention is to ignore or to leave alone. God may not intervene in the way I want, but the biblical record suggests God does not leave me alone or ignore what I am doing. He is always communicating.[8] He always pays attention to what I am doing.[9] He did not leave me alone in the past, he does not leave me alone now and will not leave me alone in the future. The biblical indication of God's constant attention still leaves open the question of what is his intervention strategy and, is it a good strategy?

Modes of intervention

Physical intrusion is not the general mode of God's intervention in human activity. The bible records a few select events of physical intrusion. Two Old Testament examples are the judgment and slaying of King Belshazzar,[10] and a scared donkey speaking in human words to a man called Balaam.[11]

The general mode of God's intervention is communication. In the Old Testament, God spoke to people in many ways, including through his word and through prophets. In the New Testament, God spoke through Jesus, the heir of everything.[12] Raymond Brown summarizes the opening of the book of Hebrews, saying, "In Christ God has closed the greatest communication gap of all time, that which exists between a holy God and sinful mankind."[13] The kingdom economy model is intervention by communication. Intervention by communication is also a good strategy. It is the most value-creating strategy for real economy organizations.

Mixed results of tight regulation and intervention

Owners of real economy organizations decide how to intervene with mistake-prone agents. My professional experience is in the institutional investment business. Industry compliance systems are an exercise in prevention and punishment. In the United States, the Securities and Exchange Commission ("SEC") is responsible for regulating the investment business. The SEC administers exams to individuals before they are permitted to work in any responsible capacity. Over 20 years, I passed six different SEC exams. Some exams were one or two hours. Other exams took all day. The SEC further intervenes with required reporting, ongoing education, and monitoring of all exchange-based securities transactions. The SEC's system is designed to prevent mistakes and fraud *ex ante*. When violations of SEC rules occur, the punishments are substantial.

Despite its approach to intervention, mistakes and fraud occur all the time. Each year, the SEC brings hundreds of enforcement actions representing billions of dollars of fraud and mistakes.[14] The annual SEC enforcement report is a real-life story of human agency failure. Some of the failures are innocent oversights and some are intentional fraud. Either type of failure can decimate the financial future of thousands of individuals.

Small players lose the intervention game

The SEC itself does not always achieve just and fair outcomes. SEC resources are limited. New investment products are invented all the time. Bad actors come up with new ways to defraud individuals and avoid SEC monitoring. It can be difficult for the SEC to keep up. Further, it is expensive to bring enforcement action against large organizations compared to small organizations.

Large firms have substantial legal resources. The SEC's cost-benefit favors going after the small firms first. Research has shown large firms fare better than small firms in at least three ways.[15] The SEC is less likely to bring legal charges against individuals at large firms and it is less likely to take a large firm to court. For the same violation, individuals at large firms are also less likely to be banned from the investment industry.

The SEC serves an important regulatory function but its intervention is not completely fair and just. The noteworthy postscript to the flaws in SEC intervention is the United States regularly ranks at the top of global capital markets despite all the regulatory issues. The U.S. has the most favorable investment climate,[16] the highest amount of foreign direct investment[17] and the highest value-traded stock exchanges.[18] Imperfect intervention can still be associated with growth.

"Words speak louder without actions."[19]

There is a better way than tight regulation and direct intervention. Finance scholar Doron Levit's model indicates communication is the optimal mode of owner intervention. The big new idea of the research is an owner is better off voluntarily limiting direct intervention into the decision-making processes of her agents. In the setup of the model, owners first choose whether to influence the actions of their agents by communication or direct intervention. Direct intervention means to stop or redirect the agent's actions. Levit's paper offers a formal model and mathematical proof that ex ante *stopping intervention* [emphasis added] should be limited to maintain effective communication of ideals. This appears to support the biblical model of limited ex ante intervention.

Even though an owner may have the ability and the right to intervene in the actions of agents, the net effect of a preemptive intervention is negative for all involved. Micro-managed agents communicate less with the owner and respond less well to instructions. Agents that expect preemptive owner intervention get further and further away from the ideal. Managers propose worse and worse risk-adjusted investments over time. When owners use a preemptive intervention strategy the value of the business and its potential size is lower.

The superior strategy of intervention by communication has obvious implications for the model of human agency. I may wonder why God didn't intervene and stop me from making a bad decision with a poor life outcome. However, intervention would ultimately inhibit my communication with God. I would perceive his instructions less well and communicate less. I would read the Bible less, pray less and seek less input from wise counselors. Over time I would take more foolish actions.

Communication with God maximizes the scale of the kingdom

In later chapters, I analyze the economic resources of the kingdom economy. Land, labor, and capital are unlimited. As a result, the owner of the kingdom doesn't have the same need to intervene to stop me from losing money, for example. God is not seeking a higher stock price. God is looking to continuously increase the size of his realm called peace. Growth is achieved by agent-disciples communicating with the owner, developing personal virtues, being salt and light, and bringing the kingdom to the real economy now. Human mistakes still produce pain and suffering. But the virtuous actions of agents produce growth, life, and peace. In the way preventative intervention may damage real economy outcomes, it would also work against the kingdom objective of maximizing growth, life, and peace.

I consider James chapter one, verse 12 as a partial comfort amidst the tension of intervention by communication and the problem of human suffering.

> Blessed [happy, spiritually prosperous, favored by God] is the man who is steadfast under trial and perseveres when tempted; for when he has passed the test and been approved, he will receive the [victor's] crown of life which the Lord has promised to those who love him.[20]

So far, I propose: 1) God's general mode of intervention is communication, and 2) Communication is an optimal strategy for owners in the real economy. What follows next is a biblical survey of the tactics of God's communication strategy over time. The chapter will finish with practical steps to engage and activate the communication strategy of the owner.

Owner communication over time

I have split the biblical survey of owner communication into three parts, corresponding to three periods of history. The first era of time is the beginning of human history up to the beginning of Jesus' public ministry around 24 AD. The date 24AD assumes Jesus was born somewhere between four BC and six BC, based on the timing of the rule of Herod the Great.[21] Jesus was 30 years old when he was baptized by John.[22] The public ministry of Jesus lasts three years. Following Votaw, it is assumed that around 27 AD Jesus was crucified, resurrected, and ascended back to heaven to sit down at the right hand of God.[23] The final period, beginning after Jesus' ascension around 27 AD, is the messianic era of today. *The Theory of the Kingdom* applies to this current messianic era. The Bible prophesies a fourth period. It is the second coming of Jesus, at which point the real economy dissolves, and the model of human agency and time as it is currently experienced, fades away.[24]

A common element of Judeo-Christian terminology is to say *God is speaking*, or *God said*.[25] I will use the same terminology. The present tense is a consequence of a biblical sentiment the word of God is alive, is itself at work, and will remain so.[26]

Period 1: Ancient communication

During the first period of biblical history, God himself had a leading role in communication with human agents. God spoke in person to Adam and Eve,[27] Noah,[28] Abraham,[29] and Moses. God spoke directly to Old Testament prophets, priests, and kings. Prominent examples include the prophets Samuel, Elijah, and Isaiah. God communicated with kings of many different nations. David, Solomon, and Saul received instructions from God. Solomon was asked in a dream by God what he wanted most. Solomon asked for wisdom. God granted his request and Solomon is believed to have written, directly or indirectly, large parts of the bible's wisdom literature books including Proverbs, Ecclesiastes, and Song of Solomon.[30]

The first period includes a diverse set of modes of communication. God spoke in direct personal encounters, in dreams, with written words, via angelic messengers, out of a burning bush, out of the mouth of a donkey, out of weather events, in fire, and even in a hushed voice. God communicated directly with characters as diverse as Elijah the prophet and the corrupt King Belshazzar. According to Gay's review of *Divine Discourse*, the purpose of God's "speech-act" communication strategy is interventionist and establishes the "moral integrity" of human agency.[31] In ancient times God deployed an extensive, personal communication program to activate his model of human agency. In the first period of history, God leads the discourse.

The content of communication was often a general encouragement to not give in to fear, to take risks, to take new territory, or to build. The first series of communications from God to Joshua includes three instructions to take risk, to be bold, and to not fear. Joshua received both general and specific instructions from the owner.[32]

There is a line of comparison between Old Testament kings and modern-day leaders. The record of kings in the first and second Chronicles includes notable construction projects. Making a large investment implies taking a large risk. The biblical record of building projects indicates how much of a risk-taker a particular leader was. The ability of kings to invest and grow their realms was an indication of their ability to overcome fear by faith in God. The record of kings also tends to include a statement on the level of obedience to God's law. The level of obedience, particularly in terms of idolatry, resulted in being described as good or bad.

A theme of first period communication was a system of blessings for obedience and curses for disobedience.[33] The list of blessings was extensive and included success in relationships, a good reputation, and economic prosperity. The list of curses for disobedience was as negative as the blessings were positive. Disobedience would result in a difficult life in every dimension and confusion as to how to make things better. Thankfully I do not live in the first period of history. As Blomberg notes God changes what constitutes obedience from one period of time to another.[34] Jesus' arrival marks a transition from an external Mosaic law to one that is now within. Owner instructions are now understood in the context of New Testament teaching, particularly the teaching of Jesus and his fulfillment of the Mosaic law.[35]

Period 2: Communication in Jesus' lifetime

The transition point from the first period of communication marked the beginning of a change from external communication by God to an internal program. From the point of Jesus' baptism to his resurrection, communication is led by Jesus with several points of help from the Holy Spirit. The writer of Hebrews clearly indicates the transition from God speaking through prophets to speaking through Jesus.[36] The transition point from the first period to the second period sets up Jesus' public ministry and leadership. The transition point coincides with a significant decline in the number of recorded direct communications of God. God speaks in the New Testament at the baptism of Jesus and at the transfiguration.[37]

The water baptism of Jesus is recorded in all four gospels.[38] Present at the baptism were the three members of the ownership group. In addition to Jesus himself, God was present and spoke in an audible voice. The Holy Spirit was present and confirmed the identity of Jesus to John the Baptist. Holy Spirit communication at Jesus' baptism was symbolic and visual. God's audible statements affirmed Jesus' identity and also declared love and approval. In the transfiguration statement, God uses the same words as at the water baptism, adding a final instruction to *listen* to his son. As parents know, hearing an instruction is not by itself sufficient. Listening is hearing and doing. The final phrase of God in the New Testament emphasizes the need for agents to demonstrate hearing through action.

Ownership communication at the point of transition

The event of transition to the second era brings about a practical application for businesses at points of leadership transition. Commissioning a new leader into an agency role should be confirmed by the clear communication of the owner(s). The words spoken by God and the actions of Jesus and the Holy Spirit marked the beginning of Jesus' earth-bound ministry and the beginning of his kingdom, or reign, with authority over all things. The unity and agreement of the Father, Son, and Spirit marked a clear beginning for the new phase.

The theme of Jesus' teaching is the kingdom of God. There are approximately 80 instances of Jesus speaking about the kingdom of God or the kingdom of heaven.[39] Jesus' realm includes everything. It is not any particular real economy political territory. The introduction of the kingdom comes in the sermon on the mount. Stott summarizes the theme of the sermon as everything is different now.[40] The central thought is Jesus' statement, "do not be like them". Everything about the kingdom is different. Indeed, the theme of this study is the economy of God is completely different from the real economy. Agents of the kingdom economy are to act based on the character of the owner, his sacrificial love, and unlimited resources. I am to take as much risk as I can stand to invest in the kingdom, being salt and light to bring the resources of the kingdom across the messianic membrane into the real economy now. The real economy desperately needs the life and peace of Jesus' realm.

Jesus was a clear communicator. When he wanted to offend the power structure, he did so. When Jesus wanted to confound or provoke his foes with deft rhetoric he did so.[41] Jesus was a skilled teacher. The crowds often marveled at his simple yet authoritative teaching. The brief, clever word pictures of Jesus' teaching were unique at the time. After his ascension, Jesus' techniques were copied extensively by religious teachers.[42]

Jesus spoke in parables. Parables were stories with a spiritual dimension. Parables had the effect of bringing revelation to some and concealing revelation to others. I might be physically capable of hearing the parable. Yet only if I open my heart in the hearing, as an act of my will, will I understand and receive the message.[43]

A second important element of Jesus' teaching was to prepare humankind to live in the third phase of history. The four gospels teach us about the communication role of the Holy Spirit. The Holy Spirit communicated the identity of Jesus. The spirit of God also compelled Jesus to go into the wilderness to be tempted by the Devil. The fact the Holy Spirit sent Jesus to be tempted will be taken up again in a later chapter on the testing construct of the model.

The Holy Spirit is a personal guide

Jesus said the Holy Spirit will be a personal guide for agents. It is the role of the Holy Spirit to be at my side, teaching me everything I need to know and reminding me of important information for each situation.[44] The holy spirit serves as a memory aid and interpreter.[45] Being able to recall information is important for kingdom agents. On several occasions, the disciples were told not to worry about what to say when confronted regarding their beliefs, truth, and conduct.[46] It is the designated job of the Holy Spirit to bring to an agent's memory what to say in difficult moments. The final instruction to the disciples defines the point of transition to the third era of history. It included an admonition to wait for the spiritual empowerment of the Holy Spirit.[47]

The events of the day of Pentecost in Acts chapter two mark the founding of New Testament Christianity and the beginning of the current era of divine discourse. The internalization of divine communication is complete. Jesus' final sacrifice instituted a communication era where everyone could have access to the daily guidance of the Holy Spirit.[48]

Period 3: Communication after the day of Pentecost

A transition from the Old Testament narrative of physical battles to the New Testament narrative of spiritual battles coincides with an internalized divine discourse. I am not engaged in a battle with any other person.[49] My battles are spiritual and fought with heart labors such as prayer and fasting. I do well to remember this when interacting with work colleagues and people in online and social media forums. There is no place in the model of human agency for vitriolic personal attacks, which are so common in modern society.

Communication tools common to every era include the word of God and natural environmental processes. However, in the third period, the apostle Paul was the most prolific written communicator. Paul reiterates the value of the inspired word of God in his second letter to Timothy.[50] In addition to the inspired word of God, the body of Christ, the church, is a key vehicle of organizational communication, accountability, and governance. Most unique in this kingdom era, however, is the communication role of the Holy Spirit. Paul considers it vital enough to write about it in the sense of being continuously filled with the Holy Spirit.[51]

Holy Spirit communicates sonship to me

The Holy Spirit is the one that carries on important elements of the last message of God for the benefit of each agent. God affirmed Jesus' identity. God affirmed his love for Jesus. The Holy Spirit does the same for me. On the eve of his death, the Aramaic/Greek pair of Abba and Father together are the same words Jesus used to pray in the Garden of Gethsemane. It is by the internal witness of the Holy Spirit a person knows their identity as a daughter or son of God. The cultural context of Greco-Roman adoption was different than modern day. In antiquity, adopted children were chosen by the father to be the heir to continue the family line, often ahead of natural-born children. The era of Holy Spirit divine discourse is one of clear identity and promotional love.

God's commands are now a promise

The ultimate benefit of internalized owner-agent communication was made clear to me by the story of a United Kingdom ex-convict. Charles Price of Peoples Church in Toronto, Canada, was known to tell the story of an ex-convict visiting an Anglican cathedral. The man had become a born-again Christian during his time in jail. Upon his release, and determined to live a reformed life, he went to church. Sitting in the seats, the man looked up to see a stained-glass window inscribed with the Ten Commandments. Reading the law of God on the window made him very discouraged. The man knew his weaknesses. He knew he could not live up to the Ten Commandments. However, in that moment of discouragement, the man later told the pastor he heard the phrase 'what was a command is now a promise'. At that moment, God told him, by the witness of the Holy Spirit, that he was now able to keep the law because it was written on his heart. *Thou shalt not steal* had become *thou will not steal* [emphasis added]. Receiving the spirit of adoption meant he had a guide to enable him to live a life of true freedom. I am thankful to be alive in the messianic era and have the Holy Spirit to guide me in doing what is right and true.[52]

Application. Embrace voluntary disclosure

Living in the messianic era with the Holy Spirit as a personal guide gives me the confidence I will do the right things. It is the same offer for every person. All may receive the Spirit and be salt and light in business, bringing life and peace to all co-workers, customers, and communities. The purpose of the Spirit is life and peace.[53] Every family, workplace, community, and nation needs more life and peace. The purpose of third-era divine discourse is to facilitate the model of human agency.

In modern businesses, agents make both mandatory and voluntary disclosures to owners. Chief Executive Officers and Chief Financial Officers ("CEO" and "CFO") tend to disclose what is mandatory and any additional information that puts them in a positive light. CEOs and CFOs want to maximize their pay and job security. It is natural for CEOs and CFOs to try and inflate the value of the firm through their disclosures.[54] Local laws, regulations, and accounting standards act to govern the impulse of agents who would otherwise provide insufficient or inaccurate information about the business. However, as with SEC enforcement, mandatory disclosure communication plans are only partially effective. The tension between owners and agents over disclosure in real economy organizations is absent in *The Theory of the Kingdom.* The kingdom model is full transparency. Disclosures intended to hide or manipulate the truth are unacceptable. I do well to voluntarily confess to my owners as much data as possible.

Direct access

I may not pray or read the Bible for weeks at a time. The owner still continues to communicate with me. The offer of communication from the owner does not change with my level of devotion, though the degree of intimacy may. It is up to me to take advantage of the opportunity, even though it is only on offer because of the initiative of the owner.[55] My wife will often say, "you need to talk to Jesus about that". She understands the current pattern of divine discourse. I don't go through a priest or anyone else to speak with God.[56] Jesus even experienced my sufferings and empathizes with my problems.[57] There is no problem or pain Jesus cannot relate to. God invites me to pray with boldness and shovel all of my problems onto him.[58] The model of the Holy Spirit personally guiding me to make wise choices and to know the truth, and a messiah willing to listen is a most open owner-agent construct. The strategy of intervention by communication supports freedom and risk-taking to bring life, peace, and growth to the real economy.

Notes

[1] Lewis, C. S. (2001). *The problem of pain.* Zondervan.

[2] Revelation 21:4.

[3] Blomberg, C. L. (2020). *Can We Still Believe in God?: Answering Ten Contemporary Challenges to Christianity.* Brazos Press.

[4] Luke 6:38. New American Standard Bible, 1971, 2 Corinthians 9:6. New American Standard Bible, 1971, Galatians 6:7-8. Robertson, P., & Slosser, B. (1982). *The Secret Kingdom: A Promise of Hope and Freedom in a World of Turmoil.* T. Nelson.

[5] New American Standard Bible, 1971, Luke 13:1-5.

[6] Bubola, E. (2022, June 14). The Grenfell Fire, 5 Years Later. *The New York Times.* https://www.nytimes.com/2022/06/14/world/europe/grenfell-fire-london-explainer.html.

[7] 1 Peter 2:19.
[8] New American Standard Bible, 1971, Psalm 19:1-6. New American Standard Bible, 1971, 121:1-4. New American Standard Bible, 1971, Zephaniah 3:17. John 5:17. New American Standard Bible, 1971, Romans 1:20-23.
[9] Matthew 25:31-46. Hebrews 9:27. Revelations 20:11-15.
[10] New American Standard Bible, 1971, Daniel 5:24-30.
[11] New American Standard Bible, 1971, Numbers 22:31-38.
[12] New American Standard Bible, 1971, Hebrews 1:1-2.
[13] Brown, R. (1982). *The Bible Speaks Today: The Message of Hebrews* (p. 27). InterVarsity Press.
[14] US Securities and Exchange Commission. (2021). *SEC Announces Enforcement Results for FY 2021*. https://www.sec.gov/news/press-release/2021-238.
[15] Gadinis, S. (2012). The SEC and the financial industry: Evidence from enforcement against broker-dealers. *The Business Lawyer*, 679-728. http://dx.doi.org/10.2139/ssrn.1333717.
[16] Groh, A. Liechtenstein, H. Lieser, K. & Biesinger, M. (2022, September 15). The Venture Capital and Private Equity Country Attractiveness Index. *IESE Business School.* https://blog.iese.edu/vcpeindex/.
[17] Sanchez-Munoz et al. (2021, December 16). The World's Top Recipients of Foreign Direct Investments. *International Monetary Fund.* https://blogs.imf.org/2021/12/16/the-worlds-top-recipients-of-foreign-direct-investment/.
[18] Statista Research Department. (2022, October 9). Largest stock exchange operators worldwide as of August 2022, by market capitalization of listed companies. *Statista.* https://www.statista.com/statistics/270126/largest-stock-exchange-operators-by-market-capitalization-of-listed-companies/.
[19] Levit, D. (2020). Words speak louder without actions. *The Journal of Finance, 75*(1), 91-131. http://dx.doi.org/10.1111/jofi.12834.
[20] The Amplified Bible, 1987, James 1:12.
[21] Filmer, W. E. (1966). The Chronology of the Reign of Herod the Great. *The Journal of Theological Studies*, 283-298. http://dx.doi.org/10.1093/jts/XVII.2.283.
[22] New American Standard Bible, 1971, Luke 3:23.
[23] Votaw, C. W. (1905). The Chronology of Jesus' Public Ministry. *The Biblical World, 26*(6), 425-430. http://dx.doi.org/10.1086/473674.
[24] John 14:3. Acts 1:10-11. 2 Peter 3:10, Revelation 1:7. New American Standard Bible, 1971, Revelation 22:20.
[25] Wolterstorff, N. (1998). Divine discourse: Philosophical reflections on the claim that God speaks. *Pro Ecclesia, 7*(2), 242-244. p8. http://dx.doi.org/10.1177/106385129800700210.
[26] Hebrews 4:12. Matthew 24:35.
[27] Multiple instances including Genesis 3:8-24.
[28] Multiple instances beginning in New American Standard Bible, 1971, Genesis 6:13.
[29] Genesis 12:1-3. First instance in this passage was a call to go.
[30] Pfeiffer, C., & Harrison, E. (Eds.). (1962). *The Wycliffe Bible Commentary* (pp. 554, 585, 595). Moody Publishers.
[31] Gay, D. (1996). Book Review: Divine Discourse: Philosophical Reflections on the Claim That God Speaks. *Christianity & literature, 45*(3/4), 401-403. http://dx.doi.org/10.1177/014833319604500314.

[32] New American Standard Bible, 1971, Joshua chapter 1.
[33] New American Standard Bible, 1971, Leviticus chapter 28.
[34] Blomberg, C. L. (2020). *Can We Still Believe in God?: Answering Ten Contemporary Challenges to Christianity* (p. 87). Brazos Press.
[35] Matthew 5:17-18.
[36] Hebrews 1:1-2.
[37] Matthew 17:5. A minority of commentators also believe God speaks in the book of Revelation, including in chapter 1, verse 8. However, it is more commonly said the alpha and omega, and speaker, is Jesus.
[38] Matthew 3:13-17. Mark 1:9-11. Luke 3:21-22,
[39] Burge, G. M., & Green, G. L. (2020). *The New Testament in Antiquity: A Survey of the New Testament Within Its Cultural Contexts Second Edition* (p. 191), Zondervan Academic.
[40] Stott, J. (2014). *The Message of the Sermon on the Mount* (p. 4). InterVarsity Press.
[41] Carson, D. A. (1999). God Is Love. *BIBLIOTHECA SACRA-DALLAS-*, *156*, 131-142.
[42] Stott, J. (2014). *The Message of the Sermon on the Mount* (p. 187). InterVarsity Press.
[43] Blomberg, C. L. (1992). *Matthew: An exegetical and theological exposition of Holy Scripture* (Vol. 22, pp. 216-217). B&H Publishing Group.
[44] John 14:23-31.
[45] Bruce, F. F. (1994). *The Gospel of John: Introduction, Exposition, Notes* (pp. 305). Wm. B. Eerdmans Publishing.
[46] Luke 12:11. Mark 13:11. Matthew 10:19.
[47] Luke 24:49. Acts 1:4. Note that both verses were written by Luke.
[48] Ephesians 1:13. Romans 8:11. John 3:5.
[49] Ephesians 6:12.
[50] 2 Timothy 3:16.
[51] New American Standard Bible, 1971, Ephesians 5:18.
[52] New American Standard Bible, 1971, John 16:13.
[53] Romans 8:6.
[54] Healy, P. M., & Palepu, K. G. (2001). Information asymmetry, corporate disclosure, and the capital markets: A review of the empirical disclosure literature. *Journal of accounting and economics, 31*(1-3), 405-440. http://dx.doi.org/10.1016/S0165-4101(01)00018-0.
[55] New American Standard Bible, 1971, 1 John 4:19-21.
[56] New American Standard Bible, 1971, Ephesians 3:11-13.
[57] Hebrews 4:14-16.
[58] 1 Peter 5:7.

Chapter 5

Objective function

The ruling political body of each nation sets its economic objectives. Nations may want to maximize employment, trade, or even stability. Individuals also set economic objectives. In general, individuals want to maximize personal enjoyment. Nations and individuals make choices to meet their objectives. In this chapter, I motivate the discussion with an example of an individual objective. Second, I briefly present the objective functions of notable modern nations. Third, I offer and analyze the life, peace and growth objective function of the kingdom of God. The chapter concludes with an application of the kingdom objective function in daily life.

Individual level objective

I want to succeed. To succeed, I first define one or more objectives. Once objectives are defined, I set up a model for achieving them. Achieving my objectives represents success. Objectives may be monetary or non-monetary. Monetary success may be earning one billion dollars, or it may be much more modest. A modest objective may be to earn enough money to pay for health care and school and to save for retirement. Citizens of less developed economies may define wealth as owning a car. In non-monetary terms, an objective may be for educational attainment or a family with a certain number of children. I have been asked how I define success. Success, for me, is non-monetary. A high-order personal objective is to live out my marriage vows. The objective is mostly behavioral. I do need to earn an income to meet this objective. Income is just a small part of a non-monetary end. Behavioral choices play a greater role in meeting a marital fidelity objective.

With success defined, I set up a family behavioral model, including an economy, targeting my objectives. The first part of my family model involves developing antecedents to interim goals such as romantic fidelity. The setup of our family economy, including job selection, and specific actions my wife and I take, are oriented to the objective.

A monetary aspect of the model is joint accounts of all types. My wife and I have visibility into all sources of income and spending. A non-monetary, behavioral, example of the model relates to business travel. I make every effort to sleep at home rather than in a hotel room. It is a self-imposed rule, an antecedent to the objective of marital fidelity. At different points in my career, I have traveled extensively. However, whenever possible, I slept at home. If I had a two-day conference, I would make every effort to leave early on the morning the conference began and fly home late at night on the second day. I often turned a three night trip into a one night trip. Turning a three-night hotel stay into a one-night stay supports marital fidelity. During one season of time, I had regular business in Boston. I would arrange meetings in a way to make a series of day trips possible. Downtown Boston was a three-hour trip. It was three hours, whether by car, airplane, or rail. I could leave the house at five AM and arrive on time for an eight AM breakfast. I would generally finish meetings before six PM and then head home. My non-monetary definition of success and behavioral model led me back home whenever possible. It is possible my income potential was reduced by fewer late-night client dinners and events. Maximizing income ranked below marital fidelity.

Kingdom economy is for life, peace and growth

Chapter One introduced the model of human agency and the mechanism of how it is God accomplishes his objectives through the actions of human agents. This moment in history is an overlapping period where both the present-day real economy and the future permanent economy of the kingdom of God are in operation.[1] The arrival of Jesus in Bethlehem[2] marked the beginning of the messianic era. In this overlapping period, it is unequivocally positive for the global economy to grow and to have more jobs and more wealth. I need to earn money in the real economy to keep the wheels of my family economy turning. It is also true more jobs and more wealth are not the highest-order objectives of Jesus' kingdom economy.

The model of human agency assumes God has unlimited resources. The kingdom economy is not oriented to consistent GDP growth, low inflation or a stable currency in the way of a modern central bank. A nation's central bank objectives change over time. The kingdom economy terms of trade to acquire heart capital and spiritual products do not change. The products of the Holy Spirit in my life are defined in the Bible[3] and God, the owner, will not change his economic objectives or policies.[4] The objective function of the kingdom is not for individuals to maximize wealth in this age or to maximize the value of a business or property. Real economy wealth cannot be the objective of God's economy. Real economy wealth is at odds with several Bible passages.[5] If the economy of God is not oriented to stable prices, stable currencies, or wealth accumulation, what is it oriented to?

The objective function of the economy of the kingdom of God is to maximize life, peace, and growth. The kingdom economy produces other monetary and non-monetary outcomes. Many behavioral models have embedded secondary objectives around the high-level objectives. The life, peace, and growth objectives are the foundation for understanding the terms of trade and the required actions of human agents, and they are developed based on a survey of scripture. Before studying each of the three components of the objective function of the kingdom economy I have prepared a comparative analysis of central bank macroeconomic objectives in the real economy.

Presenting an objective function of the kingdom economy is a new idea on at least two dimensions. First, it is a new to propose a macroeconomic purpose of the kingdom of God. Second, the majority of real economy objectives are monetary. I look forward to the future research by others on the objective function of the kingdom economy.

Real economy objectives

Small groups, communities, nations, and groups of nations organize around particular objectives.

The central banks of large modern economies present clear statements of their objectives. Objectives are most often, though not exclusively, tied to monetary outcomes. For nations, the responsibility to implement specific actions to achieve monetary objectives falls to the central bank. The most important national and regional economies of the twenty-first century are the United States, China, Europe and Japan.

The objective of the Central Bank of the United States is to meet a dual mandate of maximum employment and stable prices.[6] The actions of the board of the Federal Reserve Bank are intended to achieve these two high-order goals. In an idealized world, the United States would have about 4% unemployment and an inflation rate averaging 2% per year. The objective function of the People's Bank of China is to maintain a stable currency. A stable currency is considered an important antecedent to sustainable economic growth and a general increase in China's prosperity and power.[7] Most nations of Europe have adopted a common currency. The actions of the European Central Bank ("ECB") are intended to safeguard the common currency by controlling inflation.[8] The ECB believes a stable currency will support economic growth and job creation across Europe. The Bank of Japan ("BOJ") has a slightly different purpose. The BOJ is seeking to maintain the stability of the Japanese financial system.[9] The BOJ works toward its objective of financial stability by issuing currency and developing systems to ensure the smooth functioning of individual banks.

Nations want calm and more cash

Themes emerge in a survey of national monetary objectives. First, central banks and politicians that supervise central banks, like calm. It is undesirable to have wild swings in prices, currencies and economic output. Economic volatility is undesirable because of the association between economic crises and political regime change.[10] Second, economic objectives are intended to facilitate growth in both economic output and individual prosperity. Political leaders want economic stability, more wealth, and more jobs. Third, based on changes in political regimes, objective functions also change over time.

The U.S. Federal Reserve mandate has evolved. The United States Congress established the U.S. central bank in 1913. The U.S. Congress has also amended the governing law and changed the mandate of the Federal Reserve several times.[11] The changes are generally in response to a combination of economic crisis and political pressure. The Federal Reserve's purpose has evolved from issuing currency to maintain growth, to a lender of last resort, to an inflation fighter, and most recently to achieving a dual mandate of maximum employment and stable prices.

The kingdom economy is different

There are stark contrasts between real economy objectives and kingdom economy objectives. First, the kingdom economy is not linearly connected to real economy monetary outcomes. God is the creator and owner of all things. He can manifest new resources in the real economy out of nothing.[12] Creation *ex nihilo* is a foundational element of Judeo-Christian theology.[13] Second, the real economy is temporary and the kingdom economy is permanent. Third, political leadership and objectives change, but God does not change.[14] It is safe to assume the objective function of the kingdom is the same now as it was in the time of Moses and in the time of Jesus on earth. Jesus indicated the teaching of the law and the prophets remain in effect.[15] The plan of the Gospel of God, to send Jesus to earth, was put in place even before the earth was put in place.[16] Third, money[17] is not the medium of exchange in the messianic era model of human agency, rather it is life by the Holy Spirit.

Not all economies use traditional currency nor are they oriented to a monetary outcome. There is an extensive branch of research on barter economies that function based on exchange due to the double coincidence of wants,[18] and without a uniform medium of exchange.[19] There is also a branch of economic literature studying non-monetary economies and social objective functions.[20] Further, Iannaccone attributes the lack of progress on new theories explaining the sociology of religion to an overly narrow focus on "time and money."[21] Exchange according to *The law of proportion* is the subject of chapter 12. I will have more to say on the essential role of the Holy Spirit in later chapters regarding the interaction of the real economy and kingdom economy. For now, I reference the thesis of Witness Lee. According to Lee's study, in the first instance, the economy of God depends on the endowment of the Holy Spirit.[22]

Life

The first element of the objective of the economy of the kingdom of God is to maximize life. If I am living and working according to the model of human agency, I am making life-giving, life-promoting, and life-sustaining choices. No government can stop me from choosing to promote life in my family, my community, my workplace and in my management of the environment. John's gospel records Jesus' purpose. Jesus came so that I might have eternal life and live an abundant life, starting right now.[23] A key narrative of the Bible is God created humankind to experience loving relationships and abundant life.[24] All of us have, at some point, chosen to rebel against God's authority and plan. Human rebellion is the cause of real economy injustice and suffering. No real economy administration can alleviate suffering. Humanistic rational choice actions often cause suffering. Jesus came to earth to die in my place and provide a way for redemption back to life and life abundantly. If I choose to take the path Jesus provided back to life, I must make every effort to promote the objectives of Jesus' kingdom now. Jesus' death and resurrection replaced the sacrificial system of the Old Testament, transmuting the real economy problems into spiritual issues.[25]

Human agency is the mechanism by which the kingdom economy is activated. God confines himself, for the most part, to work through human agents. Life is what Jesus came for. It is up to me to be salt and light and to bring life to my circle of relationships.

Where created life and eternal life meet is abundant life

The book of John chapter 10 comes with a sub-heading "Jesus the Good Shepherd." The Good Shepherd section of John contains a clear, exclusive claim Jesus is the source of salvation and new life.[26] The analogy of a shepherd highlights an important virtue in the model of human agency. Jesus identifies as a shepherd and "draws to himself every epithet which the picture of sheep and shepherds"[27] evokes. Jesus' humility emphasizes a trait of effective agency in God's kingdom.[28]

In a modern economy context, shepherding, sheep and humility is a ridiculous setup to promote an economic system. Imagine you are writing a speech to convince people of the superiority of your economic model. The key argument you settle on is to compare your leadership, governance, and power to the lowest, least respected, and least desirable vocation in the economy. The argument Jesus made was, "follow me because I am employed on the lowest rung of the ladder". The economy of God and the model of human agency is completely different from competing models.

Much has been written about John chapter 10. Wycliffe's commentary says the clear sentiment is the work of the shepherd is good and constructive.[29] The first part of the shepherd's work is to save, and the second part is to provide for a good life beginning now. The model of human agency is for saving life, preserving life, and promoting a good life for all humankind right now. Past and present economic systems do not always promote life. Many fabulously wealthy people obtained wealth by destroying human life and despoiling the environment. Success in the kingdom economy only comes by making every effort to promote life.

John chapter 10 can be extended by noting the life-saving and life-giving purpose of the collective.[30] The purpose of life and abundance is for groups and nations. In that way, the life-giving objective is suitable for an economy. Merrill Tenney notes the connection of the good shepherd terminology to Psalm 23.[31] The pasture represents food for survival and restoration of the soul.[32] The good shepherd gives access to a pasture with abundant provision of food and space. The language of abundance calls to the reader's memory decadent miraculous provision of wine at the marriage of Cana or an unrestrained supply of fish and bread.[33] The economic resources in the kingdom of God are unlimited and more than sufficient for me to promote life now. Thompson goes on to write, "abundant life is found at the intersection of created life and eternal life."[34] The intersection of created life and eternal life is reflected by two nested circles in the model of human agency. Finally, the life-giving objective of the kingdom of God is further supported within the book of John.[35] I expect the *life* component of the objective will be strengthened by additional future research.

Peace

Peace is the second component of the objective function of the kingdom economy. The prophet Isaiah indicates Jesus' kingdom is one of peace and growth.[36] It will be supported by its perfect justice and moral code. It will grow forever and it will last forever. Isaiah gives Jesus the royal title of Prince of Peace. The royal title provides direction as four or five-component compound names were common for ancient royals.[37]

A title for every territory

In both ancient and modern times, formal royal titles are typically associated with particular territories. Modern royal titles have included the King of Saudi Arabia, the Queen of England, the Prince of Wales, and the Princess of

Monaco. Isaiah could have prophesied Jesus would be Prince of the Roman Empire, or Prince of the Earth, or even the King of the Universe for that matter. Isaiah did not attach Jesus' royalty to something as small or temporary as a real economy territory. Jesus is called the Prince of Peace. Peace is the name of the territory associated with the economy of God. The Hebrew word in both Isaiah 9:6 and 9:7 is *shalom*. The term is well-known and connotes not an absence of conflict but all-encompassing well-being. Shalom peace is safety, prosperity, favor, friendship, rest, welfare, and happiness.[38]

The arrival of the Messianic era, as told in the traditional Christmas story of Luke's gospel, confirms an objective of peace. The first introduction of the good news of Jesus' birth to a group of shepherds is a declaration of peace on earth and goodwill to humankind.[39] Angelic messengers did not declare war on an oppressive Roman Empire. Jesus arrived with a declaration of peace. Peace is an individual and group-level benefit of the messianic era.[40]

Kingdom economy peace if for groups

The peace objective of the kingdom economy is for groups. Peace with God is indeed the greatest benefit for people, throughout all time, that choose to receive Jesus as Lord. Individuals personally receive peace with God through justification and reconciliation. However, in the Bible, there is a distinct theme of collective peace. In the Old Testament, the peace offering of Leviticus chapter three demonstrates peace with God is for our vertical relationship with Him, and also for horizontal community relationships now. The unique instruction for the peace offering was to consume all the food in one day, or perhaps two, depending on the offering sub-type. The only way to consume a large quantity of food in such a short period of time is with a large number of people. The peace offering and associated feast was a community event.[41] The New Testament records several other bits of evidence for group-level peace with God. Jesus prayed his disciples would be united.[42] In Romans chapter five, the apostle Paul switched from the singular to the plural, referring to a shared peace.[43] Later, Paul introduces the imagery of the followers of Jesus being part of one body.[44] Maximizing peace is a high-order, group-level objective in the messianic era of human history.

The Prince of Peace title given to Jesus connects with the King of Salem.[45] In the book of Genesis, Abram, soon to be renamed Abraham, meets a person called Melchizedek, the King of Salem. Abram had won a battle and saved his nephew Lot's family and all their belongings. Following the victory, Abram received bread, wine, and a blessing from Melchizedek. Abram responded by offering Melchizedek 10% of all his wealth. The mode of Abram's wealth acquisition and to whom he was offering a tenth share is unique in ancient literature.[46] Melchizedek is referred to as the priest of the most high God. Two additional Bible passages suggest Melchizedek foreshadowed Jesus, namely as a righteous king and priest.[47] The bread and wine served by Melchizedek to Abram, the future father of many nations,[48] is a harbinger of the Last Supper scene.[49]

The name Melchizedek means "king of righteousness". The name is not a proper name such as John or Matthew, but rather an attribute. The righteousness attribute aligns with Isaiah's prophecy about how the economy of God would function.[50] The territory Melchizedek is over is called Salem. The meaning of Salem is shalom, or cosmic harmonious peace. I summarize the story of Melchizedek as an ancient king of righteousness, reigning over a realm of peace, blessing Abram, foreshadowing a righteous messiah Jesus, who would rule over a realm called peace. There is much more that can be said about peace in the kingdom economy. For example, consider the apostle Paul's tendency to use *grace and peace* as the salutation in his pastoral epistles.[51] The bottom line is I propose peace is a defining outcome for individual Christ followers and for the growing Christian community on earth.

Growth

The third component of the objective function of the kingdom economy is growth. From a starting point of just a few tens of followers, the global Christian community has well surpassed 2,000,000,000.[52] Empirical evidence abounds for the increase Isaiah prophesied.[53] My methodology, however is not to use real economy evidence to develop a theory. Rather the theory of the kingdom is arrived at by a bibliology. On the basis of a bibliology, it is clear God is ambitious and has a plan for continuous growth.

At first, I thought it was curious. Isaiah said the government of the realm of peace will increase forever. Upon closer inspection, growth is a consistent component of the biblical story, the history of humanity and what is known about the universe. The Bible indicates it is God's wish that every person would choose to be a citizen of his kingdom.[54] The offer of eternal life is actively made to any person that would believe.[55] It is also clear from scripture not all humans will choose Jesus, yet God's patience reflects his saving desires. Even the Bible character Jezebel, who was given to idolatry, corrupt political ambition, and murder,[56] was offered time to repent and choose life.[57] The offer of salvation and kingdom citizenship is made to every person. It is the height of ambition to offer kingdom entry to tens of billions of human souls.

The Bible indicates God is prepared to shelter and supply for all the people he wishes to redeem. The city of God described in Revelation has the resources and scale to make good on a universal offer of redemption.[58] The volume of space described in Revelation chapter 21 is equivalent to a cube reaching from Toronto, Canada, west to Denver, USA, south to Mexico City, Mexico, and then up into the earth's exosphere. If I assume a past and present human population of approximately 100,000,000,000, then each person is allocated at least 478 cubic meters. The biblical record of God's love and ambition for humankind is beyond comprehension.

Sustainability is part of the design

In the creation narrative of Genesis chapter one, God creates the heavens and the earth and his intention is for all living creatures and humans to multiply and fill the earth. The heavens continue to expand. This has been known for some time. However, the expansion of the universe is happening at a rate faster than the ability of current astrological models to explain.[59] For our part, humans have done well multiplying. Economists and data scientists of all types have noted people are healthier, better educated, richer, less likely to die in war, and likely to live longer, despite, or because of, being more numerous now than at any point.[60] The kingdom economy's intention for living creatures to multiply is also important. All living creatures are to multiply, not just humans. Sustainability is built into the design of the heavens and the earth. Human agency is being abused when animal populations are shrinking or facing extinction, for example.

In terms of social and national development, I note the royal records in the books of Chronicles regularly include significant building projects. The record of a king revolves in part around cities built or restored and substantial new building projects. Capital investments are important markers in the reign of political leaders. In contrast, choosing to stop investing in favor of leisure can have dire personal consequences.[61] Humankind is created in the image and likeness of God.[62] God is ambitious. Humanity is, therefore, ambitious and hard-wired to pursue growth. The economy of the kingdom of God will grow. The model of human agency is designed to simultaneously facilitate growth in the real economy and kingdom economy.

Application

Applications of the kingdom economy objectives are many. Success, defined as growth, life, and peace, will change how I speak, how I parent, how aggressively I invest and how community-minded I am. Individual and group-level applications of the model of human agency are the subject of much of the rest of this book. For now, I propose a fill-in-the-blank exercise.

"____________" for peace.

I can put any individual or group-level activity in the blank. For me, I can insert husbanding, parenting, coaching, neighboring, teaching, or working. Coaching my son's little league baseball team to maximize peace looks very different than coaching to maximize wins. I am certain parenting for peace is different than parenting to maximize my child's future income potential. At a group level, the blank may be filled in with serving on a board, managing, setting investment priorities, seeking new opportunities and working in the environment. Coming up with real economy applications to insert in the blank is easier than living them out.

Notes

[1] Burge, G. M., & Green, G. L. (2020). *The New Testament in Antiquity: A Survey of the New Testament Within Its Cultural Contexts Second Edition.* Zondervan Academic.

[2] Luke chapter 2.

[3] Galatians 5:22-23.

[4] Psalm 33:11, Malachi 3:6. James 1:17.

[5] New American Standard Bible, 1971, Proverbs 23:4-5. Matthew 6:19-21. New American Standard Bible, 1971, Mark 4:9. New American Standard Bible, 1971, Proverbs 20:21. New American Standard Bible, 1971, Proverbs 13:11.

[6] Board of Governors of the Federal Reserve. (2022). *Monetary Policy: What Are Its Goals? How Does It Work?* https://www.federalreserve.gov/monetarypolicy/monetary-policy-what-are-its-goals-how-does-it-work.htm.

[7] People's Bank of China. (2003). *Law of the People's Republic of China on The People's Bank of China.* http://www.pbc.gov.cn/english/130733/2941519/2015082610501049304.pdf.

[8] European Central Bank. (2022). *Introduction.* https://www.ecb.europa.eu/mopo/intro/html/index.en.html.

[9] Bank of Japan. (2022) *About the Bank.* https://www.boj.or.jp/en/about/outline/index.htm/.

[10] Gasiorowski, M. J. (1995). Economic crisis and political regime change: An event history analysis. *American political science review, 89*(4), 882-897. http://dx.doi.org/10.2307/2082515.

[11] Board of Governors of the Federal Reserve. (2022). *Monetary policy objectives. Section 2A.* https://www.federalreserve.gov/aboutthefed/section2a.htm.

[12] Exodus chapter 15. Exodus chapter 16. John chapter 2. Matthew chapter 14.

[13] New American Standard Bible, 1971, Romans 4:17. Keener, C. S., & Walton, J. H. (Eds.). (2016). *NIV, Cultural Backgrounds Study Bible: Bringing to Life the Ancient World of Scripture* (p. 2029). Zondervan.

[14] Psalm 33:11, Malachi 3:6 and James 1:17.

[15] Matthew 5:17. Matthew 7:12. Matthew 22:37-40.

[16] 1 Peter 1:19-21. New American Standard Bible, 1971, Titus 1:1-3.

[17] New American Standard Bible, 1971, Isaiah 55:1-2.

[18] Starr, R. M. (1989). The structure of exchange in barter and monetary economies. In *General Equilibrium Models of Monetary Economies* (pp. 129-143). Academic Press. http://dx.doi.org/10.1016/B978-0-12-663970-4.50014-1.

[19] Williams, C. C. (1996). The new barter economy: an appraisal of Local Exchange and Trading Systems (LETS). *Journal of Public Policy, 16*(1), 85-101. http://dx.doi.org/10.1017/S0143814X0000787X..
[20] Heller, W. P., & Starr, R. M. (1976). Equilibrium with non-convex transactions costs: monetary and non-monetary economies. *The Review of Economic Studies, 43*(2), 195-215. 176-185. http://dx.doi.org/10.2307/2297318. & Howard, K., & Sharp, J. A. (1985). Social indicators and policy selection: An experiment in constructing a social objective function. *European Journal of Operational Research, 19*(2). http://dx.doi.org/10.1016/0377-2217(85)90170-5.
[21] Iannaccone, L. R. (1988). A formal model of church and sect. *American journal of sociology, 94*, S241-S268. http://dx.doi.org/10.1086/228948.
[22] Lee, W. (1986). *God's New Testament Economy.* Living Stream Ministry.
[23] John 3:16. John 10:10.
[24] Eskola, T. (2015). *A narrative theology of the New Testament: exploring the metanarrative of exile and restoration* (Vol. 350). Mohr Siebeck.
[25] Tyndale, & Tyndale House Publishers. (2004). *Life Application Study Bible: New Living Translation* (p. 160). Tyndale House Publishers, Inc..
[26] Barrett, C. K. (1978). *The Gospel according to St. John: An introduction with commentary and notes on the Greek Text* (p. 368) Westminster John Knox Press.
[27] Barrett, C. K. (1978). *The Gospel according to St. John: An introduction with commentary and notes on the Greek Text* (p. 372). Westminster John Knox Press.
[28] Matthew 5:5.
[29] Pfeiffer, C., & Harrison, E. (Eds.). (1962). *The Wycliffe Bible Commentary.* Moody Publishers.
[30] Tenney, M. C. (1997). *John: the gospel of belief* (p. 162). Wm. B. Eerdmans Publishing.
[31] Tenney, M. C. (1997). *John: the gospel of belief* (p. 162). Wm. B. Eerdmans Publishing.
[32] New American Standard Bible, 1971, Psalm 23:3.
[33] Thompson, M. M. (2001). *The God of the gospel of John.* Wm. B. Eerdmans Publishing.
[34] Thompson, M. M. (2001). *The God of the gospel of John* (p. 224). Wm. B. Eerdmans Publishing.
[35] John 10:10. John 6:33. John 10:28. John 3:16.
[36] Isaiah 9:6-7. Note the transition point to messianic era chapters in Isaiah is later in chapter 40. Isaiah 40:2 indicates the arrival of Jesus means the war has ended.
[37] Keener, C. S., & Walton, J. H. (Eds.). (2016). *NIV, Cultural Backgrounds Study Bible: Bringing to Life the Ancient World of Scripture* (p. 1167). Zondervan.
[38] Strong, J. (2009). *Strong's exhaustive concordance of the Bible* (Hebrew and Chaldee Dictionary, p116). Hendrickson Publishers.
[39] Luke 2:14.
[40] Stott, J. (2014). *The message of Romans: God's good news for the world* (p. 139). InterVarsity Press.
[41] Kidner, D. (1982). Sacrifice—Metaphors and Meaning. *Tyndale Bulletin, 33*, 119-136. http://dx.doi.org/10.53751/001c.30604.
[42] John 17:22.
[43] Stott, J. (2014). *The message of Romans: God's good news for the world* (p. 138). InterVarsity Press.
[44] New American Standard Bible, 1971, 1 Corinthians chapter 12.
[45] Genesis chapter 14.

[46] Keener, C. S., & Walton, J. H. (Eds.). (2016). *NIV, Cultural Backgrounds Study Bible: Bringing to Life the Ancient World of Scripture* (p. 42). Zondervan.
[47] Psalms chapter 110, Hebrews 7:3.
[48] New American Standard Bible, 1971, Genesis 17:5.
[49] New American Standard Bible, 1971, Matthew chapter 26. Mark chapter 14. Luke chapter 22. John chapter 13.
[50] Isaiah 9:6-7.
[51] Romans chapter 1. 1 Corinthians chapter 1. 2 Corinthians chapter 1, Galatians chapter 1, Ephesians chapter 1.
[52] Pew Research Center. (2011, December 19). *Global Christianity – A Report on the Size and Distribution of the World's Christian Population.* https://www.pewresearch.org/religion/2011/12/19/global-christianity-exec/.
[53] Isaiah 9:6-7.
[54] 2 Peter 3:9.
[55] John 3:16. New American Standard Bible, 1971, Revelation 3:20.
[56] Stark, T., & Van Deventer, H. J. (2009). The 'Jezebel spirit': A scholarly inquiry. *Verbum et Ecclesia, 30*(2), 68-76. http://dx.doi.org/10.4102/ve.v30i2.301.
[57] New American Standard Bible, 1971, Revelation 2:21.
[58] Revelation 21:16-17.
[59] Greshko, M. (2021, December 17). *The Universe is expanding faster than it should be.* https://www.nationalgeographic.com/science/article/the-universe-is-expanding-faster-than-it-should-be.
[60] Radelet, S. (2015). *The great surge: The ascent of the developing world.* Simon and Schuster. & Piketty, T. (2014). *Capital in the twenty-first century.* Harvard University Press. http://dx.doi.org/10.4159/9780674369542.
[61] Luke 12:13-21.
[62] Genesis 1:27.

Chapter 6

Economic resources

Every economy has a resource base. In this chapter, I study unlimited dimensions of kingdom economy resources and apply it to everyday agency. The next chapter, on resource allocation, analyzes endowment, acquisition and utilization of kingdom resources. Chapter six, chapter seven and later application chapters 13, 14, and 15 together make up a complete exploration into the economic resource construct of the kingdom economy.

Humankind lives with a real economy reality of limited resources and rationing. God has unlimited resources. The kingdom of heaven has abundant resources. However, abundant resources do not mean I receive an allocation according to my unlimited wants. One difference in the kingdom economy is my potential getting is unlimited and is synergistic with everyone else's getting.

A central element of Judeo-Christian doctrine is creation out of nothing. God, the owner, is the primary cause of all the tangible and intangible resources in the universe. Human agents are made in God's image. Humans are creative. If I create a small kitchen table for an apartment where my wife and I live, which I did, I am the secondary cause of the table.[1] God is the primary causal agent of all resources. I say *is* because the Bible indicates God is the owner, is working, and is building the future realm and time is subject to him.[2] That God is the primary cause of resources is the reason kingdom agency is different from real economy agency.

The owner with unlimited resources offers me an agency role as a resource conduit rather than a resource depository. I am the salt and light of the real economy.[3] I am a conduit transporting kingdom economic resources into the real economy to produce life, peace, and growth. This is part of the meaning of a line in Jesus' model prayer, "Your kingdom come. Your will be done, on earth as it is in heaven."[4] The essential function of salt in antiquity was as a food preservative. Kingdom agency includes arresting resource spoilage and corruption in the real economy. The meaning of light is to illuminate the truth of God's word.[5] The purpose of this chapter is to illuminate the resources and associated economic policies found in the Bible.[6]

Managing small circle resource scarcity

Economic resources are used as inputs in the production of goods and services. The real economy has limited resources. Humankind has unlimited wants. The real economy, therefore, suffers from a scarcity of resources. Humankind has a natural drive to grow and consume more. The limited resources of the real economy and the sins of people[7] are associated with human suffering. I suffer, for example, if I do not have the resources to access proper health care to treat a sickness. I may also suffer if someone happens to want one of my valuable possessions and takes it from me by force.

If I remove the kingdom of God from the model of human agency, what is left is the small circle of the real economy. In the real economy, the problem of limited resources and human suffering is left to politicians and economists to manage, often according to a secular economic faith. The communism of Karl Marx and his followers managed the economic resources of land, labor, and capital to achieve a "secularized kingdom of heaven on earth."[8] Common parts of the different visions of communism include the elimination of private property and the elimination of individualism in favor of a new collective where economic resources are allocated by a group of "secular saints" to ensure all citizens are equal.[9] A common resource vision is still popular amongst academics. Moving on from individually owned private property to a collective social order remains a popular idea in some circles.[10] However, the effect of communism has been to cause human suffering rather than to alleviate it. It is interesting, therefore, that some religious people seem to prefer centrally planned economies over market economies.[11]

A market-based real economy deals with resource scarcity through the voluntary exchange of goods and services. The supply of goods and services finds an equilibrium where the quantity of demand and quantity of supply meet at a price agreed upon in the market. The equilibrium price is not set by government policy. The price is reached through many voluntary transactions. The market-based model of supply and demand was described in detail in the late 1800's by Alfred Marshall in his book Principles of Economics.[12] Humankind has benefited from the growing popularity of market-based economies.[13]

In market-based economies, supply is rationed by price and the resources are owned by private individuals and organizations. An alternative to price is to ration resources by time or by force. If governments own the majority of the resources, equilibrium is reached by government regulation, or sometimes not at all. All humans are fallible, including government regulators. Economies operate more efficiently and grow closer to potential with individuals making decisions to set prices, as opposed to central governments.[14] Market-based economies have a superior track record in terms of growth and alleviation of human suffering. At this moment in history, more humans are earning more money per person, are healthier, and are better educated.[15] Despite this, market-based economies on their own are not virtuous and don't deal satisfactorily with the wealth distribution question.

Kingdom economy dimensions of land, labor, and capital

The resources of the kingdom economy are multi-dimensional. In the kingdom economy, real economy resources of land, labor, and capital include additional dimensions of spiritual territory, heart labor, and heart capital. I introduce each additional resource type in this chapter and study them in more detail later.

Labor

The real economy labor resource includes physical and intellectual labor. The kingdom labor resource also includes spiritual labor. The construct of emotional or spiritual labor is a frequent topic of prior studies.[16] Reggie McNeal calls spiritual labor a work of the heart.[17] The author works extensively with religious leaders whose primary vocation deals with the spiritual well-being of humankind.

The heart labor concept reflects the additional dimension of work done in the kingdom economy. Luke 6:45 in the new living translation reads, "A good person produces good things from the treasury of a good heart, an evil person produces evil things from the treasury of an evil heart. What you say flows from what is in your heart." The connection point of the real economy to the kingdom economy is through heart labor.

Core elements of heart labor are prayer, fasting and giving

Three core elements of Catholic Lent, Jewish piety, and Jesus' sermon on the Mount are prayer, fasting, and almsgiving.[18] These three activities are the essentials of heart labor. Heart labor is the mechanism that drives kingdom growth and present output, including life and peace. Seeing biblical teaching as heart labor opens up new and different ways to work in the world. Additional heart labors, such as meekness, are listed in the sermon on the mount.[19] Meekness is restrained or yielded strength. The word for meek is sometimes translated as gentle or humble. As a young person, I considered meekness a vice, at least in competitive sports. A favorite t-shirt read, "the meek might inherit the earth but they won't get any rebounds". It was not clear why I would want to yield strength in sports or the workplace. It is clear now. I see meekness as heart labor intended to bring the kingdom reality to the real economy now, producing life, peace, and growth, even if it costs me money or position.

Capital

I most naturally think of capital as money. Part of my capital is the total of all the cash, stocks, and bonds I own. In addition to financial capital, I have fixed capital. Fixed capital includes assets like a house. Land with a house or building on it becomes real estate. My capital also includes machinery such as a car, a boat, and even a lawn mower. The accumulated total value of money, real estate, and equipment is my capital. Irving Fisher defined capital as the amount of useful material things I own at a moment in time.[20]

Fisher's view is outdated. Capital is more than material things. Intangible capital is the most highly valued type of capital. For example, Coca-Cola's value is in its intangible brand and syrup formulas, more than any manufacturing line or building. Microsoft's value is in its computer code, patents, way of hiring, training, and doing business. Small businesses are valuable because of the know-how of the founder and intangibles such as reliability and an ability to price a job well. Researchers often study the value of intangible assets. Investors value intangible assets more highly than material things.[21] In a study I co-authored with Kenneth Yung, we found intangible organization capital was significantly associated with the value of a firm.[22]

Biblical heart capital is different from spiritual capital

Academic literature considers the nature and value of a full list of intangibles. Social capital, intellectual capital, organization capital, environmental capital, and spiritual capital are all frequent topics, with hundreds of thousands of journal articles easily found on each topic in online libraries.[23] The focus of this study is to consider and define heart capital. Heart capital is a specific type of spiritual capital, as defined by a survey of the Bible. A detailed study of heart capital and its link to kingdom agent productivity is the subject of chapter 13.

The terms spiritual capital and religious capital are sometimes used interchangeably.[24] I draw a distinction between biblical heart capital and spiritual capital in general. For example, biblical heart capital is very different from the concept of spiritual capital in Zohar & Marshall's *Spiritual Capital: Wealth We Can Live By*.[25] Spiritual capital, in some instances, means an almost religion-free intangible owned by individuals or groups. Irving Fisher viewed an article of wealth as a useful material thing. Spiritual wealth is sometimes defined as the intangible items that enrich non-material components of human existence. With general spiritual capital, it is less important from whom or where the asset is received. Zohar and Marshall draw direct links between humanity-based spiritual capital, spiritual intelligence, and environmental sustainability. I find the earth-friendly line of thinking more akin to a pagan form of spirituality than any biblical definition of spirituality.

Sources of biblical heart capital

Heart capital is not a general form of spiritual capital. Heart capital is a spiritual treasure endowed by God according to the pattern of scripture. Heart capital is activated and made more productive by the Holy Spirit as a consequence of being spiritually reborn, according to Jesus' statement to the religious leader Nicodemus.[26] Acquiring heart capital is a prerequisite to being salt and light in the real economy, producing goods and services that result in the growth of the Kingdom of Heaven, and the spread of life and peace now.

All humanity is endowed with beginning heart capital and has equal opportunity to obtain an unlimited amount of additional heart capital. The initial endowment comes from the fact every person is created in the image of God.[27] Additional heart capital comes from receiving the Holy Spirit in my life. The Holy Spirit is responsible for spiritual rebirth.[28] Five times in the Bible, the Holy Spirit is called a *parakletos*, often translated as the one who is my advocate or comforter. The Holy Spirit comes alongside me to advocate, comfort, and guide me in truth on a day-to-day basis.[29] Witness Lee, in his book *The Economy of God*, argues the source of wealth for Kingdom agents is the endowment of the Holy Spirit.[30]

The third key form of heart capital is the word of God. The word of God is a treasure I can store in my heart.[31] It is used to produce good works that benefit humankind.[32] Other sources of heart capital come from my interaction with nature[33] and the community of other spiritually reborn agents.[34] All humankind begins life with heart capital and acquires more over time. Those who are born again and receive the Holy Spirit become agents according to the model of human agency.

Land and territory

The final category of resource to introduce is land. My father is fond of saying, "they stopped inventing land a long time ago". I am not sure it is original to my dad, but he gets the credit here. Usable land on earth is in limited supply. However, humankind has become adept at discovering, taking, or creating additional dimensions of territory. The United States government's Apollo missions and Artemis missions have an eye on someday colonizing the moon. The international space station has been continuously occupied since November 2000.[35] SpaceX founder Elon Musk believes colonizing Mars will be important to increase the survivability of the human race and human consciousness.[36] The eschatology of *The Theory of the Kingdom* is different, but the impulse for humankind to grow and take new territory is God-given.

Not all territory is physical. The Internet was invented in the 1960s. The Internet started as a government project to improve the resiliency of U.S. data communications in the case of nuclear war.[37] Businesses now routinely purchase and trade internet domains. Domain names such as *lasvegas.com* and *insurance.com* have sold for $10's of millions. High prices for internet domains are surprising, given the near limitless supply of new domain names. Following the internet, a new, more immersive virtual reality territory called the metaverse was invented. The future commercial potential of the metaverse is highly thought of and caused social media company Facebook to change its name to Meta.[38]

The Theory of the Kingdom is connected to land. The Bible makes frequent reference to physical territory and spiritual territory. The Old Testament temple, and the holy of holies in particular, was a place where physical territory encountered heavenly territory. Physical and spiritual territory are each important for the production of goods and services that produce life, peace, and growth on the earth. All types of territory are valuable in the messianic era.

Land and territory with kingdom economy value

Physical land has spiritual value. Much of the Old Testament revolves around God's promise of land to Abraham.[39] John Anderson developed an economic model to understand the Old Testament relationship of physical property to covenantal relationships.[40] The connection of physical territory to the human spirit is noted in Moses' encounter with God at the burning bush. God tells Moses he is standing on holy ground.[41] Old Testament writing also refers to invisible spiritual territory. In the Old Testament alone, the word heaven is mentioned 327 times. The book of Daniel includes the vision of an angelic messenger. The angelic messenger tells Daniel of a battle that took place between angelic forces in an unseen spiritual realm.[42]

In the New Testament, Jesus speaks of heavenly places and the value of physical land. Jesus' teaching on the kingdom of heaven is a reference to his reign over an unseen realm that envelops observable physical territory. Of particular interest is Jesus' statements regarding the value of physical land. "Fields" is included in a list of valuable things Jesus' followers may give up as agents in the kingdom of God. The list of surrendered valuables includes homes, brothers, mothers, fathers, sisters, and fields.[43] Homes represent capital, relationships represent familial love and community, and land represents real economy territory. Jesus promises an extravagant return for leaving land.

Later in the New Testament, the Apostle Paul emphasizes the importance of spiritual territory and transmutes my attention away from battles fought over physical land to those fought against powers in their spiritual place of authority.[44] The cosmic space and order Paul is referring to is sometimes called a *second space*, which is a reference to intangible territory with control over knowledge.[45] In antiquity, Jewish people regarded the battle over invisible spiritual territory to be more important than battles over physical territory. The ancient imagery of making a public spectacle of demonic powers evokes the exhibition of Roman emperors dressed up as the god Jupiter, dragging humiliated and defeated foes behind a victorious parade.[46]

Application. Diagnosing a resource deficit

To apply the concept of kingdom economic resources, consider the dilemma of a sin I have committed over the years. At times, I may quickly go from calm and engaging to hostile and threatening. I sometimes justify my hostility based on a personal offense, defending my real economy rights, or perhaps as a necessity of competition. However, acting in a hostile and threatening manner toward people does not produce life and peace.

I can analyze hostile attitudes and actions from the perspective of kingdom resources. An episode of sudden hostility may be due to a deficit of heart capital. I may not have been reading the Bible. I may not have memorized Bible verses indicating I should be slow to speak and slow to anger.[47] The Bible also teaches it is to my credit to overlook an offense.[48] Sudden hostility may also indicate a heart labor problem. I may be out of spiritual shape. I may not have spent much time in the cardinal Jewish labors of prayer, fasting, and almsgiving. It is more difficult to be hostile toward someone I am praying for. Finally, I may have a spiritual territory problem. Perhaps I grew up an a hostile environment. Hostility may be embedded in the culture of my community or workplace. Regardless of the source of my hostile impulse, the Bible indicates I am to tear down strongholds. Strongholds are wrong ways of thinking.[49] The hostile response may be protected by a negative spiritual stronghold.

I raise the example of hostility not to offer any particular solution. Rather, I am suggesting a methodology to analyze hostility according to the model of human agency. A resource-based analysis can help me plan to acquire kingdom resources I need in order to tear down a hostility stronghold and move me to a new life-giving and peacemaking posture. The problem of hostility toward one's neighbor is its own viral pandemic. A kingdom resource-based analysis of bad behaviors will lead to more productive agents and a better world.

Notes

[1] Donnelly, J. (1970, July). Creation ex nihilo. In *Proceedings of the American Catholic Philosophical Association* (Vol. 44, pp. 172-184).
[2] John 5:17. John 14:3.
[3] Matthew 5:13-14.
[4] Matthew 6:10.
[5] Blomberg, C. L. (1992). *Matthew: An exegetical and theological exposition of Holy Scripture* (Vol. 22, pp102-103). B&H Publishing Group.
[6] Rhodes, M., Holt, R., & Fikkert, B. (2018). *Practicing the King's Economy: Honoring Jesus in how We Work, Earn, Spend, Save, and Give* (p. 39). Baker Books.
[7] Blank, R. M., & McGurn, W. (2003). *Is the market moral?: a dialogue on religion, economics and justice.* Rowman & Littlefield.
[8] Nelson, R. H. (2015). *Economics as religion: From Samuelson to Chicago and beyond* (pp 24-25). Penn State Press. http://dx.doi.org/10.5325/j.ctv1rnpjqb.
[9] Rothbard, M. N. (1990). Karl Marx: Communist as religious eschatologist. In *The Review of Austrian Economics* (pp. 123-179). Springer, Dordrecht. http://dx.doi.org/10.1007/BF02426366.
[10] Piketty, T. (2020). *Capital and ideology.* Harvard University Press. http://dx.doi.org/10.4159/9780674245075.
[11] Henderson, J. W., Pisciotta, J. O., & Pisciotta, J. L. (Eds.). (2005). *Faithful economics: the moral worlds of a neutral science* (p. 11). Baylor University Press.
[12] Marshall, A. (2009). *Principles of economics: unabridged eighth edition.* Cosimo, Inc. http://dx.doi.org/10.1057/9781137375261.
[13] Radelet, S. (2015). *The great surge: The ascent of the developing world.* Simon and Schuster.
[14] Hayek, F. A. (2009). The use of knowledge in society. In *Knowledge management and organizational design* (pp. 7-15). Routledge. http://dx.doi.org/10.1017/CBO9780511817410.007.
[15] Radelet, S. (2015). *The great surge: The ascent of the developing world.* Simon and Schuster.
[16] McGuire, T. (2010). From emotions to spirituality: "Spiritual labor" as the commodification, codification, and regulation of organizational members' spirituality. *Management Communication Quarterly, 24*(1), 74-103. http://dx.doi.org/10.1177/0893318909351432.
[17] McNeal, R. (2011). *A work of heart: Understanding how God shapes spiritual leaders* (Vol. 60, p. xix.). John Wiley & Sons.
[18] Blomberg, C. L. (1992). *Matthew: An exegetical and theological exposition of Holy Scripture* (Vol. 22, p. 116). B&H Publishing Group.; Archdiocese of New Orleans. (2022). *The Three Pillars of Lent: Prayer, Fasting and Almsgiving* (Spring). https://nolacatholic.org/prayer-fasting-and-almsgiving.; Matthew 6:1-18.
[19] Matthew 5:5.
[20] Fisher, I. (1906). *The nature of capital and income.* Macmillan and Cie. http://dx.doi.org/10.1515/9783112351369.
[21] Lev, B., & Radhakrishnan, S. (2005). The valuation of organization capital. In *Measuring capital in the new economy* (pp. 73-110). University of Chicago Press. http://dx.doi.org/10.7208/chicago/9780226116174.003.0004.

[22] Root, A., & Yung, K. (2022). Resolving agency and product market views of cash holdings. *Research in International Business and Finance, 59*, 101518. http://dx.doi.org/10.1016/j.ribaf.2021.101518.
[23] A very brief search on Google Scholar reveals millions of articles available for each of social, intellectual and organization capital theory, and approximately 1 million for Spiritual Capital theory,
[24] Finke, R. (2003). Spiritual capital: Definitions, applications, and new frontiers. *Retrieved April, 24*, 2005. http://www.metanexus.net/archive/spiritualcapitalresearchprogram/pdf/finke.pdf.
[25] Zohar, D., & Marshall, I. (2004). *Spiritual capital: Wealth we can live by.* Berrett-Koehler Publishers.
[26] John 3:5.
[27] Genesis 1:27.
[28] John 3:5.
[29] John 14:16. John 14:26. John 15:26. John 16:7. 1 John 2:1.
[30] Lee, W. (1986). *God's New Testament Economy.* Living Stream Ministry.
[31] Psalm 119:11.
[32] Luke 6:45. New American Standard Bible, 1971, 2 Timothy 3:16-17.
[33] Psalm 19:11. Romans 1:20.
[34] Ephesians 4:11-13. New American Standard Bible, 1971, Hebrews 10:24-25. New American Standard Bible, 1971, James 5:16. Matthew 18:19-20.
[35] Garcia, M. (2023, January 4). *International Space Station Facts and Figures.* National Aeronautics and Space Administration. https://www.nasa.gov/feature/facts-and-figures.
[36] Kay, G. (2022, April 19). Elon Musk said life on Mars won't be luxurious – it will be 'cramped, difficult, hard work'. *Insider.* https://www.businessinsider.com/elon-musk-mars-trip-cramped-difficult-hard-work-2022-4.
[37] Online Library Learning Center. (2022). *A Network of Networks.* Board of Regents of the University System of Georgia. https://www.usg.edu/galileo/skills/unit07/internet07_02.phtml.
[38] Meta. (2021, October 28). *Introducing Meta: A Social Technology Company.* https://about.fb.com/news/2021/10/facebook-company-is-now-meta/.
[39] Genesis 12:1.
[40] Anderson, J. E. (2005). A biblical and economic analysis of jubilee property provisions. *Faith and Economics, 46*, 25-41.
[41] Exodus 3:5.
[42] Daniel 10:12-14.
[43] New American Standard Bible, 1971, Mark 10:29. Matthew 19:29.
[44] Ephesians 6:12.
[45] Stewart, E. C. (2012). New Testament space/spatiality. *Biblical Theology Bulletin, 42*(3), 139-150. http://dx.doi.org/10.1177/0146107912452245.
[46] Keener, C. S., & Walton, J. H. (Eds.). (2016). *NIV, Cultural Backgrounds Study Bible: Bringing to Life the Ancient World of Scripture* (p. 2160, p 2143). Zondervan.
[47] James 1:19.
[48] Proverbs 19:11.
[49] New American Standard Bible, 1971, 2 Corinthians 10:3-5.

Chapter 7

Resource allocation

The subject of this chapter is the distribution of real economy and kingdom resources in the context of owner-agent relationships. I choose to analyze the interaction of resources and relationships across two dimensions. One dimension is owners and agents. The other dimension is the kingdom economy and real economy. The purpose of a brief dimensional analysis is, as Detective Hercule Poirot says, to activate *the little grey cells.* Each interaction in Figure 7.1 could be the subject of its own literature review. I will focus on the implication of each dimension for the model of human agency. The chapter ends with a practical application to real economy ethnic-based inequality.

Two dimensions of relationships and resources

Real economy resources are allocated in small part based on relationships and in large part based on money. Kingdom economy resources are allocated based on relationships. Resource allocation in the model of human agency is not an instrumental ethic or one that operates by human vices. In contrast, in the real economy, self-interested, greedy, and even evil people can work together and earn huge financial or political returns. Not so in the kingdom economy. To love God is to follow him regardless of what he might give me in return. In chapter two, I showed the biblical character of God is holy, loving, sovereign, and unlimited. I know following God means I will receive sufficient resources.[1]

Figure 7.1. Dimensions of relationships and resources.

Relationship	Real Economy ("Small Circle")	Kingdom Economy ("Big Circle")
Owner-Agent	Shareholders and CEOs.	God and people.
Owner-Owner	Business partners or family members.	Father, Son, and Holy Spirit.
Agent-Agent	CEO and managers.	Kings, Prophets or Apostles, and followers.

Figure 7.1 major message: Owners and agents interact in three different types of relationships. Relationships dictate the allocation of resources in the kingdom economy.

The model of human agency is defined by the Love of God for humankind and was modeled in the obedience, self-sacrifice, and servanthood of Jesus on earth. The model of loving God by sacrifice[2] is repeated throughout the Old Testament and New Testament. My lifetime journey of living sacrifice is the topic of chapter 12, called *The Law of Proportion.*

Owner-Agent in the real economy

The owner-agent model of real economy businesses was introduced in chapter one. Owners of large modern businesses appoint a board of directors to govern the actions of managers. I am interested in how owner-agent relationships influence resource allocation. Board members can be classified as business insiders or outsiders. Board insiders serve the dual role of manager and owner representative. Senior executives, such as Jamie Dimon of JP Morgan Chase Bank, may act as both CEO and Chairman of the Board of Directors.[3] Managers that are members of the board of directors are called inside directors. Academics make frequent studies of board independence, firm performance, and resource allocation. The resource allocation decisions of boards include how much to pay the CEO and whether to support strategic investment plans.

Large public businesses are required to disclose the level of board independence. Boards with a higher proportion of outside directors may be more objective about CEO performance and therefore, pay the CEO less. However, findings of one large study found board independence is not associated with CEO pay.[4] Shareholders would naturally expect CEO pay is most closely linked to firm performance. The real economy evidence on CEO pay is murky. One of the most interesting studies consolidated over 200 prior studies to draw definitive conclusions on CEO pay versus performance. The study concluded powerful directors, with a high percentage of ownership, can dictate tighter links between pay and performance.[5]

There is also concern friendly and conflicted boards will not be effective in monitoring management activities. An interesting study in this stream was undertaken by James Westphal.[6] Westphal considered how the social ties of independent directors and CEOs might increase board oversight. It is plausible a higher level of social relationship may result in more counsel being transmitted from owners to managers. At the core of the debate is the difference between the board as management partner and the board as management police. The big new idea of the study is greater social ties do not hurt management monitoring, but it does help transmit more strategic advice. Evidence in terms of the benefit of social interactions to firm investment performance is not as clear. Less independent, management-friendly boards are associated with less value-creating merger investments.[7]

Owner-owner in the real economy

Some real economy businesses are organized as partnerships. On three occasions, I have worked at partner-owned firms. At private firms, culture, the particular way business is done, and values are emphasized. Shared risk and shared profits can promote a close relationship-centric culture. Medical practices are a common form of business partnership with extensive owner-owner interactions. Somewhat surprisingly, total sharing of owner resources, responsibilities, and compensation tends to be ineffective in real economy partnerships. Shared resources lead some partners to shirk their responsibilities and reduce overall output. Owner-owner interactions work well when production responsibilities are specifically assigned and linked to compensation.[8]

Agent-agent relationships in the real economy

Resource allocation decisions are made between agents in the real economy. Senior managers have authority over the pay and responsibilities of subordinates. In large modern businesses, the Chief Financial Officer ("CFO") is often considered to be number two in the organization.[9] The CFO reports directly to the Chief Executive Officer and also interacts extensively with the owners of the business. Owners of the business use reports prepared by the CFO to monitor the CEO. This puts the CFO in a somewhat conflicted role of holding the CEO accountable on behalf of the owners while also working for the CEO. As one might expect, the risk-taking and financial reporting choices of the CFO are linked to compensation.[10] To understand how CFOs are paid, a team of researchers led by Ariel Caglio created a measure called CEO-likeness. The more a CFO is like the CEO and is considered a partner rather than a senior manager, the higher the compensation. The tighter the CEO-CFO relationship, the higher the pay. CEO likeness, in terms of manager political ideology, also influences resource allocation. CEOs allocate more resources to ideologically aligned business managers, particularly when there is a compensation incentive.[11]

Money over relationships

One theme of a review of research on dimensions of the real economy owner and agent relationships indicates relationships are important to resource allocation. However, resource allocation decisions are subject to monetary incentives. Even owner-owner relationships are mediated by money. Partners simply working for one another is not enough. Job functions must still be well-defined and linked to compensation.

Owner-owner in the kingdom economy

The stark contrast of owner-owner relationships in the kingdom economy versus the real economy is an opportune place to move the analysis to the right-hand side of Figure 7.1. The owners in the Bible are God the Father, the Son, Jesus, and the Holy Spirit. There are several indications of how the kingdom owners interact and work together. I will draw out key economic points without getting too far into trinitarian theology. Discussing specific roles of the three fully God members of the trinity can be in the mode of the *economic trinity,* according to R.C. Sproul.[12] The purpose of the allocation of resources and roles amongst the Father, Son, and Holy Spirit is the "economy of redemption". I am redeemed and reborn. The life component of the objective function of the kingdom economy is supported by owner interactions within the trinity.

Owner-owner motivation is love

The motivation for owner-owner resource allocation is love. God declares in an audible voice he loves his son Jesus. Jesus acknowledges the love of the father in John 17:23. Jesus associates love with obedient service. Jesus indicates his obedient service is evidence of his love for the father.[13] The mutual love of Jesus and the Father is so intimate Jesus describes the Father and Son as one. The unity of the father and son is in contrast to divisions in real economy ownership and governing bodies of all types.[14] The Holy Spirit was the agent of the immaculate conception of Jesus and was with Jesus to enable him to accomplish his earthly ministry. The Holy Spirit also identified Jesus as Messiah for John the Baptist.[15]

Loving relationships lead to generous resource allocation. God the Father raised Jesus from the dead and put all things under his authority.[16] The father did not hold anything back from the son.[17] God showed the Son all that he is doing so the Son could fulfill his messianic mission on earth.[18] The Holy Spirit came forth from the father and also was sent by Jesus as he returned to the father. In a scriptural analysis of *mutual love* theory of the immanent and economic trinity, David Coffey indicates the Holy Spirit is the embodiment of the Father's love for Jesus and, of Jesus' love for the Father.[19] The owner-owner relationship and productive partnership is evident in the creation story of Genesis One and the opening of the book of John. At the beginning of the Bible, God is creating, and the Holy Spirit is hovering over the face of the waters.[20] The disciple John wrote that Jesus was with God in creation and that everything, including humankind, was made through him.[21]

The three great Christian virtues are faith, hope, and love. Love is the greatest. Love is the nature of the owner-owner relationship in the kingdom of God.

Creation activities were shared. Jesus now maintains what he and the father created.[22] Governing for life and peace are shared by the son and spirit.[23] The father shows the son all he is doing and gives him all authority over human agents. There is no productivity problem that I see in some real economy partnerships. There is no shirking of responsibilities or free riding due to a lack of incentives. Owner-owner partnership in the kingdom runs on love.

Owner-Agent and Christian virtues

Owner-agent resource allocation is based on relationships that depend on love. God loved me, so he sent his son to die and when I was reborn, I received the Holy Spirit. This new covenant is the basis for my relationship with God and the foundation from which I receive kingdom resources. This is one part of the model of human agency where things get very good indeed.

A biblical survey of owner-agent resource allocation requires consideration of the other two great Christian virtues of faith and hope[24] and the model of covenantal relationships. The kingdom owner-agent relationship is the New Testament covenant instituted by Jesus at the Last Supper.[25] The Old Covenant was the one God made with Abraham. The Old Covenant is based on the Mosaic law and sacrificial system of the Old Testament. Important economic elements of the Mosaic law included instructions regarding circumcision, seven-year sabbatical cycles and jubilee.

Faith, hope and love in the sabbath

In an innovative study economist John Anderson analyzed the allocation of land resources to the Israelite people.[26] The covenant relationship was governed by the mosaic law, which includes sabbatical years and the jubilee provision. The sabbatical law required farmland to be left fallow every seventh year. The owner-agent covenantal promise was for enough of a harvest in the sixth year to supply food for the three years affected by the sabbatical provision. Being obedient to such an instruction requires faith God will do what he promised and placing your hope for the future solely in the owner rather than in the efforts of any human agent. It is a unique provision that, by faith and hope, produces owner-agent relational intimacy and a sabbatical rest for agents.

The jubilee provision pertained to every fiftieth year, after seven sabbatical cycles. In the fiftieth year, the land reverted to the original owner, and debts were forgiven. Anderson makes the point the Jubilee provision was a metaphor for the new covenant of Jesus that would mark the arrival of the kingdom of God. The key institution at the time was the extended family. Anderson refers to an explanation of the Jubilee provision as God's way to keep the family land economic units viable. This maintained the way God related to the nation of Israel. From a purely real economy perspective, the Jubilee year would require a very high degree of obedience and trust in God's provision. In the modern economy, it is difficult to conceive of widespread implementation of the law of jubilee.

Agency duty of obedience

Obedience is important in the covenant of real economy businesses. According to legal scholars, there are three key duties owed to owners of a firm. Senior agents owe a duty of care and a duty of loyalty to the owners of the business. The third duty owed to owners is a duty of obedience. The third duty has gone through seasons of being forgotten and then remembered by senior corporate officers. In the mid-twentieth century, obedience was considered the first duty of corporate officers.[27] The duty of obedience arises out of the legal duty of good faith. Wake Forest University law professor Alan Palmiter argues that the duty of obedience is required for the institution of the modern corporation to remain viable.

Faith-motivated obedience is required for a sustainable model of agency in both the real economy and kingdom economy. Abraham received the first covenant and a promise of land resources for the nation God was going to build from his family line. Hebrews chapter 11 is sub-titled *The Triumphs of Faith*. Verse six says I cannot please God without faith.

Resources received by faith are for groups

Hebrews 11 includes a series of historical examples of what kingdom agents have received by faith. Abraham started a journey by faith and received a new land from God. When Abraham started the journey he did not know where he was going. Paul writes about the faith of Abraham in Romans chapter four. The title of Romans four is *Justification by Faith*. Three times in Romans chapter four it says Abraham's faith was credited to him as righteousness.[28] The Abrahamic covenant came out of Abraham's relationship with God, including his faith, his fear of God, and obedience.[29]

Kingdom resources supplied out of owner-agent love relationships are for groups of people, not just for individuals. One example from the Old Testament and New Testament provides additional evidence of the real economy resources the owner supplies to his agents. In my personal study notes I label the book of Joshua the book of resources. Joshua succeeds Moses as the leader of Israel. Through obedience and overcoming the fear of man, Joshua leads the nation into the promised land. In chapter eight, Joshua received a plunder of food, flocks, and weapons to continue the mission. The provision benefited everyone in the community and served the larger mission of the owner, including care for the poor. Kingdom resources are for individuals and groups.

The New Testament miracle of turning water to wine is well-known in popular culture.[30] Faith, obedience, and hope are all seen in the love relationship between Mary and her son Jesus. When the wine ran out at a wedding in Cana of Galilee, Mary the mother of Jesus, simply told the banquet manager to do whatever Jesus tells you. Jesus' public ministry had not started. No one there knew Jesus was the Messiah. Also, at that moment, no one on earth loved Jesus as Mary did. Jesus loved his mother. Mary knew her son. Mary had faith in Jesus' goodness and miracle-working power. Mary was full of hope that Jesus would honor her and do what she asked him to.

The banquet servant's obedience benefited a community

Mary's faith, hope and love set the stage to receive real economy resources to benefit a group. However, Mary understood the key to solving the resource problem at the wedding was to obey Jesus. Jesus responded to Mary's request for wine with a most extravagant provision. The provision of wine benefited an entire community of people. It is interesting to estimate just how extravagant the provision of wine was. Approximately 760 bottles of wine were produced out of plain water.[31,32] The banquet manager graded the wine as the best that had been served at the wedding. A reasonable current estimate for the range of value of good wedding wine would be $100 to $200 per bottle. Jesus responded to faith and obedience with $76,000 to $152,000 worth of wine. Mary brought hope to a business owner in a tough spot, to an embarrassed family, and to a married couple at the beginning of their covenantal marriage relationship. Coupled with obedience kingdom resources we transported into the real economy to benefit a community.

Agents are expected to give to the poor

The final points to consider on owner-agent kingdom resource allocation come out of individual and community generosity.[33] Individual generosity includes giving alms to the poor. The owner expects me to give to the poor. In back-to-back verses, Matthew records Jesus saying, "when you give to the poor."[34] Matthew does not write *if*, rather it is *when* I give to the poor. Even though it is a command to obey, giving to the poor receives a promised repayment from God.[35]

Community generosity includes communal benevolence[36] and support for other kingdom agents. In Paul's letter to the Philippian church, I learn they have a pattern of generosity to Paul and his missionary work. In the context of their volitional and generous giving, Paul promises the owner will keep them well-supplied based on His unlimited resources. The Philippian community freely gave of their limited resources without any noted expectation of reciprocity from Paul or God. The Philippian community received back a promise of unlimited kingdom resources. Giving generously, in humility,[37] out of love for the owner facilitates the movement of kingdom resources into the real economy to produce life, peace, and growth.

Challenges of agent-agent relationships in the kingdom economy

The agent-agent resource allocation interactions are the most fraught. Even though I make every effort to live for the kingdom economy, I live in the real economy. Relationships in the real economy tend to run on money rather than love. It is challenging for kingdom-oriented organizations to remember their identity in the body of Christ over their place in the real economy. The biblical record and modern day record of conflicts created by agent-agent resource allocation decisions is extensive.

In the first book of the Bible herdsman of Abraham (nee Abram) and his nephew Lot quarrel over pastureland.[38] Abraham freely surrendered the better land to his nephew Lot. Immediately following the surrender, God promised Abraham and his descendants as much land as Abraham could see.[39] In his surrender to Lot, Abraham demonstrated he believed provision was based on his relationship with God. Abraham's faith released resources already allocated to him by the owner. There was no need to fight with Lot over resources. It remains challenging to make an Abrahamic choice. However, the apostle Paul[40] endorsed the Abrahamic choice in the kingdom era.

Later in the book of Genesis, Jacob's youngest son, Joseph, acted as an agent of Pharoah in allocating grain during a famine. Joseph had previously gained the prime-ministerial position by interpreting a dream of Pharoah to mean there would be seven years of abundant harvest, followed by seven years of famine.[41] During the seven abundant years, Joseph collected grain for Pharoah's inventory. By the time the famine was affecting the entire region of the world, Joseph was selling grain to Egyptians and foreigners. As the famine progressed, the Bible says Joseph had collected all the money in Egypt. All the money was followed by all the livestock, then all the land, and even individual freedom.[42]

Joseph was said to be in charge during the famine. Though it is very likely Pharoah was still closely monitoring Joseph. It has been suggested Joseph's actions could be seen as either an endorsement of hoarding or a prohibition of hoarding.[43] I do not agree the story endorses hoarding. The story is an example of God's mercy. There would have been no food in the region but for

Joseph's system of storehouses. Joseph's initial intent appears to be to store grain in the form of a trust for the Egyptian people. Grain was to be returned during the famine as needed. Soller suggests Joseph did not take payment when the grain storehouses were first opened. It is proposed that Pharoah used Joseph as chief administrator and a *scapegoat* in a plan to extract a huge return from a monopoly position in grain.[44] Regardless of each agent's motivations, it is clear real economy agent-agent relationships cause unnecessary shortages and suffering for the ends of power and profit.

Perhaps lost in the story of Joseph and the famine is there is no record of mass starvation. God sent the necessary information to human agents and provided enough grain for the period of famine. Famine in Egypt didn't cause mass starvation, but perhaps a real economy motivation to maximize profit and power produced suffering and inequality. The outcome in Egypt can be compared to Lot and Abraham's dispute. Abraham's love, generosity, mercy, and faith in God's provision produced life, peace, and growth.

Modern governance lesson in the book of Acts

In the present-day messianic kingdom era, agent-agent resource allocation decisions still create conflicts. My favorite Bible passage to raise issues of governance and economic distribution is found in the book of Acts. It is believed the Book of Acts was written around 70 AD. The first-century church had decided to share its possessions.[45] Wealthier Christ-followers shared with the poor and widows as needed. The distribution process involved wealthier individuals bringing money to the former disciples of Jesus, including Peter and John. The disciples were Jewish. The leaders then distributed the provisions as they saw fit. The Acts chapter four example of communal living is not an argument for or against socialism. It is an example of wealthy Christ-followers being motivated by the love of God and love for each other to donate real economy resources for the benefit of widows and the poor. Note there were wealthy Christians in the first place.

The communal arrangement did not eliminate agent-agent resource conflict. Sometime after the communal arrangement was in effect, a dispute arose. Acts chapter six records Greek Christians complaining to the Jewish leaders. The complaint was Greek widows were being overlooked in the daily distribution of food. The Jewish leadership council included the 12 disciples of Jesus.[46] The 12 were being accused of religious and ethnic bias, favoring their kind over another. The cause of providing for widows was valid. Widows are worthy recipients of food and assistance.[47] The distribution should continue but the system needed to change.

To solve the resource allocation problem the Jewish leaders needed to act according to kingdom economy principles of love, generosity, and faith in God. Jewish leaders instructed the larger group of Jewish and Greek Christians to select a group of wise and devout men from among them to take over the daily distribution of food. To settle the issue the group chose seven men.[48]

1. Stephen – Hellenist. Foreign-born Jew who spoke Greek. First recorded martyr.
2. Philip - Greek name, Hellenist
3. Procorus – Likely a nephew of Stephen. A Hellenist. May have directed the first choir.
4. Nicanor – The name means conqueror or victory. The name is derived from the Greek word *Nike,* meaning victory. It may be the same person in Maccabees who was a Syrian general. His name indicated he was also a Hellenist Christian.
5. Timon – Hellenized Jew who became a bishop in Greece.
6. Parmenas – Also a martyr. He was likely a Hellenist Christian, given his Greek name.
7. Nicolas of Antioch - Born a gentile (non-Jew) who went by a Greek name.

The list of seven men that the early Jewish Christian church leaders chose to solve the resourcing problem is entirely Greek. The Jewish leadership solved the first economic equity and ethnic bias problem in the Christian church by turning control of the resources over to the aggrieved party. The very current message is that group-level bias may be solved by the privileged group surrendering control of disputed resources to jointly selected mature individuals in the aggrieved party.

> Group-level economic bias may be solved by the privileged group surrendering control of disputed resources to jointly selected mature individuals in the aggrieved party.

Application. Act to resolve inequity

Peter, John, and the rest of the 12 Jewish disciples acted to resolve the issue. The author, Luke, does not record the disciples appointing a study group to analyze the issue. I am not told the Jewish leaders assessed the legitimacy of the grievance. They did not appear to debate whether or not they were biased against Greek widows. The Old Testament prayer of David seems to indicate I may be biased even though not aware.[49] Peter, John and the apostles did not unduly concern themselves with the risk of a public backlash based on inadequate Greek leadership or ill intentions. The Jewish leaders did not collect data on the actual timing of food distribution by ethnicity. The leaders simply, and apparently quickly sought a solution that was met with broad approval. Two particular elements of what the Jewish leaders did bear further consideration.

Always risky to resolve agent-agent disputes

First, it may be in situations of bias the privileged party is concerned about aggrieved party reprisals or competence. Perhaps, I might reason, the privileged party should retain control of the resources because the aggrieved party is inexperienced, incapable, or biased. The risk did not stop the leadership from acting despite later evidence showing such a concern was real. In a few chapters in Acts, the Jewish apostle Paul is preaching to a group of Greeks. The Greeks were so offended by Paul's message they tried to murder him. To protect Paul, Jewish disciples sent him away to Tarsus.[50] The important point is the risk of reprisal is always real. If I am in the aggrieved party, it would be difficult to at least not consider payback. There are perhaps not many Nelson Mandela type persons that can forgive right as they walk out of prison.[51] The risk of aggrieved party reprisal is not a reason for kingdom agents to do nothing.

Second, the Bible does not state whether the economic unfairness was real or perceived. In modern times, a charge of racism or gender bias can be met with a flurry of data. Presenting data is important, but it also can be a distraction. In my experience as a data scientist, it is not especially challenging to present data in support of the status quo. One practical message of Act Chapter Six is, do not waste time looking for data to justify moving on from the status quo. Whether perceived or real, economic inequity must be quickly addressed.

As a final postscript to the real or perceived question implied in Acts six, it is likely the inequity was real. Peter's bias against non-Jews was on display in Acts chapter ten. The Spirit of God explicitly told Peter to go into the house of the Roman soldier and non-Jew, Cornelius. Upon entering his house, Peter told Cornelius he would not normally enter his house. It was against Jewish law to visit unclean non-Jews.[52] Peter told Cornelius God showed him he should not call anyone unclean.

The Book of Acts, including Peter's interaction with Cornelius, reveals the kingdom economy is for all equally. Ethnic bias in tangible reality may only be resolved by kingdom agents being salt and light, transporting the resources of the kingdom into the real economy to produce life and peace. Real economy, love of money produces death, but the kingdom economy of love produces life and peace.[53] In the words of Bob Dylan "You gotta serve somebody". Serve God and not money and economic resources will flow where they are needed.

Notes

[1] Matthew 6:25-34.
[2] Romans 12:1. John 15:13.
[3] As of the time of writing, Jamie Dimon had been the CEO of U.S. bank J.P. Morgan Chase since 2005, and Chairman of the Board since 2006.
[4] Guthrie, K., Sokolowsky, J., & Wan, K. M. (2012). CEO compensation and board structure revisited. *The Journal of Finance, 67*(3), 1149-1168. http://dx.doi.org/10.1111/j.1540-6261.2012.01744.x.
[5] Van Essen, M., Otten, J., & Carberry, E. J. (2015). Assessing managerial power theory: A meta-analytic approach to understanding the determinants of CEO compensation. *Journal of management, 41*(1), 164-202. http://dx.doi.org/10.1177/0149206311429378.
[6] Westphal, J. D. (1999). Collaboration in the boardroom: Behavioral and performance consequences of CEO-board social ties. *Academy of management Journal, 42*(1), 7-24. http://dx.doi.org/10.2307/256871.
[7] Boubakri, N., Dionne, G., & Triki, T. (2008). Consolidation and value creation in the insurance industry: The role of governance. *Journal of Banking & Finance, 32*(1), 56-68. http://dx.doi.org/10.1016/j.jbankfin.2007.09.004.
[8] Gaynor, M., & Pauly, M. (1987). *Alternative compensation arrangements and productive efficiency in partnerships: evidence from medical group practice [Working paper].* National Bureau of Economic Research. https://www.nber.org/papers/w2170.
[9] Caglio, A., Dossi, A., & Van der Stede, W. A. (2018). CFO role and CFO compensation: An empirical analysis of their implications. *Journal of Accounting and Public Policy, 37*(4), 265-281. http://dx.doi.org/10.1016/j.jaccpubpol.2018.07.002.
[10] Chava, S., & Purnanandam, A. (2010). CEOs versus CFOs: Incentives and corporate policies. *Journal of financial Economics, 97*(2), 263-278. http://dx.doi.org/10.1016/j.jfineco.2010.03.018.
[11] Gupta, A., Briscoe, F., & Hambrick, D. C. (2018). Evenhandedness in resource allocation: Its relationship with CEO ideology, organizational discretion, and firm performance. *Academy of Management Journal, 61*(5), 1848-1868. http://dx.doi.org/10.5465/amj.2016.1155.
[12] Sproul, R.C. (2014, August 15). What's the Difference between the Ontological and Economic Trinity. *Ligonier.* https://www.ligonier.org/learn/articles/whats-difference-between-ontological-and-economic-trinity.
[13] John 14:31.
[14] Keener, C. S., & Walton, J. H. (Eds.). (2016). *NIV, Cultural Backgrounds Study Bible: Bringing to Life the Ancient World of Scripture* (p. 1918). Zondervan.
[15] John 1:32-34.
[16] Ephesians 1:15-22. 1 Corinthians 15:27-28.
[17] John 3:34.
[18] Carson, D. A. (1999). God Is Love. *Bibliotheca Sacra-Dallas-, 156*, 131-142.
[19] Coffey, D. (1990). The Holy Spirit as the mutual love of the Father and the Son. *Theological Studies, 51*(2), 193-229. http://dx.doi.org/10.1177/004056399005100202.
[20] Genesis 1:1-2

21 John 1:1-3.
22 Colossians 1:16-17.
23 Isaiah 9:6-7. John 10:10. Romans 8:6.
24 1 Corinthians 13:13.
25 Luke 22:20. Matthew 26:28.
26 Anderson, J. E. (2005). A biblical and economic analysis of jubilee property provisions. *Faith and Economics, 46*, 25-41.
27 Ballantine, H. W. (1946). *Corporations*. Callagham.
28 Romans 4:3. Romans 4:9. Romans 4:22.
29 New American Standard Bible, 1971, Genesis 22:12-18.
30 John 2:1-12.
31 Cardarelli, F. (2003). *Encyclopaedia of Scientific units, weights and measures: their SI equivalences and origins*. Springer Science & Business Media.
32 Six ancient water pots averaging 25 gallons, at 3.8 liters per gallon equals approximately 570 liters of wine. Modern bottles of wine are ¾ of one liter. Based on John 2:6 and easily obtained conversions, Jesus produced 760 bottles of fine wine on the spot.
33 New American Standard Bible, 1971, Proverbs chapter 11 (note especially verse 25).
34 Matthew 6:2-3.
35 Proverbs 19:17.
36 Acts 4:32-35.
37 Luke 18:14.
38 New American Standard Bible, 1971, Genesis 13.
39 Genesis 13:14-17.
40 New American Standard Bible, 1971, 1 Corinthians 6:1-8.
41 New American Standard Bible, 1971, Genesis chapter 41.
42 New American Standard Bible, 1971, Genesis chapter 47.
43 Sharfman, K. (2006). The Law and Economics of Hoarding. *Loyola Consumer Law Review, 19*(2), 179.
44 Soller, M. (2019). Joseph and the enslavement of the Egyptians. *The Jewish Bible quarterly, 47*(1), 39-44.
45 Acts 4:32.
46 Acts 6:2.
47 New American Standard Bible, 1971, Psalm 68:5. James 1:27.
48 Schnabel, E. J. (2010). *Acts* (p. 334). Zondervan Academic. http://dx.doi.org/10.2307/26424315; Feldman, L. H. (1994). Josephus' portrayal of the Hasmoneans compared with 1 Maccabees (pp 41-68. In *Josephus and the History of the Greco-Roman Period.* http://dx.doi.org/10.1163/9789004509122_006; Yancey, P., & Stafford, T. (2011). *NIV, Student Bible* (p. 1167). Zondervan.
49 Psalm 19:12.
50 New American Standard Bible, 1971, Acts 9:29-30.
51 Mandela, N. (2008). *Long walk to freedom: The autobiography of Nelson Mandela* (pp. 364-365). Hachette UK.
52 New American Standard Bible, 1971, Acts 10:28.
53 John 10:10. Romans 8:6.

Chapter 8

Risk, returns & rewards

The next four chapters are a quartet on the topic of investment. In this first chapter of the quartet, I discuss real economy returns and kingdom economy returns. I also introduce a new construct called the hierarchy of temptation. The temptation always before me is to serve money rather than God. The chapter finishes with a review of the types of kingdom economy rewards.

To make an investment I save some income and then take a risk. Investment occurs along individual and group dimensions. The group can be a business, a non-profit, a community, or even national political bodies. I invest because I have not spent all of my income and because I want to earn a return. The purpose of earning a return is to build wealth for future consumption or future charity. Prior books such as *The Law of Rewards*[1] might suggest kingdom agents are investing to build treasure in heaven. The specific meaning of treasure in heaven is hotly debated.[2] The body of literature on investment and returns in the real economy and kingdom economy is extensive. My perspective on investment and returns is informed by decades of professional and academic experience analyzing real economy investments and returns. The goal of this chapter is to provide enough analysis of returns to suggest investing more in the kingdom economy is a rational choice.

This study focuses on the generation and interaction of returns and rewards across the messianic membrane. There are many studies and sermons on how to accumulate eternal riches. Some suggest a primary motivation of accumulating a large stock of riches in heaven. Such motivation may risk turning charity into just another, "act of vanity." John Stott references C.S. Lewis in describing the reward for kingdom economy investment as the restorative desire fulfilled.[3] For example the appropriate reward for giving to a destitute widow is to see her fed and her family cared for, and to have a share in the same charity everywhere in the kingdom. My ultimate inheritance and source of riches is to be with God in his eternal home.[4] Eternity with the owner is my reward. Jesus is the mediator of my inheritance. The Holy Spirit is the essential companion to produce kingdom returns now. The analysis of returns contained in this chapter focuses on the interaction and two-way flow of returns and rewards across the messianic membrane.

Patience rewarded in the real economy

Returns in the real economy are influenced by resource scarcity and the preferred timing of consumption of individuals. In the real economy, I choose how much of my income to consume and how much to save. The relative patience of individuals to consume is the basis for interest rates.[5] Interest rates are also influenced by inflation expectations.[6] Inflation expectations are influenced by resource scarcity in the real economy and the supply of money printed by modern central banks.[7]

Fisher's original theory of interest rates is sometimes called the theory of (im)patience. Individuals differ in terms of a desire to consume now or later. *The Marshmallow Test: Why Self-Control is the Engine of Success*[8] studies the concept of time preference of consumption. In one experiment, children are given a single marshmallow and a choice. The marshmallow represents, for most children, a desirable treat. It may be eaten immediately. If the child can delay consumption, an additional marshmallow will be given as a reward. Delayed consumption of one marshmallow now, for two later, shows a substantial measure of self-control for a child. The benefit of self-control was associated with many positive outcomes over a lifetime. The positive benefits of self-control include higher standardized test scores, lower body mass indexes, and lower rates of adult mental illness.

Figure 8.1. Return component of the model of human agency.

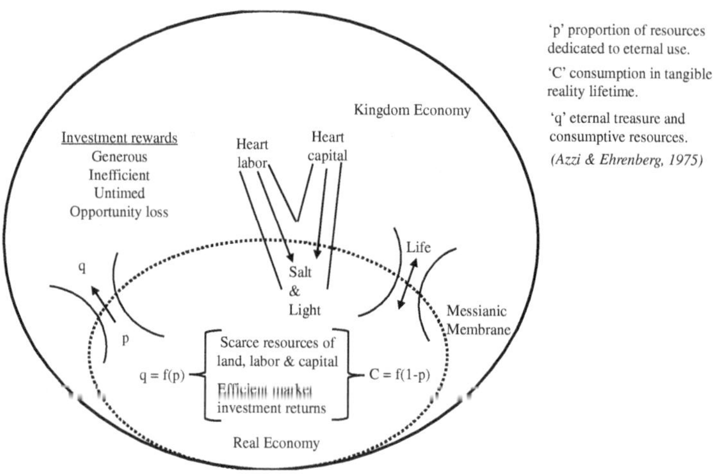

Figure 8.1 major message: Returns in the small circle real economy are efficient. Information is processed quickly and returns are associated with risk. Returns in the large circle kingdom realm are inefficient in the sense the reward may far exceeds the risk. Heart labor and giving of time and money for kingdom purposes of life, peace and

growth activates the flow of resources between the two realms. The conversion of time and money into eternal treasure ("q")[9] happens by giving the proportion of resources for kingdom purposes ("p"). As I reduce my real economy consumption ("C") I increase my proportion and eternal treasure.

Self-control is associated with real economy returns. The academic discipline of behavioral finance studies how investment risk causes humans to make irrational decisions.[10] One of the most common irrational decisions people make is to sell a winning investment too quickly while holding on to losses too long.[11] Fortunately, in the messianic era, I can increase in self-control. I receive self-control through the work of the Holy Spirit in my heart. The fruits of the Holy Spirit include love, joy, peace, patience, kindness, goodness, faith, gentleness, and self-control. The contrasting motif in Galatians of living by the Spirit or by the Flesh is an important repeating contrast in an analysis of kingdom returns.[12] According to the model in Figure 8.1, the products of the Holy Spirit are different types of heart capital I acquire in the kingdom economy. The benefits of heart capital are realized individually and collectively in the real economy.[13]

Transmutation of wealth into the kingdom economy

The perception of time changes with age. An empirical study of 499 individuals showed all aspects of the perception of time are influenced by age.[14] Time does indeed move faster with age. The model of human agency (Figure 8.1) leads to a proposition: I make consumption choices based in part on my perception of time. I choose between real economy consumption (labeled 'C') and deferred consumption. Following a study called *Household Allocation of Time and Church Attendance*,[15] I label the deferred consumption 'q', which is an eternal treasure. The ratio of deferred consumption to present consumption is the proportion of resources used for the kingdom economy (labeled 'p'). Resources allocated to kingdom purposes of life and peace are transmuted into returns in the kingdom economy. A.W. Tozer comments on the transmutation of wealth, "Whatever is given to Christ is immediately touched with immortality."[16]

Human perception of the transmutation of wealth and a two-phase reality is real. The real economy is timed. The kingdom economy is eternal. Evidence for belief in an untimed eternal realm has been demonstrated at the individual and corporate levels. Cory Azzi & Ronald Ehrenberg[17] developed a model of household production intended to maximize utility based on consumption in the real economy and the afterlife. The influence of belief in eternity is not confined to individuals. Religiosity influences corporations.

Gilles Hillary & Kai Wai Hui showed religiosity influences corporate investment policy and risk-taking.[18]

Returning to marshmallows, when I eat a marshmallow, I gain a unit of satisfaction. Economists call satisfaction utility ("U"). Real economy models are based on an expectation that individuals choose the highest level of satisfaction possible. I am expected to make rational choices based on scarce resources to experience maximum happiness. The unique element of the model of Azzi & Ehrenberg is the inclusion of consumption in eternity.[19]

Christ-follower transmutation of wealth increases with age

Azzi & Ehrenberg show the satisfaction of a household of Christians is based on tradeoffs in consumption between the real economy and eternity. The big new idea of the study is religious activity and fervency increase with age. If human existence ends at death, there is less incentive to delay consumption with age. Yet, with eternity closer in view, the pace of individual transmutation of wealth increases. I would extend the discussion with two points. First, the study is evidence in favor of the biblical teaching God "has set eternity in the human heart."[20] Second, the trade-off has a positive feedback loop in the model of human agency.

If I give up a marshmallow now to someone in need, several kingdom processes are set in motion. The marshmallow gift fills a real economy need for the receiver, producing a small bit of life and peace in the community.[21] I receive a future reward,[22] partly contingent on secrecy or doing it specifically as an act of sowing in the kingdom realm.[23] Laboring in giving, I build up a generous spirit and receive heart capital, enabling me to give away more future marshmallows, thereby deferring more consumption into eternity. It is to my benefit and the benefit of my community to increase my proportion, the percent of consumption deferred into eternity, as high as possible. The concept of proportion can motivate me to exceed the commonly cited 10% giving standard.[24]

Real economy wealth building associated with inequality

In the real economy, money-motivated return dynamics are consistently associated with inequality. *Capital in the 21st Century*[25] uses the Gini coefficient and other measures of distribution to detail inequality based on income and return on wealth. Author Thomas Piketty outlines fundamental forces driving inequity, such as the return on wealth exceeding the return on labor. It is not especially difficult to find data showing the distribution of income across many political settings is extreme in the real economy. A simple contemporary example of inequity is the pay of U.S. public company Chief Executive Officers ("CEOs").

CEOs who are members of the leadership group the U.S. Business Roundtable have earned between 200 times and 300 times the median employee pay every year for the past 10 years.[26] The model of human agency takes a different approach from *Capital,* measuring wealth, assets, and the timing of returns differently. Measurement of assets in *Capital* excludes intangible human capital altogether. The kingdom economy is spirit-based. In the kingdom economy, my heart is my most valuable asset, and the high return labor is heart labor. I invest because I love God, not because I love money. Kingdom returns are unquantifiable ex-ante and concentrated in eternity. They are unquantifiable because God himself is the sole payor.[27]

Returns in the real economy are measured in relative and absolute terms. Relative measures require a point of comparison. Building a benchmark for comparison starts with the risk-free rate of return and then adding a premium for risk. In 1958, Franco Modigliani and Merton Miller published an article entitled *The Cost of Capital, Corporation Finance and the Theory of Investment.*[28] The article handled the research question of determining an organization's required return in a world of uncertainty. The real economy is a rather uncertain realm. William Sharpe and other researchers added to this by developing a formula to relate the risk of an investment to its required rate of return.[29] The capital asset pricing model ('CAPM') is given by:

> Expected Return = Risk Free Return + Beta*[Expected Stock Market Return – Risk Free Return]

Beta is a measure of how risky an organization or an investment is relative to the average. A higher beta means more risk and a larger required return. Zero risk means I don't invest in anything. The lowest risk means putting my money in a hole in the ground to protect it from robbers. This is a losing strategy. In the parable of the talents, the risk-averse servant put his money in a hole and was excoriated by the owner.[30] Money in a hole is a negative return. Inflation means when I take the money out of the hole, it is worth less than when it went in.

The next level of risk is investing in risk-free government debt. In the United States, my expected return is between 3% and 6% over the long term. Even though government debt is called risk-free, I lose money about one out of every four years. The term risk-free means I will be paid the contracted interest and principal. I may not like being paid in U.S. dollars, but I will get paid. Buying debt is synonymous with lending. There is sometimes a discussion in religious circles if kingdom agents should charge interest, and if so, at what point does it become usury? I define usury as the victimization of people, particularly the poor, through excessive interest. There is a strong case to be made for not charging interest to the poor or brothers and sisters in the body of Christ.[31] On the other hand, the parables of the talents imply that lending is happening in the economy around Jesus, and it is generally better to loan money for interest than do nothing with it.[32]

Some interest rates are hard to justify in the kingdom economy

I do not know for certain the answer to what level of interest constitutes usury. However, Investment Bank Merrill Lynch published a chart of interest rates from 3000 BC to the present day.[33] The median rate is approximately 5%, with a range of 0% to 20%. The real rate of interest, after inflation, is likely around 2%. Interest rates were highest in the distant past when markets were inefficient. Modern capital markets price risk efficiently. This is a significant positive for investors of all types. For my purpose, charging 2% to 3% interest on top of inflation seems fair. To charge much more indicates the borrower is very risky. Biblical synonyms for a risky borrower include *the poor* or *foreigner*. Charging very high rates of interest to risky borrowers is not a business for kingdom agents.

The next level of risk is owning individual businesses in the stock market. For this extra unit of risk, represented by Beta in the CAPM formula, I can expect to earn a total of 8% per year, or more. I can expect to lose money one year in four, and the annual return dispersion is much wider for stocks than for debt. This is a rough cut of my analysis of data presented in *Financial Management Core Concepts*.[34] The key point is the real economy is risky. The more risk I am willing to take, the more money I will make over time. There are exceptions to the rule. Some of the risk premium earned by stocks is rational, but some appear irrational. Academics call the irrational element the *equity return premium puzzle*.[35] Not all investment outcomes in the real economy are rational.

The link between risk and kingdom agency is through the channel of fear. Fearful people become more risk-averse.[36] Effective kingdom agency requires fearing rightly. When Joshua took over the leadership of the nation of Israel, God repeatedly told Joshua not to fear.[37] God's instructions refer to the fear of man. The Bible is clear that the beginning of wisdom and knowledge is the fear of God.[38] I will take the right risks and produce the right returns in the kingdom economy if my fear is properly directed into the obedience of the holy owner. The two economies are made distinct by motivations in terms of fear of man or fear of money, the love of money or the love of God.[39] and what Paul calls sowing in the flesh or sowing in the spirit.[40]

Choosing what to fear and who to serve distinguishes the two realms

The central element of the kingdom economy return analysis is temptation. There is a strong theme of returns for obedience throughout the Bible.[41] I choose for brevity to focus on the book of Hebrews. Hebrews contains two important facts to understand how to generate returns. First, Jesus is the mediator of the new covenant.[42] Second, Jesus can empathize with the temptations I experience in the real economy.[43] Luke records one instance of Jesus being tempted by Satan.[44] The Devil is the opposing force to the kingdom of God. Luke's writing is notable here in that it was more common for him to use the *love of money* as an opposing force.[45]

There are four categories of temptations in the first 13 verses of Luke 4. The first category is identity. The opening phrase, "If you are the son of God" challenges the identity previously confirmed by God the Father at the baptism of Jesus.[46] The phrase "turn this stone to bread" introduces the second category of temptation. Jesus was at the end of a 40-day fast and had a physiological need for food. The third category of temptation was rulership over the real economy realm. The final category of temptation was physical safety.

Figure 8.2. Hierarchy of temptation and rewards.

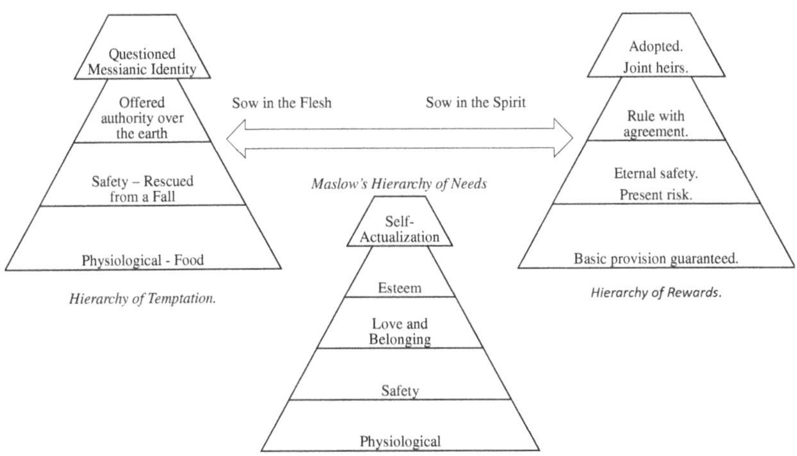

Figure 8.2 major message: Abraham Maslow developed a useful hierarchy to understand the basic needs of people.[47] The temptation of Jesus, as recorded in Luke's gospel chapter four, proceeds along a hierarchy that bears some prima facie resemblance to Maslow's hierarchy. To give in to temptation and move left on Figure 8.2 is to satisfy needs by the fear of man and love money. To fear God and serve him alone, I move right to receive kingdom economy rewards that satisfy my needs. Jesus demonstrates knowing and quoting the word of God is an excellent method of overcoming temptation.

The last phrase of the passage reads the Devil "left him until an opportune time."[48] I may take comfort in the last phrase. Jesus was repeatedly tempted and I may expect the same. Further study shows Jesus faced each temptation several times. For example, Peter tempts Jesus with the thought of rulership.[49] Peter has not yet understood Jesus as the *suffering Messiah*.[50] The rebuke of Peter to 'get behind me Satan' is best understood in the context of the overall temptation strategy of the Devil. Jesus appears to be talking to and through Peter to the opposing spirit. Blomberg writes Peter was "no longer acting like the foundation block of the church but like a stumbling block."[51] I expect to repeatedly face temptation. My expectations can keep me alert.

Kingdom rewards satisfy my needs for all time

There is a parallel between evidence for the empathetic Messiah in the temptations recorded by Luke and Maslow's Dynamic Theory of Human Motivation.[52] Maslow lists five areas of human needs. The center of Figure 8.2 includes a hierarchical pyramid commonly used to communicate Maslow's theory. The left-hand side of Figure 8.2 includes the four categories of temptation Jesus experienced in Luke chapter 4. Maslow's concept of my psychological needs supports the idea Jesus is empathetic to his agents. It is an interesting parallel, but how do temptation and core human needs link to a study of kingdom returns?

A typology of biblical rewards is the mirror image of the typology of temptation. The typology of temptations and rewards also has parallels with Maslow. The temptations faced and rewards promised to kingdom agents are both in the categories of identity, rulership, safety, and provision. Kingdom rewards can be for now, for the future, or both.

Tradeoffs

The theory of the kingdom involves understanding the choices and tradeoffs I make each day. To understand the returns I will generate, I begin with Maslow's hierarchy of human needs in the center of Figure 8.2. If I choose to live for God and not money, I act with Holy Spirit led intentions and produce life and peace. The returns I earn, listed in the Bible, are mediated by Jesus[53] and satisfy my human needs. The returns last and have positive externalities for humanity now. Externalities include less corruption of society and the environment and more revelation of truth. If, on the other hand, I choose to satisfy my needs by giving in to the temptation for money or to mitigate excessive worry, returns will be temporary. If I am motivated by money, then community externalities are negative. Negative outcomes include hypocrisy, economic inequities, and environmental damage. Returns generated from a love of money are not transmutable into the kingdom realm, regardless of the moral quality of the action itself.

Returns earned for the love of money in the real economy satisfy the flesh. Money for money returns do not translate. There is no transmutation of ill-gotten gains. Crime generally pays in the sense it earns a positive risk-adjusted return.[54] Humility is a biblical virtue and hubris is a vice. However, CEO Hubris in the real economy often helps companies to be highly innovative.[55] On the other hand, financial history is full of stories of greed destroying lives. Roger Lowenstein's *When Genius Failed* is a spectacular case study of the best and brightest of the real economy failing due to pride and greed.[56]

Weber's *The Protestant Ethic and the Spirit of Capitalism*[57] attributed the rise of Western economies to a Protestant work ethic. The empirical evidence is not as conclusive. While the protestant work ethic may help nations, there is no evidence individual devotion to kingdom agency is broadly associated with real economy wealth. On the other hand, studies associating kingdom economy commitment with less money are common. For example, in the United States, families that attend church more and believe the Bible is the inerrant word of God tend to have less money.[58] In Luke, Jesus indicates his kingdom is not associated with real economy wealth, charging the Pharisees, the religious leadership class, with a love of money.[59]

The distinction between general religiosity and a commitment to kingdom agency is the love of money. The Pharisees were highly devout and engaged in giving alms to the poor. However, their motivation moved them to the left of Figure 8.2. The moral act of almsgiving resulted in a temporary reward. The Pharisees quickly ate their marshmallows. Jesus instructed his followers to give in private, as unto the Lord. If I give in secret, my gift to the poor is transmuted into the kingdom economy.[60] The reason to live for God is not to outperform my investor peers now; it is to produce life, peace, and growth in the kingdom.

One payor of kingdom rewards

Rewards, profit, and loss are thoroughly discussed in the Bible. A survey of the teachings of Jesus reveals over 50 sayings regarding rewards. The apostle Paul regularly teaches about rewards. The five opening books of the Bible, the Pentateuch, regularly teach rewards based on the theme of blessings for obedience and curses for disobedience. King Solomon teaches how to accumulate rewards in Proverbs and teaches of the nature of rewards in Ecclesiastes. The terms gain, profit, and reward are used throughout the Bible. There are over 100 references to rewards. The owner is the source of rewards. Of the various uses of the word reward, the word translated *rewarder* in

Hebrews 11:6, *misthapodotes*, is used only one time and is about God.[61] The sole payor of kingdom rewards is the owner. At times, God himself is described as the reward.[62]

> Of the hundreds of biblical references to rewards, gain and profit, the sole rewarder, the one *misthapodotes*, in the kingdom economy is God.

Restoration and returns on loss and suffering

In the real economy, I may lose money, I may lose a job and I will experience suffering. Everyone experiences monetary gains and losses in the real economy.[63] The best stock traders are quick to recognize losses.[64] The biggest loss of wealth occurs at the end of life. I will not leave the world with anything in my pockets.[65] One rejoinder may be money goes to designated heirs as an inheritance. True enough. However, there is not a clear consensus on the effects of inheritances. Already wealthy heirs tend to remain wealthy, but less than wealthy heirs have been shown to deplete an inheritance within 10 years.[66] A lifetime of work consumed within 10 years is an example of the vanity of Ecclesiastes.[67]

In the kingdom economy, the owner may make up for my losses. Years of recession can be made up.[68] Severe military losses can be miraculously made up.[69] Personal losses of family, honor, and wealth can be healed and repaid with greater future glory.[70] Nothing of value is ever lost in the kingdom economy. The owner has the unlimited resources to refill, resupply, or restore anything I need to be productive.

Everyone experiences suffering in the real economy. Suffering may be self-inflicted. Disobedience, pride, love of money, and laziness are some of the vices that cause suffering.[71] The Bible includes a consistent juxtaposition between the losses of pride and the gains of humility. God opposes the proud. He gives grace to the humble. God may even deliver members of my family from their problems because of my humility and righteousness.[72] Humility is associated with the inheritance of the kingdom of heaven.[73]

Perhaps most often, suffering is a consequence of living in an imperfect world. Dorothee Solle opens *Suffering* with existential questions of meaning.[74] Through no fault of my own, I may fall ill or I may be in the wrong place at the wrong time and suffer.[75] This study addresses a very narrow part of suffering. Suffering may produce returns in the kingdom economy. Suffering can return a reward of endurance.[76] The suffering of Jesus in the flesh destroyed the power of sin and made a way for me to find peace with God.[77] If I suffer for being a Christ-follower, I will be *supremely blest, fortunate, and well-off.*[78] Clearly, this is mostly a future realm reward. There is a reward for persecution in the kingdom of God.[79] The life of a kingdom agent includes suffering.[80] I certainly do not seek suffering but it is a comfort that God takes my suffering, humbly submitted to him, to produce a return of life and peace.

Rewards of identity, authority, provision and protection

Rewards can be categorized in the same manner as temptations. The analysis of kingdom rewards requires considering whether the rewards are for the real economy now, for the kingdom economy, or both realms. If I fear God and choose to love God rather than money, my needs are satisfied according to the hierarchy on the right-hand side of Figure 8.2. The categories I use for rewards are identity, authority, provision, and protection. The investment activities associated with rewards are the subject of the chapters following.

Basic physiological provision is the foundation of Maslow's hierarchy. Humans don't progress toward identity without food and water. Fear of God, the love of God, and a degree of obedience are the antecedents to moving to the right in Figure 8.2. Kingdom agents are promised physiological provisions in the real economy. I receive this provision with the hopeful expectation God will satisfy my needs. Physiological provision is the risk-free return of serving God. Jarvis Williams writes kingdom agents "should know God will provide for them as a loving father."[81]

Blessings for obedience in the Old Testament include agricultural harvest and bread.[82] Sincere kingdom agents will be able to provide food for their children.[83] Even though the real economy situation may appear bleak, people who live according to the law of the land and deal fairly will provide food for their families.[84] Being content with basic provision is a *great* return.[85] The promise of provision in difficulty can be for groups as well as individuals.[86] Jesus emphasized a guarantee of real economy provision. The concern over food was not trivial at the time of Jesus. The Roman government often maintained order by giving away food. Even to satisfy my most basic need, I must decide who to trust.

The criteria for provision and rewards in Jesus' sermon in Matthew chapter six includes a command to love God rather than money.[87] The love of money causes me to take the burden of being the source of provision. In addition to a love of money and desire to be rich,[88] I may be triggered by worry and thereby move left on Figure 8.2 into temptation. Blomberg quotes R. Mounce saying, "worry is practical atheism and an affront to God."[89] If I trust him, God will supply my basic physiological needs.

Eternal security is a promised reward

It is obvious a Christ-follower can die of physical starvation or exposure because of the intentional act of an evil person. The reality of persecution and abuse in a sinful world links to the second level of returns. God will provide food and water for me. However, evil people may still harm me. A life of kingdom agency does include some promise of security for the real economy.[90] However, ultimate security is for the kingdom realm. I am not guaranteed physical security in this realm. Many friends and family die far too young. By the virtues of faith, hope in the future, and love for God, I bridge the gap from likely but not guaranteed physical security in the real economy, to eternal security in the kingdom realm.

Jesus said there was no one greater than John the Baptist.[91] Yet John was unjustly beheaded.[92] Even John did not have a guarantee of physical security. Jesus knew he was going to die by crucifixion. Yet in John chapter ten, Jesus made a clear declaration of my absolute security in the kingdom of God.[93] The allegory Jesus used was the good shepherd securing his sheep. In this short section of the Bible, Jesus indicates he has the authority to protect the sheep; he will protect sheep of any ethnicity, he will protect the sheep with his life and no robber may steal away any of the sheep.[94] I am told to pray to be kept from evil and believe I am likely to be kept physically safe in the real economy, but I am certainly secure in the future.

Need for authority

The next level of kingdom returns addresses authority. I want to be in charge and I want the compensation and honor of being in charge. The temptation is to take authority over a real economy realm for my wealth and honor. Jesus was offered real economy rulership.[95] The correct response to an offer of rulership is the response Jesus gave, "You shall worship the Lord your God and serve him only."[96] Jesus came as a servant of all. Jesus' service included the voluntary humiliation of washing the disciple's feet and death by crucifixion.[97] Sometimes, serving others in the real economy results in their promotion and my stagnation. The path to authority in the kingdom economy is always service.

The path to authority in the kingdom economy is service.

The authority of kingdom agents comes from Jesus and is for teaching, baptizing, and making disciples.[98] I use my authority over unseen principalities and power to produce life, peace, and kingdom growth now.[99] The full exercise of authority requires my agreement with other Christ-followers and faith and heart labors of prayer and fasting.[100] Faithful service now earns a return of authority in the future realm.[101] Risk-taking and the returns of faithful service are the basis for future authority.[102] I do not use my authority to satisfy my love of money and honor. Returns of money for the sake of money do not transmute into the kingdom economy. The New Testament church included slaves, the poor, the wealthy, and the politically connected. The church is to live in unity and work together in agreement.[103] I resist the temptation to take authority by worshiping God and serving everyone, particularly serving fellow kingdom agents. My obedient service is the productivity engine of the kingdom economy.

The first need and first temptation is identity

The ultimate category of rewards is identity. Maslow's top human need is self-actualization. The top human need in biblical typology is identity. I receive the reward of knowing my identity. Identity is the first target of the Devil.[104] Titles matter in real economy businesses. Partners have more authority than new analysts. In academic circles, I quickly learned the difference between a lecturer and a full professor. Titles and names matter. It is a source of pride to be identified by a senior title.

The biblical account contains many identity rewards. I receive salvation because I am identified in the Book of Life.[105] The Holy Spirit is the first part of my kingdom inheritance and identifies me as an adopted child of God. In suffering, I am made a joint heir with Jesus.[106] John Stott's analysis of joint heir indicates a potential duality of rewards. The first is the obvious suggestion of future valuables being kept in heaven. The second is the inheritance of God himself. Stott notes the comments of Murray and the pattern of the Old Testament Levites. God himself was the inheritance of the Levites.[107] I am a friend. I received insight as a friend of the owner. Jesus said to his disciples, "No longer do I call you slaves, for the slave does not know what his master is doing; but I have called you friends because all things that I have heard from my Father I have made known to you." Jesus informs me about it because I am his friend. Information is highly valuable in real economy businesses as well. In Christ, I have all the information I need. Next, Jesus intercedes to identify me in front of the father.[108] Finally, in the future, I am given a new name, written on a white stone.[109]

Renaming of agents is a common motif in the Bible. Abram was renamed Abraham. Sarai was renamed Sarah. Saul became Paul and Simon became Cephas (Peter). The new names gave identity and purpose in the kingdom economy. I will be rewarded with a white stone inscribed with a new name that only the owner and I know. The white stone reward may be compared to stones associated with determining the will of God, upon which the name of God was inscribed. Revelation 2:17 includes the white stone together with manna. For 40 years, God miraculously fed the Israelites with manna. Jesus is quoting this fact when he tells Satan, "man shall not live by bread alone but by every word of God."[110] The special manna and white stone are eternal provision and a God given identity, respectively. The reward of food and identity was given for overcoming the temptations of idolatry, sexual immorality and false doctrine. Glasson notes the white stone and manna are listed together as high-priestly rights, which God imparts to me as a king and priest.[111] I will be fulfilled by a kingly and priestly identity in the fully arrived kingdom economy. My agency task is to resist the temptation to find identity in money and honor or to choose my own identity. I will be eternally satisfied with the reward of my God-given identity in Jesus.

Notes

[1] Alcorn, R. (2003). *The Law of Rewards: Giving What You Can't Keep to Gain What You Can't Lose.* Tyndale House Publishers, Inc.

[2] Roller, B. (2021). The Treasure Principle Reconsidered: Storing Up True Treasures in Heaven. *Journal of Biblical Integration in Business, 24*(1).

[3] Stott, J. (2014). *The Message of the Sermon on the Mount* (p. 110-111). InterVarsity Press.

[4] Harris, D. M. (2009). *The eternal inheritance in Hebrews: The appropriation of the Old Testament inheritance motif by the author of Hebrews.* Trinity International University.

[5] Fisher, I. (1930). *Theory of interest: as determined by impatience to spend income and opportunity to invest it.* Augustusm Kelly Publishers, Clifton.

[6] Tanzi, V. (1980). Inflationary expectations, economic activity, taxes, and interest rates. *The American Economic Review, 70*(1), 12-21.

[7] Coibion, O., Gorodnichenko, Y., & Wieland, J. (2012). The optimal inflation rate in New Keynesian models: should central banks raise their inflation targets in light of the zero lower bound?. *Review of Economic Studies, 79*(4), 1371-1406. http://dx.doi.org/10.1093/restud/rds013.

[8] Mischel, W. (2015). *The marshmallow test: Why self-control is the engine of success.* New York: Little, Brown.

[9] Azzi, C., & Ehrenberg, R. (1975). Household allocation of time and church attendance. *Journal of political Economy, 83*(1), 27-56. http://dx.doi.org/10.1086/260305.

[10] Kahneman, D., & Tversky, A. (2013). Prospect theory: An analysis of decision under risk. In *Handbook of the fundamentals of financial decision making: Part I* (pp. 99-127). http://dx.doi.org/10.1142/9789814417358_0006.

[11] Shefrin, H., & Statman, M. (1985). The disposition to sell winners too early and ride losers too long: Theory and evidence. *The Journal of finance, 40*(3), 777-790. http://dx.doi.org/10.1111/j.1540-6261.1985.tb05002.x.

[12] Galatians 5:16-25.

[13] Luke 6:45.

[14] Wittmann, M., & Lehnhoff, S. (2005). Age effects in perception of time. *Psychological reports, 97*(3), 921-935. http://dx.doi.org/10.2466/pr0.97.3.921-935.

[15] Azzi, C., & Ehrenberg, R. (1975). Household allocation of time and church attendance. *Journal of political Economy, 83*(1), 27-56. http://dx.doi.org/10.1086/260305.

[16] Tozer, A. W. (1959). The Transmutation of Wealth. *Born after Midnight.*
[17] Azzi, C., & Ehrenberg, R. (1975). Household allocation of time and church attendance. *Journal of political Economy, 83*(1), 27-56. http://dx.doi.org/10.1086/260305.
[18] Hilary, G., & Hui, K. W. (2009). Does religion matter in corporate decision making in America?. *Journal of financial economics, 93*(3), 455-473. http://dx.doi.org/10.1016/j.jfineco.2008.10.001.
[19] The future consumption variable is called "q", with a utility function of the form $U = U(C_1, C_2, \ldots C_t, q)$.
[20] New American Standard Bible, 1971, Ecclesiastes 3:11.
[21] Romans 8:6.
[22] Matthew 10:42. Proverbs 19:17.
[23] Matthew 6:3-4.
[24] Malachi 3:8-12.
[25] Piketty, T. (2014). *Capital in the twenty-first century.* Harvard University Press. http://dx.doi.org/10.4159/9780674369542.
[26] Root, A. (2022, September). *LeBron gets it more than Jamie does.* LinkedIn. https://www.linkedin.com/pulse/lebron-gets-more-than-jamie-does-andrew-root/?trackingId=fM3ICdlZ0TZpic38pMADVA%3D%3D
[27] Hebrews 11:6.
[28] Modigliani, F., & Miller, M. H. (1958). The cost of capital, corporation finance and the theory of investment. *The American economic review, 48*(3), 261-297.
[29] Sharpe, W. F. (1977). The capital asset pricing model: a "multi-beta" interpretation. In *Financial Dec Making Under Uncertainty* (pp. 127-135). Academic Press. http://dx.doi.org/10.1016/B978-0-12-445850-5.50011-8.
[30] Matthew 25:26.
[31] New American Standard Bible, 1971, Deuteronomy 23:19-20. New American Standard Bible, 1971, Nehemiah 5:10. Matthew 5:42, Proverbs 19:17, New American Standard Bible, 1971, Exodus 22:25, New American Standard Bible, 1971, Leviticus 25:35-37. The verses address not charging interest to brothers and sisters, or to the poor.
[32] Luke 19:23. Matthew 25:27.
[33] Chart is available on request in an electronic appendix. Contact the author at aroot@regent.edu.
[34] Brooks, R. (2013). *Financial management: core concepts* (p. 220). Pearson.
[35] Benartzi, S., & Thaler, R. H. (1995). Myopic loss aversion and the equity premium puzzle. *The quarterly journal of Economics, 110*(1), 73-92. http://dx.doi.org/10.2307/2118511.
[36] Lerner, J. S., & Keltner, D. (2001). Fear, anger, and risk. *Journal of personality and social psychology, 81*(1), 146. http://dx.doi.org/10.1037/0022-3514.81.1.146.
[37] Joshua chapter 1.
[38] New American Standard Bible, 1971, Proverbs 1:7. New American Standard Bible, 1971, Proverbs 9:10. New American Standard Bible, 1971, Psalm 111:10.
[39] Mathew 6:24.
[40] Romans 8:5-6. Ephesians 6:7-8.
[41] New American Standard Bible, 1971, Deuteronomy 11:26-29. New American Standard Bible, 1971, Deuteronomy chapter 28. Leviticus chapter 26.
[42] Hebrews 9:15.
[43] Hebrews 4:15.

[44] New American Standard Bible, 1971, Luke 4:1-13.
[45] Moxnes, H. (2004). *The economy of the kingdom: Social conflict and economic relations in Luke's Gospel* (Vol. 23, p. 152). Wipf and Stock Publishers.
[46] Luke 3:21-22.
[47] Maslow, A. H. (1958). A Dynamic Theory of Human Motivation. http://dx.doi.org/10.1037/11305-004.
[48] Luke 4:13.
[49] Matthew 16:22.
[50] Blomberg, C. L. (1992). *Matthew: An exegetical and theological exposition of Holy Scripture* (Vol. 22, p. 259). B&H Publishing Group.
[51] Blomberg, C. L. (1992). *Matthew: An exegetical and theological exposition of Holy Scripture* (Vol. 22, p. 259). B&H Publishing Group.
[52] Maslow, A. H. (1958). A Dynamic Theory of Human Motivation. http://dx.doi.org/10.1037/11305-004.
[53] 1 Timothy 2:5. Hebrews 9:15.
[54] Freeman, R. B. (1999). The economics of crime. *Handbook of labor economics, 3*, 3529-3571.
[55] Hirshleifer, D., Low, A., & Teoh, S. H. (2012). Are overconfident CEOs better innovators?. *The journal of finance, 67*(4), 1457-1498. http://dx.doi.org/10.1111/j.1540-6261.2012.01753.x.
[56] Lowenstein, R. (2001). *When genius failed: The rise and fall of Long-Term Capital Management.* Random House trade paperbacks.
[57] Weber, M., Parsons, T., & Tawney, R. H. (1930). *The Protestant Ethic and the Spirit of Capitalism. Translated by Talcott Parsons... With a Foreword by RH Tawney.* G. Allen & Unwin. http://dx.doi.org/10.4324/9780203995808.
[58] Keister, L. A. (2011). *Faith and money: How religion contributes to wealth and poverty* (pp. 26-29). Cambridge University Press. http://dx.doi.org/10.1017/CBO9781139028547.
[59] Luke 16:14-15.
[60] Matthew 6:1-4.
[61] Strong, J. (2009). *Strong's exhaustive concordance of the Bible* (p. 844). Hendrickson Publishers.
[62] New American Standard Bible, 1971, Genesis 15:1. New American Standard Bible, 1971, Numbers 18:20.
[63] Ecclesiastes 3:6.
[64] Garvey, R., & Murphy, A. (2004). Are professional traders too slow to realize their losses?. *Financial Analysts Journal, 60*(4), 35-43. http://dx.doi.org/10.2469/faj.v60.n4.2635.
[65] New American Standard Bible, 1971, 1 Timothy 6:7. Job 1:21. Ecclesiastes 5:15.
[66] Nekoei, A., & Seim, D. (2023). How do inheritances shape wealth inequality? Theory and evidence from Sweden. *The Review of Economic Studies, 90*(1), 463-498. http://dx.doi.org/10.1093/restud/rdac016.
[67] Ecclesiastes 6:1-2.
[68] Joel 2:25.
[69] New American Standard Bible, 1971, 1 Samuel 30:1-19.
[70] Job 42:10.
[71] Deuteronomy 28:15-68. New American Standard Bible, 1971, Proverbs 24:33-34. Galatians 5:13-21. 1 Timothy 6:10.
[72] New American Standard Bible, 1971, Job 22:29-30.

[73] Matthew 5:3.
[74] Soelle, D. (1989). *Suffering* (p. 1). Fortress Press.
[75] Luke 13:1-5.
[76] James 1:2.
[77] Colossians 1:19-29.
[78] 1 Peter 3:14.; Strong, J. (2009). *Strong's exhaustive concordance of the Bible. Greek Dictionary of the New Testament* (p46). Hendrickson Publishers.
[79] Matthew 5:10. Mark 10:29-30. Luke 6:22. New American Standard Bible, 1971, Revelation 6:9-11. Revelation 20:4-5.
[80] Matthew 16:24. Mark 8:34. Luke 9:23.
[81] Williams, J. J. (2021). *Redemptive Kingdom Diversity: A Biblical Theology of the People of God* (p. 84). Baker Academic.
[82] Deuteronomy 28:4-5.
[83] New American Standard Bible, 1971, Psalm 37:25.
[84] New American Standard Bible, 1971, Isaiah 3:10.
[85] 1 Timothy 6:6-8.
[86] Genesis 47:27.
[87] Matthew 6:25-34.
[88] 1 Timothy 6:9. Proverbs 23:4.
[89] Blomberg, C. L. (1992). *Matthew: An exegetical and theological exposition of Holy Scripture* (Vol. 22, p. 126). B&H Publishing Group.
[90] New American Standard Bible, 1971, Psalm 34:19-20.
[91] New American Standard Bible, 1971, Matthew 11:11. New American Standard Bible, 1971, Luke 7:28.
[92] Luke 7:7-9. Matthew 14:1-12. New American Standard Bible, 1971, Mark 6:14-29.
[93] John 10:26-29.
[94] Tenney, M. C. (1997). *John: the gospel of belief* (pp. 161-166). Wm. B. Eerdmans Publishing.
[95] Luke 4:5-7.
[96] Luke 4:8.
[97] Matthew 20:28. Mark 10:45. John 13:1-17.
[98] Matthew 28:18-20.
[99] New American Standard Bible, 1971, Luke 10:17-20.
[100] Matthew 17:14-21. Mark 9:14-29.
[101] Matthew 25:23.
[102] Matthew 25:21-23.
[103] Matthew 18:19-20. Psalm 133:1-3. Ephesians chapter 4. The latter is a treatise on the need for unity amongst kingdom agents.
[104] Luke 4:3.
[105] New American Standard Bible, 1971, Daniel 12:1. Luke 10:20. Philippians 4:3. Revelation 3:5.
[106] Romans 8:14-17.
[107] Stott, J. (2014). *The message of Romans: God's good news for the world* (pp. 234-235). InterVarsity Press.
[108] Romans 8:33-35.
[109] Revelation 2:17.
[110] New International Version Bible, 1978, Luke 4:4.
[111] Glasson, T. F. (1965). *The Revelation of John* (Vol. 63, p. 29). CUP Archive.

Chapter 9

Risk aversion

This is the second chapter of four on kingdom investment. The most basic problem with using agents is risk aversion. Risk aversion is a common agency problem in the real economy and kingdom economy. Business owners want agents to make new investments and win new clients. The value of a business is heavily influenced by its future growth prospects. In the same way, the kingdom economy highly values growth. According to the book of Isaiah, the kingdom is growing.[1] God's sincere wish is that everyone would be born again.[2] God is the causal force driving growth[3] and he wants kingdom agents to make disciples, take new territory and participate in the increase. To contribute to the growth of any organization, I must take risks.

Owner diversification lowers risk

Real economy owners have an easier time reducing risk than their agents do. Owners can diversify across different companies. King Solomon had the right idea to divide his money across different ventures. In modern times, I can do better than dividing my money across seven or eight businesses.[4] It has long been known the effect of owning 40 different individual companies, as opposed to one, reduces risk by over half.[5,6] The rise of exchange-traded funds ("ETFs") has made it easy for owners to diversify. An exchange-traded fund is a cost-effective way for an investor to buy a small piece of hundreds of companies in one purchase. If I buy an ETF representing the U.S. Standard & Poor's 500 index, I own a very small amount of 500 large companies. Efficient diversification means I am not especially concerned if any one company goes out of business. I want the leaders of the 500 companies to invest as aggressively as possible. Aggressive aggregate investment drives up the average growth rate. Faster growth is what I want, almost regardless of how many individual firms fail. If I happen to work at a business that fails, it is very bad for me, but not as bad for a diversified owner.

Agent risk aversion overcome with incentives

In comparison to owners, agents are not as able to diversify their risk. My current salary, future income, and promotion prospects are tightly associated with my current owner. Owners handle the mismatch of risk profiles by implementing incentives. Owners set up rewards and punishments for agents to do business according to their desires. The most common incentive for CEOs is very large pay packages. CEOs are already relatively wealthy. They have a natural tendency to try and keep from losing money or position.[7] To keep a wealthy CEO taking new risks, shareholders pay enormous amounts in the stock of the company. Enormous is defined as approximately 300 times the median worker pay.[8] Academic research defends CEO pay as being set by market forces and largely associated with firm performance.[9] Whether or not CEO pay is fair has no bearing on how kingdom agents deal with risks.

Risk-taking and growth

Risk-taking produces growth. Risk aversion leads to stagnation and decline. A common instruction for kingdom agents is 'do not be afraid'. The phrase appears over 300 times in the Bible. As I experience God's love and receive the virtuous traits produced by the Holy Spirit, I can take risks, despite fears I may feel. Obedient risk-taking and investment of time and money, enabled by a robust stock of heart capital, allows me to participate in the growth of the kingdom. Dimensions of risk can be analyzed on the same basis as the hierarchy of temptation. It is appropriate to apply the risks Jesus felt to the modern day. Laurence Iannaccone in *Rational Choice Theory and Religion*[10] assumes people assess costs and benefits in much the same way, regardless of time and place. The type of risk is different according to the hierarchy of human needs in Figure 8.2, but the construct travels well.

C.T. and Priscilla Studd's risky business

To animate an analysis of kingdom risk-taking and to incorporate higher risk less developed economy settings[11] consider the unusual story of Charles Thomas ("C.T.") and Priscilla Studd, according to the biography by Norman Grubb. The story begins in the year 1780 with the formation of the *London Society of West Indian Planters and Merchants.* Society members acted as sugar traders and United Kingdom colonial agents. Edward Studd was a successful member of society. Returning to England a wealthy man, Edward became a cricket enthusiast, fox hunter, and racehorse owner. Under the preaching of evangelist D.L. Moody, Edward Studd repented and became a born-again Christ follower.

Edward continued to ride horses and hunt, but he sold the racehorses and converted part of the family estate in Tedworth to an evangelism center. Edward died two years after the conversion of the Tedworth property. Before Edward's death, several members of his family, including his son C.T., followed in Christian conversion. C.T. Studd was attending Eton College when he was born again. C.T. was captain of the Eton cricket club. However, C.T. decided to give up his promising career as a cricketer and wealthy scion of

London Society. C.T. Studd decided to move away from England to preach about Jesus in developing economies. C.T. became a different type of planter and merchant.

Edward Studd left his son an inheritance of 29,000-pound sterling. Bank of England data shows the current value of the 1887 inheritance is over 4,000,000-pound sterling. C.T. decided to give away his inheritance before leaving for missionary work. On July 25, 1887, in a letter sent to his soon-to-be fiancé Priscilla, C.T. wrote he was inviting her to marry him for a life of service, toil, and hardship. The only certainty they would know would be a secure place in the kingdom of God. The couple was prepared to take an extraordinary risk. In faith, they were laying up treasures in heaven.[12]

The act of young C.T. to give away so much money so young was highly unusual. Jesus himself had said it is difficult for a rich man to choose the kingdom of heaven over money.[13] To effect the donations, C.T. needed the signature of the U.K. Consul. The Consul was hesitant to sign and required C.T. to take two weeks to reconsider. After two weeks, C.T. went ahead with the donations. In one pre-marital correspondence recorded in Norman Grubb's biography of his father-in-law,[14] C.T. informed Priscilla he had given away almost all of the money, investing it in a variety of ministries. Donations went to venerable organizations such as The Salvation Army and the Moody Bible Institute and organizations serving orphans and the poor.

In planning for retirement many years away, C.T. informed Priscilla there was a few thousand pound sterling that remained. Priscilla's reply to C.T. was to give the rest of the money away so they could start marriage with a clean slate before God. C.T. and Priscilla risked it all. They risked all of their time and money to follow Jesus. The same opportunity was given to another rich young person in Matthew chapter 19.[15] The rich young ruler had the benefit of seeing Jesus and watching him work. The rich young ruler did not take the risk.

The Studd's worked in China, India, and the Democratic Republic of Congo ("DRC"). They suffered periods of hunger, danger, and untreated illnesses that eventually led to death. C.T. Studd did not retire in England. He died in the DRC. C.T. did not regret the risk taken so young. C.T.'s last retrospective letter to home provides evidence of his state of mind. He was most pleased first, that he had ignored family opposition to move to China. Second, he was pleased his entire inheritance was safely invested in an eternal kingdom. Third, he was satisfied his life was invested to preach Jesus as Savior to the developing world. C.T. and Priscilla Studd risked very nearly 100% of their time and money in the kingdom economy, with apparently no final regrets.

Challenge to risk it like the Studd's

The story is instructive because it does not appear to fit with Jesus' metaphor about camels traversing the eye of a needle,[16] or with academic evidence of the present day. Beginning with data presented by Dean Hoge, studies have consistently shown a negative association between wealth and the percentage given to churches.[17] In the bottom decile of income, U.S. churchgoers were found to give between 5% and 8% of income, depending on denomination. In the top income decile, giving is between 2% and 4% of income. The wealthy do give more in total dollars but empirical findings more closely track the commentary of Jesus. Two of the four gospels recount the story of a widow giving two small coins.[18] Wealthier people put in more money, but the widow put in *all she had to live on.* Prior studies suggest the story is in praise of a widow for a higher proportionate gift. However, Addison Wright believes it is a lament of Jesus that the widow could be religiously compelled to give all her money when she in fact, needed it.[19] Blomberg criticizes Wright's religious compulsion view as the temple was funded by the wealthy and the widow's gift was voluntary and unusual in historical context.[20] The most direct message is the most likely; proportional giving is the relevant measure in the kingdom economy. Kingdom economy risk-taking is measured in personal relative proportion.

Most economists consider the risks and investment decisions of kingdom agents to revolve, somewhat obviously, around choices regarding time and money. However, additional subdivisions are required when considering Maslow's hierarchy of human needs and the record of Jesus' temptation in Luke chapter four. The risks of rational Christ-followers are multidimensional compared to rational real economy actors. Christ-followers believe in an omnipotent owner. Here Iannaccone's analysis introduces the prospects of rewards that can only be obtained in God: "eternal life, peace on earth, unending bliss."[21] The list of rewards is similar to my proposition that the objective function of the kingdom economy is to maximize life, peace, and growth. The specific assumption is that "most religious commodities are risky, promising large but uncertain benefits."[22]

Religious risk is largely rewarded in spiritual credence goods

The risks of kingdom agents is unique in that religious goods are credence goods.[23,24] Credence goods are those products I might buy where I am also concerned with fraud. For example, on a trip to the dentist, I don't know what I need before I am examined. I also don't know for certain if the diagnosis and treatment are correct. I don't know if I paid the right price and after the dentist is finished. I cannot be sure for some time the problem is fixed. Credence goods are subject to fraud.

The common New Testament Greek word translated faith is *pistis.* The writer of Hebrews says without faith, without *pistis,* it is impossible to please God. *Pistis* can also be translated as credence or persuasion. It is true, for example, the products of the Holy Spirit in my life are credence goods. What prior studies appear to miss is credence goods are subject to fraud except in one important case. A monopolist credence good seller is honest.[25] If the monopolist seller is dishonest, as word of mouth spreads in the marketplace, the number of transactions will decline and eventually cease. God is the monopolist seller of Holy Spirit goods. I have more to say on credence goods in chapter 12, *the Law of Proportion.* To be productive, agents must believe that God is the sole payor of those who diligently seek him.[26]

Analysis of religious risk is highly Westernized. Dominant theory, models, and empirical tests originate in developed Western economies. Data gathering may be too westernized to be globally useful in moving the discipline forward. Most of the cross-border analysis of religious risk relates to freedom to practice.[27,28] In Western economies, the risk of religious practice translates into an individual loss of freedom and loss of income. In developing economies, personal risk is often severe, including loss of life. The life of Samuel Lamb in China is an example of experiencing incarceration and loss of money and property for the practice of protestant religion.[29]

Rich young ruler indicted by omission

A list of risks I take by believing in Jesus includes misplaced faith, free riders using community resources without contributing, social stigma, and sacrifice. Misplaced faith is associated with all country settings and levels of human need. Social stigma and sacrifice appear to be the specific form of risk aversion the rich young ruler was not able to overcome.[30] Halvor Moxnes notes the sacrifice and stigma associated with the extreme social distance between the rich young ruler and the life of Jesus' followers.[31] One commandment Jesus omitted in an exchange with the young ruler was "you shall not covet your neighbor's house...or anything that belongs to your neighbor."[32] It is an indictment by omission. A yearning to possess money and relationships is a block to kingdom economy risk taking. The love of money causes me to forgo risk and fulfill my rulership needs apart from God (left-hand side of Figure 8.2).

Social stigma and extreme sacrifice were highly relevant in the cultural setting of the four gospels. The risk of following Jesus included family rejection. For the disciples specifically, the risk included being arrested and severely punished or executed. Notably, three gospels include a forecast of being arrested for following Jesus. Further, John's gospel notes a prediction the disciples will be *put out* of the synagogue. F.F. Bruce notes by the time the gospel was written, Nazarenes may have been cursed in synagogue prayers and hunted by zealots, such as Saul.[33] It is *when*, not *if*, the governmental authorities impose costs for kingdom agency.[34] The timing and degree of persecution may change.

In each of the four instances, the strategy is to listen to the leading of the Holy Spirit. The purpose of Holy Spirit guidance was not exoneration. The purpose of Holy Spirit guidance was to reveal the truth and communicate the gospel message. In the cases of Stephen,[35] Peter, and John[36] obediently following the Holy Spirit in front of governmental authorities substantially increased risk. Interestingly, raising the cost of discipleship addresses the general problem of risks and religiosity.[37] Casually interested free riders can be assumed to fall away when the price is high.

Risk in the time of Rome

The risk of being a Christ-follower was very high at the time the gospels were written. First and second century brutality of the Roman empire toward Christians is hard to fathom in modern times. The book *The Roman Empire a Very Short Introduction* includes an analysis of the common spectacle of Christians being tortured and killed for entertainment. It was not disorderly rabble that attended and enjoyed the murder of Christians. It was the solid citizens of Rome and Emperor Claudius in particular. Even seating in amphitheaters and coliseums was carefully arranged to give prominent access to the most honored guests.[38] The chants and habits of the crowd showed their social distance from the criminals and Christians they had come to see *butchered.*[39]

Risk mitigation was not on the minds of Christ-followers. Total sacrifice, stigma, and total obedience were embraced. The record of the death of Polycarp, the Bishop of Smyrna (in Turkey) reveals a heart fixed on risky investment. Polycarp had only to say "Lord Caesar" and offer a sacrifice to avoid being burned alive. Before his death, Polycarp prayed "I bless you (God) because you have considered me worthy of this day and hour". Brannan's record of the death of Polycarp includes a section on rewards. His reward was the crown of immortality, rejoicing with apostles gone before him, and giving glory to God by his testimony and sacrifice.[40] The risks of kingdom agency were well known in the time of Rome. The martyrs invested their lives and "turned the Roman world upside down."[41] The martyr's investment is participating in the kingdom economy return of over 1,200,000,000 current members of the Catholic Church.[42] Great risk taken and great reward realized.

Fear and the hierarchy of temptation

The Bible gives hundreds of commands to not be afraid. I study biblical cases of agency fear using the hierarchy of temptation. Faith is required overcome fear of provision. Numbers chapter 20 is the story of the Israelites telling Moses they would be better off dead because there was no water for them to drink. God miraculously delivered water. However, because of the sin of unbelief, that group of Israelites was not able to receive its promised inheritance of land.[43] At the need of provision, the Israelites succumbed to the temptation to not believe in God for water.

The second level of temptation and associated human need is physical security. Moses reached the point of preparing to enter the land God had promised. 12 leaders were selected to spy out the land. 10 of the 12 spies came back afraid and stirred up the rest of the nation to rebel against the plan to enter the land. None of the 10 risk averse spies received a share in the land.[44] Believing testimony about God and choosing to obey are prerequisites to making risky investments. Facing the risk of physical harm, 10 of the 12 Israeli agents succumbed to the temptation of retreat and forfeited their share of the promised land.

The life of King Saul illustrates is a case study in a recurring temptation over rulership and authority. Saul began his rule at 40 years old and lasted in power until he was 72. The first part of the account of Saul shows a fear of man and lack of confidence. The prophet in Saul's time was the powerful Samuel. When the time came for Saul to become king he was shy about dining with Samuel. Later, on the day of his coronation, Saul was found hiding among some baggage. The bible does report Saul had moments of overcoming his fear of man and acting in his God-given authority. In one instance the Holy Spirit came upon Saul to prophesy and in another Saul fought to deliver the people of a place called Jabesh-Gilead.[45] With the Holy Spirit's help, Saul was able to be a risk taker.

When Saul acted in his own strength, out of the fear of man, he disobeyed God's instructions.[46] Fear of man and disobedience caused Saul to die on the battlefield. The prophet Samuel identified a litany of Saul's sins. Saul has disobeyed, disregarded and rebelled against God, he had been insubordinate and idolatrous.[47] Saul committed the sin of idolatry when he set up a monument to himself, as was common for kings in the ancient near east.[48] Saul confessed his struggle was a fear of man saying, "I have sinned, I have transgressed the command of the Lord and your words because I feared the people and listened to their voice."[49]

Finally, the Old Testament judge Gideon is a case study in misplaced identity. The introduction of Gideon, a judge of Israel, takes place in a winepress. Gideon is hiding wheat from Israel's oppressors by threshing in a winepress.[50] Gideon had to be reminded he was a "mighty man of valor", and he even then asked for a supernatural sign that God was with him. The sign God gave caused Gideon to fall under the fear of the Lord. Able to operate in his God given identity as a man of valor, the Holy Spirit came on Gideon and he was eventually able to subdue his enemies. Reminded of his identity, reminded that God was with him, fearing God more than man and under the power of the Holy Spirit Gideon accomplished his assignment.

A survey of these four cases suggests variables associated with risky decision making. It is important to know God, but I must also believe God. Faith is required to overcome risk aversion and act in obedience. Faith may be closely associated with overcoming basic physiological and safety risks. I must know God, believe God, and be humble enough to obey. The Israelites had experienced God yet they still chose not to believe and obey. Pride is the antecedent of rebellion. Pride and fear of man cause me to give in to temptation. Humility and fear of God make me more likely to overcome risk aversion and invest in the kingdom. The love of money may lead me to lose my identity as a born-again son of God. Hearing the testimony of other Christ-followers helps build my faith. In addition, in the messianic era the Holy Spirit is my personal counsellor to encourage me to take risks.

Final case application and future research direction

Why did C.T. and Priscilla Studd give away a large inheritance and become an exception to both Jesus' heuristic about rich people and empirical evidence that the wealthy are less generous then the poor? The Studd's biography includes direct quotes from personal letters addressing the choices of fear of God versus fear of man, love of God, or love of money and sowing in the Spirit or sowing in the flesh. It is quite clear they did not fear man.[51] Life in the Spirit was embraced and life in the flesh was rejected.[52] The Studds loved God more than family[53] and gave away millions (in present day value) before leaving for China.[54] Their normal mode was to spend every last dollar to accomplish their assignment. The Studds relied on God to satisfy their hierarchy of needs. Food was often in short supply but they never ran out. Their health was quite poor but C.T. pressed on with his assignment.[55] The Studds knew and used their authority in Christ to pray for the sick. Their identity was firmly rooted in Christ and his eternal kingdom.

C.T. and Priscilla were able to be so prolific because of their heart labors. C.T. was often up very early to pray and read the Bible.[56] Long periods of prayer and fasting were common.[57] They were baptized in the Holy Spirit. They exhibited an astounding level of love, trust, obedience, unity and extensive collaboration with a diverse group of kingdom agents.[58] Heart labor and heart capital produced a lifetime of risk taking in the kingdom economy.

Future research could use natural language processing to evaluate the writing of different religious leaders. The frequency and type of owner-agent communication, including prayer and Bible study, is proposed to be associated with risk-taking. This follows the main theoretical conclusion of the paper *Words Speak Louder Without Actions.*[59] There is a large supply of archival religious biographical writing to empirically test the temptation hierarchy associations shown in Figure 8.2.

Notes

1 Isaiah 9:7.

2 2 Peter 3:8-10.

3 New American Standard Bible, 1971, 1 Corinthians 3:5-9.

4 New American Standard Bible, 1971, Ecclesiastes 11:2.

5 Evans, J. L., & Archer, S. H. (1968). Diversification and the reduction of dispersion: an empirical analysis. *The Journal of Finance, 23*(5), 761-767. http://dx.doi.org/10.2307/2325905.

6 Lintner, J. (1965). Security prices, risk, and maximal gains from diversification. *The journal of finance, 20*(4), 587-615. http://dx.doi.org/10.2307/2977249.

7 Bertrand, M., & Mullainathan, S. (2003). Enjoying the quiet life? Corporate governance and managerial preferences. *Journal of political Economy, 111*(5), 1043-1075. http://dx.doi.org/10.1086/376950.

8 Root, A. (2022, September). *LeBron gets it more than Jamie does.* LinkedIn. https://www.linkedin.com/pulse/lebron-gets-more-than-jamie-does-andrew-root/?trackingId=fM3ICdlZ0TZpic38pMADVA%3D%3D

9 Kaplan, S. N. (2008). Are US CEOs Overpaid?. *Academy of Management Perspectives, 22*(2), 5-20.

10 Young, L. A. (2016). *Rational choice theory and religion: Summary and assessment* (p. 26). Routledge.

11 Current academic literature on religious risk is very (hopelessly) western economy oriented. Empirical data is available mostly in the United States. Biblical risks of bodily harm and governmental mistreatment are most acute in less developed economic settings.

12 Matthew 6:19-21.

13 Matthew 19:24.

14 Grubb, N. (2014). *CT Studd: cricketer and pioneer.* The Lutterworth Press. The details of the C.T. Studd story are taken from several sections of Grubb's work. Norman Grubb was C.T. Studd's son-in-law and co-laborer in Africa.

15 Matthew 19:22-24.

16 Mathew 19:24.

17 Hoge, D. R. (Ed.). (1996). *Money matters: Personal giving in American churches* (p. 60). Westminster John Knox Press.

18 Mark 12:41-44. Luke 21:1-4.

[19] Wright, A. G. (1982). The Widow's Mites: Praise or Lament?—A Matter of Context. *The Catholic Biblical Quarterly, 44*(2), 256-265.
[20] Blomberg, C. L. (2001). Neither poverty nor riches: A biblical theology of material possessions. *Pro Ecclesia, 10*(2), 235-237. http://dx.doi.org/10.1177/106385120101000209.
[21] Young, L. A. (2016). *Rational choice theory and religion: Summary and assessment* (p. 33). Routledge.
[22] Young, L. A. (2016). *Rational choice theory and religion: Summary and assessment* (p. 33). Routledge.
[23] Iannaccone, L. R. (1998). Introduction to the Economics of Religion. *Journal of economic literature, 36*(3), 1465-1495.
[24] Stark, R., & Bainbridge, W. S. (1985). *The future of religion: Secularization, revival, and cult formation.* Univ of California Press. http://dx.doi.org/10.1525/9780520341340.
[25] Emons, W. (2001). Credence goods monopolists. *International Journal of Industrial Organization, 19*(3-4), 375-389. http://dx.doi.org/10.1016/S0167-7187(99)00023-5.
[26] Hebrews 11:6. The word for rewarder appears only one time in Greek manuscripts. God is the sole payor in the kingdom economy.
[27] Hurd, E. S. (2015). Beyond religious freedom. In *Beyond Religious Freedom.* Princeton University Press. http://dx.doi.org/10.1515/9781400873814.
[28] Hertzke, A. D. (2008). International religious freedom policy: Taking stock. *The Review of Faith & International Affairs, 6*(2), 17-23. http://dx.doi.org/10.1080/15570274.2008.9523333.
[29] Qin, D. (2020). Samuel Lamb's Exhortation Regarding Eternal Rewards: A Socio-Political Perspective. *Studies in World Christianity, 26*(1), 63-83. http://dx.doi.org/10.3366/swc.2020.0282.
[30] Luke 18:18-27.
[31] Moxnes, H. (2004). *The economy of the kingdom: Social conflict and economic relations in Luke's Gospel* (Vol. 23, p. 119). Wipf and Stock Publishers.
[32] Exodus 20:17.
[33] Bruce, F. F. (1994). *The Gospel of John: Introduction, Exposition, Notes* (p. 317). Wm. B. Eerdmans Publishing.
[34] Mark 13:11. Matthew 10:19. Luke 12:11. The respective phrases to note are: "When they arrest you", "But whenever they hand you over", When they bring you before the synagogues and the rulers and the authorities", respectively.
[35] New American Standard Bible, 1971, Acts chapter 7.
[36] Acts chapter 4.
[37] Young, L. A. (2016). *Rational choice theory and religion: Summary and assessment* (p. 26). Routledge.
[38] Kelly, C. (2006). *The Roman Empire: a very short introduction* (pp. 78-79). OUP Oxford. http://dx.doi.org/10.1093/actrade/9780192803917.001.0001.
[39] Kelly, C. (2006). *The Roman Empire: a very short introduction* (p. 82). OUP Oxford. http://dx.doi.org/10.1093/actrade/9780192803917.001.0001.
[40] Brannan, R. (2017). *The Apostolic Fathers: A New Translation* (pp. 263-276). Lexham Press.
[41] Kelly, C. (2006). *The Roman Empire: a very short introduction* (p. 86). OUP Oxford. http://dx.doi.org/10.1093/actrade/9780192803917.001.0001.
[42] BBC News. (2013, March 14). How many Roman Catholics are there in the world? *British Broadcasting Corporation.* https://www.bbc.com/news/world-21443313.

[43] New American Standard Bible, 1971, Numbers 20:11-13.
[44] New American Standard Bible, 1971, Numbers chapter 13. New American Standard Bible, 1971, Numbers chapter 14.
[45] New American Standard Bible, 1971, 1 Samuel chapter 11.
[46] New American Standard Bible, 1971, 1 Samuel 13:8-14.
[47] New American Standard Bible, 1971, 1 Samuel 15:22-23.
[48] Keener, C. S., & Walton, J. H. (Eds.). (2016). *NIV, Cultural Backgrounds Study Bible: Bringing to Life the Ancient World of Scripture* (p. 506). Zondervan.
[49] 1 Samuel 15:24.
[50] New American Standard Bible, 1971, Judges 6:11.
[51] Grubb, N. (2014). *CT Studd: cricketer and pioneer* (p. 89). The Lutterworth Press. "She doesn't' fear the face of man or woman a little bit."
[52] Grubb, N. (2014). *CT Studd: cricketer and pioneer* (p. 78, p. 40). The Lutterworth Press. "After all, the one great qualification, as in the days of old, is the baptism of the Holy Spirit."; "What a life the Spirit lives out in us when He possesses us?" "But this time I determined not to consult with flesh and blood, but just wait until God would show me."
[53] Grubb, N. (2014). *CT Studd: cricketer and pioneer* (p. 42). The Lutterworth Press. "I felt there was one thing that could keep me from going, and that was the love of my mother; but I read that passage, Whoever loves father and mother more than me is not worthy of me".
[54] Grubb, N. (2014). *CT Studd: cricketer and pioneer* (p. 70). The Lutterworth Press. "Charlie, what did the Lord tell the rich young man to do? Sell all. Well then, we will start clear with the Lord at our wedding."
[55] Grubb, N. (2014). *CT Studd: cricketer and pioneer* (p. 131). The Lutterworth Press. "Penniless, turned down by the doctor, dropped by the committee, yet told by God to go (to Africa), what was he to do? The only honest thing. Once more he staked all on obedience to God."
[56] Grubb, N. (2014). *CT Studd: cricketer and pioneer* (p. 86). The Lutterworth Press. "I got up at four o'clock this morning, Christ always knows when I have had sleep enough, and he wakes me to have a good time with him."
[57] Grubb, N. (2014). *CT Studd: cricketer and pioneer* (p. 86). The Lutterworth Press. "after eight days spent alone in prayer and fasting."
[58] Grubb, N. (2014). *CT Studd: cricketer and pioneer* (p. 127). The Lutterworth Press. "I observe in the New Testament, is not apparent politeness and manifest disobedience, but filial or childlike obedience, trust and love."
[59] Levit, D. (2020). Words speak louder without actions. *The Journal of Finance, 75*(1), 91-131. http://dx.doi.org/10.1111/jofi.12834.

Chapter 10

Individual investment

This is the third of four chapters on the topic of investment. I find individual investment a difficult topic to write about. After the Bible, I have read more textbooks, more articles, and more books on investing than on any other topic. My professional career has been dedicated to investing. I have often been asked what the Bible says about *how to get rich*. I have spent decades investing my own time and money. Yet investing my own money has not produced above-average results. At points, I have felt like an all-time great investor. Often, after a substantial loss, I have felt like a failure. At a few low points, I have felt condemned for losses motivated by greed. This chapter is a personal reconstruction of my view of investing according to the model of human agency. I start by developing a definition of investing. Second, I survey real economy data and literature on investment. Third, I develop a practical approach to investing time and money in the real economy, but for the kingdom economy. Finally, I close with a fresh look at a parable of the talents juxtaposed against the parable of the rich fool. A kingdom agency investment strategy assumes the owner is holy, loving, sovereign, and unlimited.[1]

Real economy investing

The process of investing begins when I defer consumption. I defer consumption in two ways. First, I defer consumption by spending less than my income. Second, I defer consumption of my time when I use it for education[2] or worship and service,[3] rather than income generating work or leisure. Education, in particular, is relevant to the theory of the kingdom. Evidence for the value of teaching and learning includes the great commission mandate to make and teach disciples.[4] The kingdom model is an apprenticeship model in the mode of communication between Jesus and God the Father[5] and the ministry office of teachers in the New Testament church.[6]

The deferred consumption of money for investment is for my future needs. Deferred consumption of time, investment of time, has both current and future utility. Gary Becker applies rational choice theory to all aspects of human behavior, including the investment of time in education. Becker won the Nobel prize in economic science for extending rational choice theory to non-market behaviors.[7] Real economy investors make choices about money in an attempt to maximize risk-adjusted returns. Kingdom agents invest both money and time to maximize non-monetary objectives of life, peace, and growth in the Christian church.

Tangible and intangible returns on education

I defer the consumption of time and money because I expect to realize a future increase in value. The future value may be to cover future physiological and security needs, or it may be to achieve a substantially higher level of future consumption and utility. *Financial Peace* author Dave Ramsay exhorts readers to use a zero-based budget to maximize income deferral and "live like no one else so (in the future) you can live like no one else".[8]

If I invest my time in education rather than consuming it for employment and current income, I expect to earn future income that more than repays for lost income. From almost any level of education and whether the setting is a developed or developing economy, educational attainment is associated with higher income.[9,10]

The antecedent to investing is deferred consumption of time or money. The deferral results in the accumulation of surplus time and money for future gain. Investment is the accumulation and deployment of time and money for an expected future tangible or intangible payoff. For example, I invest in education for tangible and intangible returns. Individuals and families in the United States invest large sums in higher education. According to the U.S. Department of Labor, in general, obtaining a post-high school degree pays off for the student. Mark Kantrowitz used detailed calculations to estimate a lifetime return on a bachelor's degree at 27%.[11] More recent studies accounting for the increase in university costs estimate mid-teens returns with a stronger result for science disciplines relative to humanities.[12] The median gross return on a bachelor's degree is well above historical stock market returns.[13]

In some fields of study, tangible rewards are unattractive. One example is social work. The return on a social work degree is a single-digit percentage. Yet in the early part of the twenty-first century, almost 400,000 individuals with a Bachelor of Social Work (BSW) degree worked in the field across the United States. BSW graduates are assumed to be rational, and therefore, the return on a BSW degree is partly intangible. A survey of University of Wisconsin adult-learner bachelor's graduates indicated that expected intangible returns of the satisfaction of earning a degree included an enhanced sense of identity and expanding social networks.[14] Individuals and families choose to defer consumption and leisure, to invest in education on an expectation of tangible and intangible rewards.

Real economy investing in theory

The theoretical answer to how much income I should defer is, more at a young age and less at an older age.[15] If I save and invest early, I will have more wealth to consume later when the incentive to defer consumption is lower. In practice, deferring consumption may be difficult for young families. Studies such as *Age Structure and the Personal Savings Rate* consistently show the ratio of minors to the working-age population reduces income deferral.[16] The study also shows that the savings rate declines with age. Once retired, however, consumption tends to rise less than expected,[17] in part due to a desire to leave an inheritance, expectations of the cost of an adverse health event, or misestimation of the living costs of retirement.

Real economy investing in practice

According to the U.S. Federal Reserve, the long-run rate of income deferral (i.e., savings rate) in the United States is approximately 9%.[18] The Federal Reserve also reports the long-run increase in prices for all types of things I buy is approximately 3.5% per year.[19] To develop a rule of thumb of how my income deferral translates to investment and then future income, I start with an assumption my mid-career household income is around the average of $70,000. If I have an average savings rate of 9%, the annual deferred income is $6300.[20]

I can take my deferred income and use it to purchase different types of assets. The assets include owning part of a business, lending money, or owning real estate. Historical returns of various investment types are available on the website of New York University Professor Ashwath Damodaran.[21] Damodaran's data is U.S.-oriented and covers 95 years. The data shows a return for owning stocks of 9.5% per year, a risk-free short-term government bills return of 3.5%, riskier bonds returning between 5% and 7% per year, and real estate of 4.2% per year. Recall, as a point of comparison, the Chapter Eight report shows a median interest rate of 6% over the past five thousand years.

To keep the analysis simple, I assume I will work for 45 years. Further, I assume the split of my investments is 60% in stocks, 10% in risk-free bills, 10% in riskier bonds, and 20% in real estate. Using this split and almost 100 years of data, I expect to earn 7.7% per year on an investment portfolio (see Figure 10.1 below). After I retire, it is rational to choose to reduce risk. I assume a 5.6% return in retirement.

Figure 10.1. Sample of real economy investment portfolio and expected return.

Investment Type	Allocation	Trailing 95-Year Return	Weighted Return
Stocks	60%	9.6%	5.7%
Risk-Free Treasury Bills	10%	3.3%	0.3%
U.S. Government and Corporate Bonds	20%	5.9%	1.2%
Real Estate	10%	4.2%	0.4%
		Total	7.7%

Figure 10.1 major message: Over the long run a diversified, United States based portfolio, has an expected pre-tax return of 7% to 8%. Source: Author's original analysis of data presented at https://pages.stern.nyu.edu/~adamodar/New_Home_Page/datafile/histretSP.html as of September 15, 2022.

Savings rate of 15% sufficient for future consumption

The bottom line is if I save 9% of my income each year and want to consume in retirement the way I did at the end of my working career, I will be out of money as early as 78 years old. If I cut my consumption by 25% in retirement, I push the likely depletion date to 85 years old. A savings rate of 15% changes the picture significantly. The retirement fund depletion date is pushed to near 100 years old. A 20% savings rate gives my retirement savings a substantial margin of safety. Overall a savings rate of 10% to 15% of gross income is likely a good rule of thumb because at retirement, I no longer need to defer income for savings.[22] The allocation of investment assets shown in Figure 10.1 is easy to implement in market-based economies.

God designed the earth to support investment returns

Investment returns do not happen by accident. Returns happen by God's design. The population of the earth grows. Each year, technology advances and human productivity increases. Savings, investment, and advances in technology, in particular, have a very positive effect on future economic activity and well-being. Robert Solow won a Nobel prize in economics for pioneering research on *Growth Theory*, and the positive long-run effects of investments in research, innovation, and education on economic output.[23] The economic output of a nation is called gross domestic product ("GDP"). GDP grows decade after decade and century after century. The earnings of businesses grow alongside GDP. As earnings grow, the cash flow and dividends paid out to business owners grow. Over time, stock prices go up with dividends and cash flow. My first research supervisor at Dominion Securities owned a stock so long that the annual dividend he received became more than what he paid for the stock. In the short run owning stocks is risky. Over the long run, because of economic growth, owning small parts of many businesses is a rational way to invest and accumulate wealth.

The second reason returns happen by design is resource scarcity. With each passing year, the world is home to more people with unlimited wants. The productivity of the planet grows with innovation and trade, yet the price of goods and services rises to ration scarce resources. Scarcity causes real estate prices to rise. Rising prices cause humans to balance consumption and savings, to invest in new technology and increase efficiency. Further, the rate at which prices rise is a key component of the rate of interest on debt and the return required on owning a business.[24] Human ambition and resource scarcity make investing a worthwhile activity, continuously raising human living conditions.

Kingdom investing principles in the real economy

The model of human agency shows the real economy exists within and is subject to the kingdom economy. Religious beliefs influence investing decisions of all types.[25] A growing trend in exchange-traded fund investing is to use negative screening to eliminate owning companies with objectionable products or business practices. This is a type of so-called *sin stock* screening some investment firms have done for many decades. A *sin stock* traditionally involved a business involved with alcohol, tobacco, gaming, and adult entertainment.

The name given to Christian negative investment screens is biblically responsible investing ("BRI").[26] It is possible the return outcome from a biblically responsible investing screen would be performance that is comparable to other broadly diversified portfolios. BRI investing is a somewhat higher cost compared to straight index investing. As a result, the most likely outcome is slight underperformance of BRI funds versus broad market index funds.

Investments to avoid

Is BRI the best approach? *The Theory of the Kingdom* begins with the character of the owner. The owner is holy. The opposite of holy is corrupt or profane. The opposite of holy can also be common. Just because the low-cost method of investing is the most common does not imply it is acceptable. It is straightforward to propose a list of business types to avoid. Agents of a holy owner must avoid profiting from bribes or environmental damage. A sampling of investment agents must avoid or include prostitution, harmful addictive behaviors, human trafficking, infanticide, and victimization of the poor or foreigners.

The counterpoint to any list of prohibited investments may be no real economy business is holy. Further, God himself, by the words of the prophet Jeremiah, encouraged Israelite captives to make investments that would benefit their Babylonian captors. The reason to invest and thrive was that an improvement in the general welfare of Babylon would be good for the Israelite captives.[27] If I buy a broad, diversified market index exchange-traded fund, I am linked to the welfare of the country the index covers.

I do not have *the* right answer. I don't believe there is only one right answer. I am proposing because God is Holy, I carefully consider each investment I make. Choosing the most common path may be incompatible with God's holiness. Giving up a few basis points of return to avoid a corrupt business is easily made up, as necessary, by the overseer of kingdom economy. One of the best statements on a sound approach to kingdom-based investing was written by the Ouachita Baptist University Student Investment Club. "Team members are forced to examine their beliefs, consider how those beliefs should impact their decision-making process, and learn how to best articulate those beliefs to others."[28]

Investing according to the ultra-wealthy

Warren Buffett has the nickname the Oracle of Omaha. At several points, he has been the richest man in the world. An annual charity auction to have lunch with Buffett raises millions from the winning bidder. Whether it is Buffett, Bezos, Rockefeller or Rothschild, humankind seeks investment advice from the ultra-wealthy.

The best place to begin a search for wisdom on kingdom investing is the world's richest person from around 950 BC. King Solomon wrote substantial parts of Proverbs and Ecclesiastes. Ecclesiastes chapter 11, verses one to six (New Living Translation) real economy investing advice stands up well to modern scrutiny.

> [1]Cast your bread on the surface of the waters, for you will find it after
> many days.[2] Divide your portion to seven, or even to eight, for you do
> not know what misfortune may occur on the earth.[3] If the clouds are
> full, they pour out rain on the earth; and whether a tree falls toward the
> south or toward the north, wherever the tree falls, there it lies.[4] One
> who watches the wind will not sow and one who looks at the clouds
> will not harvest.[5] Just as you do not know the path of the wind, and
> how bones are formed in the womb of the pregnant woman, so you do

> not know the activity of God who makes everything.[6] Sow your seed in the morning and do not be idle in the evening, for you do not know whether one or the other will succeed, or whether both of them alike will be good.

This short part of Ecclesiastes includes 1) international trade and investing, 2) diversification, 3) hedging, 4) counter-cyclical investment, 5) random walk, and 6) dollar cost averaging. International trade is a benefit to almost all economies[29] and emerging market investing tends to earn higher returns compared to developed economy investing. In modern portfolio theory, it is well known owning several stocks lowers risk and improves risk-adjusted returns.[30] The randomness of nature described in verse three, with the connection to agricultural uncertainty in verse six imply the need for hedging as a risk mitigation technique.[31] One predictor of future returns is often immediately past returns, suggesting it may be good to invest when most cloudy.[32,33]

Solomon's investing advice is well-supported in academic literature

Aranidhar Subrahmanyan summarizes past evidence on expected stock returns with several studies affirming Solomon's heuristics.[34] The mysterious path to growth of Ecclesiastes 11:5 has a resemblance to the random walk theory.[35] A very good summary of the popular and effective dollar-cost averaging approach to investing can be found in Meir Statman's article.[36] Finally, a strong theme in Solomon's writing is the connection of the variation of nature to the variation in economic processes. Variation is a risk when investing. Consistently acting on the principles of Ecclesiastes 11 is almost enough personal investing advice for one lifetime.

Writing in the book of Proverbs, Solomon adds several elements to real economy investing insight. Consistent diligence leads to success. Diligence benefits include generating income for investment and monitoring investment plans.[37] Using excessive leverage is a danger.[38] Lending at high-interest rates and using excessive leverage is for the express purpose of getting rich quickly. Lending at high rates of interest exhibits a love of money over the second greatest commandment to love my neighbor.[39] Returns generated by corruption are at risk of sudden loss.[40] In particular, money made at the expense of the defenseless will be opposed by God. Proverbs includes the admonition to not work to get rich.[41]

Do not work for the purpose of being rich

The apostle Paul picks up on the theme of not working for the goal of being rich. The desire to be rich is a trap that leads to ruin. Paul wrote, "for the love of money is the root of all sorts of evil, and some by longing for it have wandered away from the faith and pierced themselves with many griefs."[42] The internal consistency of biblical teaching on the love of money versus the love of God is striking. The teachings of Jesus, Paul, and Solomon all affirm the proposition of the hierarchy of temptation in Figure 8.2. My love of money causes me to satisfy my human needs by giving in to temptation, sowing in the flesh, and reaping more inequality and corruption in the real economy.[43] The consequence is deterministic based on God's design. If I invest out of the fear of God, love of God, and love of my neighbor, and with the help of the Holy Spirit, I will avoid corruption and realize a return sufficient to meet all my needs and produce life, peace, and growth in my community.

Kingdom investing for now and then

Investing in the kingdom is associated with choosing to use my time and money to consume kingdom goods rather than real economy goods. Azzi & Ehrenberg theorize this is done by deferring consumption for a future larger benefit in the afterlife.[44] Laurence Iannaccone is critical of the afterlife theory. The criticism is partly based on a lack of input from other social sciences. Perhaps influenced by his Ph.D. advisor, Gary Becker, Iannaccone takes a different approach.[45] Gary Becker is the founder of the human capital school of microeconomics and extended the discipline into the analysis of non-market behaviors such as religiosity.[46] Iannaccone assumes I can maximize my enjoyment in the present life through the tradeoff of secular and religious consumption. Jesus' purpose of abundant life supports a view kingdom agency can include enjoyment now.

The arrival of Jesus marked the beginning of the messianic age. The arrival of the kingdom of God is the key theme of Jesus' teaching.[47] The model of human agency is for individuals who have been born again. The model is a way to conceptualize life now, such that I make rational decisions about how to allocate my time and money. My physical life will indeed end. But my spiritual life will continue. Further, the kingdom of heaven has arrived. Individuals who are born again are part of the kingdom both now and going forward. In that sense, I agree with Iannaccone it is not necessary to use afterlife consumption as the motivator for devout behavior now. Further past satisfaction from religious consumption can result in a positive feedback cycle. However, religious goods need to be better defined using a biblical survey and theological literature. In the chapter called *The Law of Proportion,* I define kingdom religious goods, the price of those goods, and how I rationally maximize utility.

Jesus' teaching on the kingdom of God explains how to transmute time and money into the kingdom. One focus of transmuted wealth can be on accumulating riches at a rate of up to 100 times return.[48] Rewards earned are inefficiently allocated. Jesus' offer of a large reward is not always conditioned on the risk of the investment. Craig Keener indicates the 100 times return would be associated with the exceptional harvest of Isaac in Genesis and the benefit of being part of the Christian community and sharing.[49,50]

Investment rewards are based on the holy, loving, sovereign, and unlimited character of the owner. Time and money committed to kingdom purposes are exchanged for some tangible goods such as guaranteed physiological provision.[51] The exchange of time, money and relationships for a hundredfold return "envisages an eternal family and future dwelling place unspeakably more wonderful than anything this earth has to offer."[52]

Figure 10.2. Time and money exchanged for religious goods with utility in the real economy.

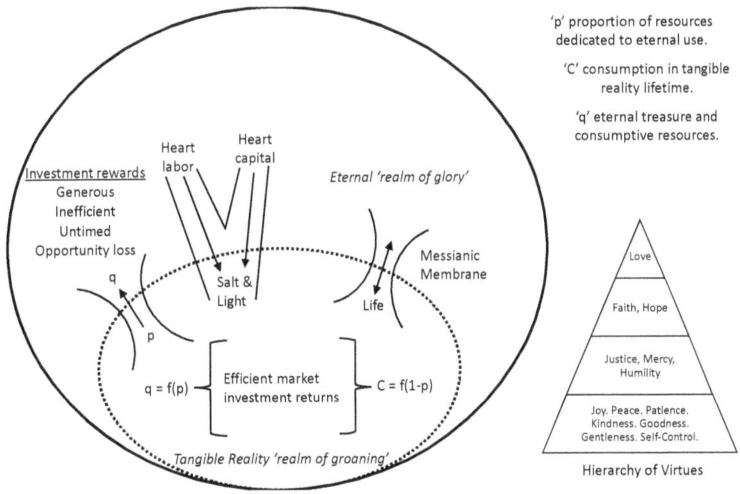

Figure 10.2 major message: Investment of time, money and relationships receives more than just a risk-adjusted in the future realm. In the present realm my kingdom investment receives a reward of heart capital and a greater capacity to do heart labor. The heart capital received includes love, faith, hope, humility, the ability to do justice, and patience.

Kingdom investment rewards includes spiritual virtue

Highly productive goods for the present day are intangible spiritual goods. A proposed list of spiritual goods is shown in the pyramid at the lower right of Figure 10.2. The hierarchy of virtues in Figure 10.2 is ordinal, not cardinal. It is a relative ranking based on a scriptural survey and not given as a fixed value or with absolute certainty, as is sometimes offered by lists of *cardinal virtues*.

There is, however, a high degree of certainty; the top three virtues are love, faith, and hope.[53]

Justice, mercy, and humility are also high-order virtues mentioned in several scriptural contexts. The prophet Micah wrote to the people of Israel, "And what does the Lord require of you but to do justice, love mercy and walk humbly with your God?"[54] John Walton notes the ancient world would have viewed this as the most basic list of virtues needed for any well-functioning society. Justice, mercy, and humility are the starting points for obedient service in the kingdom, not the endpoint.[55] Jesus quotes the prophet Hosea's saying that God wants mercy and not sacrifice.[56] Jesus represents the intersection point of mercy and justice.[57] The word for mercy in Hosea is associated with the nation of Israel "carrying through on covenant commitment both to exclusive worship of the Lord and to communal justice."[58] Humility is required to receive God's grace,[59] to work with other agents,[60] and is characteristic of the exercise of Godly wisdom that produces the desired products of the kingdom economy.[61] The final level in the pyramid of virtues is straightforward. It is a virtue dispensed by the Holy Spirit, not already included in the three higher tiers.[62]

The tithe

The most common proportional benchmark to measure the exchange of money and time for kingdom investment is the tithe. The tithe is a useful benchmark. The tithe was a requirement of the Mosaic law.[63] The tithe is associated with an Old Testament promise of provision. There is a vibrant current debate over the tithe in the kingdom era. George Davis presents most of the relevant arguments for and against a standard of giving 10%, concluding by deduction tithing is a recommended action. Empirically, most studies show the average U.S. church adherent does not give a full tithe, a full 10% of income.[64] A definitive statement on tithing is not required to draw specific conclusions with the model of human agency. I tithe in part because it has been a learned discipline passed on and because of the benefits associated with generous giving. I find it an essential discipline in a sincere daily attempt to serve God rather than money. I tithe because Jesus did not come to abolish any part of the teaching of the law and the prophets. The prophet Malachi emphasized the tithe.[65] However, an excessive focus on the tithe risks the same mistake of the religious leaders of Jesus' day. A focus on the exchange of 10% of time and money for religious goods risks "missing the forest for the trees."[66]

Giving is servanthood and an act of worship

A feature of the giving forest that has perhaps been lost is servanthood and worship. When tempted by real economy authority, Jesus replied with a requirement of worship and service. The personal requirement becomes more significant in light of Romans chapter 12 verse one, "Therefore I urge you brothers and sisters, in view of God's mercy, to offer your bodies as a living sacrifice, holy and pleasing to God – this is your true and proper worship." Focus on a hurdle rate of 10% of money may obscure the requirement I exchange as much of my life as possible in service.

High earners should invest more than money in kingdom service and worship

There is evidence the wealthiest Christ-followers, those with a high value of money per unit of their time, choose to give a larger proportion of money than time.[67] The reasoning may be along the lines the church is better off with the high time-value person generating income and donating money rather than time. The thinking presupposes three facts. First, it assumes there is a valid trade-off in the model between time and money. Second, if the tradeoff exists the value of money is equal to or greater than the value of time. Third, the assumption seems to be God needs money to achieve his objectives.

The reasoning can be challenged on theoretical and empirical lines. Empirically, survey data generally indicates wealth is negatively associated with giving percentage. Some surveys show an uptick in percentage for the ultra-wealthy that comes close to matching the lowest deciles of income, but it does not exceed the giving rate of the lowest income. Second, time spent in religious practice is most closely associated with age. The thinner the messianic membrane gets, the more urgently I realize I must invest in the kingdom economy.[68]

The theoretical breakdown begins with God, who is not in need of anything humankind produces.[69] It is a self-indictment to believe the kingdom economy is better with my money than my time. The thinking reflects the teachings of Epicurus and Aristotle that denied God was the creator and owner of all.[70] God is in fact, the owner and unlimited source of all the earth. He doesn't need one dollar from me. I am offered a chance to invest my time in service and worship for His Glory. Peter and Paul indicated God is no respecter of persons, regardless of class or ethnicity.[71] No one is exempt from following the example of Jesus, who came to serve.[72] If an agency task requires resources, God can reallocate money[73] or produce the resource out of nothing.[74] The false teaching of Epicurus and Aristotle also robs the rich man of a reward of heart capital and heart labor capacity. Kingdom service has a joint product benefit of the outcome of the act itself, as well as building greater capacity and capital stores for future service.

Exchange of the highest order

Finally, the resources exchanged with the owner must be of the highest order. Elements of high-order exchange might include: 1) Agents give out of freedom,[75] not out of any compulsion. 2) I give the first fruits of my income,[76] not out of what is left over. 3) I give time and resources[77] that are truly costly, not what is left over. 4) I give as unto the Lord, often in secret, rather than for honor from the crowd.[78]

What might an exchange of high-value time with the owner mean in a modern developed economy context? A simple example may be serving on a church board or committee. Arrive early and be well prepared. Contribute to the group at least as well as the normal practice for a business meeting. There are many applications to every aspect of service within a family, a church, or a community.

The individual investment model can be summarized with the salt and light metaphor of Jesus. As I use an increasing amount of my time and money for service and worship according to kingdom principles I receive back spiritual goods as virtues. Over time, I become saltier and brighter, producing more peace, life, and growth in the real economy now. The amount of any particular good I receive now or in the future is dispensed by the Holy Spirit according to the Bible and the will of an owner who is holy, loving, and unlimited.

Application. Reconsidering losses and staying in the game

Risky investment sometimes results in a loss. Losses make the parable of the talents a curiosity in a real economy context. The gospels of Matthew and Luke contain variations of the same parable.[79] Both versions begin with an owner assigning money for investment to slaves before leaving on a long trip. In Matthew, the owner allocates five bags of gold to one servant, two bags to another, and one bag to the third. In Luke, the owner allocates 10 minas to 10 different servants. One mina was equal to about three months' pay.[80] There are no specific instructions on how to invest. There is no indication of how long the owner will be away. The story in Luke contains a simple instruction, "Do business with this money until I come back."[81] The parable is an illustration of how the economy of the kingdom runs on agency.

In both versions of the story, the owner returned to receive an account from the investors. In both versions, the first two servants earned a large gain and were given more responsibility. In both versions, the third servant did not invest. In Matthew, the third servant reported no investment and no return.

The verdict is the third servant is wicked and lazy. The correct interpretation of lazy is to hesitate or shrink back. The third servant succumbed to fear and risk-aversion. The penalty for underinvesting and risk avoidance is severe. The third servant was cast out by the owner. In Luke's version, the failure of the third servant is carelessness. The money should not have been put in a handkerchief in the ground. According to ancient cultural norms, even if no investment was made a strong box would have been a superior way to store money.[82]

The three most salient points in the parable are summarized by Blomberg.[83] First, every person receives resources from the owner. Second, agents that faithfully invest and earn positive returns will be rewarded. Agents who do not invest, whether due to carelessness (Luke) or refusing to take a risk (Matthew) will be judged severely. The most direct message is clear. Invest what the owner has allocated to you or it will be taken from you, at your great peril.

The real economy curiosity is there is no fourth scenario in Matthew and no report from servants four through 10 in Luke. The curiosity began to bother me very much after a business I started failed. I believe I started the business for a righteous kingdom purpose. I had left an excellent job to take a risk and I failed spectacularly. Where in the parable was the investor who took a risk and lost the owner's money? Risk taking and loss are a fact of life in the real economy. If I *do business* until the owner returns, I might lose money. From my perspective, the two versions of the parable of the talents were incomplete. Well after the business failed and I have moved on I received an answer from the Holy Spirit. The answer came in two parts and it gave me new hope to take new risks in the kingdom economy.

It is by design there is no fourth investor in the book of Matthew. Any particular loss I may incur can be made up by the owner. All of my resources came from God in the first place. Despite any personal loss, he will meet my basic physiological needs according to his resources. I must keep investing my time and money as aggressively and as diligently as possible until the count is finally taken. The owner of the kingdom economy is highly diversified. He has unlimited resources. Any good faith loss I suffer is not a setback for the kingdom of God. It may produce pain for me now, but it can be redeemed for life and peace in the kingdom. God is well-diversified and wants each agent to take risk. The story of ten minas in Luke fits well with Matthew. Three out of 10 servants were called to account. I am not told if the owner required a final report from the other seven servants. Any particular loss I suffer is only one part of a long journey of investing time and money for the kingdom. My final report is not yet due. If I keep taking risks for life, peace and growth, when the owners calls for my report, it will be all good.

The second part of the answer is in the parable of the rich fool.[84] The story starts with a highly successful landowner. The success was so great the rich fool built two new barns to double his inventory. The rich man then decided to retire and "eat, drink and enjoy yourself." As the landowner sat back to enjoy his wealth, God said to him, "you fool! This very night, your soul will be demanded of you." The man's assets went to people he did not even know. Jesus told the story after being presented with a dispute over a family inheritance. The story is told as a caution against greed and believing life is about real economy wealth. Life is about exchanging time and money now for kingdom output and credence (*pistis*) goods dispensed by the owner.

The answer for agents is clear. There is no fourth person in Matthew's story, and the reports of the majority of investors from Luke's story were not yet due. I must continue to invest, knowing the owner is unlimited. The moment I stop allocating time and money to advance the kingdom, I become useless. As I continue to take risks, I contribute to the growth of the kingdom, regardless of the real economy tally at any moment in time. Nothing is ever lost for the owner of the kingdom economy. I invest as aggressively and prudently as possible.

Notes

[1] See Chapter 2, "Characteristics of the Owner".

[2] Becker, G. S. (2009). *Human capital: A theoretical and empirical analysis, with special reference to education* (p. 17). University of Chicago Press. http://dx.doi.org/10.7208/chicago/9780226041223.001.0001.

[3] Luke 4:8. Jesus' response to temptation sets a good direction for considering investment in the kingdom economy. "You shall worship the Lord your God and serve him only". Worship and service is the path to authority, as this is the area of human need over which the Devil was tempting Jesus.

[4] Matthew 28:19-20.

[5] John 5:18-24.

[6] Ephesians 4:11-12.

[7] Becker, G. S. (1992, October 13) Nobel Prize Outreach AB 2023. *NobelPrize.org*. https://www.nobelprize.org/prizes/economic-sciences/1992/becker/facts/

[8] Ramsey, D., & Ramsey, S. (1997). *Financial peace*. Viking.

[9] Kane, T. J., & Rouse, C. E. (1995). Labor-Market Returns to Two-and Four-Year College. *The American Economic Review, 85*(3), 600.

[10] Chen, J., Kanjilal-Bhaduri, S., & Pastore, F. (2022). *Updates on Returns to Education in India: Analysis using PLFS 2018-19 Data* (No. 1016). GLO Discussion Paper. http://dx.doi.org/10.2139/ssrn.4114527.

[11] Kantrowitz, M. (2007). The financial value of a higher education. *Journal of Student Financial Aid, 37*(1), 5. http://dx.doi.org/10.55504/0884-9153.1075.

[12] Abel, J. R., & Deitz, R. (2014). Do the benefits of college still outweigh the costs?. *Current issues in economics and finance, 20*(3).

[13] 2018 data from the U.S. department of education indicates median weekly earnings of U.S. Bachelors degree holders is $1156, much higher than the $692 per week earned by high school graduates. Investment in comparable dollars for four years of public university tuition, including room and board, is approximately $150,000. The $24,000 in additional pre-tax income equates to a gross yield of 16%, well higher than student loan interest rates.
[14] Mishler, C. J. (1983). Adults' perceptions of the benefits of a college degree. *Research in Higher Education, 19*(2), 213-230. http://dx.doi.org/10.1007/BF00974760.
[15] Phelps, E. S. (1962). The accumulation of risky capital: A sequential utility analysis. *Econometrica: Journal of the Econometric Society*, 729-743. http://dx.doi.org/10.2307/1909322.
[16] Thornton, J. (2001). Age Structure and the Personal Savings Rate in the United States, 1956-1995. *Southern Economic Journal, 68*(1), 166-170.
[17] Banks, J., Blundell, R., & Tanner, S. (1998). Is there a retirement-savings puzzle?. *American Economic Review*, 769-788.
[18] Federal Reserve Bank of St. Louis. (2022, September 15). *Personal Saving Rate*. The Federal Reserve, Federal Reserve Bank of St. Louis. https://fred.stlouisfed.org/series/PSAVERT
[19] The Federal Reserve data for all items for the past 75 years (1947 to 2022) yields a compound rate of increase of 3.5% per year. The index level went from 22.0 in April 1947 to 295.3 in July 2022.
[20] The calculations can easily be updated for median income at a future time of reading.
[21] Damodaran, A. (2022, January). Historic Returns on Stocks, Bonds and Bills: 1928-2021. NYU Stern School of Business. https://pages.stern.nyu.edu/~adamodar/New_Home_Page/datafile/histretSP.html
[22] An electronic spreadsheet of the calculations is available upon request.
[23] Solow, R. M. (1987, December 8). Growth Theory and After. *NobelPrize.org*. https://www.nobelprize.org/prizes/economic-sciences/1987/solow/lecture/
[24] Summers, L. H. (1982). *The Nonadjustment of Nominal Interest Rates: A Study of the Fisher Effect* (No. 0836). National Bureau of Economic Research, Inc.
[25] Shu, T., Sulaeman, J., & Yeung, P. E. (2012). Local religious beliefs and mutual fund risk-taking behaviors. *Management Science, 58*(10), 1779-1796. http://dx.doi.org/10.1287/mnsc.1120.1525; León, A. K., & Pfeifer, C. (2013). *Religious activity, risk taking preferences, and financial behaviour: Empirical evidence from German survey data*. Inst. für Volkswirtschaftslehre. http://dx.doi.org/10.1016/j.socec.2017.05.005; Parboteeah, K. P., Walter, S. G., & Block, J. H. (2015). When does Christian religion matter for entrepreneurial activity? The contingent effect of a country's investments into knowledge. *Journal of Business Ethics, 130*(2), 447-465. http://dx.doi.org/10.1007/s10551-014-2239-z
[26] Graham, L. (2017). *Investing with integrity*. Kingdom Life Publishing.
[27] Jeremiah 29:4-7.
[28] Brune, C., & Files, J. (2019). Biblical screens and the stock selection process: applications for a student-managed fund. *Christian Business Academy Review, 14*.
[29] Krugman, P. R. (1979). Increasing returns, monopolistic competition, and international trade. *Journal of international Economics, 9*(4), 469-479. http://dx.doi.org/10.1016/0022-1996(79)90017-5.

[30] Wagner, W. H., & Lau, S. C. (1971). The effect of diversification on risk. *Financial Analysts Journal, 27*(6), 48-53. http://dx.doi.org/10.2469/faj.v27.n5.48.

[31] Whitwell, C. (2009). The variation of nature in Ecclesiastes 11. *Journal for the Study of the Old Testament, 34*(1), 81-97. http://dx.doi.org/10.1177/0309089209346354.

[32] Jegadeesh, N. (1990). Evidence of predictable behavior of security returns. *The Journal of finance, 45*(3), 881-898. http://dx.doi.org/10.1111/j.1540-6261.1990.tb05110.x. I note because of the efficient nature of capital markets mean-reversion strategies wax and wane in terms of empirical proof. Regardless, the axiom it is best to be bold when others are fearful, generally holds.

[33] Loughran, T., & Ritter, J. R. (1996). Long-term market overreaction: The effect of low-priced stocks. *The Journal of Finance, 51*(5), 1959-1970. http://dx.doi.org/10.1111/j.1540-6261.1996.tb05234.x.

[34] Subrahmanyam, A. (2010). The cross-section of expected stock returns: what have we learnt from the past twenty-five years of research?. *European Financial Management, 16*(1), 27-42. http://dx.doi.org/10.1111/j.1468-036X.2009.00520.x.

[35] Malkiel, B. G. (1999). *A random walk down Wall Street: including a life-cycle guide to personal investing.* WW Norton & Company.

[36] Statman, M. (1995). A Behavioral Framework for Dollar-Cost Averaging. *The Journal of Portfolio Management, 22*(1), 70-78. http://dx.doi.org/10.3905/jpm.1995.409537.

[37] Proverb 6:6-11.

[38] New American Standard Bible, 1971, Proverbs 22:7. New American Standard Bible, 1971, Proverbs 28:8. Proverbs 6:4-5.

[39] Matthew 22:36-40.

[40] Proverbs 6:12-15.

[41] Proverbs 23:4.

[42] 1 Timothy 6:10.

[43] 1 Corinthians 6:9-10, Galatians 6:4-10. Galatians 4 says I examine my own work. Verse 5 says I bear my own load. This is pertinent to the individual nature of personal financial planning and the reference in note 28.

[44] Azzi, C., & Ehrenberg, R. (1975). Household allocation of time and church attendance. *Journal of political Economy, 83*(1), 27-56. http://dx.doi.org/10.1086/260305.

[45] Iannaccone, L. R. (1984). *Consumption Capital and Habit Formation with an Application to Religious Participation* (Publication No. T29220) [Doctoral dissertation, The University of Chicago]. ProQuest Dissertations & Theses Global.

[46] Becker, G. S. (1992, October 13) Nobel Prize Outreach AB 2023. *NobelPrize.org.* https://www.nobelprize.org/prizes/economic-sciences/1992/becker/facts/

[47] Burge, G. M., & Green, G. L. (2020). *The New Testament in Antiquity: A Survey of the New Testament Within Its Cultural Contexts Second Edition.* Zondervan Academic.

[48] Matthew 19:29. Mark 10:30.

[49] Keener, C. S., & Walton, J. H. (Eds.). (2016). *NIV, Cultural Backgrounds Study Bible: Bringing to Life the Ancient World of Scripture* (p. 1776). Zondervan.

[50] New American Standard Bible, 1971, Genesis 26:12.

[51] Keener, C. S., & Walton, J. H. (Eds.). (2016). *NIV, Cultural Backgrounds Study Bible: Bringing to Life the Ancient World of Scripture* (p. 2153). Zondervan.

[52] Blomberg, C. L. (1992). *Matthew: An exegetical and theological exposition of Holy Scripture* (Vol. 22, p. 300-301). B&H Publishing Group.

[53] 1 Corinthians 13:13. New American Standard Bible, 1971, Deuteronomy 6:5. New American Standard Bible, 1971, Leviticus 19:17-18. Matthew 22:37-40.
[54] New American Standard Bible, 1971, Micah 6:8.
[55] Keener, C. S., & Walton, J. H. (Eds.). (2016). *NIV, Cultural Backgrounds Study Bible: Bringing to Life the Ancient World of Scripture* (p. 1579). Zondervan.
[56] New American Standard Bible, 1971, Hosea 6:8.
[57] New American Standard Bible, 1971, Psalm 85:10.
[58] Edin, M. H. (1998). Learning what righteousness means. Hosea 6: 6 and the ethic of mercy in Matthew's gospel. *Word & world, 18*(4), 355-363.
[59] New American Standard Bible, 1971, Proverbs 3:34. Repeated for emphasis in New American Standard Bible, 1971, James 4:6 and 1 Peter 5:5.
[60] Psalm 133:1-3. I Corinthians chapter 12.
[61] James 3:13-18.
[62] Galatians 5:22.
[63] Leviticus 27:30-33, Malachi 3:8-10.
[64] James III, R. N., & Jones, K. S. (2011). Tithing and religious charitable giving in America. *Applied Economics, 43*(19), 2441-2450. http://dx.doi.org/10.1080/0003684090 3213384.
[65] Micah 6:8.
[66] Keener, C. S., & Walton, J. H. (Eds.). (2016). *NIV, Cultural Backgrounds Study Bible: Bringing to Life the Ancient World of Scripture* (p. 1579). Zondervan.
[67] Young, L. A. (2016). *Rational choice theory and religion: Summary and assessment* (pp. 30-31). Routledge.
[68] Azzi, C., & Ehrenberg, R. (1975). Household allocation of time and church attendance. *Journal of political Economy, 83*(1), 27-56. http://dx.doi.org/10.1086/260305.
[69] Acts 17:24-28.
[70] Henry, M. (1991). *Matthew Henry's commentary on the whole Bible* (Vol. 5, Acts 17). Peabody^ eMA MA: Hendrickson Publishers.
[71] Acts 10:34. New American Standard Bible, 1971, Romans 2:11.
[72] Luke 22:24-27.
[73] Proverbs 13:22. Examples include the gift of Egyptians to Israel at the Exodus, the gifts to the exiles with Nehemiah and Ezra.
[74] John 2:1-12.
[75] Matthew 10:5-8. Galatians 5:1.
[76] Proverbs 3:9
[77] New American Standard Bible, 1971, 1 Chronicles 21:24. New American Standard Bible, 1971, 2 Samuel 24:24.
[78] Matthew 6:1-4.
[79] Luke 19:11-27. Matthew 25:14-30.
[80] Keener, C. S., & Walton, J. H. (Eds.). (2016). *NIV, Cultural Backgrounds Study Bible: Bringing to Life the Ancient World of Scripture* (p. 1857). Zondervan.
[81] Luke 19:13.
[82] Keener, C. S., & Walton, J. H. (Eds.). (2016). *NIV, Cultural Backgrounds Study Bible: Bringing to Life the Ancient World of Scripture* (p. 1857). Zondervan.
[83] Blomberg, C. L. (1992). *Matthew: An exegetical and theological exposition of Holy Scripture* (Vol. 22, pp. 373-375). B&H Publishing Group.
[84] Luke 12:13-21.

Chapter 11

Organization investment

> "The two great forming agencies of the world's history have been the religious and economic.[1]"
>
> Alfred Marshall

> "But the law has upon many occasions attempted to raise the wages of curates, and for the dignity of the church, to oblige the rectors of parishes to give them more than the wretched maintenance which they themselves might be willing to accept of.[2]"
>
> Adam Smith

> "It is the prosperity gospel preached by an array of fast-expanding Christian evangelical churches across the world (generating) engaging debates on the affinity between market and religion."[3]
>
> Osella & Rudnyckyj

Growing organizations take risks and invest. The purpose of kingdom-oriented organizational investment is to participate in the growth of kingdom economy. The quotations identify an area of particular interest for this study. Religious institutions have influenced human development, but is the impetus for investment by religious organizations self-interest or kingdom economy growth, or both? Self-interest in the form of high pay is a reliable risk-taking incentive for business leaders. However, at least in the time of Adam Smith, pay for curates and rectors was unattractive. Modern studies suggest real economy prosperity is at least part of the incentive scheme at rapidly growing churches. The importance of religion to human development and the time inconsistency of monetary incentives in the Christian church leaves open a question regarding what other incentives, besides money, motivate organizational risk-taking in the kingdom economy.

This chapter is not a study of the influence of religiosity on the investment activity of businesses with traditional profit or stakeholder motivations. There is a large body of literature on the influence of religiosity on investment policies of for-profit businesses.[4,5] This chapter studies why some religious organizations push to grow, others do not and what is a recommended approach to grow. Kingdom economy organizations include more than churches. Organizations such as Compassion International[6] or Operation

Blessing[7] are important to the advancement of the kingdom of God now. Compassion International is focused on holistic child development in poor regions of the world, and Operation Blessing's mission is to demonstrate the love of God by alleviating human suffering. Both organizations have a mission compatible with life, peace, and growth. The chapter concludes with a set of organizational investing guidelines.

A substantial percentage of business investment literature is motivated by agency theory.[8] Agency theory has been discussed extensively so far. Strategic management has several other equally important theories explaining the success of choices made within an organization. One important theory is the institution-based view of organizations.[9] The quote above by Alfred Marshall alludes to religious organizations as important formative institutions. Churches and non-profits function as normative, informal institutions in the real economy. The upper echelon theory is also highly relevant to churches. Upper echelon theory means the experience, personality, and values of a lead pastor will influence church investments.[10]

A church is not a for-profit business

Prior literature has postulated the Church writ-large or individual churches can be analyzed as business enterprises. *Towards an Economic Theory of the Church*[11] indicates the church has a positive normative function in the economy by enforcing private property rights and lowering transaction costs. Hull & Bold expect churches will seek to maximize wealth by selling happiness, social goods such as education, and an altered eternal fate. According to Hull & Bold churches are in the business of selling spiritual credence goods.

Prior literature has also analyzed the medieval era church as a single enterprise. The medieval era analysis reformulates "the spiritual hypothesis in economic terms."[12] Robert Ekelund and his colleagues motivate their analysis with government public interest theory. Religious organizations can be thought of as oriented to the general good of a community, nation, or even the world. Here I add the comments of John Walton on what God requires of his followers. Kingdom agents are required to do justice, love mercy and walk humbly. The three virtues of justice, mercy, and humility were considered the basics of a well-functioning society.[13] To those virtues I add the cardinal Christian virtues of love, faith, and hope.[14] These virtues dispensed by the Holy Spirit, shown previously in Figure 10.2, are intended to produce the outputs of the kingdom economy.[15]

The mandate of the messianic era church is to make disciples everywhere. Looking at the church as a quasi-governmental entity or single business enterprise may be of academic interest. However, there are a large number of organization-level investments described in the Bible. The Old Testament case studies and New Testament instructions leads to a more usable set of guidelines and propositions for church and ministry investment. A fresh biblical survey is also preferable to a survey of consultants. I have found the strategy advice provided to churches and ministries, particularly on turning around a shrinking organization, often reads like any other for-profit consulting report. There is, of course, wisdom in real economy advice for kingdom-oriented for-profit businesses. I see little value in repeating the advice here because churches and ministries are not businesses.[16]

Incredible ambition

The ambition of God is unfathomable. Genesis chapter one reports God created the heavens and the earth. Father, son, and Holy Spirit were present at the creation of the world. Jesus actively maintains creation. The known universe continues to expand in the present day. God's wish is all humankind would choose to know him through the salvation work of Jesus. He sends out billions of kingdom agents to teach about Jesus, arrest corruption in the real economy, and to partner in a renewal that will make all things new. Now, in the present, Jesus has gone to prepare a future home of incomprehensible scale and beauty. God is ambitious.

Every human is created in the image of God. "Let us make mankind in Our image according to Our likeness."[17] In ancient culture, the image speaks of the essence of something for an image bearer to carry out necessary work. The likeness indicates a type of resemblance.[18] God has made humankind with what is needed to perform agency tasks and to bear a resemblance of the owner. The doctrine of *Imago Dei* and the ambition of God bring understanding to the human capacity to invest and meet the growth objective of the economy of the kingdom.

The first building project in Genesis, Noah's ark, was enormous. Noah received specific instructions. It is recorded he did everything he had been commanded. Noah's obedience saved his family while all others were judged.[19] The second project of note was also ambitious. The Tower of Babel was intended to reach heaven. God himself stopped the construction by disrupting communication. Jarvis Williams notes the tower may have been an ancient ziggurat to provide a path for a god to descend to earth.[20] The one true God put a stop to the project. Noah's Ark and the Tower of Babel projects show human ambition, communication, unity, and ingenuity are powerful and important elements of completing new and difficult tasks.

A very expensive tent built by generosity and Holy Spirit inspiration

During a time of sojourn in the desert, the Israelites were instructed to build a tabernacle. God supplied very specific instructions for the project. At least three elements of the project bear on organization investment now. The project was (over)funded with willingly supplied gifts from the people.[21] The project was not funded by coercing valuables out of the children of Israel. God handpicked artisans named Bezalel and Uri to lead construction. The first recorded impartation of the Holy Spirit is for Bezalel and Uri to work on the building project in "wisdom, in understanding, in knowledge, and in all kinds of craftsmanship, to create artistic designs for work in gold, in silver, and bronze, and in the cutting of stones for settings, and the carving of wood, so that he may work in all kinds of craftsmanship."[22]

The Holy Spirit activates God-ordained leaders to execute the project. The accounting of the materials used in the tabernacle showed its extraordinary value. The materials list includes approximately 35,000 ounces of gold and 121,000 ounces of silver, plus bronze, valuable linens, and gemstones. The present-day value of gold and silver in the tabernacle is approximately $62,000,000.[23] The value of other raw materials and labor would potentially double the estimated market value of the tabernacle. The modern-day value of the tabernacle project described in Exodus is well over $100,000,000. The total enclosed area of the tabernacle was 11,250 square feet.[24] My rough estimation puts the cost of the tabernacle project per square foot at $8888 per square foot.

Kings were hard-wired to invest and build

The second book of Chronicles supplies a record of the ancient kings of Israel. The record of a king often includes a note on building activity. The record of Rehoboam[25] noted he built 15 cities, including Bethlehem, Hebron, and Tekoa. Rehoboam fortified strongholds, and he reigned for 17 years. Asa, son of Abijah, built cities in a time of rest from war. Asa declared a period of peace is the time to build cities and make walls, towers, gates, and bars.[26] Jehoshaphat invested in education and built fortresses and storage cities. Jehoshaphat set judges in the land at fortified cities and reigned for 25 years.

Investment activity reveals the priorities of the leaders. Some kings built out of pride and disobedience to God. Jehoram, son of Jehoshaphat, got the throne "because he was the firstborn."[27] Jehoram killed all his brothers, built high places for idol worship, and led his subjects into sin. Manasseh also disobeyed God and rebuilt high places for Baal worship. Manasseh suffered military defeat and eventually humbled himself. God delivered him and Manasseh built the wall on the west side to the Fish gate. He rebuilt the altar of the Lord and tore down idols. Investment projects reveal the contents of a leader's heart.

Joash became king after Jehoram. Joash was only 7 years old when he became king. Joash reigned for 40 years. Initially, Joash was obedient to the law of the Lord and started a building project to renovate the Temple. Joash collected money and hired masons, carpenters, ironworkers, and bronze workers. Joash restored the temple to its original condition. Joash is also a case-let in upper echelon theory. Joash's top advisor in the obedient years was Jehoida. However, when Jehoiada died, Joash listened to new senior advisors. Joash went so far as to kill Jehoiada's son. The year after the murder of Zechariah, Joash was killed by an invading army and was not buried with the kings.

King Uzziah built Elath. Uzziah built towers at the gates and other fortifications. Uzziah invested in weapons and invented new technology. He was obedient and reigned for 52 years. King Jothan rebuilt an upper gate, rebuilt a wall at the hill of Ophelia, and built towns in the hill country of Judah. Finally, Jothan constructed fortresses and towers in wooded areas. The list in Chronicles goes on to include investments made by Hezekiah and Josiah.

Worthwhile investments meet the needs of provision, security, authority and identity

The record of kings confirms senior leaders are hard-wired to invest and advance. The report of Chronicles appears to indicate investment activity shows royal performance. Obedience, humility, and faith are antecedents of worthwhile kingdom investments. Worthwhile investments are associated with community worship, security, and provision. The product of good investment satisfies human needs of physiological provision, security, authority, and identity. Pride and idol worship leads to corruption, captivity, and community loss. The temptation strategy of the devil is on display in Luke chapter four. The tactics appear to be a repeat of the lives of Israel's kings. Leaders making investments for the right reasons is vital to the ongoing growth of the kingdom economy.

The coincidence with for-profit firms is new investment is the main driver of value. Franco Modigliani and Merton Miller, both Nobel prize winners, theory of investment states value is created by the investment activity of the firm.[28] Value is not created through any particular source of funding or dividend policy. Investment activity includes new spending on production facilities, buildings, and land. Investments are also made when a business buys another business. Investments can be in intangible assets such as research and development and organization capital. There are, of course, nuances and exceptions to the Modigliani and Miller theorem, but the main point remains valid. Value is created through investment activity.

The extravagant temple built in a time of peace

The temple investment is a recurring part of the meta-narrative of the people of Israel. In the ancient world, a temple was often constructed as a home for gods. The greatest king of Israel was David. Messiah Jesus was born out of the tribe of Judah, the house and line of David. Around 1000 BC, King David and the people of Israel had peace on all borders.[29] As suggested by past king Asa, peace is a time to invest and build. David wanted to build a temple in Jerusalem for YHWH. God replied David was not the person for the job and that since the Exodus, a tent and tabernacle had been sufficient. It is not easy for a king, President, or CEO to pass up a landmark investment opportunity. David was obedient and did not begin construction even though it was his desire. David turned his attention to preparation and instructing Solomon on how to serve the people and secure the royal line by obeying the Mosaic law.[30]

The agent with the mandate to build the temple was David's son Solomon. David played a large role in planning for the temple. David commissioned both Solomon and the project in front of the nation. David gave Solomon detailed architectural and workforce plans. David made a large donation of gold, silver, bronze, onyx, marble, iron, and wood. David then asked the assembly of Israelites who would be willing to donate time and money to the project. The people "offered willingly with a loyal heart."[31] The project was set up for success because it was conceived and funded out of a love for God[32] rather than a love of money. Detailed plans were inspired by the owner rather than the pride of the agents.[33] The people were unified and in agreement. It was the right time for the temple investment.

David's investment, over and above basic preparations, was equivalent to 3000 talents of gold and 7000 talents of silver.[34] The people gave 5000 talents of gold, 10,000 darics of gold, and 10,000 talents of silver, plus bronze, iron, and gemstones. The present value of David's investment in gold and silver is approximately $6.1 billion. The present value of the people's investment is approximately $10.4 billion. The value of the gemstones, cedar, labor, fabrics, iron, and bronze is unknown. I make the conservative assumption the value of the gold and silver makes up the majority of the value of the project. If I assume at least two-thirds of the project was in gold and silver, the total project cost was on the order of $25 billion.

The first temple investment may have been an order of magnitude more expensive than the current tallest building in the world. The unprecedented grandeur of the temple was attested to by the Queen of Sheba, who proclaimed Solomon's achievement far exceeded any of the stories she had heard.[35] The Queen presented Solomon with gold worth $245,000,000.[36] In geopolitics, money is power. Solomon's temple was a demonstration of the change in Israel's fortunes over the 40 years of David's reign. Israel had become the near east seat of wealth and power.

Solomon's temple stood for 400 years. It was destroyed around 590 BC. King Nebuchadnezzar burned down the temple, destroyed the wall around Jerusalem, and took all the valuable artifacts back to Babylon. The citizens of Jerusalem who didn't die by the sword were carried off to be slaves in Babylon.[37] Seventy years later, and after the Babylonian empire had fallen, Cyrus of Persia allowed the Jewish exiles to return home to Jerusalem.[38]

Jerusalem wall and interim temple

The return of the exiles to Jerusalem in 537 AD began one of the last periods of group-level investment before the arrival of Jesus. The first project was a temple repair project. Solomon's temple had been destroyed. The repair project was modest in scope. The repair met with opposition and insufficient resources and took a long time. It took approximately 21 years for a greatly scaled-down version of Solomon's temple to be rebuilt. The temple's repaired structure included the return of 5400 stolen articles of gold and silver. The repair work was so inferior to the first temple, returners who had seen the old temple wept, at least in part out of sadness for its lack of grandeur, at its dedication.[39]

Passionate and bold leadership needed to repair a city wall

It was 78 years from the first exiles' return to the arrival of Ezra the scribe. In the intervening years, only the more modest temple had been rebuilt in Jerusalem. The city wall was still broken down and the people were susceptible to attacks. It was a mixture of "apathy and fear" that caused the Jews living in Jerusalem to fail to invest in fixing the wall.[40] The opposite of apathy and fear is passion and boldness.

Successful capital projects require passionate and bold leaders. Enter Ezra, the scribe. His purpose in going to Jerusalem was to teach the law of God to the returners. Ezra also brought the favor of the king and investment capital. King Artaxerxes sent Ezra with $200,000,000 in gold and suspended taxes for the period of rebuilding.[41] Ezra called the people to account. Eventually, the Israelites gave a freewill offering worth over $220,000,000.[42] Altogether, resources for teaching, reconstruction of the wall, and future temple improvements came to around $500,000,000, plus the value of Artaxerxes tax relief. Ezra began teaching the returning exiles and instituted a severe form of religious reformation. Ezra is the first scribe who implemented the continuing modern requirement that the Torah is known. At the beginning of Jesus' time, the Torah was the final revelation of God to Israel and the source of knowledge and supreme authority.[43]

The next bold leader to join the project was Nehemiah. Nehemiah started by taking a risk with King Artaxerxes to request resources and a release to go to Jerusalem. The king granted Nehemiah's request. Fourteen years after the arrival of Ezra, Nehemiah arrived in Jerusalem. Like the first wave of returners, Nehemiah's city wall capital project was met with threats and opposition. There is much to be learned from Nehemiah's management of the project. The essential message of this study is risk-taking, determination, and leadership enabled the wall to be completed in 52 days. Jerusalem was without a wall for almost 150 years. Nehemiah started and finished the job in 52 days. The leadership of Ezra and Nehemiah changed the situation in Jerusalem. Investments in religious education and the city wall filled the community's needs for physical security and identity.

New Testament era investment

The upper echelon at the universal level of the kingdom is Jesus. He is the owner and head of the church.[44] The final instructions of Jesus to his followers include waiting for the Holy Spirit to come for empowerment and then going and making disciples in every part of the earth.[45] The work of the Holy Spirit enables agents to represent the owner "with authority."[46] Authority satisfies an essential need according to the hierarchy of temptation shown previously in Figure 8.2. Being born of water and spirit[47] realigns an agent's investment priorities to life and peace.[48] The *go* part of Jesus' great commission instructions requires taking a risk and making investments of time and money.

A key assumption of *The Theory of the Kingdom* is the transmutation of real economy warfare, wealth, investment, and power into the spiritual realm.[49,50] Jewish leaders in the time of Jesus had a 1000-year-old vision of the glory of a $25 billion temple as the seat of global political and economic power. Jewish leaders also remembered Nehemiah's tactic of working on the wall with one hand while holding a sword in the other. The former visions were now obsolete. Jesus instituted a new era of authority in the heavenly realm. The case of the building and destruction of the second temple illustrates the new paradigm.

Herod the Great built the second temple

Herod the Great began construction of the second temple around BC 19. Herod may have been motivated by pride and the political expedience of religious diplomacy. Herod needed to maintain peace in his territory. Herod also gained valuable information from the Jewish leadership.[51] Herod celebrated the completion of the first and main phase of construction after 10 years.[52] After another 36 years, around AD 27, after the first phase was completed, additional phases were still under construction. Around AD 27 is when Jesus stated, "destroy this temple and in three days I will raise it up." The Jewish audience protested. The second temple had been under construction for 46 years. It could obviously not be rebuilt in three days. The second temple investment was finally finished in 63 AD. The second temple stood for only seven years. The misplaced attempt of the Jewish zealots to overthrow the Roman army resulted in the destruction of Jerusalem and the second temple in 70 AD.[53] The second temple was never rebuilt.

F.F. Bruce explains the third-day resurrection of Jesus and the destruction of the second temple signified God's living habitation on earth is now in the hearts of born-again kingdom agents.[54]

> Real economy wealth and power demonstrated by Solomon's temple are not relevant in the messianic era. Kingdom of God investment is now for the increase of the government of peace, making disciples, revealing the truth, arresting corruption, and producing life.[55]

The messianic era is not a battle of flesh and blood.[56] Jesus made no effort to take over any physical realm of the real economy, even though he has authority over everything. The kingdom economy is made up of individual hearts. The apostle Paul made no apparent attempt to invest and build wealth. Paul had influence and had many opportunities to speak with the highest authorities in Rome. Yet instead of using his position to raise money and acquire power, he preached the gospel to everyone, even King Agrippa.[57]

The doctrine of the transmutation of investment to the spiritual realm can be taken too far. The parable of the talents includes the instruction to 'do business with this money until I get back."[58] The job of making disciples all over the earth requires risk-taking, investment, and infrastructure. Infrastructure will inevitably include computers, vehicles and buildings.

To some, the transmutation of kingdom investment may mean an austere existence where churches don't own anything. Kingdom investors and risk-takers may find themselves opposed even inside the church. The opposition may be well-placed, as I will discuss in a moment. However, intra-church criticism in the book *Pagan Christianity*, represented by chapter titles such as, "The Church Building: Inheriting the Edifice Complex,"[59] is well off the mark. Arguments made in *Pagan Christianity* go too far. An example of an off-base criticism is saying that D.L. Moody was overly focused on evangelism.[60] The enemy of Jesus and his church is called the accuser of the brethren.[61] I prefer not to hurl intra-church accusations. Paul indicates there is one body with many parts,[62] parts with different ways of working,[63] and each part with a responsibility to make its own investment decisions.[64]

Practical approach

The purpose of kingdom economy organizational investment is to facilitate group-level work toward the increase of the government of peace, making disciples, revealing the truth, arresting corruption, and producing life.[65] All organizations invest. Therefore, the best way to finish this chapter is with how to invest. The question of what to invest in is for the Holy Spirit to communicate to each organization.

A. Invest. The field is white

Capital heavy - The size and range of acceptable investments in the kingdom economy are wide. When evaluating potential projects, I eliminate the upper end of luxury and scale. Outside the upper bound of acceptable is purchasing high-value per unit buildings or capacity. It is also clear erecting the most valuable building in a city or nation, in total dollars or per square foot, is likely for the glory of a person rather than God. Power projects with the grandeur of Solomon's temple are excluded. Investment activity revealed the heart of kings. Modern day proposals will reveal the heart of the leadership.

No capital - On the other end of the continuum, it is impractical for a church or kingdom economy oriented non-profit to rule out investment entirely. Even if I stipulate a church should not own a building, it will still make investments. The church will rent an auditorium, rent office space, rent a house, or perhaps use the house of a church member. If the church somehow avoids any rented space, it is still likely to own a computer, sound equipment, teaching tools, and perhaps a vehicle. When the church does rent space, a rental agreement is an investment. Signing a lease obtains an asset and incurs a liability. The asset is the right to use the space. The liability is an obligation to make future lease payments. All kingdom organizations make real economy investments.

Capital light - Capital-light organizations tend to be more efficient and is the preferred approach. However, if being a capital-light organization is interfering with the group's purpose in the kingdom economy, it is time to take a risk and increase the level of investment. If the church or non-profit forgoes an investment because of risk or apathy, some other group will be given the assignment. One proposition of *The Theory of the Kingdom* is churches that cease to invest due to apathy or fear will shrink. Risk aversion takes the form of accumulating large cash reserves or refusing to use any amount of leverage. Apathy may be expressed in less emphasis on sending missions programs or cutbacks in Christian education.

B. Obedience to the Holy Spirit

Kings that obeyed were successful. David was obedient to the point of deferring the construction of the temple. David had the plans, the money, and the capacity. Yet he was obedient. His obedience secured his royal line. Jesus was born out of the "house and line of David."[66] In the kingdom era, groups are to use unity and open communication to see what investments "seem good to us and the Holy Spirit."[67] The Holy Spirit is the differentiator. He will offer counsel to a group that seeks it.

C. Real economy problems

In some cases, the obstacle to kingdom investment is real economy uncertainty. Investments in scripture are not associated with any one phase of the economic cycle. However, economic or political uncertainty has a negative influence on investment activity. Former U.S. Federal Reserve Chairman Ben Bernanke showed there is real economy value to delaying large investments when uncertainty rises.[68] When uncertainty rises, for-profit businesses may be better off waiting to retain the future option value of that investment. The investment can be made at a later date when the cash flow and return are more certain. The kingdom economy has unlimited resources. If a group believes the Holy Spirit is leading it to invest, it must take the risk and forge ahead. There may be practical problems, such as banks being reluctant to lend or unemployed church members. However, the obedience principle requires investments to be made despite economic uncertainty.

D. Law of unity[69]

The law of unity term was presented in the book the *Secret Kingdom.* Unity of the Spirit in the bond of peace mitigates the risk of making the wrong investment. Creation was a united event in which each owner participated. The Babel project started well because of unity. In the New Testament era, authority and resources are released by agreement in prayer. Unity is an explosive force in the kingdom.[70] Unity releases a commanded blessing on a group.[71] The day before Jesus died, he prayed the disciples would be one as the trinity is one.[72]

E. Humility

The virtue of humility unlocks the ability of an investment group to operate in unity. Humility recognizes the investment group is not responsible for growth.

Humble leaders are transparent and accountable. It is God that causes the increase in kingdom organizations. The investment itself is conceived and communicated by the owner. The investment facilitates a specific part of the overall growth plan of the kingdom economy. Humility recognizes the owner is responsible for investment success.

F. Freewill offerings

The offerings taken for the tabernacle of meeting, Solomon's temple, and by Ezra for repairs were freewill offerings. I have been part of seven capital campaigns for church investment. New projects require money. Some non-profit religious organizations have enough margin in regular operations to fund new investments. More often, new investments require raising new money. High-pressure tactics, including some capital campaigns, tip over into coercion. Kingdom projects are to be funded with joyfully given freewill offerings. At the same time, I am personally thankful for every church investment project I have participated in. Each has been a unique opportunity to participate in a high-return investment.

G. Leadership matters

Leaders of investment projects need to be diligent, bold, and finishers. Nehemiah repaired the Jerusalem wall in 52 days. Returning exiles had done nothing on the wall project for almost 150 years. The community suffered from apathetic and risk-averse leadership. Groups should make every effort to choose the right leader who can finish the job.

H. Failure does not have to end in failure

All things work together for good and the owner's resources are unlimited. Not all current failures are ultimately failures. I have seen the building of a bankrupt church sold to another thriving church for cents on the dollar. I have seen a dwindling congregation sell its $6,000,000 church building for $10 dollars. The shrinking congregation was investing in the next generation and setting itself up for a large kingdom return. Thomas Ranier includes the gift of discounted real estate sales as a way for shrinking churches to invest in the future.[73] Even the products of the reorganized Big Idea Productions, creator of Veggie Tales, have tremendous ongoing kingdom economy value. Veggie Tales programming for children remains widely distributed and some of the founders are active in new kingdom media and animation projects. Kingdom agents absolutely suffer and experience the personal pain of a loss. But like Peter, when they have returned, their losses and remaining assets can strengthen the body.

I. Grace and peace in all things

Kingdom organization investing is not easy. Sincere teams take risks and sometimes good-looking deals go bad. Churches are not generally well diversified and a bad deal can seriously impair the future outlook. Ultimately, all things work together for good. The increase is accomplished by God, and Jesus will build his church. If you have led an organization in a great venture for the kingdom economy and lost, forget about it. The lost assets can be reallocated, refunded, and reused by the owner. Wherever you find yourself, strengthen the body of Christ, lead, invest and run. The field is still white.

Notes

[1] Marshall, A. (2009). *Principles of economics: unabridged eighth edition.* Cosimo, Inc. http://dx.doi.org/10.1057/9781137375261.

[2] Smith, A. (1869). *An Inquiry into the Nature and Causes of the Wealth of Nations, volume 1* (Vol. 1). Oxford: Clarendon Press. http://dx.doi.org/10.1093/oseo/instance.00043218.

[3] Osella, F., & Rudnyckyj, D. (2017). Introduction: Assembling market and religious moralities. *Religion and the Morality of the Market,* 1-28. http://dx.doi.org/10.1017/9781316888704.001.

[4] Hilary, G., & Hui, K. W. (2009). Does religion matter in corporate decision making in America?. *Journal of financial economics, 93*(3), 455-473. http://dx.doi.org/10.1016/j.jfineco.2008.10.001.

[5] McGuire, S. T., Omer, T. C., & Sharp, N. Y. (2012). The impact of religion on financial reporting irregularities. *The Accounting Review, 87*(2), 645-673. http://dx.doi.org/10.2308/accr-10206.

[6] Compassion International. (2022, October). Releasing Children from Poverty in Jesus' Name. *Compassion International.* https://www.compassion.com/about/about-us.htm

[7] Operation Blessing. (2022, October). What We Do. *Operation Blessing.* https://www.ob.org/what-we-do/

[8] Jensen, M. C., & Meckling, W. H. (2019). Theory of the firm: Managerial behavior, agency costs and ownership structure. In *Corporate Governance* (pp. 77-132). Gower.

[9] North, D. C. (1990). *Institutions, institutional change and economic performance.* Cambridge university press. http://dx.doi.org/10.1017/CBO9780511808678.; Scott, W. R. (2008). *Institutions and organizations: Ideas and interests.* Sage.

[10] Hambrick, D. C., & Mason, P. A. (1984). Upper echelons: The organization as a reflection of its top managers. *Academy of management review, 9*(2), 193-206. http://dx.doi.org/10.2307/258434.

[11] Hull, B. B., & Bold, F. (1989). Towards an economic theory of the church. *International Journal of Social Economics.* http://dx.doi.org/10.1108/EUM0000000000444.

[12] Ekelund, R. B., Tollison, R. D., Anderson, G. M., Hébert, R. F., & Davidson, A. B. (1996). *Sacred trust: the medieval church as an economic firm* (p. 6). Oxford University Press.

[13] Keener, C. S., & Walton, J. H. (Eds.). (2016). *NIV, Cultural Backgrounds Study Bible: Bringing to Life the Ancient World of Scripture* (p. 1579). Zondervan.

[14] 1 Corinthians 13:13.

[15] Isaiah 9:6-7, Romans 8:6, John 10:10.

[16] Barna, G. (1993). *Turn Around Churches.* Regal Books. The Barna Group is well known in Christian leadership circles. The ideas presented in *Turnaround Churches* could be the advice of any strategy consultant looking to reinvigorate growth at any type of organization. In order for a spirit led organization to grow it must sow in the Spirit (see Romans 8:5 and Galatians 6:8). The truth of the kingdom is revealed by the Spirit of wisdom and truth (Isaiah 11:1-3 and John 16:13).
[17] Genesis 1:26.
[18] Keener, C. S., & Walton, J. H. (Eds.). (2016). *NIV, Cultural Backgrounds Study Bible: Bringing to Life the Ancient World of Scripture* (p. 8). Zondervan.
[19] Genesis chapter 6. Genesis chapter 7. Genesis chapter 8.
[20] Williams, J. J. (2021). *Redemptive Kingdom Diversity: A Biblical Theology of the People of God* (p. 16). Baker Academic.
[21] New American Standard Bible, 1971, Exodus 25:1-2. New American Standard Bible, 1971, Exodus 35:20-21. New American Standard Bible, 1971, Exodus 36:2-7.
[22] New American Standard Bible, 1971, Exodus 31:3-5.
[23] One talent was approximately 75 pounds or 1200 ounces. One shekel was approximately one-half ounce. The price of gold and silver changes but for convenience I choose a representative price of $1700/ounce of gold and $20/ounce of silver. 35,000 ounces of gold is therefore worth $59.5 million and 121,000 ounces of silver is worth $2.4million.
[24] Keener, C. S., & Walton, J. H. (Eds.). (2016). *NIV, Cultural Backgrounds Study Bible: Bringing to Life the Ancient World of Scripture* (pp. 162-163). Zondervan.
[25] New American Standard Bible, 1971, 2 Chronicles chapter 10. New American Standard Bible, 1971, 2 Chronicles chapter 11. New American Standard Bible, 1971, 2 Chronicles chapter 12.
[26] New American Standard Bible, 1971, 2 Chronicles chapter 14. New American Standard Bible, 1971, 2 Chronicles chapter 15. New American Standard Bible, 1971, 2 Chronicles chapter 16.
[27] New American Standard Bible, 1971, 2 Chronicles 21:3.
[28] Modigliani, F., & Miller, M. H. (1958). The cost of capital, corporation finance and the theory of investment. *The American economic review, 48*(3), 261-297.
[29] Keener, C. S., & Walton, J. H. (Eds.). (2016). *NIV, Cultural Backgrounds Study Bible: Bringing to Life the Ancient World of Scripture* (p. 547). Zondervan.
[30] New American Standard Bible, 1971, 1 Kings chapter 2.
[31] New American Standard Bible, 1971, 1 Chronicles 29:9.
[32] 1 Chronicles 29:3.
[33] New American Standard Bible, 1971, 1 Chronicles 28:19.
[34] David's gift was 3000 talents of gold and 7000 talents of silver, equal to 3.6 million ounces of gold and 8.4 million ounces of silver. At $1700/oz for gold and $20/oz for silver the value of David's silver and gold was approximately $6.3 billion ($6.1 billion + $168 hundred million) The people gave 5000 talents of gold, 10 thousand darics (1/4 ounce) of gold, 10 thousand talents of silver, plus bronze, iron and gemstones. The people offered approximately 6 million ounces of gold and 12 million ounces of silver. The value of the gold and silver from the people was approximately $10.4 billion ($10.2 billion + $240 hundred million).
[35] 1 Kings 10:6-17.
[36] 1 Kings 10:10. 120 talents equals 144,000 ounces, worth $245 million at $1700/ounce. The Queen also brought spices and gemstones. Diplomacy can be an expensive endeavor.

[37] New American Standard Bible, 1971, 2 Chronicles 36:15-21.
[38] 2 Chronicles 36:22-23.
[39] New American Standard Bible, 1971, Ezra 3:12.
[40] Keener, C. S., & Walton, J. H. (Eds.). (2016). *NIV, Cultural Backgrounds Study Bible: Bringing to Life the Ancient World of Scripture* (p. 806). Zondervan.
[41] New American Standard Bible, 1971, Ezra 7:21-26.
[42] New American Standard Bible, 1971, Ezra 8:24.
[43] Herford, R. T. (2006). *Christianity in Talmud and Midrash.* KTAV Publishing House, Inc.
[44] New American Standard Bible, 1971, Psalm 118:22. Colossians 1:15-20. Ephesians 1:22.
[45] Matthew 28:18-20. New American Standard Bible, 1971, Mark 16:15. Acts 1:4-9.
[46] Rackham, R. B. (1901). *Westminster Commentaries* (Vol. 44, 1.1, p. 5). Methuen.
[47] John 3:5.
[48] Romans 8:5-6.
[49] Blomberg, C. L. (2020). *Can We Still Believe in God?: Answering Ten Contemporary Challenges to Christianity* (p. 87). Brazos Press.
[50] Tozer, A. W. (2015). *Born after midnight.* Moody Publishers.
[51] New American Standard Bible, 1971, Matthew 2:1-8.
[52] Schürer, E. (1891). *A history of the Jewish people in the time of Jesus Christ* (Vol. 5, pp. 409-410). Scribner.
[53] Docherty, S. (2015). *The Jewish Pseudepigrapha: An Introduction to the Literature of the Second Temple Period* (p. 5). Fortress Press.
[54] Bruce, F. F. (1994). *The Gospel of John: Introduction, Exposition, Notes* (pp. 76-77). Wm. B. Eerdmans Publishing.
[55] Isaiah 9:6-7. Matthew 28:18-20. Matthew 5:13-16. John 10:10.
[56] Ephesians 6:12.
[57] New American Standard Bible, 1971, Acts 26:24-30.
[58] Luke 19:13.
[59] Viola, F., & Barna, G. (2010). *Pagan Christianity?: Exploring the roots of our church practices* (p. 9). Tyndale House Publishers, Inc.
[60] Viola, F., & Barna, G. (2010). *Pagan Christianity?: Exploring the roots of our church practices* (p. 70). Tyndale House Publishers, Inc.
[61] New American Standard Bible, 1971, Revelation 12:10.
[62] 1 Corinthians 12:12-27.
[63] 1 Corinthians 3:1-9.
[64] Philippians 2:12.
[65] Isaiah 9:6-7. Matthew 28:18-20. Matthew 5:13-16. John 10:10.
[66] Luke 2:4.
[67] New American Standard Bible, 1971, Acts 15:28.
[68] Bernanke, B. S. (1983). Irreversibility, uncertainty, and cyclical investment. *The quarterly journal of economics, 98*(1), 85-106. http://dx.doi.org/10.2307/1885568.
[69] Robertson, P., & Slosser, B. (1982). *The Secret Kingdom: A Promise of Hope and Freedom in a World of Turmoil.* T. Nelson.
[70] Leviticus 26:2-8.
[71] Psalm 133:1-3.
[72] John 17:20-23.

[73] Rainer, T. S. (2014). *Autopsy of a deceased church: 12 ways to keep yours alive.* B&H Publishing Group.

Chapter 12

The law of proportion

> And without faith it is impossible to please Him, for the one who comes to God must believe he exists, and that He proves to be One who rewards those who seek him.[1]
>
> - Hebrews 11:6, NASB.

Entry into the kingdom of heaven is salvation by grace through faith in Jesus.[2] Hebrews chapter 11 is sometimes subtitled *heroes of the faith*. The nature and quality of faith include the acceptance of God's word, winning God's approval through response to the word, and recognition of God's power.[3] The word translated as faith in Hebrews 11:6 is the Greek word *pistis*. It is most often translated as faith. However, the first listed possible meaning in Strong's Greek dictionary is credence, "especially in reliance on Jesus for salvation."[4] Spiritual goods, including salvation, are a type of credence goods.[5] There is a consensus among economists who study rational choice theory that religious goods are credence goods.[6,7] This chapter introduces a model for the supply and demand of kingdom economy faith goods.

Credence goods

Credence goods are a special category of economic goods and have unique properties. Consumers cannot easily understand credence goods before purchase or completely perceive their utility after consumption. An example of a credence good is auto repair. If my car isn't running well, I take it to a mechanic. The mechanic is the expert. The mechanic diagnoses the problem, prescribes a solution, performs a service, and then I pay the bill. Even after the bill is paid, it is not certain the mechanic had the correct diagnosis or was telling me the truth. It is not certain the job was done well. It is not certain the price was fair.

The auto repair example illustrates the problem of fraud and credence goods. A prior review of 15 years of credence goods literature identified other categories of credence goods sellers, such as lawyers, financial advisors, doctors, and computer technicians. In each case, the seller is the expert and the buyer is relatively naïve.[8] In almost each case, sellers have some incentives to defraud buyers. Fraud based on monetary incentives can be very damaging to victimized consumers. One study showed a change in medical fees and incentives caused doctors to perform significantly more births by cesarean section than was necessary.[9]

The problem of fraud and credence goods may be alleviated if consumers have a common problem and equally value a solution. The problem of sin and the desire for eternal life may fit this condition. The second condition to solve fraud is simultaneous consumer commitment to accept the solution and owner commitment to honor a preset price. The preset price for salvation was the once and for all sacrifice Jesus made on the cross. Despite positive points of comparison, neither of the first two conditions appears totally satisfying in the context of the range of spiritual goods listed in the Bible. Most credence goods models assume a competitive market, with more than one seller of credence goods. Biblical credence goods are not offered by more than one seller.

The kingdom economy is a monopolist credence goods market

The biblical credence goods market is a monopolist case. An analysis of different credence goods markets, with a selfish seller or a conscientious seller, shows the consumer generally loses.[10] However, Winand Emons considers a monopolist market structure with one seller only. The monopolist credence goods market compares well to the kingdom economy.[11] In a monopoly market where customers don't know how much of a credence good they need but eventually understand what they received, the monopolist is always honest and fair. If the monopolist does not act fairly, no transaction takes place. The expert monopolist, credence goods seller, maximizes profits by serving the entire market honestly. The clearing price of the credence goods for efficient production equals the minimum average cost. In economic theory, the most reliable case for an honest credence goods market is the monopoly case.

The kingdom economy is a monopoly. Spiritual credence goods are exchanged with one seller. The phrase "One who rewards" in Hebrews 11:6 is translated from a unique Greek word. The literal translation of the word is rewarder. The Greek root word occurs one time in the Bible. There are hundreds of other instances of the word reward in the Bible, with a few different root words, each being repeated many times. The emphasis in Hebrews 11:6 is God is the only one with whom I can make an exchange for kingdom economy spiritual credence goods.

> The emphasis in Hebrews 11:6 is God is the only one with whom I can make an exchange for kingdom economy spiritual credence goods.

Monopolist seller capacity is also an important commitment device. If the capacity of the seller is observed by the buyer, transactions take place. In this way, notably, Christian doctrine includes God's wish that none should perish, that he is omnipotent and that all creation demonstrates his glory. God's capacity is unlimited. If the capacity of the seller is unknown or perhaps not yet believed, a clear publication of the price of the service can still persuade customers of the monopolist's honesty. When the price is published, the maximum number of transactions can take place. In the kingdom economy, the price of the product is Jesus. The price was posted long ago. God has unlimited capacity and has posted the pre-set price for all that I need for life and godliness.[12]

Holy Spirit as distributor

In the messianic era, the Holy Spirit distributes spiritual goods, spiritual gifts and designates spiritual offices of responsibility. The biblical metaphor for spiritual goods is fruit. The fruit of the Holy Spirit includes love, joy, peace, patience, kindness, goodness, faithfulness, gentleness, and self-control.[13] The list of fruits is equivalent to a selection of human virtues and character traits. The three cardinal Christian virtues are faith, hope, and love.[14] Jesus used a similar metaphor saying kingdom agents are branches of his vine. To bear fruit kingdom agents "abide" in the vine.[15] The metaphor was carefully chosen as Jesus spoke it just one day before his crucifixion. The metaphor fits with the nature of the market and the mechanism of agency bonding discussed later in chapter 17.

Abiding indicates the loving intimacy of knowing Jesus, even as God the Father and Jesus know one another. Intimacy produces a Jesus "likeness" from receiving the fruit of the Holy Spirit.[16] Peter gives a similar list of moral virtues. Peter's second letter reads, "Now for this very reason also, applying all diligence, in your faith supplies moral excellence, and in your moral excellence, knowledge, and in your knowledge, self-control, and in your self-control, perseverance, and in your perseverance, godliness, and in your godliness, brotherly kindness, and in your brotherly kindness, love. For if these qualities are yours and are increasing, they do not make you useless nor unproductive in the true knowledge of our Lord Jesus Christ."[17]

Unlimited supply of goods for life in the real economy

The purpose of Peter's list is to live life in the real economy based on "God's own goodness."[18] The practice of the virtues is both a means of production in the kingdom economy and an end in itself. I receive virtue from the Holy Spirit for my benefit and also to be a servant of all. Peter's list begins and ends with a grounding in God's goodness rather than in the characteristics of humanity. The virtues are credence goods from God and in God. That the virtues are to be increasing suggests supply is not fixed.

My quantity of virtues is variable based on my spiritual diligence. Peter's virtue of knowledge requires effort on my part and is coincident with the instructions to study and to be prepared to answer questions about hope in Christ.[19] The means and ends argumentation of Reuschling bridges some of the differences between economic models of religiosity. Salvation, eternal life, and time remaining before realizing an eternal consumptive state is an appropriate motivation for examining rational choice.[20] In addition, there is a positive habituating loop of increasing virtuous character in the real economy.[21]

The named offices and leadership functions of the kingdom economy are apostles, prophets, evangelists, pastors, teachers, and deacons.[22] The bible includes formal structures and the means of marshaling kingdom resources for the production of life, peace, and growth. The seven spiritual gifts are also types of special credence goods and include words of wisdom, words of knowledge, faith, healing, miracles, prophecy, discernment, tongues, and interpretation of tongues. The Holy Spirit is the distributor of the gifts. The gifts represent a division of labor for an efficient, productive, and well-functioning kingdom organization. The originator of the gifts is God.[23] He is also the causal agent of growth that comes from agents using their gifts.[24]

Supply demand in the kingdom economy

Before proposing a graphical representation of demand and supply for kingdom credence goods, there are two points to be made on the acquisition of credence goods and the supply of goods. First, on the acquisition of credence goods, in the monopolist case of a credence goods seller, the number of transactions is maximized by an honest exchange of goods priced at average cost.[25] The kingdom of God has been fully transmuted into the spiritual realm. The average cost of supply to God is not measured in dollars. The cost is measured in sacrifice. God was motivated by love to give his son Jesus so that I could obtain eternal life.[26] Jesus was obedient and paid the price of suffering and shame because of the future joy of billions of people being saved.[27] Eternal life is not the only spiritual good of value but it is the highest order good. The price of supply was the willing sacrifice of God's own son, a price that was known by the owner before the first humans ever walked on the earth.[28]

The exchange requires no money and it is open to everyone at all times. Scripture repeatedly indicates I can purchase the water of life without money.[29] In the messianic section of the prophecy of Isaiah, it is emphatically written, "You there! Everyone who thirsts, come to the waters; And you who have no money come, buy and eat. Come, buy wine and milk without money and without cost. Why do you spend money for what is not bread and your wages for what does not satisfy? Listen carefully to Me, and eat what is good, and delight yourself in abundance."[30]

Entry and advancement by non-monetary means

The water, wine, and milk of the kingdom economy cannot be purchased with real economy money. David Guzik notes both entrance and advancement within the kingdom economy do not require money.[31] The goods available range from the most necessary to the most luxurious. In addition to the security of eternal life, there are credence goods that satisfy every higher-order human need for authority and identity. Wisdom, knowledge, hope, the spirit of adoption, peace, and agency assignments are supplied without money. The emphatic language commends to the reader resources for a new life that is supplied "far more liberally and abundant in Christ."[32] It was known that previous biblical figures, such as David, had experienced the "goodness" of God.[33] The prophecy is for a higher level of experience and enjoyment of blessings of spiritual goods. The new and abundant supply of resources in Christ is the reason for a second supply curve shown to the right of the old covenant supply curve (Figure 12.1). The arrival of Jesus marked the arrival of the kingdom of God and a greater supply of spiritual resources.

Figure 12.1. Law of proportion. Spiritual goods supply demand.

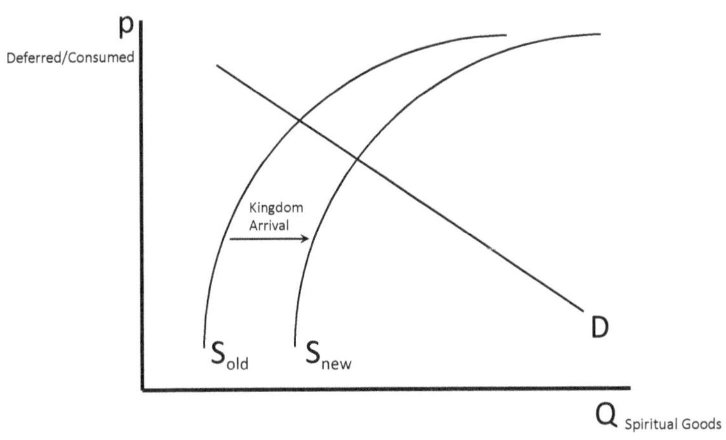

Figure 12.1 major message: The supply demand graph represents an aggregate snapshot of all Christ-followers at a point in time. During a lifetime, individuals move up and down the vertical axis. The price of exchange in the kingdom economy is a proportional living sacrifice according to Romans 12:1.[34] The average cost is God's gift is according to John 3:16.[35] The quantity of goods received are spiritual, according to the will of God and an individual's proportional offering.

I purchase the spiritual goods by offering myself in the same way Jesus obediently offered himself. The measurement of the degree of my offering is my proportion of time, effort, and money. The effort is noted in the biblical theme of active agency and diligence.[36] There is an extremely long list of spiritual labors that I can engage in to be productive in the kingdom economy. The most obvious are the cardinal Jewish labors of prayer, fasting, and almsgiving to the poor. Jesus identifies the three labors as practices of righteousness. The phrasing is not if but when I give to the poor, when I pray, and whenever I fast. Each labor is vital, but serving the poor is at the top of the list.[37] The practice of righteousness necessarily includes serving the poor in the real economy. Considering Paul's statement in Romans, I conclude it is expected serving the poor, prayer and fasting would feel like sacrificial service.[38] If my service to the poor does not require sacrifice, perhaps it is insufficient.

Proportional sacrifice is the reasonable price of exchange

The price of the exchange is proportional to sacrifice. Paul urges Christ-followers to "present your bodies as a living and holy sacrifice, acceptable to God, which is your spiritual service of worship."[39] In the kingdom economy the owner is a fair monopolist and the cost to produce salvation for humanity was giving his son Jesus. The price of purchase is, therefore, my real economy life as a living sacrifice, an act of service and worship. I thereby acquire spiritual goods already granted to me to do the works already set out for me to do.

Paul's argumentation of living sacrifice appeared to some ancient hearers as oxymoronic. Animals were sometimes killed in religious rituals. Rather than sacrifice an animal, I choose to die for a love of money and fear of people to be transformed to love God and prove what is good to Him. Stott explains Paul's logic succinctly in stating because of the owner's mercies to me, I offer my body, mind, and spirit in rational worship to Him.[40] Stott's quotation of Stoic Philosopher Epictetus drives home the point. "If I were a nightingale, I would do what is proper to a nightingale, and if I were a swan what is proper to a swan. In fact I am *logikos* (a rational being), so I just praise God."[41]

In Marshallian economics[42] the law of supply and demand explains the rationing of scarce resources by price. The real economy, inside the small circle of the model of human agency, is best explained by Marshallian models of supply and demand. Victor Klaar and Robin Klay explain how real economy markets facilitate the "highest forms of cultural and spiritual expression."[43] The rationing of scarce resources directs production to the most efficient outcomes. Scarcity sometimes imposes helpful discipline on wasteful humans. Sometimes scarcity causes suffering, especially when bad actors accumulate resources for evil purposes. The overall market function is supported by rational human agents acting in their self-interest. Acting in self-interest does not necessarily mean being *selfish*. In general, the discipline of the market directs resources to more efficient outcomes that cause economies to grow. The long-run record of neoclassical economics is positive for raising living standards.

The cost of discipleship means average demand slopes down

The kingdom economy has unlimited resources. However, the resources are still rationed based on the proportional exchange of my body, mind, and spirit for spiritual goods needed to thrive now and be salt and light in the real economy. The vertical axis of Figure 12.1 is the variable called proportion. Proportion is the price, a degree of living sacrifice, measured by the use of an individual's time, money, and effort relative to the total available. The demand line in Figure 12.1, labeled "D" is an aggregate function. It is the snapshot picture of all kingdom agents. Demand slopes down because I would naturally prefer more spiritual gifts for less sacrifice. As the cost of worship and service in the kingdom rises, fewer are willing to make the sacrifice.

Individual agents will be at different points of proportion at different times in life. Even though the aggregate demand function slopes down the individual goal is to increase in proportion. The design is for individuals to be transformed over a lifetime,[44] moving on to more robust spiritual labor and resources,[45] advancing in spiritual gifts,[46] and traversing to continuously higher levels of devotion,[47] kingdom productivity, and proportion. Studies consistently show as Christ-followers age, they give more time and money to the church.

Supply of goods slopes up

Supply is upward-sloping. In the real economy, supply slopes upward as existing, idle and new producers respond to higher prices with an increase in production. Businesses have an incentive to produce more of a product at higher prices. In the law of proportion, neither higher costs nor increasing production is the reason for the upward-sloping supply curve. The cost of salvation, and the cost of distribution to dispense gifts and fruits stay the same. God knew before "the foundation of the world"[48] the cost of salvation would be Jesus. Earl Richard's commentary on 1 Peter 1:20 begins with the heading "God's redemptive plan."[49] Because of the love of the owner, the long-decided plan for the production of salvation was the incarnation, death and resurrection of Jesus. It follows the cost of salvation was determined before the first human sinned.

The production process has been completed and a full complement of spiritual goods has been allocated for whosoever will receive the messiah.[50] Continuing with the letter of Peter shows, "His divine power has granted to us everything pertaining to life and godliness, through the true knowledge of Him who called us by His own glory and excellence." This means God by his power has already granted me everything I need according to his unlimited resources.[51,52] The Holy Spirit distributes spiritual goods and supports me as I labor to live a godly life. The resources have already been granted to me. In a real economy research grant, I may be awarded a grant, but receive the money only as milestones and dates are reached and the correct evidence is supplied to the grantor.[53]

Kingdom spiritual goods are supplied equally, without consideration of ethnicity, economic class, or gender. People of all ethnicities are grafted into the Christian vine as living sacrifices.[54] Paul's appeal in Romans 12 is for one international family of sisters and brothers, regardless of ethnic origin.[55] Real economy wealth is negatively associated with the demand for spiritual goods.[56] The rich young ruler did give some money but he could not see his way clear to giving all his money and time to follow Jesus.

A large proportionate gift

Artists including Gustave Dore, James Tissot, and William Giles have captured the New Testament widow's offering of two small coins. Modern surveys consistently show wealthy people give more money to the church than poor people, but they give a lower percentage. The poor woman put in *all she had to live on*[57] and was commended by the Lord. The view of the substantial majority of expository commentators is the gift was voluntary and unusual and indicated the giving standard in the kingdom economy is proportional.[58] The kingdom marketplace is the proportional exchange of my time, effort, and money for spiritual fruit, gifts, and assignments.

The supply curve is also thought to slope up according to relative proportion because of repeated examples of higher levels of agent activity and obedience being associated with higher rewards and relationship intimacy. The parable of the talents sees a reward of greater future realm responsibility for faithful servants.[59] Diligence is rewarded.[60] The list of virtues in 2 Peter chapter one implies receiving additional virtues because of my faithful agency effort.

It is also certain salvation is by grace through faith alone.[61] To account for this, the concave supply function has a steep initial slope. The asymptotic slope is an indication of the grace of God in immediately changing my heart condition not based on any work of righteousness.[62] At the point of being born again, I immediately receive a deposit of the Holy Spirit. I can't be extra-saved or max-saved. However, interesting biblical cases of variable rewards for variable effort suggest an upward sloping supply curve.

Variable reward of information for variable effort

A relatable example of a variable reward is given in the gospel of Luke. Luke writes of a reward dispensed to the elderly prophet Anna. Anna was a widow from her seventh year of marriage. For the rest of her life, approximately 60 years, Anna lived in the temple in Jerusalem. The Bible records Anna's 60 years were invested in worshipping God with fasting and prayer. The Bible also records Anna was the second person to know, by the Holy Spirit, with certainty, the baby Jesus was the long-awaited Messiah. Anna's very high individual proportion, comprised of worship, prayer, and fasting, was exchanged for special kingdom knowledge and access to Jesus. Information is extremely valuable in every marketplace and economy. Anna's heart labor was rewarded with relational intimacy and special knowledge. Later in this study I apply the law of proportion to the kingdom economy-specific resources of territory, heart labor, and heart capital.

Two additional features of the supply of spiritual goods require a brief explanation. First, the supply curve does not return to the origin. The law of proportion applies to kingdom economy agents. However, if someone has not yet decided to be a Christ-follower, and is theoretically at zero proportion, they still have the God-given capacity to do good. Each human is created in the image and likeness of God. As such, each human is endowed with some beginning spiritual goods. The human capacity to do good is further supported by interaction with nature[63] and the influence of kingdom agents who reveal the truth. Second, the arrival of the kingdom of God shifted the supply curve to the right. The present messianic era curve on Figure 12.1 is called "Snew", for the new covenant. Jesus brought a greater glory which the profit Isaiah referred to, including the individual deposit of the Holy Spirit in the messianic age. The curve may continue to shift right according to the prophecy of Joel 2:28 and some empirical evidence of periodic Christian revival.[64,65,66]

Practical implications and future research questions

The most obvious implication of kingdom supply and demand is I should be diligent about increasing my proportion over time. The supply of kingdom spiritual goods is unlimited, and the goods I need are already allocated to me, but the goods are supplied according to my diligence in faith.[67] I have not discussed the tithe or focused on how much money a Christ-follower should give. It is obvious a devoted Christian will give money to the church. Further, it is likely a proportional goal of 10% of income is a good beginning. However, the emphasis is on the lifelong work to transmute as much time, money, and effort as possible to kingdom purposes. Jesus asked for the rich young ruler to give away his money because that is what the young man valued most. I believe the same call, in different forms, comes to all Christ-followers. The accumulation of the stock of credence goods is heart capital. The law of proportion is the beginning point of an analysis of the allocation of productive kingdom resources.

Several empirical questions are raised by the law of proportion. First, at an individual level, do surveys measuring spiritual devotion show significantly positive associations with spiritual virtues, such as patience or hope? Second, following periods of revival, do group-level measures of life and peace change significantly? Third, it remains for the relationship of proportion and quantity of spiritual goods to be formalized in a model to determine if a single equilibrium exists.

Notes

[1] Tyndale, & Tyndale House Publishers. (2004). *Life Application Study Bible: New Living Translation.* Tyndale House Publishers, Inc. Hebrews 11:6.
[2] Ephesians 2:8-9
[3] Brown, R. (1982). *The Bible Speaks Today: The Message of Hebrews* (pp. 198-199). InterVarsity Press.
[4] Strong, J. (2009). *Strong's exhaustive concordance of the Bible* (Greek Dictionary p. 58). Hendrickson Publishers.
[5] Hull, B. B., & Bold, F. (1989). Towards an economic theory of the church. *International Journal of Social Economics.* http://dx.doi.org/10.1108/EUM0000000000444.
[6] Stark, R., & Bainbridge, W. S. (1985). *The future of religion: Secularization, revival, and cult formation.* Univ of California Press. http://dx.doi.org/10.1525/9780520341340.
[7] Young, L. A. (2016). *Rational choice theory and religion: Summary and assessment.* Routledge.
[8] Balafoutas, L., & Kerschbamer, R. (2020). Credence goods in the literature: What the past fifteen years have taught us about fraud, incentives, and the role of institutions. *Journal of Behavioral and Experimental Finance, 26,* 100285. http://dx.doi.org/10.1016/j.jbef.2020.100285.
[9] Gruber, J., & Owings, M. (1996). Physician Financial Incentives and Cesarean Section Delivery. *The RAND Journal of Economics, 27*(1), 99. http://dx.doi.org/10.2307/2555794.
[10] Liu, T. (2011). Credence goods markets with conscientious and selfish experts. *International Economic Review, 52*(1), 227-244. http://dx.doi.org/10.1111/j.1468-2354.2010.00626.x.
[11] Emons, W. (2001). Credence goods monopolists. *International Journal of Industrial Organization, 19*(3-4), 375-389. http://dx.doi.org/10.1016/S0167-7187(99)00023-5.
[12] 2 Peter 1:3
[13] Galatians 5:22-23.
[14] 1 Corinthians 13:13. Jeremiah 29:11. Matthew 22:37. Luke 10:27.
[15] John 15:1-11.

[16] Bruce, F. F. (1994). *The Gospel of John: Introduction, Exposition, Notes* (pp. 309-311). Wm. B. Eerdmans Publishing.
[17] 2 Peter 1:5-8.
[18] Reuschling, W. C. (2014). The Means and End in 2 Peter 1: 3—11: The Theological and Moral Significance of" Theōsis". *Journal of Theological Interpretation, 8*(2), 275-286. http://dx.doi.org/10.2307/26373929.
[19] 2 Timothy 2:15. 1 Peter 3:15.
[20] Azzi, C., & Ehrenberg, R. (1975). Household allocation of time and church attendance. *Journal of political Economy, 83*(1), 27-56. http://dx.doi.org/10.1086/260305.
[21] Iannaccone, L. R. (1984). *Consumption Capital and Habit Formation with an Application to Religious Participation* (Publication No. T29220, Chapter 2 & 3) [Doctoral dissertation, The University of Chicago]. ProQuest Dissertations & Theses Global.
[22] Ephesians 4:11. Acts 6:1-15.
[23] 1 Corinthians 12:1-7.
[24] 1 Corinthians 3:6-8.
[25] Emons, W. (2001). Credence goods monopolists. *International Journal of Industrial Organization, 19*(3-4), 375-389. http://dx.doi.org/10.1016/S0167-7187(99)00023-5.
[26] John 3:16.
[27] Hebrews 12:2.
[28] 2 Peter 1:20.
[29] Isaiah 55:10. New American Standard Bible, 1971, John 7:37. Revelation 21:6. Revelation 22:17.
[30] Isaiah 55:1.
[31] Guzik, D. (2021). Isaiah 55: An Invitation to Receive the Glory of the Lord's Restoration. *Enduring Word.* https://enduringword.com/bible-commentary/isaiah-55/
[32] Haroutunian, J. (1958). *Calvin: Commentaries* (p. 155). L. P. Smith (Ed.). London: SCM Press.
[33] New American Standard Bible, 1971, Psalm 31:19.
[34] Roman 12:1
[35] John 3:16.
[36] Hebrews 11:6. "a rewarder of those who diligently seek him."
[37] Matthew 6:1-18.
[38] Romans 12:1
[39] Romans 12:1.
[40] Stott, J. (2014). *The message of Romans: God's good news for the world* (p. 320). InterVarsity Press.
[41] Long, G. *The Discourses of Epictetus: With the Encheiridion and Fragments.* G. Bell and sons, 1890.
[42] Marshall, A. (2009). *Principles of economics: unabridged eighth edition.* Cosimo, Inc. http://dx.doi.org/10.1057/9781137375261. Alfred Marshall was the founder of the neoclassical school of economics.
[43] Claar, V. V., & Klay, R. J. (2015). *Economics in Christian Perspective: Theory, Policy and Life Choices* (p. 28). InterVarsity Press.
[44] Romans 12:2.
[45] 1 Corinthians 3:1-3.
[46] Hebrews 5:12.

[47] New American Standard Bible, 1971, Psalm 84:7-12. 1 Corinthians 3:18. Romans chapter 12.
[48] 1 Peter 1:20.
[49] Richard, E. (2000). *Reading 1 Peter, Jude, and 2 Peter: A literary and theological commentary* (pp. 65-66). Smyth & Helwys Publishing, Inc.
[50] Ephesians 1:3-14.
[51] Walls, D., & Anders, M. E. (1999). *Holman New Testament Commentary-1 and 2 Peter, 1 2 and 3 John and Jude* (Vol. 11, pp. 108-109). B&H Publishing Group.
[52] Philippians 4:19.
[53] University of Rochester. (2022, October). Research and Innovation Grants. *University of Rochester, Arts, Science and Engineering, Office of Undergraduate Research.* http://www.rochester.edu/college/ugresearch/funding/rig.html. The grants page gives instructions and criteria regarding how grants are made, funds are allocated, and then resources are distributed over time based on a clear list of criteria.
[54] Williams, J. J. (2021). *Redemptive Kingdom Diversity: A Biblical Theology of the People of God* (p. 112). Baker Academic.
[55] Stott, J. (2014). *The message of Romans: God's good news for the world* (p. 321). InterVarsity Press.
[56] Mark 10:25. Matthew 19:24.
[57] New Living Translation Bible, 1996, Mark 12:44.
[58] Blomberg, C. L. (2001). Neither poverty nor riches: A biblical theology of material possessions. *Pro Ecclesia, 10*(2), 235-237. http://dx.doi.org/10.1177/106385120101000209.
[59] Luke chapter 19. Matthew chapter 25.
[60] Hebrews 11:6.
[61] Ephesians 2:8.
[62] New American Standard Bible, 1971, Titus 3:5-7.
[63] Psalm 19:1. Romans 1:20.
[64] Shaw, M. R. (2010). *Global awakening: How 20th-century revivals triggered a Christian revolution.* InterVarsity Press.
[65] Blumhofer, E. (2006). Azusa Street revival. *Christian Century, 123*(5), 20-22.
[66] Stegemann, E., & Stegemann, W. (1999). *Jesus movement: A social history of its first century.* A&C Black.
[67] 2 Peter 1:5. James 2:18. Ephesians 2:8.

Chapter 13

Heart capital

Introduction to capital

This chapter studies a particular type of capital, the heart capital of the kingdom economy. The chapter begins with a brief review of real economy capital. I then define heart capital and identify types of heart capital. The chapter ends with case studies on the productive effects of heart capital.

Capital theory is concerned with "the allocation of resources."[1] In order to generate cash flow and grow all businesses allocate capital, invest in new capital and maintain existing capital. Capital is the total stock of tangible and intangible assets used for the production of goods and services. Some capital is tangible items such as equipment. Intangible capital includes entrepreneurship, patents, a valuable brand, or a unique organizational process. The productivity of entrepreneurship and the success of new business ventures are sometimes linked to an entrepreneur's "faith orientation."[2] Capital can also be financial. The cash and securities owned by a company are financial capital. Capital markets, such as the stock market, are for the raising and trading of financial capital.

How a business uses capital

Consider the example of a small property management business. The business may own equipment such as trucks, vacuums, lawnmowers, and leaf blowers. The business may have a trademark or logo on the side of its trucks. The business may have high Google ratings and a good reputation with its customers. The business would have money in a bank account to pay its employees and a longer-term savings account for investment opportunities. The business will face competition and operational difficulties. Its success will be linked to the entrepreneurial qualities of the owner. Labor and capital are combined to produce services that earn income. In the real economy, financial capital can be invested in other businesses and earn a passive return. I have not yet found a kingdom economy example of a return on purely passive capital.

Real economy capital is scarce and mobile

Two important characteristics of real economy capital are scarcity and mobility.[3] The scarcity of capital at times causes the return on capital to be higher than the return on labor. Long periods of capital returns exceeding labor returns are associated with economic inequality.[4] Capital is mobile. Owners of capital will move it to the highest return opportunities. Efficient capital markets facilitate the low-cost movement of capital from low return opportunities to high-return opportunities. A business with higher margins and better prospects can pay the highest amount for necessary equipment and will have the best access to financing. The most valuable capital is human capital. Human capital is the source of intangible capital in the real economy. Each human carries the image and likeness of God.[5] A business may buy a shiny new Caterpillar dump truck, but it is the human operator and collective firm know-how that makes the equipment valuable and productive.

The return on capital is the most critical component of any theory of capital.[6] A business or individual must earn a return on capital that meets or exceeds its cost of capital. Earning above the required return on capital creates new value. Earning below the required return means a business will not generate enough cash to maintain its capital or stay competitive.

Introduction to heart capital

> "The good person out of the good treasure of his heart brings forth what is good, and the evil *person* out of the evil *treasure* brings forth what is evil; for his mouth speaks from that which fills *his* heart".
>
> – Luke 6:45. New Living Translation.

Heart Capital is spiritual treasure endowed by God according to scripture. It is the treasure stored in human hearts that enables the production of good works. Real economy capital is scarce, mobile, and finite. God is the source of heart capital and his resources are infinite. Heart capital is not scarce. Nobel Prize winner Robert Solow wrote, "It does not really matter whether the period of production process involving fixed capital is finite or infinite, or even if it can be well defined at all." In the context of Solow's comment, it is notable Abraham received a partial return of heart capital of faith in his lifetime and the rest in eternity.[7] Abraham received his inheritance of the kingdom of God only after the salvation work of Jesus. I define the sources and types heart capital with a biblical survey, including its character, and returns.

Sources of heart capital

God has given every human a starting endowment of heart capital. Some sources of heart capital are common to humankind. Other sources of heart capital are specific to a born-again person receiving the Holy Spirit through a personal relationship with Jesus. Humankind is created in the likeness and image of God.[8] Mathematician Blaise Pascal famously said humankind has a *God-shaped hole* in her heart.[9] The essence of Pascal's sentiment mirrors the writer of Ecclesiastes, declaring "God has set eternity in their heart."[10] Quoting from Martin Luther's lectures on the book of Genesis, Stanley Grenz discusses two views of the Imago Dei. One view is the reflection of God was blocked out by the sin of humankind. Grenz' goes on to cite the more commonly held view of John Calvin that despite the damage done by sin, humankind and even all of creation is a "sphere of divine glory."[11]

Common heart capital of creation

I subscribe to the second view. Creation itself is an ongoing source of divine glory and heart capital for humankind. The human capacity to do good is supported by interaction with the natural world.[12] The apostle Paul makes the claim God is *clearly seen* in creation. In the past, the divine glory and testimony of new scientific discovery has convinced skeptics to dedicate their lives to Jesus. Francis Collins led the human genome project. He was part of the first team of scientists to completely sequence human DNA.[13] Collins' book *The Language of God* details his kingdom conversion experience.[14] Even Stephen Hawking observed the universe had a beginning or else the night sky would be brightly lit.[15] Hawking, so far as I have read in his books, did not use the fact of the dark night sky to decide God was the originating force in the universe, rather just that He couldn't rule it out.

Human interaction with other humans, particularly Christ-followers intent on being salt and light in the real economy, presents people with daily opportunities to receive additional heart capital. The caution to humankind is to avoid the pagan trap of worshiping parts of the created universe rather than the creator.[16] Humankind can fall victim to the lie that people, creatures, and creation are in themselves worthy of worship rather than God.[17] The natural environment is indeed a marvelous wonder. There is joy embedded in creation.[18] It is a source of common God-given heart capital and, above all, a reason to worship the owner of it all.

Endowment of the Holy Spirit and the word of God

The specific and much larger stock of heart capital is available to humans who have been born again. The first component is the Holy Spirit. He is given to any person who receives Jesus.[19] Jesus told the disciples, "It is to your advantage I am leaving; for if I do not leave, the Helper will not come to you; but if I go, I will send him to you."[20] The Greek word for advantage is profit. It is to my profit I have one member of the ownership trinity as my guide.[21] In perhaps a crude way, I see an analogy of the Holy Spirit as an investment banker. He is the one who guides, counsels, empowers,[22] and raises heart capital in the form of fruits of the spirit and gifts of the Spirit. The endowment of the Holy Spirit in a Christ-follower's life is evidence of repentance and salvation by grace through faith.[23] The Holy Spirit is a gift from the father, a source of spiritual capital, and the sign of salvation and life. A major message of Witness Lee's *The Economy of God* is the endowment of the Holy Spirit is the most critical resource in a Christian's life.[24]

The second treasure trove of specific heart capital is the word of God. The word is heart capital because I put it in my heart. King David hid the word of God in his heart. The word was the machinery that enabled him to be obedient.[25] Jesus himself is the pre-eternal word of God. John's gospel opens with, "In the beginning was the Word, and the Word was with God and the Word was God."[26] The word is Jesus. FF Bruce notes the intentionality of the writer opening the gospel of John with the same three words as the creation account of Genesis. The causal force of creation is the Word of God.[27]

Figure 13.1. Heart Capital crosses the messianic membrane to produce life, peace, and growth.

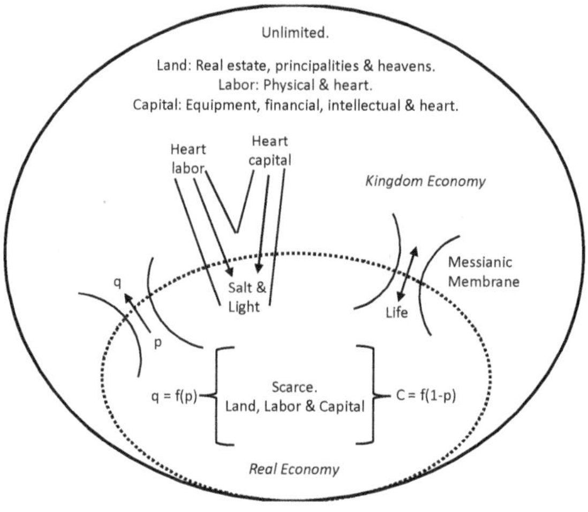

Figure 13.1 major message: Agents improve and increase their stock of heart capital by heart labors including prayer, bible study, fasting, almsgiving and service of all types. Heart capital is the internal machinery enabling agents to be salt and light, producing life, peace, and growth in the real economy.

"Heaven and Earth" will pass away but none of the words of Jesus will.[28] The context of Jesus' statement is an indication that even though the destruction of the temple was not many years off, nothing will destroy his words and teaching.[29] After Jesus' resurrection, the teaching of scripture caused the hearts of hearers to burn.[30] The word is alive and it judges the unseen intent of my heart.[31] God told the prophet Samuel that man judges based on the outside of a person but God looks inside the heart.[32] The word is for both defense and offense. The apostle Paul describes it as a sword.[33] All of the weaponry of the armor of God is on the balance sheet of a Christ-follower. Jesus uses the word of God to repel and counterattack the temptations of Satan.[34] In the parable of the sower, Jesus uses the imagery of seeds to explain the word of God being planted in my heart and growing.[35] The seed must fall on good ground to germinate and grow. For receptive kingdom agents, the word of God is a vast, powerful and productive form of heart capital. The word of God and the Holy Spirit are complementary heart capital.

Heart capital produces life, wisdom and virtue

In Figure 13.1, heart capital is deposited into me by the owner. As I work for the kingdom economy, my heart capital travels across the messianic membrane and is activated to produce life, peace and growth in the real economy. If my heart is full of good capital,[36] I will be salt and light and speak and act in a way that produces the kingdom economy outputs. In the most general sense, I have a high level of capability, creativity, power, and resourcefulness. In the messianic era, the use of my heart capital may not be as it was for Samson in tearing apart a lion,[37] but it can be to give a faithful testimony in the face of accusers that would do me grave bodily harm. The New Testament witness Stephen was so full of heart capital that he asked God to forgive his killers, even as they were engaged in the act of stoning him.[38]

Heart capital produces life. The apostle Paul wrote in Romans, "But if the Spirit of Him who raised Jesus from the dead dwells in you, He who raised Christ Jesus from the dead will also give life to your mortal bodies through His Spirit who dwells in you."[39] New Testament scholar Craig Keener associates the verse with the Holy Spirit resurrecting the dead in the valley of the dry bones.[40] The story of the Valley of the Dry Bones resurrection is an example of human agency. God could have directed the operation. Instead, he delegated the authority to the prophet Ezekiel. Ezekiel, acting on behalf of the owner, did as he was 'commanded' to a life-giving effect. The mind, fruit, and function of the Holy Spirit is life and peace.[41]

Heart capital gives the wisdom to guide decision-making. The fear of the Lord is the beginning of wisdom and knowledge,[42] and it is how I even understand what the fear of the Lord is. Through wisdom, I can understand right and wrong, how to do justice, and how to correctly walk each day.[43] The wisdom of the Holy Spirit is for individuals and groups. The New Testament governing body, the Jerusalem Council, used the guidance of the Holy Spirit to lead the church.[44] Unity in decision making can serve as a guardrail in discerning the mind of the Holy Spirit.[45]

Heart capital enables me to be virtuous. The fruits of the Holy Spirit include valuable real economy virtues of love, patience, kindness, and self-control. There are three cardinal Christian virtues of love, faith, and hope and a total of nine fruits of the Spirit. The purpose of being virtuous is not an end to itself in the sense of Stoicism. Rather it is to enable me to produce life, peace, and growth in the real economy. Hope, according to Hope Theory founder Charles R. Snyder, is an agency construct. Hopeful people meet with obstacles and problems the same way despairing people do. However, people high on the hope scale have a greater ability to find alternative paths to success.[46] Successful kingdom agency depends on the hope and encouragement of the Holy Spirit.

Heart capital used for the common good

Heart capital includes gifts of specific ability for the common good. Bezalel was given wisdom and knowledge by the Holy Spirit for making artistic designs in gold, silver, and bronze.[47] The Holy Spirit is the one who knows the mind of God and is the distributor of spiritual gifts.[48] The spiritual gifts are not earned, they are divinely allocated for the maximum overall productivity of the kingdom economy.[49] Paul's specific instruction on spiritual gifts follows after the general instruction for me to offer myself as a living sacrifice.[50] The instruction is to think of myself in the context of my faith and the spiritual gifts I have received.[51] The first list of spiritual gifts in Romans includes prophecy, acts of service, teaching, encouraging, generous giving, leadership, and showing mercy. Paul follows the list of spiritual gifts with heart labors, including prayer, blessing those who persecute me, and weeping with those who weep.

Labor applied to capital produces real economy work. It is the same in the kingdom economy. The purpose of the gifts is to use them for the "common good."[52] Gifts truly benefit the recipient only insofar as they are used to serve all. There is a further list of seven gifts of the spirit listed in 1 Corinthians 12. The second list includes wisdom, word of knowledge, faith, healing, miracles, prophesy, discernment, speaking in unknown tongues, and interpretation. The analysis of the functions of heart capital is not exhaustive. However, it does serve to show the extent of the generosity of the owner to provide heart capital for my good, the good of my community, and the world. I have a full complement of resources to produce life and peace in the real economy.

Acquiring heart capital through agency activity

Idealized systems of political economy and equality, such as *Sovereign Virtue*,[53] or a system based on the elimination of private property rights, fail for the exclusion of the consequences of sin in the real economy. The desire for fairness is a sign of the basic virtues God has embedded in humankind. However, without the life-giving work of the Holy Spirit, life and peace cannot be achieved. All humankind has an equal opportunity to acquire an unlimited amount of good heart capital. Good heart capital is obtained with obedient surrender and not with money. All who are thirsty for the "free gift of the water of life" are invited to come and receive forgiveness and the Holy Spirit. The offer is made repeatedly in the Bible.[54]

Heart capital is acquired through agency activity. Heart capital is not passively acquired. Jesus instructed his followers to ask, seek, and knock to receive good gifts from God.[55] During the time of the Roman empire, it was unusual for religious leaders or philosophers to encourage followers to pursue God with the enthusiasm of a child.[56] The active part for agents is in the asking. The construction of the passage in Greek indicates the receiving is passive. God responds to my asking with good gifts, such as what I need, perhaps not what I specifically ask for.[57] The immediately preceding context for the asking is for me to pray the Lord's prayer which includes the phrase "God's will be done." Proverbs indicate I should search for the precious treasure that is wisdom. James indicates if I am lacking in wisdom I should ask God, knowing I will be supplied with what I need.[58] Finally, when I ask, I must realize that God alone is the rewarder of my pursuit.[59] These and many other examples in scripture show the pursuit of heart capital is intended to be active, diligent, and continuous.

Heart capital is acquired through study. The final commission of Jesus to his disciples includes an instruction to teach people how to follow his commands. The implication is I must be taught how to be an effective kingdom agent. In the book of Acts, Luke records the conversion experience of a senior Ethiopian government official. The official was traveling in the Middle East between Jerusalem and Gaza. One of the early converts and church leaders, Philip, was sent to find him. Philip ran alongside the man's chariot and heard him reading from Isaiah 53. Philip asked the government official if he comprehended Isaiah's prophecy. The Ethiopian official responded, "how can I unless someone guides me?"[60] The official needed a teacher.

An important component of acquiring heart capital is self-study. As I study the Bible, I can understand the word of God and handle it accurately.[61] Every part of the Bible is useful for training in righteousness.[62] As I study the Bible, it is deposited into my heart as good capital. The second form of self-study is prayer. I am taught by the Holy Spirit when I pray and wait on God for answers.[63] The writings of the apostle Paul teach me to pray at all times.[64] I am also taught in community. Regular church attendance and interaction with other Christ-followers produces personal accountability and opportunities to learn from one another. I acquire heart capital through community worship and service.

The work involved in acquiring heart capital is the heart labor of kingdom agency. Heart labor is discussed in the following chapter. Heart capital itself is a joint product. A joint product is something that is made in combination with another product from a common input. For example, organization capital is built when a business wins a large new customer. The customer win results in new income for the business. The process of bidding for the business and managing the sales team also increases the intangible know-how of the firm. In the case of kingdom agency, if I serve food in a homeless shelter I produce a small bit of life and peace in the real economy, and I receive additional heart capital to increase my capacity and enjoyment in serving in the future. In this way, heart capital bears some similarities to intangible organizational capital in the real economy.[65] The joint product nature of heart capital helps me raise my kingdom productivity.

Maintaining and refining heart capital

Capital must be maintained and protected. Maintenance requires a new investment. It has been experimentally shown the useful life of real economy organization capital is two to three years.[66] To stay competitive, firms must continually invest in their intangible capital. Physical capital, such as a manufacturing plant or a building, may have a fairly long useful life. New machinery may last up to 10 years, and new buildings may last 50 years or longer. Firms can increase the useful life of physical capital through maintenance. Each year, firms spend on maintenance capital. Heart capital can also dissipate. One sign that my heart capital is dissipating is my lack of spiritual authority. Perhaps where I once felt sharp and bold, I feel timid. Paul encouraged Timothy to "kindle afresh the gift of God which is in you through the laying on of hands."[67] Timothy needed to maintain the gift of heart capital he had received from the Holy Spirit.

Heart capital must be protected. Proverbs 4:23 in the New Living Translation says, "Guard your heart above all else, for it determines the course of your life." In the real economy, I cannot make a product or deliver a service if I don't have the right equipment. So, it is in the kingdom economy. If I want to be salt and light and produce life, peace, and growth, I must have the right capital in my heart. Heart capital is valuable. Humans guard what is valuable to them. Proverbs emphasizes the point by stating the contents of my heart dictate my life. The conceptual connection between Luke 6:45 and Proverbs 4:23 is sometimes noted by Bible editors and commentators.[68]

Viewing my heart as a lock box of valuable capital puts the work of the devil in a new light. John 10:10 says, "The thief comes only to steal, kill and destroy. I have come that they might have life and have it more abundantly." The second half of the verse is part of the life objective of the economy of God. The first part of the verse indicates how the enemy opposes the kingdom of God. A first thought when reading this may be the enemy wants to steal real economy resources. That is a small part of the enemy's plan. It is not terribly important if someone were to steal my car. Physical goods can be replaced. The enemy opposes humanity by attempting to steal valuable heart capital. If he can steal heart capital, I may treat my wife less well and lose my family. If I do not guard my heart, I may lose peace and patience. I may lose humility to a temptation of pride. I may even simultaneously become wealthier and lose my heart capital because of a growing love of money. When my stock of heart capital declines, I produce less life and peace in the real economy. Eventually, my actions may even cause corruption and death. I must be on the alert for traps that cause me to be susceptible to attack. Two biblical antecedents to the loss of heart capital are pride and worry.[69]

Case examples of the capital theory of the kingdom economy

Robert Solow taught, "Capital theory is the study of causes and consequences of acts of savings and investments."[70] Payment for labor is wages and payment for capital is interest. In the real economy, in equilibrium, the rate of return on investment must equal the rate of interest.[71] The cost of heart capital in the kingdom is sacrifice. God gave his only son[72] and therefore the reasonable return should be my equal living sacrifice of worship and service. The capital theory of the kingdom economy is to offer myself as a living sacrifice to produce good works here on earth in the same way Jesus did.[73] The payment for capital is according to the love and unlimited resources of the owner. I close this chapter with two examples of world-changing heart capital. The first example of heart capital in action is Jesus' work on the cross. The second example is the abolition of slavery in the United Kingdom.

Merciful Jesus

Jesus came to establish the kingdom of God on earth and give all people an opportunity to have peace with God.[74] Jesus, the man, had a full stock of heart capital, including humility, righteousness, peace, justice, mercy, and forgiveness. The stock of mercy was so great the Bible records that during an unjust execution by crucifixion, Jesus said, "Father forgive them, for they do not know what they are doing."[75]

At first glance, it strains credulity to think, at least on a superficial level the crowd did not know anything about what was happening. At the time of his execution, Jesus was famous. Jesus had traveled throughout Israel. Jesus had taught indoors and outside. Jesus preached on hilltops and healed so many people; John the Disciple wrote there were not enough pages to record all the details of his exploits. The Bible records there was a sign atop Jesus' cross that read *King of the Jews*. The crowd did not understand because of willful blindness. The poetry of Psalms captures the meaning of Jesus' mercy on the cross, "Surely his salvation is nigh them that fear him; that glory may dwell in our land. Mercy and truth are met together; righteousness and peace have kissed each other. Truth shall spring out of the earth, and righteousness shall look down from heaven."[76]

William Wilberforce and Psalms chapter 119

The second case shows the power of the word of God stored in a person's heart can change the world. William Wilberforce and his spiritual mentor, John Newton, were driving forces behind the abolition of slavery and the slave trade. Wilberforce and Newton had in common young adult conversions to Christianity, followed by a period of discipleship and ultimately strong drives for economic and social justice. Newton had been a sailor involved in the slave trade before his conversion. Ultimately, Newton became an abolitionist, acting as one of Wilberforce's spiritual mentors. Wilberforce spent his political capital in the U.K. parliament on the abolition of the slave trade and the emancipation of slaves. He became indignant at times with political colleagues worried only about the real economy, contemporary society, and "concerns of this world (rather than) thoughts of heavenly treasure."[77] It bears considering how the privileged Wilberforce became a tireless advocate for the defenseless and oppressed of his country. Wilberforce became a reformer by being taught the Bible, studying the Bible, and praying.

Wilberforce was taught in part by his mentor, John Newton, Rector of St Mary Woolnoth. Newton is credited with writing perhaps the most famous of religious hymns, Amazing Grace. On December 17, 1819, Wilberforce wrote "It is only by educating our people in Christian principles that we can hope to advance in strength, greatness, and happiness." In his role in the U.K. government, Wilberforce responded by requiring the East India Trading Company to supply chaplains and teachers to the citizens of India.

Wilberforce became a reformer by self-study and memorizing Bible passages. In the middle of December 1819, Wilberforce made a journal entry that described the United Kingdom's political state as "near combustion."[78] In a following entry, Wilberforce simply records, "walked from Hyde Park Corner, repeating the 119th Psalm in great comfort". On his walk to work, Wilberforce kept his heart and mind focused on the work of abolishing slavery by reciting Psalm 119. At 60 years of age, the experienced social reformer chose to spend 30 valuable minutes meditating on Psalm 119. In Psalm 119, David wrote about the perfection of God's law, its protection against sin, its drive for justice, and keeping the law in his heart. God's word is a source of good heart capital that produces the good work of social reform. May I learn the lesson of Wilberforce and go and do likewise.

Notes

[1] Solow, R. M. (1963). *Capital theory and the rate of return* (p. 14). Amsterdam: North-Holland Publishing Company.
[2] Judge, W. Q., & Douglas, T. J. (2013). Entrepreneurship as a leap of faith. *Journal of management, spirituality & religion, 10*(1), 37-65. http://dx.doi.org/10.1080/14766086.2012.758047.
[3] Barro, R. J., Mankiw, N. G., & Sala-i-Martin, X. (1992). *Capital mobility in neoclassical models of growth* (No. w4206). National Bureau of Economic Research.
[4] Piketty, T. (2014). *Capital in the twenty-first century.* Harvard University Press. http://dx.doi.org/10.4159/9780674369542.
[5] Genesis 1:26-28.
[6] Solow, R. M. (1963). *Capital theory and the rate of return* (p. 16). Amsterdam: North-Holland Publishing Company.
[7] Harris, D. M. (2019). *Hebrews.* B&H Publishing Group.; Hebrews 11:39-40.
[8] Genesis 1:26-28.
[9] Nowalk, N. (2011, May). Pascal's God-Shaped Hole. *Harvard Ichthus.* https://harvardichthus.org/2011/05/pascal_hole/
[10] Ecclesiastes 3:11.
[11] Grenz, S. J. (2001). *The social God and the relational self: A Trinitarian theology of the imago Dei* (Vol. 1, pp 165-166.). Westminster John Knox Press.
[12] Psalm 19:1. Romans 1:20.
[13] The Genome Sequencing Consortium. (2001). Initial sequencing and analysis of the human genome. *Nature.409 (6822),* 860-921. https://doi.org/10.1073/pnas.90.10.4338
[14] Collins, F. S. (2006). *The language of God: A scientist presents evidence for belief* (No. 111). Simon and Schuster.
[15] Hawking, S. (1996). *The illustrated a brief history of time* (p. 11, figure 1.4). Bantam.
[16] Romans 1:25.
[17] Stott, J. (2014). *The message of Romans: God's good news for the world* (pp. 76-77). InterVarsity Press.
[18] New American Standard Bible, 1971, Proverbs 8:30-31.
[19] Luke 11:13.
[20] John 16:7-8.
[21] Tenney, M. C. (1997). *John: the gospel of belief* (p. 233). Wm. B. Eerdmans Publishing.
[22] Acts 1:8.
[23] Acts 11:17.
[24] Lee, W. (2005). *The economy of God.* Living Stream Ministry.
[25] Psalm 119:11.
[26] John 1:1-3.

[27] Bruce, F. F. (1994). *The Gospel of John: Introduction, Exposition, Notes* (pp. 28-29). Wm. B. Eerdmans Publishing.
[28] Matthew 24:35. Luke 21:33.
[29] Blomberg, C. L. (1992). *Matthew: An exegetical and theological exposition of Holy Scripture* (Vol. 22, pp. 364-365). B&H Publishing Group.
[30] Luke 24:32
[31] Hebrews 11:4.
[32] 1 Samuel 16:7.
[33] Ephesians 6:17.
[34] Luke 4:4. Luke 4:8. Luke 4:12.
[35] New American Standard Bible, 1971, Luke 8:11.
[36] Luke 6:45.
[37] New American Standard Bible, 1971, Judges 14:6.
[38] Acts 7:59-60.
[39] Romans 8:11.
[40] Ezekiel chapter 37.
[41] Romans 8:6.
[42] Proverbs 1:7. Proverbs 9:10.
[43] Proverbs 2:1-9.
[44] Acts 15:25-29. The Jerusalem council was the governing body of the early church.
[45] Psalm 133:1-3.
[46] Snyder, C. R. (2002). Hope theory: Rainbows in the mind. *Psychological inquiry, 13*(4), 249-275.
[47] Exodus 31:2-11.
[48] New American Standard Bible, 1971, 1 Corinthians 2:1-11.
[49] Romans 12:3-8.
[50] See the analysis of Romans 12:1 in Chapter 12, "The Law of Proportion".
[51] Stott, J. (2014). *The message of Romans: God's good news for the world* (p. 325). InterVarsity Press.
[52] Stott, J. (2014). *The message of Romans: God's good news for the world* (pp. 326-326). InterVarsity Press.
[53] Dworkin, R. (2002). *Sovereign virtue: The theory and practice of equality.* Harvard university press. http://dx.doi.org/10.2307/j.ctv1c3pd0r.
[54] Isaiah 55:10. John 7:37. Revelation 21:6. Revelation 22:17.
[55] Mathew 7:7-12
[56] Keener, C. S., & Walton, J. H. (Eds.). (2016). *NIV, Cultural Backgrounds Study Bible: Bringing to Life the Ancient World of Scripture* (p. 1682). Zondervan.
[57] Blomberg, C. L. (1992). *Matthew: An exegetical and theological exposition of Holy Scripture* (Vol. 22, p. 130). B&H Publishing Group.
[58] James 1:5-6.
[59] Hebrews 11:6.
[60] New American Standard Bible, 1971, Acts 8:31.
[61] 2 Timothy 2:15.
[62] 2 Timothy 3:16-17.
[63] Isaiah 40:31.
[64] Ephesians 6:18.

[65] Prescott, E. C., & Visscher, M. (1980). Organization capital. *Journal of political Economy, 88*(3), 446-461. http://dx.doi.org/10.1086/260879.
[66] Root, A., & Yung, K. (2022). Resolving agency and product market views of cash holdings. *Research in International Business and Finance, 59*, 101518. http://dx.doi.org/10.1016/j.ribaf.2021.101518.
[67] 2 Timothy 1:6-7.
[68] Tyndale, & Tyndale House Publishers. (2004). *Life Application Study Bible: New Living Translation.* Tyndale House Publishers, Inc..
[69] 1 Peter 5:6-8
[70] Solow, R. M. (1963). *Capital theory and the rate of return* (p. 14). Amsterdam: North-Holland Publishing Company.
[71] Solow, R. M. (1963). *Capital theory and the rate of return* (p. 33). Amsterdam: North-Holland Publishing Company.
[72] John 3:16.
[73] John 14:12, Romans 12:1.
[74] Romans 5:1
[75] New American Standard Bible, 1971, Luke 23:34.
[76] Psalm 85:9-13.
[77] Wilberforce, W. (2011). *The Correspondence of William Wilberforce* (Vol. 2, p. 273). Cambridge University Press. http://dx.doi.org/10.1017/CBO9780511792052.
[78] Wilberforce, W. (2021, June). William Wilberforce papers, 1782-1837 and undated (1819 Journal, pp. 45). *Duke University Libraries, Archives & Manuscripts Collection Guides.* https://archives.lib.duke.edu/catalog/wilberf.

Chapter 14

Heart labor

Definition and purpose of heart labor

In this chapter, I study the resource heart labor. The chapter begins with a definition and purpose of heart labor. Next, we survey the bible for heart labor types and characteristics. The survey will show how the kingdom economy accounts for heart labor and the income that is credited. The chapter finishes with an example of individual heart labor producing peace and two group applications, one for Christ followers and one for business leaders.

Labor means physical strain or effort. In economic terms, labor has a variety of definitions. It may be defined as all the wage earners in a group or nation. The labor resource is the physical and mental capacity to work and produce goods and services. In the kingdom economy heart labor is the combined spiritual effort of all Christ-followers to produce life, peace and growth.

> Heart labor is the combined spiritual effort of all Christ-followers to produce life, peace and growth.

The United States Federal Reserve makes available a *circular flow model* to help understand how an economy works.[1] A modified version of the model to suit the kingdom economy, is shown in Figure 14.1. The model shows the flow of goods, services, and money in an economy. The economic interactions are between households and businesses. In more complicated circular flow models, governments are also included. Resources are required to produce any good or service.

A key point of the circular flow model is households own all resources. Businesses interact with households to make contracts and use their resources. The human labor resource is the most valuable. In the kingdom circular flow model, a household's proportional offerings, including heart capital, heart labor, territory, and deferred consumption, are used to produce a growing stream of outputs of life and peace. Households receive back spiritual wages and heart capital. The owner is the source of life, peace, and growth in the kingdom economy.[2]

Figure 14.1. Circular flow model of kingdom economy resources.

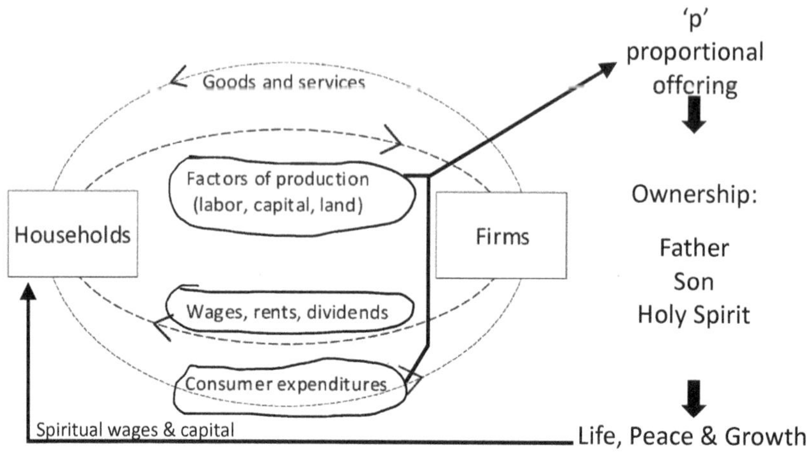

Figure 14.1 major message: In a real economy circular flow model resources are owned by households. In the kingdom economy individuals, families and communities have resources. Resources are allocated to the kingdom economy by proportional offerings of time and money. Offerings activate the owner-agent partnership, producing life, peace, and growth in both realms. Source: Original analysis of the author, modifying a circular flow model presented by the U.S. Federal Reserve.[3]

Individual and group level heart labor

The obedience and heart labor of agents activate the process. Ezekiel was obedient to speak to the dry bones and God put life into them.[4] Kingdom labor refers to a labor force rather than an individual laborer. For certain, there is individual responsibility. My individual works will be judged.[5] I individually undertake heart labors such as prayer and fasting. It is my responsibility to work out my salvation in fear and trembling.[6] However, part of the judgment of my labor is how well I serve in community with other parts of the kingdom of God.[7] It is common for heart labor instructions to reference the group. The Lord's prayer begins with "Our Father" as opposed to *my father.*[8] Paul teaches I am part of one body with many individual parts, each serving a unique function. Jesus sent the first group of kingdom ambassadors out in pairs rather than individually.[9] Spiritual authority in the kingdom is based on the agreement of at least two or three.[10]

Humankind performs better in the community. A severe natural experiment on the effects of isolation occurred with the COVID-19-induced lockdowns of the early 2020s. A meta-analysis of studies published on the effects of pandemic lockdowns showed isolated patients were worse off. An increase in anxiety and depression among isolated patients reduced quality of life and exacerbated the COVID-19 health crisis.[11] In a separate study, COVID-19 patients were discharged from the hospital to isolate at a hotel or home, based on their own choice. Patients isolated at home were significantly less depressed and anxious than patients isolated in a hotel room.[12] Humankind was designed to experience the love, strength, accountability, and challenges of living with families and communities.

Types of heart labor. King David as a model laborer

If Proverbs is the biblical book of heart capital, Psalms is the book of heart labors. David was the author of about half of the Psalms. God said, "I have found in David the son of Jesse, a man after my own heart who will do all My will."[13] Obedience is the key trait of an effective heart laborer. In Psalms chapters three through nine, David prays for help, offers thanks, pleads for mercy, fears the Lord, and worships.[14] David sings praises with his whole heart, worships God for his creation, testifies about God's goodness,[15] and declares he trusts God. David knows how to honor God by being truthful, fair in lending, avoiding bribes, and humbling himself to be tested.[16]

The intensity of David's heart labor is captured in Psalm 63. David prays early in the morning, searches for God, praises, meditates, and follows Him closely. In Psalm 37 David wrote living for God is about trust, delight, commitment, rest, waiting, patience, humility, speaking wisdom, doing justice, and being a person of peace. David writes in Psalm 133 that the unity of believers brings a commanded blessing from the owner.

The beatitudes as heart labor

In the New Testament, the sermon on the mount is known in part for its unique list of opening virtues. The main message of the opening is everything about the kingdom of God, its economy, and its practices are completely different from any other realm of the real economy.[17] Blessed are the poor in spirit, the mourners, the meek, those who hunger for righteousness, the merciful, the pure in heart, the peacemakers, and those persecuted for righteousness. The poor in spirit are sometimes called humble. Mourners repent for their sins and the sins of their community. Mourners were known to pray for a change of heart in the community and nation at large.[18] The meek yield their rights or physical strength for the benefit of others. Meekness in ancient culture would not be an obvious virtue. Each of the attributes listed is heart labor. I engage my heart to be merciful or a peacemaker. The heart labor activates the circular flow model of the kingdom economy. An act of mercy plants a seed in the object of my mercy, and God then brings the increase of the seed until it can be harvested.

The circular flow model is activated by the proportional sacrificial offering of my capital and labor. In the same chapter as the encouragement to be a living sacrifice, I find a list of the characteristics of a Christ-follower.[19] The list of heart labors in Romans 12 includes genuine love, hating evil, holding on to good, showing honor, being zealous, hopeful, patient, prayerful, giving money, and being hospitable. The list goes on saying bless those that seek to harm me, be humble, weep with those who weep, mourn with those who mourn, live peaceably with everyone, and feed my enemies.

The purpose of living in the way of the Beatitudes and Romans chapter 12 is to overcome evil with good and bring the kingdom of God to the real economy now. I have experienced how mourning with a friend can, in time, bring them a small measure of peace. It also increases love for each other and builds our capacity to comfort others in the future. John Stott summarizes Romans 12 along the theme of Christ-followers loving one another and serving all of humanity instead of retaliating for evil.[20] The only way to begin to live out this section of the Bible is through the heart labors of forgiveness and humility.

To believe God and act for the kingdom of God in faith is heart labor. The *triumph of faith* chapter in Hebrews 11 begins with a definition of faith as, "the certainty of things hoped for and the proof of things not seen."[21] Faith is a requirement. I must believe God is the creator and owner of everything and that he is my only rewarder. The wages I receive for my heart labors are from God alone. God alone *signs my paycheck.* Later, I discuss the payments to Abraham for his faith, which includes righteousness.[22]

Core heart labors are prayer, fasting and giving

Three cardinal components of Jewish piety are prayer, fasting, and giving to the poor. Blomberg links the inter-testament Book of Tobit 12:8-10[23] to Jesus' teaching on piety in Matthew chapter six.[24] Acts of piety are the work of a devoted heart. It is expected kingdom agents will pray, fast, and give to the poor. Jesus uses the imperative in describing private and devoted ways to do this. Serving and giving money to the poor is a theme throughout the Bible. According to the law of proportion, my goal is to give as much as I can stand. Deferring consumption and giving to the poor activates the circular flow model of the kingdom economy. I receive back heart capital and wages from the owner. The question of wages and rewards has previously been dealt with. Here I invoke the sentiment of C.S. Lewis,[25] also referred to by Stott, that what I receive back in spiritual wages or heart capital for almsgiving is not money per se, but the utility of the consummation of my gift. I realize the benefit of seeing a sick person made well or a low-income child well-educated.

The practice of fasting connects my real economy senses to my heart. Fasting is deliberately abstaining from food for spiritual purposes. Daily prayer and giving to the poor are well understood requirements of Christian living but fasting may be less so.[26] Fasting is an act of self-denial and humbling myself before God.[27] Fasting intensifies my prayer. The holiest day of the Jewish calendar is Yom Kippur, the *day of atonement.*[28] It is a permanent statute to fast, be humble before God, pray, and confess sins. The day is for community atonement. Fasting can be for a specific purpose. The scribe, Ezra called a fast to ask God for a safe journey from the Ahava Canal in Babylon to Jerusalem.[29]

I live in the messianic era. I have received atonement for sins through Jesus' sacrifice. Yet Jesus still expects me to fast as part of my heart labors in the kingdom economy.[30] Fasting is not token penitence. The effect of fasting, for me, has some mystery to it. However, three effects of fasting given by Stott seem pertinent to this study.[31] Fasting increases my physical hunger and is a reminder of the danger of greed and the blessing of giving and being hungry for righteousness. Fasting reminds me to give to the poor and thereby relieve injustice and lift burdens.[32] God hears my prayers when I am obedient in helping oppressed people and serving the poor. Third, when I fast, I find my prayers intensified and communication with the owner more intimate.

The final pillar of Jewish piety is prayer. Prayer is perhaps the most fundamental heart labor. In the messianic era, I can talk to the owner at any time or all the time. There is a wide variety of literature available on prayer. In addition to the Bible, I commend Rees Howells' *Intercessor,*[33] *The Power of a Praying Wife,*[34] and *Fasting: Opening the Door to a Deeper, More Intimate, More Powerful Relationship with God.*[35]

Failures activated my work in prayer

At one time, I didn't much like prayer. I had been attending church my whole life but did not enjoy time in prayer. For the better part of 20 years I had the opportunity to teach Sunday school and serve on the board of our church in Connecticut. For the first 10 years, I served on the board. I would intentionally arrive 30 minutes late to board meetings to skip the prayer time. I had a long commute from Manhattan to the church. My frequent lateness was excused for the challenging commute and a busy job. In the mid-2000s, my prayer life changed. Through a series of career disappointments and out of desperation, I began to pray early in the morning. Another desperate member of the church board and I found each other and we started praying. It was by the mercy of God that I became desperate enough to start to pray. Over the decades since, my prayer life has increased. Now, I would rather pray than do just about anything else in the church. Prayer changes my heart about other people. Prayer makes me spiritually bolder, saltier, light-er, and it activates the circular flow model of the kingdom economy in my family. Prayer, according to the will of God changes the world for the better. Prayer has changed me for the better.

Prayer is not just for me. It is done together with others in agreement. The effect of prayer in the kingdom economy can include authority over human governments. Authority does not necessarily mean a local church prays and gets its desired candidate elected. It is God who sets up one political leader and deposes another.[36] It does mean taking authority in prayer to receive good government and thereby influence the decisions and outcomes of government policy. It also means preaching the gospel to those in authority. Paul preached to King Agrippa.[37] In the Old Testament a servant girl convinced Naaman, the Syrian Army Commander, to seek out the prophet Elisha for healing. Naaman was healed and went on to confess there is only one true God.[38]

It is up to the church to pray together for good government

Regardless of *any* particular political leader or regime, the kingdom of God will increase. In three short centuries after the death of Jesus, the rapidly expanding kingdom of God turned a blood-soaked Roman regime of "age, rank, wealth and occupation"[39] upside down. At the same time, God wants good government and instructs kingdom agents to pray for it. 1 Timothy 2:1-4 presents the preferred approach to using heart labor to obtain good government.[40]

The primary heart labor of a community of kingdom agents is prayer. The first topic of prayer is rulers and authorities in the civil government. The community is to ask God for good government. God's desire is for every person to hear the good news of Jesus. The benefit of good government is an environment conducive to hearing the good news, and the cost of bad government is a social rancor that hinders hearing.[41] The instructions of 1 Timothy I are associated with 2 Chronicles 7:14, which reads, "if my people, who are called by my name, will humble themselves and pray and seek my face and turn from their wicked ways, then I will hear from heaven, and I will forgive their sin and will heal their land." It is for the community to humble itself and pray. There are innumerable examples in the Bible and in my own life of God answering prayers of agreement with miracles of economic provision and physical protection. The main message at this moment is the heart labor of community prayer improves outcomes in the real world.

Characteristics of heart labor. The kingdom economy does not have a labor-capital problem

In the real economy the return on capital ("r") often exceeds the growth of labor income ("g"). Thomas Piketty proposes that because r > g for long periods of time, economic inequality is deterministically increasing.[42] The suggested solution is for society to eliminate private property and move to a post-capitalism period. Piketty's view is common in academic circles. Piketty's two comprehensive volumes on *Capital*, published by Harvard University Press, sell very well. Most right-thinking humans share an impulse to see all humanity thrive. Most people appreciate the ideal of equality. Though I personally have many issues with Piketty's calculations and constructs I appreciate the intention, exceptional work, and treasure trove of data the author provides.

One issue I see with the thesis of *Capital* is the misestimation of the life cycle returns on capital. I estimate the average nominal pre-tax return on a typical United States-based portfolio is 7.7% (see Chapter 10, Figure 10.1). The after-tax return on wealth consumed is approximately 5%. Depending on inheritance taxes, the return on the inherited portion is around the same. After inflation, the real after-tax return on wealth is at or slightly under 2%. This is a similar level to long-run real wages. In the long run, data suggests it is more correct to say r = g. Second, Piketty excludes the intangibles of human capital from the split of labor and capital. Humankind is in the information age. Increasing the amount of intangible capital lowers the implied comprehensive return on capital. The most basic disagreement between the theory of *Capital* and the *Theory of the Kingdom* is the sinful state of man and the design of God for ongoing growth.

The sin problem remains in a proposed post-capitalist world

Most economic agents love money rather than God. Even if humanity somehow moves to a post-capitalist regime, man will still love money. Eliminating property rights would not solve inequality. God designed the real economy to grow. The increase of the kingdom economy within the real economy will never end.[43] There is an underlying concern about the unsustainability of income growth. However, if well-tended, the global economy can continue to thrive. This study, in part, takes up the challenge to offer an alternative system that, "may be more useful in transcending capitalism than simply threatening to destroy it without explaining what comes next."[44] The kingdom economy is here and next. The solution is the kingdom economy, come now, with agents doing heart labors for the love of God rather than money.

Heart labor is highly valued in the kingdom economy

The return on heart labor is not inferior to the return on heart capital. Jesus told his disciples to pray for laborers to bring in the harvest, not to pray for new technology or a farm tractor.[45] The highest value position is the servant of all.[46] Heart labor is the engine of the kingdom economy. I have heard teaching within the Christian church that implies I should save as much money as I can now so I can give a lot of money in the future. My future giving will enable me to have a large kingdom economy impact. According to the model of human agency, that thinking is flawed. The *Theory of the Kingdom* would suggest that God, the owner of all will provide me all I need to perform the heart labor I am called to do at all points in time. Real economy financial capital can come from my own savings, other Christ-followers, those opposed to Christianity, and even *ex nihilo.* Obedience to the direction of the Holy Spirit and faith that God will reward diligent labor is all that is required. Financial capital received from other Christ-followers has the additional benefit of promoting the unity of the body of Christ.

Heart labors reveal truth and arrest corruption

Heart labors reveal truth. The kingdom agency mandate includes revealing truth by *being light.*[47] A lighted city on a hill is conspicuous. In the real economy, the brightness of a city is directly related to the level of business activity.[48] More people and more activity results in more luminescence. To reveal truth I live out countercultural virtues, including peacemaking. In modern culture, hostility is easier to come by than peace. If I coach youth sports for peace rather than wins, I reveal the peace objective of the economy of the kingdom. If I overlook an offense and do good to a co-worker, I reveal the life and peace objectives of the kingdom economy. If I show mercy, I reveal the nature of Jesus on the cross. Each heart labor requires faith that God is my sole rewarder[49] and he desires that everyone would be saved.[50]

Heart labor arrests corruption in the real economy. Corruption is multi-dimensional. In general, corruption leads to suffering and death. The mind of the Holy Spirit is for life and peace. The effect of living for money and myself is corruption and death. The effect of salty heart labor produces life and peace. Four examples of heart labor arresting corruption include New Testament letters, music and the arts, environmental leadership, and ministry to the poor.

First, Paul the Apostle begins most of his pastoral New Testament letters with "Grace to you and peace from God our Father and the Lord Jesus Christ."[51] Second, Artistic expression makes the world more palatable. God gives beauty for ashes through artistic expression.[52] An example of salty music is John Newton's *Amazing Grace.* Newton wrote the song in the ashes of the slave trade and lamented his role in it. It brings a measure of peace to the wretched, the lost and the ones caught in great difficulty. Thank God music and art bring a measure of grace and peace to arrest corruption in the real economy. Third, real economic growth can cause damage. In response to the damage, in November 2019, Pope Francis introduced ecological sin to the catechism of the Catholic church. The purpose is to influence Catholics to work to slow environmental corruption. The papal pronouncement made me more circumspect about my theology and appreciative of the role played by Catholic Social Teaching in the body of Christ. Fourth, Saint Teresa of Calcutta spent almost 50 years serving the untouchables of India. Her Missionaries of Charity[53] serve the poor and manage homes for those with leprosy, HIV, and tuberculosis. Saint Teresa's heart labors arrested corruption.

Urgency and effort

Heart labors are done with fervor. Urgency is embedded throughout scripture. I take hold of the labor I have been assigned. Kingdom agency is compared to a runner in a race.[54] God rewards those who diligently seek him. Ecclesiastes says whatever I do, do it with my highest efforts.[55] Proverbs also criticize the lazy person as virtually worthless. Entry into the kingdom is not work-based. However, productivity requires I undertake heart labors fervently.

Considering how most real economy businesses work, a kingdom economy requirement to be a fervent laborer is not a surprise. In my experience, most investment firms start each day with a morning meeting. Employees that arrive early and are well-prepared to contribute ideas and energy produce more research, generate more sales, and deliver more customer wins. Anyone who is invited to the morning meeting has the opportunity to be all-in for business every day. Yet, not everyone approaches each day with the same fervency. Similarly, the fervency of my heart labors of prayer, fasting, Bible study, and worship influence how ready I am each day to be salt and light.

Work performed away from the spotlight

Heart labor is best done in secret. Matthew 6:1 says, "Take care not to practice your righteousness in the sight of people, to be noticed by them; otherwise you have no reward with your Father who is in heaven." The point is specifically emphasized for each of the three pillars of Jewish piety. Giving in secret will be rewarded by God. Praying behind closed doors will be rewarded by God. When I fast, I must groom myself and dress so people don't notice I am not eating. It is logical to choose rewards from an unlimited God over a pat on the back now. However, that is not the main purpose of secrecy. The purpose of quietly going about my kingdom business is to glorify God rather than myself. The hierarchy of temptation indicates I have a need for authority and identity. If I do good works to be seen, I satisfy my pride by receiving honor from other people. If I do good deeds in secret, the praise goes to God. I receive my reward, a satisfied need for authority and identity, from God by the Holy Spirit. God receives the glory and the kingdom economy expands. The instruction to labor away from the spotlight recognizes, "Christian righteousness is not an external manifestation only, but one of the secret things of the heart."[56]

Heart labor wages incentives and effects

In the real economy, payments to capital include rents, dividends, and interest. The payment to labor is wages. There is not a clear separation in the kingdom economy between payments to capital and labor. However, based on scriptural identification of wages for certain good heart labors and the contra for sin, I can propose kingdom accounting. The wages for sin, the heart labor of rebellion and rejection of God, is death.[57] In Romans 6:23, the contrast to the wages of sin is the free gift of salvation. The meaning of wages in antiquity included the ration paid to soldiers and the small compensation paid to slaves in the Roman empire.[58] Keener confirms that in antiquity, even slaves received wages. Approximately 20% of the entire population of the Roman empire were slaves. In portions of Italy, the fraction of slaves was greater than one in three.[59] The opposite nature of wages in the real economy and the salvation gift of kingdom economy would have stood out to any first-century reader.[60]

Wages are incentives in the real economy. Owners pay agents a certain wage to achieve the desired outcome. When wages are set and paid honestly, the incentive creates a mutual benefit. Owners also manipulate wages for the love of money. Manipulation of wages corrupts owner-agent relationships.

The word wages is used 18 times in the Bible. An example of a corrupt owner is Laban. The story of Jacob and his father-in-law Laban accounts for one-quarter of the biblical references to wages. The relationship between Jacob and Laban was dysfunctional. Laban frequently changed Jacob's wages. Laban sought a real economy benefit by manipulating Jacob's incentives.[61] An honest owner does not harm employees by changing the terms of payment. Further, wages are to be paid immediately upon service, not at the convenience of the owner. God will judge owners who exploit agents through compensation.[62]

Kingdom economy wages and accounting

There are spiritual wages for laborers in the kingdom economy.[63] There are wages for righteousness and wages for unrighteousness. Abraham's belief and God's credit of righteousness in recorded in four books of the Bible.[64] There is also a credit of death for unrighteousness. Balaam, son of Beor loved money, and it was credited to him as unrighteousness. Balaam was an Old Testament prophet who knew who God was. However, because Balaam loved money, he worked as a prophet for hire. He was paid to corrupt the people of Israel and was credited with unrighteousness, eventually dying by the sword.[65] The continuing motif throughout the Bible is the love of money versus the love of God. To love money is unrighteousness, producing corruption, conflict, and death. To love and trust God is righteousness, producing life, peace, and kingdom economy growth.

The work of Jesus on the cross cancels the credits of unrighteousness against Christ's followers. Therefore, for the remainder of this section, I focus on the wages of good-hearted labor. To motivate the analysis, consider Abraham's belief and credit of righteousness. Figure 14.2 also includes the example of hospitality towards 'the least', including children and itinerant disciples.[66] There are many more types of labor-wage entries than suggested here. The purpose of Figure 14.2 is to reveal the generosity of kingdom economy accounting.

Figure 14.2. Heart labor accounting.

Owner Entries			
Debit	Wages Expense	1 unit	
Credit	Righteousness		1 unit
Debit	Wages Expense	1 unit	
Credit	Righteousness		1 unit
Agent Entries			
Debit	Righteousness	1 unit	
Credit	Believing		1 unit
Debit	Service to the least	1 unit	
Credit	Hospitality Labor		1 unit

Figure 14.2 major message: The Bible includes specific indications of wages for righteousness and wages for sin. Further, the term used for Abraham's credit is accounting oriented. The information can be turned into journal entries. Figure 14.2 proposes journal entries for righteousness and service. Future research may propose additional entries and steps in the accounting process.

Heart labor received diverse and generous wages

The first characteristic of kingdom economy compensation is wages greatly exceed the value of the inputs. My account in the kingdom is accumulating righteousness. However, it is not by the weight of my accumulated righteousness I am compensated, but according to God's mercy and grace.[67] The blessing of righteousness includes mighty descendants, provision, stability, boldness, generosity, honor, growth, and productivity in old age.[68]

In the real economy, wages must equal the value of rewards. Businesses that have a habit of overpaying will not earn their cost of capital and eventually will go out of business. In the kingdom economy, hospitality in the form of a cup of cold water receives eternal compensation. Returning to the example of Abraham's credit of righteousness, Romans 8:16 says Abraham is the "father of us all." The belief of Abraham, credited to him as righteousness, continues to receive a wage.[69] "All believers belong to Abraham's seed and so inherit Abraham's promise."[70] Finally, the generosity of the first-century Philippian church community to Paul received a wage according to God's riches, not according to their need or in proportion to the value of the gifts.[71] God can be an extravagant payor because he is the owner, he loves his agents and he is unlimited. The balance sheet of the owner already includes all assets required to credit the activity of kingdom laborers. The wages for heart laborers are "pressed down, shaken together and running over."[72] The rational choice is to give as much heart labor to the owner as I can stand.

Wages may be money for real economy needs.[73] The wages of faith may be real economy goods and services.[74] Wages for obedience, faith, and being honorable may include territory.[75] Rewards for Jesus' obedience included joy and authority. "Looking only at Jesus, the originator and perfecter of the faith, who for the joy set before him endured the cross, despising the shame, and has sat down at the right hand at the throne of God."[76] Wages are paid for working in the kingdom economy harvest field.[77] The purpose of good-heart labor is not to accumulate wages. It is my reasonable act of worship to bring honor to the owner by whose hand I was made.[78]

Heart labor is exchanged for information. The gospel of Luke relays the stories of Simeon and Anna. Anna was called a prophet and Simeon was a devout man. Anna was a widow from her seventh year of marriage. For the rest of her life, approximately 60 years, Anna lived and worked in the temple in Jerusalem. The Bible records Anna's contribution as worshipping God with the heart labors of fasting and prayer. When Jesus was an infant he was brought to the temple for dedication. Anna met baby Jesus and it was revealed to her that this was the Messiah, born to save humankind from its sins. Her invisible heart labor of worship, prayer, and fasting was compensated in part by Holy Spirit revelation and access to Jesus.

The first recorded person to receive revelation that Jesus was the long-awaited Messiah was Simeon. In a remarkably short bio, it is learned Simeon was a man, who lived in Jerusalem, was righteous, and was devout. Devotion speaks to fervency. Righteousness speaks to personal integrity. Simeon must have been a man of faith, as he was also credited with righteousness. Some prior literature suggests Simeon was old and a priest. Simeon, like Anna, received the highest spiritual wages of the day. Simeon was introduced to Messiah Jesus.

Kingdom economy wages are immune from the biases of real economy compensation. It is noteworthy Luke records one man and one woman receiving the revelation of Jesus. God paid male and female kingdom laborers the same amount at the same time. The real economy does not always pay fairly. One essential problem is human business owners are limited in what they see. God judges the heart.[79] God told the prophet, Samuel, he could not see that David was a "man after My heart, who will do all of My will."[80]

Real economy wages are not fairly distributed

Real economy business owners are biased by virtually every visible human characteristic. There is a vast amount of evidence proving true what God told Samuel. The study of exterior trait bias began with a study by Karen Dion, Ellen Bersheid, and Elain Walster. *What is beautiful is good,*[81] revealed physical attributes are associated with social and economic outcomes in the real economy. Researchers have tested and extended the findings in several directions. Identical fake resumes were sent with different candidate headshots. Headshots rated as attractive were called for an interview 36% more often.[82] Ruffle & Shtudiner showed callbacks for attractive men are twice as high as callbacks for plain-looking men.[83] For women, the evidence is more mixed and more harmful. The differential effect of women versus men may be related to attractive women being viewed as less intelligent, being blamed for trying to sell their looks, or they may even be discriminated against by envious less attractive female hiring managers.

Cognitive ability explains higher return to labor for men but shows a bias against wages for women. However, a workplace wage bias against women extends even to the female intellect. Smart women under-earn because of bias against believing in the capability of attractive women.[84] The overall effect of all of these gender biases is called the female beauty penalty. Lest I entertain the thought the real economy is efficient in the sense beautiful people are in fact more productive, Feingold reports it is not so.[85] Physical attributes of workers are not associated with mental ability and personality. The effect of human gender bias in the workplace is corruption and death. The perception of relative attractiveness influences loneliness, anxiety, and social popularity.

The owner in the kingdom economy is just

In the kingdom economy, it doesn't matter if I am short or tall, skinny or fat, attractive or unattractive. God looks at my heart. He sees the productive heart labor I do. Luke did not report the ethnicity of Anna and Simeon or if they were physically attractive. Jesus was not himself especially physically appealing.[86] Jesus was so disfigured by the end of his crucifixion he didn't appear human.[87] Paying special attention to someone because of their appearance or relative wealth is a sin.[88] The wages received for heart labor are fair. To arrest corruption and reveal truth, I must engage the insight of the Holy Spirit to treat others fairly.

Example of heart labor producing peace

The story of Corrie and Betsy Ten Boom is an example of the heart labors of prayer and hospitality, producing life and peace, even in horrible circumstances. Corrie and Betsy were part of the Dutch reformed church. They were not Jewish. During the Second World War Corrie and Betsy chose to risk their own lives by loving their neighbors and providing hospitality to Dutch Jews. They became part of an underground movement to get as many Jews as possible away from the Nazis and to safety. Eventually, Corrie, Betsy, and their father, Casper, were arrested for helping their Jewish neighbors. It is estimated the Ten Boom's saved 800 Jews from Nazi capture, including six Jews hiding in the home the day the family was arrested.

Casper died shortly after his capture. Corrie and Betsy ended up in Ravensbruck concentration camp. Betsy died at the camp. Corrie was released due to an administrative error. Corrie told her story in the book *The Hiding Place.*[89] On a U.S. tour promoting the book in 1974, Corrie told of Betsy's prayers bringing peace to chaos.

The sisters were being held together with 700 prisoners in a room with a capacity for 200. Eventually, the overcrowding and awful conditions caused prisoners to riot. Betsy began to pray. At Corrie's encouragement, Betsy continued to pray, and the riot slowly ceased. Betsy prayed until the room fell silent and the chaos was replaced by an inexplicable blanket of peace. Betsy's prayer calmed the storm of chaos and violence in a room of 700 prisoners. The prayers of one woman and her sister's agreement appropriated peace from the kingdom of God and transported it into the real world. Each day at Ravensbruck. Corrie preached the gospel of Jesus to the prisoners.

God uses the heart labor of his agents, regardless of circumstances, to achieve his objectives of life, peace, and growth. The heart labors of prayer and agreement receive a wage of peace. Peace facilitates the preaching of the gospel so that all have a chance to hear the truth.[90]

Applications

The first application of heart labor is to pray for good government. According to 1 Timothy, I am obligated to pray for good government. To be effective, prayers should be offered in agreement with a local community of Christ-followers, according to the will of God. The purpose of the prayer is to bring a measure of peace so that the gospel can be preached and everyone has a chance to choose Jesus. One measure to evaluate what type of government is good is the one that delivers peace, life, and growth to its citizens. I am not instructed to trust in any real economy governmental leader. I only see the exterior. Further, I am told to be wary of the leaven of Herod.[91] I am wary of government leaders in part because of the corruption wrought by religious diplomacy. I simply trust God sets up one leader and takes down another for his sovereign purpose.[92] I pray for all real economy government leaders that they would do the will of God, which is to promote peace, life, and growth.

The second application is to manage businesses according to what God sees and not what man sees. I am prone, like the prophet Samuel, to look on the outside rather than the heart. However, I possess the heart capital of the Holy Spirit. With the counsel of the Holy Spirit, I can see things in people other business managers cannot. I have hired and promoted people left behind by others. Many have gone on to great success. The Holy Spirit can reveal things about a candidate and co-worker that others are not able to perceive.

Notes

1 Federal Reserve Bank of St. Louis. (2022, May 10). *Economic Lowdown Video Series* (Episode 6). The Federal Reserve, Federal Reserve Bank of St. Louis. https://www.stlouisfed.org/education/economic-lowdown-video-series/episode-6-circular-flow

2 1 Corinthians 3:5-9.

3 Federal Reserve Bank of St. Louis. (2022, May 10). *Economic Lowdown Video Series* (Episode 6). The Federal Reserve, Federal Reserve Bank of St. Louis. https://www.stlouisfed.org/education/economic-lowdown-video-series/episode-6-circular-flow.

4 Ezekiel 37:1-14, especially verses 5, 6 and 14.

5 New American Standard Bible, 1971, 2 Corinthians 3:10. Romans 2:6. New American Standard Bible, 1971, Psalm 62:2. Proverbs 24:12.

6 Philippians 2:12.

7 Mark 12:31.

8 Matthew 6:9.

9 Mark 6:7. Luke 10:1.

10 Matthew 18:19-20.

11 Sharma, A., Pillai, D. R., Lu, M., Doolan, C., Leal, J., Kim, J., & Hollis, A. (2020). Impact of isolation precautions on quality of life: a meta-analysis. *Journal of Hospital Infection, 105*(1), 35-42. http://dx.doi.org/10.1016/j.jhin.2020.02.004.

[12] Joseph, S. (2020). Isolation and Mental Health: The Psychological Impact of COVID-19 Lockdown on Children. *Mukt Shabd Journal, 9*(8), 399-405.
[13] New American Standard Bible, 1971, Acts 13:22. 1 Samuel 13:14.
[14] New American Standard Bible, 1971, Psalm 5:7.
[15] New American Standard Bible, 1971, Psalms 9:14.
[16] Psalm chapter 139.
[17] Stott, J. (2014). *The Message of the Sermon on the Mount* (p. 4). InterVarsity Press.
[18] Keener, C. S., & Walton, J. H. (Eds.). (2016). *NIV, Cultural Backgrounds Study Bible: Bringing to Life the Ancient World of Scripture* (p. 1678). Zondervan.
[19] Romans 12:1. Romans 12:9-21.
[20] Stott, J. (2014). *The message of Romans: God's good news for the world* (pp. 330-337). InterVarsity Press.
[21] Hebrews chapter 11.
[22] Hebrews 11:17-22. Genesis 15:6. Romans chapter 4. New American Standard Bible, 1971, Galatians 3:6-8.
[23] Sumney, Jerry L. (2007) *The Book of Tobit. In Saint Mary's Press College Study Bible,* 587-88. Winona, MN: Saint Mary's Press., Tobit 12:8. "Prayer with fasting is good, and so is giving to the poor with righteousness".
[24] Blomberg, C. L. (1992). *Matthew: An exegetical and theological exposition of Holy Scripture* (Vol. 22, p. 113)). B&H Publishing Group.
[25] Lewis, C. S. (1939). Learning in War-time. *The Weight of Glory and Other Addresses,* 47-63. http://www.orcuttchristian.org/Lewis_Learning%20in%20War-Time.pdf
[26] Stott, J. (2014). *The Message of the Sermon on the Mount* (p. 114). InterVarsity Press.
[27] New American Standard Bible, 1971, Psalm 35:13.
[28] New American Standard Bible, 1971, Leviticus chapter 16.
[29] Ezra chapter 8.
[30] New American Standard Bible, 1971, Matthew 9:15. New American Standard Bible, 1971, Luke 5:35.
[31] Stott, J. (2014). *The Message of the Sermon on the Mount* (pp. 117-119). InterVarsity Press.
[32] Isaiah 58:6-11.
[33] Grubb, N. (2014). *Rees Howells, Intercessor.* The Lutterworth Press.
[34] Omartian, S. (2007). *The Power of a Praying® Wife.* Harvest House Publishers.
[35] Franklin, J. (2014). *Fasting: Opening the Door to a Deeper, More Intimate, More Powerful Relationship with God.* Charisma Media.
[36] Daniel 2:21.
[37] Acts chapter 26.
[38] New American Standard Bible, 1971, 2 Kings chapter 5.
[39] Kelly, C. (2006). *The Roman Empire: a very short introduction* (p. 79). OUP Oxford. http://dx.doi.org/10.1093/actrade/9780192803917.001.0001.
[40] Prince, D. (2002). *Shaping history through prayer and fasting* (p. 42). Whitaker House.
[41] Prince, D. (2002). *Shaping history through prayer and fasting* (p. 42). Whitaker House.
[42] Piketty, T. (2014). *Capital in the twenty-first century* (p. 25). Harvard University Press. http://dx.doi.org/10.4159/9780674369542.
[43] Isaiah 9:6-7.
[44] Piketty, T. (2020). *Capital and ideology* (p. 8). Harvard University Press. http://dx.doi.org/10.4159/9780674245075.

[45] Luke 10:2. Matthew 9:38.
[46] New American Standard Bible, 1971, Matthew 23:11. Luke 22:6.
[47] Matthew 5:14-16.
[48] Elvidge, C. D., Baugh, K. E., Kihn, E. A., Kroehl, H. W., Davis, E. R., & Davis, C. W. (1997). Relation between satellite observed visible-near infrared emissions, population, economic activity and electric power consumption. *International Journal of Remote Sensing, 18*(6), 1373-1379. http://dx.doi.org/10.1080/014311697218485.
[49] Hebrews 11:6.
[50] 1 Timothy 2:4.
[51] 1 Corinthians 1:2. Galatians 1:3.
[52] New American Standard Bible, 1971, Isaiah 61:3.
[53] Missionaries of Charity. (2022, September). About Us. https://missionariesofcharity.org/
[54] 1 Corinthians 9:24.
[55] New American Standard Bible, 1971, Ecclesiastes 9:10.
[56] Stott, J. (2014). *The Message of the Sermon on the Mount* (p. 106). InterVarsity Press.
[57] New American Standard Bible, 1971, Romans 6:23.
[58] Stott, J. (2014). *The Message of the Sermon on the Mount* (p. 186). InterVarsity Press.
[59] Cartwright, M. (2013, November 1) Slavery in the Roman World. *World History Encyclopedia.* https://www.worldhistory.org/article/629/slavery-in-the-roman-world/
[60] Keener, C. S., & Walton, J. H. (Eds.). (2016). *NIV, Cultural Backgrounds Study Bible: Bringing to Life the Ancient World of Scripture* (p. 2033). Zondervan.
[61] New American Standard Bible, 1971, Genesis 31:7. Genesis 31:41.
[62] Leviticus 19:13. Malachi 3:5. Proverbs 3:28.
[63] New American Standard Bible, 1971, John 4:34-39
[64] Genesis 15:6. Romans 4:3. Romans 4:9. Romans 4:22. Galatians 3:6. Hebrews chapter 11.
[65] New American Standard Bible, 1971, Joshua 13:22.
[66] Schweizer, E. (1975). *The good news according to Matthew* (pp. 252-254). Westminster John Knox Press.
[67] Titus 3:5-7.
[68] New American Standard Bible, 1971, Psalm 112. New American Standard Bible, 1971, Psalm 92.
[69] Romans 4:16-17.
[70] Stott, J. (2014). *The Message of the Sermon on the Mount* (p. 132). InterVarsity Press.
[71] Philippians 4:10-20.
[72] Luke 6:38.
[73] Matthew 17:27.
[74] John 2:1-12. Matthew chapter 14. Mark chapter 6. Mark chapter 8.
[75] Deuteronomy chapter 11. New American Standard Bible, 1971, 2 Chronicles 4:9-10.
[76] Hebrews 12:2.
[77] John 4:36.
[78] Romans 12:1. Isaiah 43:7.
[79] 1 Samuel 13:14.
[80] Acts 13:22.
[81] Dion, K., Berscheid, E., & Walster, E. (1972). What is beautiful is good. *Journal of personality and social psychology, 24*(3), 285. http://dx.doi.org/10.1037/h0033731.
[82] Bóo, F. L., Rossi, M. A., & Urzúa, S. S. (2013). The labor market return to an attractive face: Evidence from a field experiment. *Economics Letters, 118*(1), 170-172.

[83] Ruffle, B. J., & Shtudiner, Z. E. (2015). Are good-looking people more employable?. *Management Science, 61*(8), 1760-1776. http://dx.doi.org/10.1287/mnsc.2014.1927.
[84] Böckerman, P., & Vainiomäki, J. (2013). Stature and life-time labor market outcomes: Accounting for unobserved differences. *Labour Economics, 24*, 86-96. http://dx.doi.org/10.1016/j.labeco.2013.06.003.
[85] Feingold, A. (1992). Good-looking people are not what we think. *Psychological bulletin, 111*(2), 304. http://dx.doi.org/10.1037/0033-2909.111.2.304.
[86] Isaiah 53:2-3.
[87] Isaiah 52:14
[88] James 2:3-9.
[89] Ten Boom, C., Sherrill, E., & Sherrill, J. (2006). *The hiding place.* Chosen Books.
[90] 1 Timothy 2:1-4.
[91] Mark 8:15.
[92] New American Standard Bible, 1971, Psalm 75.

Chapter 15

Territory

Types and importance

Territory is derived from the Latin roots *terra* and *torium*. *Terra* means land and *torium* means belonging to. The words were first used to refer to the small-scale ownership of land by a town or community.[1] In the real economy, territory has come to refer to geographical areas belonging to nations. Real economy businesses and individual churches, except for the Vatican, are not intrinsically territorial in the sense of geopolitics.[2] An exclusively nation-centered narrative of territory would limit this analysis, however.[3]

This chapter studies the territories of interest for *The Theory of the Kingdom*. *Terra* refers to more than physical land. Following an article by Andrea Brighenti, I choose to study territories as "working concepts," with tangible and intangible dimensions.[4] The two territories of interest are the kingdom of God and the real economy. Humankind may someday become multi-planetary, at which point this chapter may need an update. For now, tangible real economy territory is defined as physical land on the earth. Intangible real economy territory includes intellectual space, emotional space, and spiritual space.

Real economy territory is included within the kingdom of God.[5] However, the real economy is distinct given the created order by which God, at present, relates to humanity. The boundary between the two territories is the messianic membrane. The God-given order governs how relationships and resources move across the territorial border. Christ-followers are called "Ambassadors for Christ."[6] Any person who has been reconciled to God through Jesus is now an ambassador for the kingdom of God in the real economy realm.

Land is highly valued

This analysis of territory begins with physical land. Land is the scarcest type of territory. The word kingdom is a concatenation of king and domain. If there is no physical domain, there is no kingdom. Many people devote their lives to land care. Terms for land care professionals include agronomists, cartographers, and pedologists. A pedologist is a soil expert, not to be confused with an edaphologist, who is a soil expert with a particular focus on plant growth. Some people experience anxiety over land scarcity and environmental sustainability. Fear of an environmental cataclysm is called eco-anxiety. Pope Francis is a land-lover. The pontiff calls Earth our sister "Mother Earth."[7] Pope Francis' reference is to Francis of Assisi and the canticle of the creatures.

Humankind has a love for land that may be irrational at times. A behavioral analysis of real estate prices suggests the market is subject to momentum effects. Up to 80% of future real estate price changes can be explained by the prior year's price change.[8] Individuals fight over land. I was once sued for adverse possession of a small sliver of my land. I dutifully fought the claim. Governments fight with citizens over land use. Nations fight each other over land. Russia annexed Eastern Ukraine in the mid-2010s and took the fight for land further west in the 2020s.

Humans aren't the only species to fight over land. Animals, large and small, fight over land as well. Sarah Foltz and a research team in the journal *Behavioral Ecology* detailed the territorial fight of song sparrows over food. The fight of the song sparrows is more intense in urban settings. The song sparrows may not have received the message the meek shall inherit the earth.[9]

Land is scarce. Businesses use land. Families use land. Land is not just scarce; it is important. God made land for real economy use and enjoyment.[10] Inheritance of land is the subject of much of the story of ancient Israel.[11] Jesus considered the value of land in the same context as the value of family relationships.[12]

Intangible mental and spiritual territory is also valuable

Territory is also intangible. Intellectual capital, including patents and thought leadership, are part of a dimension called mental space.[13] Emotional territory can be conceived of as an individual's sphere of "action and experience."[14] When the personal sphere is stimulated or breached, an individual will exhibit emotions. Businesses stake out emotional space of a different sort. Consumer products and brands may be associated with particular feelings and consumer utility.[15] The Bible speaks of spiritual territory. In the kingdom era, physical battles of the Old Testament are transmuted into spiritual spaces. "For our struggle is not against flesh and blood, but against the rulers, against the powers, against the world forces of this darkness, against the spiritual *forces* of wickedness in the heavenly places."[16] Kingdom agency is not oriented to taking up weapons over physical land. Agents are ambassadors of the kingdom economy, speaking truth and arresting corruption, advancing one heart at a time.

The value of territory

God places a high value on land. *The Theory of the Kingdom* assumes God created the earth. God related to the Israelite people through a provision of land and he delivered the promised land to the Israelite people.[17] Joel 2:18

says God is passionate about his land. He uses it as needed, increasing or inhibiting its productivity for his economic purposes.

Humans seek to acquire land. Land represents resources and power. Land also represents current and future prosperity. An extensive review of real estate returns showed land returns beat bond returns and sometimes reach the same level as stock returns. However, buying land improves risk-adjusted portfolio returns as land prices and stock prices don't always move together.[18] Governments seek to acquire land and also tax private landholdings. Land is a prerequisite to any significant business. Even modern-day high-technology companies, which prosper based on intangible capital and territory, invest in land. One of the most valuable businesses of the twenty-first century, Apple Inc., once invested $5 billion in new headquarters buildings and owned land and buildings worth more than $30 billion.[19]

Interest rates heavily influence the value of real economy land. Interest rates are, in turn, influenced by inflation and inflation expectations.[20] Inflation is the change in the general level of prices. High inflation results in high interest rates which reduce the value of land and the incentive for investment. The growth objectives of the real economy and kingdom economy are both inhibited by an imbalance of supply and demand which causes inflation.

Inflation was a significant economic issue in ancient times. A siege on the city of Samaria caused prices to skyrocket and humans coped by engaging in vile survival practices such as cannibalism. At the height of the siege, I estimate the price of a donkey head was between $500 and $1000. God's intervention and appropriation of new supply for Samaria resulted in a snapback of supply. Prices fell from one day to the next and economic life was restored.[21]

Mosaic-era land ownership, land use, and land values were heavily influenced by inflation and interest rates. John Anderson details the four types of property covered by the Mosaic law, including raw land.[22] Land was not sold in perpetuity in the Old Testament. The right of redemption and the law of jubilee meant each family was guaranteed a future economic base. For a family unit that held a perpetual right of redemption on a particular territory the value of the territory was high. Incorporating the range of long-run interest rates presented in chapter ten, the value of $1 of farming cash flow from land owned in perpetuity would have been $5 when interest rates were high, $17 when interest rates were normal and up to $100 when interest rates were low.[23] Economic policies that support stable, appreciating land values and steady supply growth are part of good government.

Intangible mental and spiritual territory is most highly valued

As valuable as physical territory is, intangible territory is more valuable and it is unlimited. The amount of physical land is fixed. Land may be made more productive but the total land mass is constant. New intangible mental territory is staked out each year. The United States Patent and Trademark Office grants hundreds of thousands of new patents each year.[24] The new patents represent new inventions and innovations that have the promise of improving life in the real economy. New scientific discoveries and new business innovations are part of the desire of God for humankind.[25]

Spiritual territory is the most valuable type of intangible territory. In the messianic era, kingdom economy competition is over spiritual territory, not physical territory. Spiritual territorial battles influence real economy outcomes but spiritual battles are not won or lost with real economy tactics.[26] Economic productivity in the kingdom of God requires taking spiritual territory and using it for the production of life, peace, and growth.

Economic productivity in the kingdom of God requires taking spiritual territory and using it for the production of life, peace, and growth.

Jesus has authority over all territory.[27] Paul's writing in Colossians on the supremacy of Jesus over all creation is an ancient hymn in two stanzas.[28] It is a form of rhythmic, musical prose praising Jesus as Lord over all visible and invisible territory.[29] Jesus has given authority over the spiritual territory to his agents to teach the principles of the kingdom.[30] The effect of teaching is to influence mental, emotional, and spiritual space, more so than physical space.

Spiritual space has multiple dimensions. Some ancient Jewish sources diverge on the number of heavens. The most common estimate of the number of levels in heaven was either three or seven.[31] The number of levels is not crucial for *The Theory of the Kingdom*. Rather, understanding the basic distinctions of spiritual space can help motivate higher productivity. The three-heaven view in antiquity included the air, a second higher intermediate realm, and the highest heaven. The air includes the atmosphere of the earth and is occupied by creatures such as birds. A first level heaven realm of air has significant implications for environmental stewardship. Skipping ahead for a moment to the third level, called God's highest heaven, is a realm of righteousness, holiness, and beauty. The throne of God is there and a variety of creatures.[32]

Action is in second level spiritual territory

The second level was understood to include angels and territorial spiritual powers with forms of spiritual fortresses. The second level is where the action is for agents in the kingdom economy. The second level is where the spiritual weapons, given in the book of Ephesians, are effective. Truth, righteousness, the gospel of peace, faith, personal salvation, and knowledge of the Bible are weapons used to destroy spiritual strongholds.[33] The weapons are deployed with prayer and perseverance.

The strongholds I attack are wrong ways of thinking in myself, others and organizations that create patterns of destructive behavior and corrupt business practices. My tactic is not to physically oppose a bad actor. Rather, I pray and persevere, in agreement with other kingdom agents, until the thinking changes and real economy outcomes improve. It is simple to tell when real economy outcomes improve. Good output promotes life, peace, and growth. Bad output produces conflict, corruption of individuals, and corruption of the environment. I may be tempted to become impatient with a spiritual approach to real economy problems. Regardless, it is the mechanism by which the kingdom economy acquires new territory.

The human heart is territory. It can be filled and defended, and it grows

Though not defined as such in antiquity, to further the analysis along the lines of the model of human agency, I add the territory of the human heart as ground zero. The heart is territory because it is a place of residence, storage, and labor. God puts his Holy Spirit into the heart of a human who requests it.[34] The heart is a repository of various types of heart capital.[35] It can be occupied and filled up with good, for good actions, or with evil, for evil actions. The good or evil it is filled with is activated by heart labor to produce products. Good capital and good heart labors produce peace and life in the real economy.

Heart territory is not fixed. Falling in love with a person, developing a new passion, or having children all cause the heart to grow. Every heart can grow. Dr. Seuss wrote even the Grinch's heart can grow.[36] Finally, the human heart is fought over. In political circles, the battle over hearts and minds is called "soft power."[37] The essence of the territorial battle is over the human heart, as ground zero. My weapons of defense and offense in holding and taking territory are spiritual. Spiritual territory is not fixed.

Groups occupy spiritual territory

Spiritual territory is also group level territory. It is known to be group level in part because kingdom authority is given to more than one person. There is spiritual power in agreement.[38] Kingdom agents are known by their love for one another.[39] The trinity of the Father, Son, and Holy Spirit work together in unison. There is an office of group-level leadership in the gifts of the Holy Spirit.[40]

Pope John Paul II and Poles cracked open their territory

Spiritual leadership and group influence on a territory is well illustrated by Pope John Paul II's dramatic visit to Poland. Karol Wojtyla was elected Pope on October 16, 1978. At the time, Poland was under the rule of communist Russia. In June 1979, the new Pope visited Poland, his homeland. Upon arrival at the airport in Warsaw, the Pope kissed the ground and then embarked on an ambitious tour of the country. His prepared remarks are available on the Vatican website.[41] The third sentence of his first public discourse off the plane included the phrase, "I express my esteem for the State Authorities and I again renew my cordial gratitude for the kind attitude towards my visit to Poland." His statement reflected the tone and teaching of Paul in 1 Timothy 2. The Pope went on to speak of his purposes of rapprochement, collaboration among nations, and peace in the contemporary world.

The State Authorities of whom the Pope graciously spoke was the communist party. The communist leadership served the Soviet Union. The leadership had sent a memo to teachers, according to Wall Street Journal columnist Peggy Noonan, stating the Communist party and teachers in Poland must counter the activities of the Pope and Catholic Church in Poland by more intensely working "to atheize the youth" of the country. The communist authorities understood the true battle was spiritual and was being fought over the most valuable territory in Poland, the hearts of each citizen, particularly the young people.

At the time of the Pope's visit, the population of Warsaw was estimated at 1,600,000.[42] A crowd of 1,000,000 participated in the Pope's public mass. Over 60% of the city came out to hear the gospel of peace preached. The mass extended beyond the planned time and the crowd spontaneously began to chant and sing, "We Want God." The inhabitants of the capital of Poland united to reject a godless future. As Peggy Noonan noted, communism didn't fall overnight. It was November 9, 1989, when the Berlin Wall fell. However, the war taking place in spiritual territory turned that day on the efforts of united hearts under the leadership of Pope John Paul II.

Land use and productivity

In the real economy, land value is higher the closer the plot is to a city center or populated coastline. The theory and model of patterns of land use in a city are provided by William Alonso.[43] The three main types of real economy land use include agricultural, commercial/industrial, and residential. An individual family is happiest when it finds an equilibrium of the largest possible size of property within the constraints of desired consumption and the distance from the center of the city. Agricultural, commercial and industrial choices regarding land are arrived at in the same way, through trade-offs of size, location and costs.[44] Land can be made more productive over time. At some point, land use can become too intense and deplete the underlying resources.

The management of land resources for the collective good is the subject of Elinor Ostrom's controversial book *Governing the Commons.*[45] In some respects, Ostrom's book attacks current private property rights[46] in the same way as Piketty's *Capital and Ideology in the 21st Century.* The similarity I see in the two books is a message humans will deplete an underlying resource for maximum profit. It is a straightforward conclusion of any time value of money calculation, particularly when required returns are high. The challenge with both books, concerning *The Theory of the Kingdom* is a community stakeholder construct[47] does little to counteract the human impulse to serve money. The impulse to serve money will remain in any new property rights regime. So far, an attempt at stakeholder capitalism by large U.S. firms has been a failure.[48]

The assumption of *The Theory of the Kingdom* is humankind, in its sinful state, is likely to choose to serve money rather than God. Serving money breeds corruption and destroys land resources, regardless of real economy governance. In the case of real economy land, as in real economy capital, the best hope for a better future is kingdom agents motivated by the love of God.

Kingdom land use tactics cover tangible land and intangible territory. In the kingdom economy, the owners acquire or borrow real territory as required. The clearest example of land acquisition is the Israelite people settling in the land east of the Jordan River. The agency assignment was to love and serve God and be obedient to the law.[49] When the Israelites were living in Egypt, the region of Goshen was *borrowed* as a place to increase in number.[50] Notably, the Israelites didn't just live there. They built homes in Goshen. Life in Goshen can be linked to the instructions to the exiles in Jeremiah 29. In each case, the agency assignment was to acquire property, build houses, increase in number and prosper. The first principle of land use is to invest to flourish and grow, whether property use is permanent or temporary.

> The first principle of kingdom economy territory use is to invest to flourish and grow, whether property use is permanent or temporary.

The construct of borrowed territory is especially relevant to the messianic era. If I am part of the kingdom of God I become, as a first-order matter, an agent in the kingdom economy rather than the real economy. At his trial, Jesus told Pilate, "My kingdom is not of this world. If My kingdom were of this world, My servants would be fighting so that I would not be handed over to the Jews; but as it is, My kingdom is not of this realm."[51] The conclusion of the interrogation over the word *truth* is important. Jesus stated his kingdom was a kingdom of truth. "Pilate knew his business and to discuss the nature of truth was not part of it."[52] The second principle of kingdom land use is to reveal the truth. Each land use principle has a real economy and kingdom economy application. Truth can be revealed through how land is used for real economy productivity. Truth is also required to be productive with spiritual territory.

The second principle is to use territory to reveal truth.

Inappropriate land use includes inactivity and corruption. A parable of inactivity includes the rich fool of Luke 12. Halvor Moxnes' analysis notes in Luke's time being rich was associated with land ownership. Further, the economic unit of analysis was a family rather than an individual.[53] It is likely the inheritance dispute was over land. The parable Jesus tells in response directly addresses greed related to property. In the parable, a rich man is so prosperous he can't store all his grain. The rich man tore down his barns and built bigger barns to store his vast hoard. He planned to retire, sell down his inventory, and live the good life. The end of the story is the man died the same night his new barns went up. The caution against inactivity is strengthened by a command in a different story to work until the owner returns.[54] Land is valuable. The land I have authority over must be worked for a purpose other than monetary gain. Inactivity or greed will likely result in the reallocation of my resources to a more productive agent or group of agents.

The third principle is land must not lay fallow.

Obtaining and holding territory

In the real economy, land is purchased with money. The price is set at auction or by a special relationship with an owner. In the kingdom economy territory is purchased by righteousness obtained through heart labors such as faith in Jesus, obedience, prayer, fasting, and worship. The Old Testament character Jabez prayed for a larger territory and since he was honorable God granted his request.[55] Bruce Wilkinson's best-selling book *The Prayer of Jabez* details the modern-day utility of prayer in taking territory.[56] Faith and obedience receive a credit of righteousness. Abraham's faith was credited as righteousness. Jesus' obedience in water baptism was to fulfill righteousness and, "complete everything that forms part of a relationship of obedience to God."[57] A recurring theme of Jesus' teaching is kingdom agents must exhibit righteousness that exceeds outward acts of piety.[58] Faith is messiah Jesus is the credit of righteousness exceeding the Pharisees, by which I take territory to use for peace, life, and growth.

Caleb and Joshua are examples of faithful servants credited with righteousness in obtaining promised territory. When the Israelites reached the western border of the promised land, Moses sent 12 leaders to spy out the land called Canaan. The land had been set aside for Israel. 10 of the 12 spies returned to report the people living in Canaan were too strong to be conquered. Caleb agreed the inhabitants were strong but recommended moving to take over the land. Caleb believed God would be with them. Faith is not based on a made-up report about real economy conditions. It is based on an accurate report and obedience and trust that God can do what he has promised regardless of the report. The 10 spies afraid of proceeding died in the desert. Only two, Joshua and Caleb, took possession of the promised land.[59]

Valuable territory has to be protected. Territory can be sold for money. Territory can also be lost to an attack. In the kingdom economy, the source of territorial challenge is the love of money and the devil. According to the hierarchy of temptation, I choose between God and money. To hold territory, I resist the devil[60] and repeatedly choose to serve God. I say repeatedly, as the account of Jesus' temptation in Luke closes by noting the devil only left for a later opportunity to tempt him. The kingdom economy principle is agents defend valuable spiritual territory.

> The fourth principle is land is acquired and held through obedience to the owner.

Applications

The first application is in the form of beachfront land use. At the time of this writing, my family and I live next to a beach in the mid-Atlantic region of the United States. It is a public beach. The beach does not have a shower or a bathroom. Many of our friends frequent the beach. They are all welcome to use the outdoor shower and the bathrooms inside the house, whether we are home or not. I expect we would welcome pretty much any sandy passerby. The principal is to use our land as intensively as possible to bring any small measure of life and peace into the real economy.

The second application integrates the chapters on heart capital, heart labor, and territory. I analyze behaviors I would like to change along the lines of kingdom economy resources. Imagine for the moment a parent is regularly shouting at their child. The shouting does not produce peace in the child's life or the home. The shouting may be justified or it may not be. Justification, according to parenting tradition, is not important. The key point is this particular parent knows, by the witness of the Holy Spirit, that the shouting should stop. If it were as simple as knowing, that would be the end of it. Typically, it is not that simple. The analysis of the shouting proceeds on a three-step path. First, evaluate if shouting is a heart capital problem. Perhaps the parent is not spending time reading the Bible or in the Christian community being taught how to live. The parent's incoming good capital may be insufficient to displace the incoming stream of social media rage. Second, it may be a heart labor problem. Perhaps the parent does not spend time in prayer for the child or does not have a person to whom he can confess his shouting. Third, there may be a territorial problem. The parent may have learned a thought pattern that triggers shouting. Thought patterns may be learned from a parent, a hostile teacher, or even a friend. A wrong thought pattern is a stronghold. A stronghold can be torn down with the spiritual assets of warfare, including the word of God and the witness of the gospel of peace. I have found I have been able to produce more life and peace in my family and community by employing a resource-based analysis.

Notes

[1] Wendt, A. (1999). *Social theory of international politics* (Vol. 67, p. 211). Cambridge University Press. http://dx.doi.org/10.1017/CBO9780511612183.

[2] Wendt, A. (1999). *Social theory of international politics* (Vol. 67, p. 211). Cambridge University Press. http://dx.doi.org/10.1017/CBO9780511612183.

[3] Elden, S. (2010). Thinking territory historically. *Geopolitics, 15*(4), 757-761. http://dx.doi.org/10.1080/14650041003717517.

[4] Brighenti, A. (2006). On territory as relationship and law as territory. *Canadian Journal of Law and Society/La Revue Canadienne Droit et Société, 21*(2), 65-86. http://dx.doi.org/10.1017/S0829320100008954.

[5] Munroe, M. (2011). *Understanding Your Place in God's Kingdom: Your Original Purpose for Existence* (p. 115). Destiny Image Publishers.

[6] 2 Corinthians 5:17-21.

[7] The Holy Father, Francis. (2015, May 24). On Care For Our Common Home. *The Holy See.* https://www.vatican.va/content/dam/francesco/pdf/encyclicals/documents/papa-francesco_20150524_enciclica-laudato-si_en.pdf

[8] Salzman, D., & Zwinkels, R. C. (2017). Behavioral real estate. *Journal of Real Estate Literature, 25*(1), 77-106. http://dx.doi.org/10.1080/10835547.2017.12090455.

[9] Matthew 5:5

[10] Jeremiah 29:4-7

[11] Anderson, J. E. (2005). A biblical and economic analysis of jubilee property provisions. *Faith and Economics, 46,* 25-41.

[12] Matthew 19:29.

[13] Tomasi, J. (2012). Free market fairness. In *Free Market Fairness.* Princeton University Press. http://dx.doi.org/10.23943/princeton/9780691144467.001.0001.

[14] Hansson, M. G. (2007). *The private sphere: an emotional territory and its agent* (Vol. 15, p. 3). Springer Science & Business Media.

[15] Woods, R. (2004). Exploring the emotional territory for brands. *Journal of Consumer Behaviour: An International Research Review, 3*(4), 388-403. http://dx.doi.org/10.1002/cb.150.
[16] Ephesians 6:12.
[17] New American Standard Bible, 1971, Joshua 21:43-45.
[18] Norman, E., Sirmans, S., & Benjamin, J. (1995). The historical environment of real estate returns. *Journal of Real Estate Portfolio Management, 1*(1), 1-24. http://dx.doi.org/10.1080/10835547.1995.12089516.
[19] Apple Inc., (2021, October 29). SEC Form 10-K (p. 40). *Apple Inc.* chrome-extension://efaidnbmnnnibpcajpcglclefindmkaj/https://d18rn0p25nwr6d.cloudfront.net/CIK-0000320193/42ede86f-6518-450f-bc88-60211bf39c6d.pdf. The value quoted is land and buildings, gross value, plus the value of leasehold improvements.
[20] Tanzi, V. (1980). Inflationary expectations, economic activity, taxes, and interest rates. *The American Economic Review, 70*(1), 12-21.
[21] New American Standard Bible, 1971, 2 Kings chapter 7.
[22] Anderson, J. E. (2005). A biblical and economic analysis of jubilee property provisions. *Faith and Economics, 46*, 25-41.
[23] The high case historically was 20% rates and the value of $1 of farm income would be $1/0.2 = $5. In the median case the value is $1/0.06 = $17, and in the low case $1/0.01 = $100. It is a assumed the real productivity of the farm is constant at $1 of real cash flow.
[24] US Patent and Trademark Office. (2021, May 31) U.S. Patent Statistics Chart Calendar Years 1963-220. U.S. *Patent and Trademark Office, Patent Technology Monitoring Team (PTMT)*. https://www.uspto.gov/web/offices/ac/ido/oeip/taf/us_stat.htm
[25] New American Standard Bible, 1971, Proverbs 25:2.
[26] Ephesians 6:12.
[27] Mark 10:29. Matthew 28:18.
[28] Lincoln, A. T. (2004). *Paradise now and not yet: studies in the role of the heavenly dimension in Paul's thought with special reference to his eschatology* (Vol. 43). Cambridge University Press. http://dx.doi.org/10.1017/CBO9780511555008.
[29] Keener, C. S., & Walton, J. H. (Eds.). (2016). *NIV, Cultural Backgrounds Study Bible: Bringing to Life the Ancient World of Scripture* (p. 2157). Zondervan.
[30] Matthew 28:19-20.
[31] Keener, C. S., & Walton, J. H. (Eds.). (2016). *NIV, Cultural Backgrounds Study Bible: Bringing to Life the Ancient World of Scripture* (p. 2131). Zondervan.
[32] Hebrews 8:1-5. Revelation 4:10. The prophet Ezekiel's visions.
[33] Ephesians 6:14-18.
[34] New American Standard Bible, 1971, Ezekiel 36:27. New American Standard Bible, 1971, 2 Timothy 1:14. 1 John 2:27. Revelation 3:20.
[35] 1 Corinthians 3:16. Luke 6:45.
[36] Seuss. (2015). *How the Grinch Stole Christmas!*. Random House Books for Young Readers.
[37] Berenskoetter, F., & Williams, M. J. (Eds.). (2007). *Power in world politics (p. 83)*. Routledge. http://dx.doi.org/10.4324/9780203944691.
[38] Matthew 18:19.
[39] John 13:35.
[40] Ephesians 4:11.
[41] Paul, John II, His Holiness. (1979, June 2). Apostolic Journey to Poland, Welcoming Ceremony in Warsaw. *The Holy See*. https://www.vatican.va/content/john-paul-ii/en/

speeches/1979/june/documents/hf_jp-ii_spe_19790602_polonia-varsavia-okecie-arrival.html

[42] Macrotrends. (2023, August 20). Warsaw, Poland Metro Area Population 1950-2022. *Macrotrends.* https://www.macrotrends.net/cities/22161/warsaw/population

[43] Alonso, W. (2013). Location and land use. In *Location and land use.* Harvard university press. http://dx.doi.org/10.4159/harvard.9780674730854.

[44] Turvey, R. (1964). Review of Location and land use by William Alonso. *American Economic Review, 54,* 844-845.

[45] Ostrom, E. (1990). *Governing the commons: The evolution of institutions for collective action.* Cambridge university press. http://dx.doi.org/10.1017/CBO9780511807763.

[46] Block, W. E. (2011). Review of Ostrom's governing the commons. *Libertarian papers, 3,* 1.

[47] Walljasper, J. (2011). Elinor Ostrom's 8 Principles for Managing A Commons. *On the Commons, 446.*

[48] Bebchuk, L. A., & Tallarita, R. (2022). Will Corporations Deliver Value to All Stakeholders?. *Forthcoming, Vanderbilt Law Review, 75.* http://dx.doi.org/10.2139/ssrn.3899421.

[49] New American Standard Bible, 1971, Joshua 21:43 to 22:6.

[50] Genesis 47:27.

[51] John 18:36.

[52] Bruce, F. F. (1994). *The Gospel of John: Introduction, Exposition, Notes* (p. 354). Wm. B. Eerdmans Publishing.

[53] Moxnes, H. (2004). *The economy of the kingdom: Social conflict and economic relations in Luke's Gospel* (Vol. 23, pp. 56-57, p. 61). Wipf and Stock Publishers.

[54] Luke 19:13.

[55] New American Standard Bible, 1971, 1 Chronicles 4:10.

[56] Wilkinson, B. (2010). *The prayer of Jabez: Breaking through to the blessed life.* Multnomah.

[57] Blomberg, C. L. (1992). *Matthew: An exegetical and theological exposition of Holy Scripture* (Vol. 22, p. 81). B&H Publishing Group.

[58] Matthew 5:20.

[59] Numbers chapter 13. Numbers chapter 14.

[60] James 4:7.

Chapter 16

Information asymmetry

Owners and agents don't have the same information at all times. This chapter studies the effects of information gaps on kingdom economy agents. The term for owner-agent information gaps is asymmetry. Symmetry means an item has the same properties on either side of a partition. An item is asymmetrical when it appears differently based on the side of the partition from which it is viewed.

An example of an information partition is one that exists between the seller of a used car and a prospective buyer. The owner of a used car knows more about the car than a potential buyer. The buyer knows more about how much money they are willing and able to spend. To close the information gap and lower the purchase risk, a prospective buyer may spend time and money reading online reviews and searching accident records.

An information partition is also created when an owner delegates control to an agent. At the moment control is handed over, owners and agents have different information about the organization, including its performance and future prospects. Information asymmetry ("IA") creates uncertainty, raises transaction costs, and creates investment opportunities. An agent managing a business may know of an important new customer win before the owner. In order to close the information gap an owner may invest in systems to receive accurate and up-to-date information on the business. The owner invests to gather information in part because of a rational expectation the manager will report information in the most advantageous way possible. *Advantageous* means an agent will tend to report information in a way that maximizes their compensation.

Information asymmetry is different with God as the owner

Information asymmetry in the kingdom economy is unique. God is not like a real economy owner or buyer. God is all-knowing. Agents and buyers have limited knowledge. The owner has full knowledge at all times. An owner in the real economy transmits knowledge to keep agents oriented to making owners as much money as possible. God transmits information to his agents by the Holy Spirit because he loves each agent. God also transmits information to keep each agent engaged in growing the kingdom economy. Figure 16.1

provides an outline of some of the issues created by information asymmetry, how they are resolved and for what purpose information is acquired.

Figure 16.1. Information asymmetry ("IA") fundamentals are different across the messianic membrane.

	Real Economy	Kingdom Economy
	Messianic Membrane	
Source of IA	Buyers and sellers. Owners and agents.	Seller. Owner.
Resolution	Price. Investment in M,B & T.* Regulation. Communication.	Price. Investment in M,B, & T.* Created order. Communication.
Outcome	Maximum value. Inequities.	Maximum life, peace, and growth.

*M, B & T is monitoring, bonding, and testing. M, B & T are the subjects of subsequent chapters.

Figure 16.1 major message: Agents receive information to keep actions and intentions aligned with the owner's interests. In the real economy owners are interested in money. In the kingdom economy the owner is all-knowing. Motivated by love, the owner provides information to agents to keep each one engaged in maximizing life, peace, and growth. The information is provided by God's costly investment to bond agents into the realm of peace. God transmits information through the created natural order, signals in the real economy, and direct owner communications.

Information is valuable.

Michael Lewis' book *Moneyball: The Art of Winning an Unfair Game*[1] transformed professional sports from management by tradition-bound heuristics to management by data analysis. The book details the efforts of one Major League Baseball general manager to win with a relatively low payroll. In a professional league dominated by the large payroll of the New York Yankees, Oakland A's general manager Billy Beane invested time and money to create a data analytics-based informational advantage. Since *Moneyball*, data analytics has become essential to all sports, including speed skating[2] and synchronized swimming.[3] Reducing an information deficit or obtaining an information advantage has real economy value. In the aggregate, the investment to obtain information and profit from it helps markets and the economy.

Information asymmetry is costly.

In certain situations, information asymmetry can harm individuals and an economy. In a study of used cars and the "*economic costs of dishonesty,*"[4] George Akerlof considered four types of cars. There are new-good cars, new-bad cars, used-good cars, and used-bad cars. In the case of a new car, the seller doesn't have better information than the buyer. However, in the case of a used car, the seller has an advantage over the buyer. Further, if I own a good used car, I am less likely to be a seller. The market for used cars is, therefore, dominated by bad cars. The information asymmetry drives down the price of all used cars and also drives out the number of good used cars as owners of good cars don't want to sell at a discount to the real value.[5] The result is bad and good used cars sell at a similar price because the buyer doesn't know the difference.

In the case of an owner delegating authority to managers, information asymmetry results in agency costs. Owners and managers must agree on a mechanism to exchange information. Agreements may be voluntary or by coercion. The exchange of information requires an investment of time and money. The return on investment is a reduction in uncertainty (i.e., risk) for the owner and a better alignment of economic interests with the managers. The agreement to exchange information may be based on voluntary private contracts between owners and agents. Each side has information that will lower risk for the other side, maximizing incentives to invest and prosper. The benefit of exchanging information can be to the manager such that the manager would agree to voluntarily provide the owner with reports.[6]

Information gaps are costly

Price alone may not be effective in reducing information asymmetry to an acceptable level. In the example of used cars, the informational asymmetry causes a discount for bad used cars and good used cars, reducing the number of transactions and the overall value of the market. Used car sellers may offer a warranty to partially address the problem. Overall, bad sellers tend to drive out the good sellers. In financial markets, agents may lie about the true state of a business. Agents may defraud owners to enrich themselves. The cost of financial fraud is a deficit of trust in financial markets and a higher cost of investment capital for every business owner.

Business owners or agents may address the problems of information asymmetry by voluntarily agreeing on reporting standards. When the standards don't go far enough, and often in response to an economic crisis, governments may choose to regulate information disclosure. An unreliable used car is often called a *lemon*. Lemon laws have been passed to regulate the used car market, protect buyers, and promote more honest transactions. The United States government has passed several financial disclosure laws and regulations for the stock and bond markets. The Securities Acts of 1933 and 1934 followed the stock market crash of 1929. The Sarbanes-Oxley Act followed the dot-com technology stock bust, and it requires senior business managers to personally certify the accuracy of information contained in financial statements.[7]

Communication can be hindered by differences in language or religion. Information asymmetry increases between owners in different countries due to higher inter-country distance in terms of language and religion. The communication challenges increase uncertainty and lower investment. Diversity within a country improves the ability of owners to process information and raises foreign investment activity.[8] Reducing IA is worthwhile for a nation. The fair distribution of resources is often hindered when information is unequally distributed. A straightforward example concerns transparency in labor negotiations. Firms may hide information about their profits from employees to pay lower wages, to the detriment of the employees and the overall efficiency of the labor market.[9]

Prices transmit information to the uninformed

The real economy is organized by the information contained in prices. In the real economy, information asymmetry is reduced with market prices. Prices transmit information to the uninformed. I don't have much information about what the price of eggs should be. I don't know how much it costs to raise hens, collect eggs and distribute them to a grocery store. I don't need to know. I can easily discover the price of eggs. Based on the price of eggs and the price of other alternative foods, I can make consumption choices to make myself as gastronomically happy as possible. Prices influence the real economy by providing information to agents about the true condition of the market.[10] Prices give people information about where to invest for a good return.

Communication reduces the information gap

Successful communication reduces information asymmetry. Here I am referring to speaking that is not simply stating a price. Communication from one consumer to another transmits information about the social, emotional, or functional experience associated with a brand. Communication is particularly important with religious credence goods. Word of mouth is used to close information gaps regarding the intangible experience associated with credence goods.[11]

Information asymmetry cannot be eliminated in the real economy. Sanford Grossman and Joseph Stiglitz observe that perfect informational efficiency is never achieved in the real economy. Part of their proof is the popularity of arbitrage trading activity. Arbitrage trading is earning a return from risk-free trades. If there was no information asymmetry, there would be zero return in arbitrage trading.[12] Timing differences in information transmission and assimilation also make the elimination of information asymmetry difficult. Self-interest results in a constant search for an informational edge. Paradoxically, perhaps, the fact of information asymmetry in the real economy is the thing that allows a stable market equilibrium to exist.[13]

Kingdom economy and information asymmetry

The total elimination of information asymmetry is not optimal in the kingdom economy. If information asymmetry was zero, there would be very little incentive for an agent to search for information and zealously pursue owner-agent interaction. With complete information, relational intimacy and intensity is reduced. In the kingdom economy, God could choose to eliminate information asymmetry. It is obvious he does not. I was created for relational intimacy with the owner.

The informational key in the model of human agency is the owner knows everything and the agent does not. For the *Theory of the Kingdom*, I assume God is all-knowing. In the New American Standard Version of the Bible, Psalm 139 is subtitled *God's Omnipresence and Omniscience*. God is said to know my outward movements, my inward thoughts, my behavioral patterns, and even the words I will speak in the future. David writes, "such knowledge is too wonderful for me; It is too high, I cannot attain it."[14] The prophet Isaiah notes God's thoughts are far above my thoughts and God's methods well beyond my conception.[15] The things I think I know about God may be correct if based on the Bible and the witness of the Holy Spirit. However, like Job, the things I think about the owner may be entirely incorrect based on my past successes, sufferings, and biases.[16]

The owners know the agent better than the agent does. The agent doesn't even know all of their own biases and sins.[17] The owner knows everything regarding the potential future of the agent. There is no report the agent can make to the owner that would give the owner new information. All of the reduction in information asymmetry happens by informing agents and is for the benefit of agents.

The owner communicates extensively with agents

The owner informs agents in a large number of ways. Agents are informed by the price of Jesus' sacrifice, the cost of discipleship, by monitoring, bonding, testing, by the design of the universe, and the extensive communication of the word of God and the guidance of the Holy Spirit. Monitoring, bonding, and testing are the subjects of the next two chapters.

In advance of discussing how God transmits information, I want to raise an issue that is, at times, bothersome, particularly after a failure. If God is communicating with me, *why doesn't he give me more information to be more successful?* I propose one possible answer, by induction, in three parts.

First, at the point of peak career earnings, I decided to switch careers and go back to school. I had received enough information from the Holy Spirit to decide to enroll in a Ph.D. program. Based on my work experience, I assumed I would be successful in the program and the process would be about as difficult as working in the investment business. I was correct about the likelihood of earning a degree. I was incorrect about the level of difficulty. The research, math, and comprehensive exams were extremely challenging. If the Holy Spirit had given me a full picture of the difficulty *ex ante*, I may have chosen to stay exactly where I was. Evaluating it after the fact I am thankful I did not know the full picture. I gained a new level of relational intimacy with the owner. There were family and relationship benefits I didn't know were on the way. The benefit of additional intimacy with the owner is by itself worth far more than the difficulty.

The price was clearly posted and informs me of the cost of agency

My difficulties did not approach those of Job. However, Job's statement juxtaposing his hope in God against his current suffering makes more sense with each passing year.[18] It is rational to pray like Jabez and ask God for more land and to be free from pain.[19] However, when pain and suffering come it can increase hope rather than destroy it. The story of Job leads into the second part of the analysis. Price informs the kingdom economy.

> "The model is the simplest one in which prices perform a well-articulated role in conveying information from the informed to the uninformed."[20]

This quote by Sanford Grossman and Joseph Stiglitz applies to *The Theory of the Kingdom.* Observing prices is an efficient way for the uninformed to acquire information. I have previously argued in the law of proportion that the price to acquire spiritual credence goods is self-sacrifice. In a monopoly, the market equilibrium for a credence good occurs when the price is set at the average cost.[21] John's gospel says God gave his son Jesus so I could obtain eternal life. The posted price for peace with God is the life of Jesus. Isaiah says Jesus was acquainted with grief. Jesus tells the disciples he will suffer and die at the hands of religious authorities. Further, Jesus rebukes Peter for protesting against the plan of suffering. Jesus follows the rebuke by turning to the crowd and saying the price to become his follower is self-sacrifice.[22] Posting prices reduces information asymmetry.[23] The biblical account of the price Jesus paid to serve God fully informs me the price of effective agency is self-sacrifice. The outcome of Jesus' plan to transmit information was peace with God,[24] eternal life for anyone that would call on his name,[25] and the establishment of a kingdom that will grow continuously.[26]

Jesus' selective disclosure gives way to a full disclosure by agents

The third part of my analysis includes a survey of the gospel of Mark. New Testament scholar Craig Keener's survey of Mark reveals Jesus chose to supply information about his divinity in a way that precisely served his purposes.[27] The purpose of Jesus was noble. It was (is) the salvation of humankind. In the book of Mark, at times, Jesus healed people and told them to keep it a secret.[28] At other times, Jesus told a person delivered of a demon to tell everyone.[29] Jesus told Peter, James, and John to keep the transfiguration a secret until after his resurrection.[30] Jesus carefully managed the flow of information in part because his identity as *the King* of the Kingdom of God represented a direct threat to the Roman and Jewish authorities. Jesus knew he would suffer and die at their hands. However, he managed the information flow to control revelation about his kingdom so that he would fulfill all the requirements of his earthbound assignment. After Jesus was resurrected, the instruction changed to *go everywhere and tell everyone.*[31]

Several conditions inhibit communication. Owner-to-agent communication is blocked by factors identified in the hierarchy of temptation. In the gospel of Mark, the disciples focused on physiological needs and were unable to perceive Jesus as the owner of all resources. Communication is also blocked by a love of real economy, land and money.[32] Information processing can take time. One purpose of the two-stage healing of a blind man is to indicate kingdom of God information may be processed in stages.[33]

Application. Always be ready

According to prior research, information transmission is blocked by owner intervention and enhanced by owner communication.[34] In chapter four on communication, I discuss extensively the owner-to-agent communication plan. I will not repeat the details here. The communication plan is extensive and includes the Holy Spirit, the Bible, creation, and the testimony of other

Christ-followers. Credence goods are promoted through word-of-mouth customer testimonials and ratings. The strategy given by Peter in his letters is, therefore, likely to be effective, "always being ready to make a defense to everyone who asks you to give an account for the hope that is in you, yet with gentleness and reverence."[35]

During the messianic era, an effective agent will intensively seek to know as much as the owner will reveal. Revelation comes from faith and active searching. Additional revelation about the character and activities of the owner enables agents to be more effective. I can be satisfied with my incomplete knowledge, knowing it keeps me pursuing the owner, and it is for the good purpose of the owner and my good as well. A discussion of information asymmetry naturally leads to an analysis of agent monitoring, bonding, and testing.

Notes

[1] Lewis, M. (2004). Moneyball: The art of winning an unfair game. WW Norton & Company.

[2] Knobbe, A., Orie, J., Hofman, N., Van der Burgh, B., & Cachucho, R. (2017). Sports analytics for professional speed skating. Data Mining and Knowledge Discovery, 31(6), 1872-1902. http://dx.doi.org/10.1007/s10618-017-0512-3.

[3] He, L., & Luo, Q. (2021, January). The development and research of Chinese Artistic Swimming under the background of big data--compared with the world's top three teams. In 2021 International Conference on Information Technology and Contemporary Sports (TCS) (pp. 318-321). IEEE. http://dx.doi.org/10.1109/TCS52929.2021.00071.

[4] Akerlof, G. A. (1978). The market for "lemons": Quality uncertainty and the market mechanism. In Uncertainty in economics (pp. 235-251). Academic Press. http://dx.doi.org/10.1017/CBO9780511528248.007.

[5] Akerlof, G. A. (1978). The market for "lemons": Quality uncertainty and the market mechanism. In Uncertainty in economics (pp. 235-251). Academic Press. http://dx.doi.org/10.1017/CBO9780511528248.007.

[6] J Jensen, M. C., & Meckling, W. H. (1976). Theory of the Firm: Managerial Behavior, Agency Costs and Ownership Structure. Journal of Financial Economics, 3(4), 305-360. http://dx.doi.org/10.1016/0304-405X(76)90026-X.

[7] Oxley, Michael et al. (2002, July 30). H.R. 3763 - Sarbanes-Oxley Act of 2002. Congress.gov. https://www.congress.gov/bill/107th-congress/house-bill/3763

[8] Dow, D., Cuypers, I. R., & Ertug, G. (2016). The effects of within-country linguistic and religious diversity on foreign acquisitions. Journal of International Business Studies, 47(3), 319-346. http://dx.doi.org/10.1057/jibs.2016.7.

[9] İşgın, E., & Sopher, B. (2015). Information transparency, fairness and labor market efficiency. Journal of Behavioral and Experimental Economics, 58, 33-39. http://dx.doi.org/10.1016/j.socec.2015.06.005.

[10] Bond, P., Edmans, A., & Goldstein, I. (2012). The real effects of financial markets. Annu. Rev. Financ. Econ., 4(1), 339-360. http://dx.doi.org/10.1146/annurev-financial-110311-101826.

[11] Lovett, M. J., Peres, R., & Shachar, R. (2013). On brands and word of mouth. Journal of marketing research, 50(4), 427-444. http://dx.doi.org/10.1509/jmr.11.0458.
[12] Grossman, S. J., & Stiglitz, J. E. (1980). On the impossibility of informationally efficient markets. The American economic review, 70(3), 393-408.
[13] Grossman, S. J., & Stiglitz, J. E. (1980). On the impossibility of informationally efficient markets. The American economic review, 70(3), 393-408.
[14] Psalm 139:6.
[15] Isaiah 55:8-9.
[16] Job 42:7.
[17] Psalm 19:12-13. New American Standard Bible, 1971, Psalm 90:8.
[18] New American Standard Bible, 1971, Job 13:15.
[19] 1 Chronicles 4:10.
[20] Grossman, S. J., & Stiglitz, J. E. (1980). On the impossibility of informationally efficient markets. The American economic review, 70(3), 393-408.
[21] Emons, W. (2001). Credence goods monopolists. International Journal of Industrial Organization, 19(3-4), 375-389. http://dx.doi.org/10.1016/S0167-7187(99)00023-5.
[22] Mark 8:29-34.
[23] Goldstein, I., & Yang, L. (2022). Commodity financialization and information transmission. The Journal of Finance, 77(5), 2613-2667. http://dx.doi.org/10.1111/jofi.13165.
[24] Romans 5:1
[25] New American Standard Bible, 1971, Acts 2:21. Romans 10:13
[26] Isaiah 9:7.
[27] Keener, C. (2022, October 1). Mark in 51 Minutes. https://craigkeener.com/mark-in-51-minutes/
[28] Mark 1:44.
[29] New American Standard Bible, 1971, Mark 5:19-20.
[30] Mark 9:9.
[31] Matthew 28:19-20.
[32] Mark 10:21-31.
[33] Mark 8:22-25.
[34] Levit, D. (2020). Words speak louder without actions. The Journal of Finance, 75(1), 91-131. http://dx.doi.org/10.1111/jofi.12834.
[35] 1 Peter 3:15.

Chapter 17

Monitoring and bonding

Monitoring and bonding are essential operations to align the behavior of an agent with the intentions of an owner. For a sweater to be sold at Harrod's in London, for a stock to be listed and traded on the Tokyo Stock Exchange, or even for a small business to maintain the gardens of an estate in Greenwich, Connecticut, monitoring, bonding, and testing take place. Each of the three governance activities is necessary for both the real economy and kingdom economy. The difference is monitoring, bonding, and testing in the kingdom economy is for maximum life and peace rather than maximum profits or high stock prices. This chapter and the next aim to reveal truth about the governance constructs in the model of human agency. The truth will catalyze a new understanding of the extraordinary plan of the owner to offer agents a chance to produce life, peace, and growth in the real economy. This first chapter on monitoring and bonding will cover 1) definitions, 2) prior insight on optimal strategies to align agent behaviors with owner interests, and 3) a case-oriented analysis of a diverse set of biblical examples of monitoring and bonding. The chapter concludes with practical applications.

Monitoring

Susan Shapiro delineates a "cartoon version" of the many problems owners take on when using agents.[1] Owners don't know what an agent is hiding about themselves. Owners don't know the true capabilities of an agent during the recruiting phase or for much of the period of employment. Owners don't know if the agent is truly committed to the business or whether the agent is opportunistic and duplicitous, taking personal advantage of corporate perquisites and expense accounts. Owners don't know if the actual effort of each agent matches the efforts of the whole team. In general, agents are assumed to do as little as possible for the same pay and glory. Finally, agents are less diversified than owners and therefore, are more risk averse. Owners are, therefore, wise to monitor their employees.

Owners have monitoring choices

To monitor is to watch and evaluate. Consider the case of a pizza restaurant. Assume the restaurant owner employs a driver to deliver pizza. The owner could monitor driver performance by measuring delivery time and customer feedback. The owner could watch the driver with an in-car camera. The owner could install a remote tracking device in the delivery vehicle and monitor every turn from the restaurant to the customer and back again. The purpose of monitoring the driver is to collect information the owner does not have. The information is used to lower delivery costs and increase customer satisfaction. The information should also be used to fairly evaluate the driver and create pay incentives that satisfy the driver in the context of the owner's desired service level. The benefit of information collected by monitoring must exceed the cost.

For large businesses, common monitoring actions include requiring periodic financial reports, budget submissions, face-to-face meetings with a board of directors, and performance reviews. Financial reports are tested and verified by accountants. Accounting professionals are hired by owners to independently assess the truth and accuracy of financial statements. Audits may be used for more stringent tests. Audits may also be applied to the operating activities of companies to measure, for example, the environmental impact of its operations. Owners pay a reputable external accounting firm to conduct an audit. The benefit of a quality audit is lower agency costs.[2]

God does not monitor to learn something

In the model of human agency, the owner is all-knowing. The owner does not learn anything by monitoring. It is the agent that learns from monitoring. God monitors his agents to accomplish his economic objectives. Monitoring informs an agent or another related party whether the behavior and intentions of the agent are aligned with the owner. Examples of monitoring revealing owner-aligned agents include Noah,[3] Job,[4] and the guileless Nathaniel seated under a fig tree.[5] Examples of the monitoring of misaligned agents include Ananias and Saphira,[6] and Rebekah stealing her father Laban's idols.[7]

God monitoring me and sending the information along is an opportunity for me to come into alignment, or remain in alignment, with his intentions. According to scripture, even Satan monitors kingdom agents in perhaps the same way a real economy business might monitor its competitors.[8] God's all-knowing sovereignty is evident in the monitoring process throughout the Bible.[9]

Bonding increases relational intimacy and reduces costs

Bonding refers to a relational connection or adhesion of two or more things. A study sponsored by the U.S. National Institutes of Health begins with the declaration, "Mother-infant bonding is a characteristic of virtually all mammals."[10] In the case of nursing animals such as kangaroos, skin-to-skin contact during breastfeeding bonds mother to baby.[11] Humans also bond over common interests such as sports, food, culture, and religion, and even over common enemies. To a chemist and a physicist, bonding refers to the atomic level adhesion of elements. Financial economists mean something completely different by the term bonding.

Economic bonding means obtaining status in a group with desirable attributes. An example is an accountant obtaining a Certified Public Accountant ("CPA") license. A new law school graduate passes the bar exam to be admitted to a bar association. Newly admitted lawyers are added to the *Roll of Attorneys.* I may offer home repair services and seek to obtain a general contractor license to be bonded into a group that gives me additional status with customers. In addition to professional bonding, I may choose financial bonding. I may buy a surety bond to lower the risk for my customers.

Financial markets serve a bonding function. A business with a headquarters in a poorly regulated economy may want to inform investors about its relatively outstanding corporate governance. The business could transmit the information by obtaining a listing on the New York Stock Exchange ("NYSE").[12] An NYSE listing bonds the company to a reputable marketplace, with the agency benefit of lower capital costs. The bonding is not just for show. Bonding is reflected in truly better behavior. A bonded firm is more likely to fire a poor performing CEO than an unbonded firm.[13] Bonding transmits information to owners. Interestingly, as the global flow of information improves with more integrated capital markets, high-speed internet, and social media, price informativeness increases and some of the benefits of bonding decrease.[14] Overall, the effect of bonding is to make it more likely for agents to perform in a way the owner wants. Being bonded to a desirable profession or marketplace lowers agency costs, raises the value of a business, and improves its future growth prospects.

Bonding facilitates kingdom economy agency

The messianic era kingdom economy is bonding oriented rather than monitoring oriented. In the messianic era, external monitoring has been mostly transmuted into heart bonding. God is all-knowing and doesn't gain information from monitoring. Being watched inevitably impedes a sense of freedom. This is contradictory to the mission of Jesus as "it was for freedom that Christ set us free."[15] Being monitored and caught in misbehavior may be associated with a feeling of condemnation. Yet the Bible teaches, "there is now no condemnation at all for those who are in Christ Jesus."[16] God is all-knowing. *God is always watching* simply as a consequence of his character. At the same time, the principles and requirements of kingdom agency are written internally in the hearts of Christ-followers.[17] A Christ-follower is at peace with God[18] and has been made alive together with him.[19] Kingdom agents are spiritually bonded into the body of Christ.

To *remain* is to be economically bonded

Jesus' instruction to remain in the true vine takes on a new dimension in the context of an agency model.[20] If a licensed architect fails to retain his professional status and is no longer able to certify architectural drawings, his business will collapse. To be salt and light, producing life and peace in the real economy now, I must remain bonded to the true vine, which is Jesus. Remaining bonded in the vine yields in me the "likeness of Jesus."[21]

A key piece of evidence regarding the bonding proposition of the kingdom economy comes from the apprenticeship model of antiquity. New Testament scholar D.A. Carson presents the flow of thought in the story of Jesus healing a paralytic on the Sabbath. Jesus was accused of violating the Sabbath law of rest by healing a man at the Pool of Bethesda. The religious leaders sought to execute him for it.

The relevant dimension of the healing story here relates to Jesus' claim of Father to Son apprenticeship. John 5:20 says, "For the Father loves the Son and shows Him all things that He Himself is doing; and *the Father* will show Him greater works than these, so that you will be amazed." In the apprenticeship oriented agrarian and craftsman economy of antiquity, Jesus was saying his Father loves him and has shown him all the parts of the family business. Apprenticeship is a mechanism of bonding. Apprenticeship has remained an important educational and training institution in the real economy.[22] The kingdom economy is designed for bonding agents to the owner's intentions. The claim of divine sonship was clear to the Jewish leaders. In their view, the claim of divine apprenticeship deserved death.

Insight from the study of relational pairs

This point of real economy comparison for this study has been the financial economics-oriented theory of Jensen and Meckling.[23] Follow-up studies of agency tended to focus on organization-level issues solved by efficient contracting, with a particular interest in the interaction of the Board of Directors and CEO. More realistically, there are many other types of interactions within organizations. Other dyads include manager-subordinate and manager-manager. Sociologist Susan Shapiro reviews agency literature and suggests the unit of analysis should begin with relational pairs.[24] A dyadic-oriented model fits well with this study. My relationship with God is in fact a dyad first, within a much larger community. The organization is the entire global congregation of Christ-followers. However, the first point of entry into the kingdom economy is a personal relationship with Jesus.

After two decades of agency theory research, Kathleen Eisenhardt developed several new propositions regarding optimal owner strategies.[25] In the first scenario considered by Eisenhardt, the owner has complete information. Likewise, in the kingdom economy, God is all-knowing. He knows everything about the activities of an agent. The owner that knows all agent activities does not need to invest in additional information-gathering systems. For an all-knowing owner, the study shows the most efficient contract is behavior-based. The alternative is for an owner is to write an outcome-based contract. An outcome-based contract is inefficient because it "needlessly transfers risk" from the owner to the agent.[26] The agent is already more risk-averse than the owner. An outcome-based contract adds risk to the agent because outcomes are only partly under the control of the agent. Behaviors are under the agent's control. The owner, with full information about the agent's behavior, is better off retaining the outcome risk.

To illustrate the point, assume I hire a new head of sales. I can agree to pay the new head of sales based on behaviors or outcomes. Behavioral targets might include a certain number of sales calls, a certain number of trade show presentations, and a certain number of sales team training activities each month. If I have perfect knowledge of her activities, I don't have to worry about a lack of effort (i.e., moral hazard) or false reports about her skills and performance (i.e., adverse selection).

An example of an outcome-based sales manager contract is straightforward. I hire the same new head of sales with a specific dollar amount sales target. If I had no way of knowing exactly what the sales manager is doing each day, then I may choose to transfer some of my risk and write an output-based contract. However, as I know exactly what the sales manager is doing, I retain the outcome risk to allow her to efficiently perform the work.

The owner-agent construct in the kingdom is behavioral. I am not told to pray a certain number of hours each day. I am not told to give an amount of my income to the poor or the church. Kingdom agents are encouraged to seek first the kingdom of God and His Righteousness.[27] Agents are told to love God rather than money.[28] Agents are encouraged to run life's race to win[29] and to take hold of the assignment the owner has given them.[30] God is all-knowing and has an infinite capacity to support my risk-taking. The behavioral contract of the kingdom economy is, therefore, efficient.

Eisenhardt's third proposition has implications for *The Theory of the Kingdom.* The proposition says behavior-based contracts are positively related to information systems.[31] The proposition corresponds with Doron Levit's thesis that "words speak louder without actions."[32] Figure 17.1 includes a list of several modes of communication involved in the monitoring and bonding of kingdom agents. Several of the modes of communication were presented in detail in chapter four. However, in the case of monitoring and bonding, I have added testing to Figure 17.1. Testing is a mechanism of communication. The Holy Spirit speaks through testing. Testing is integral to the monitoring and bonding process.

Real economy owners do not have perfect information. As a result, owners regularly test employees to verify their skills and abilities. Employees may also voluntarily subject themselves to testing to be bonded to a well-regarded organization such as a Bar Association or a Medical Board. Testing is the subject of the next chapter.

Figure 17.1. Monitoring and bonding in the model of human agency.

<table>
<tr><th></th><th>Monitoring</th><th>Bonding</th></tr>
<tr><td rowspan="2">Owner-Agent Interests</td><td>Mis-aligned.
Ananias and Saphira.
Acts 5:1-11.</td><td>Mis-aligned.
Moses and Zipporah.
Exodus 4:24-26.</td></tr>
<tr><td>Aligned.
Job.
Job 1:1-12.</td><td>Aligned.
Ruth.
Ruth 1:16-18.</td></tr>
<tr><td>Model owner-agent alignment</td><td>King David
1 Samuel 13:14, Acts 13:22.</td><td>The Apostle Paul
Romans 1:1-7.</td></tr>
<tr><td rowspan="2">Sampling of modes of communication</td><td>Old Testament Era
Prophets.
Judges.</td><td>Messianic Era
Jesus.
Holy Spirit.</td></tr>
<tr><td colspan="2">Time Invariant
Word of God.
Testing.
Community.
Nature.
Signs and wonders.</td></tr>
</table>

Figure 17.1 major message: The present messianic era is characterized by bonding. Kingdom agents are bonded into the body of Christ by the work of the Holy Spirit in spiritual rebirth and witness regarding individual identification as daughters and sons of God. Agents are generally employed in activities directly related to the conditions of their bonding.

Monitoring misbehavior

The third part of an analysis of monitoring and bonding proceeds, according to Figure 17.1. An example of monitoring misbehaving agents is observed in Acts chapter five. The context for the demise of Ananias and Saphira begins in the preceding chapter. The new church was growing, and the new believers held their property in common.[33] This passage is sometimes used as evidence the kingdom economy favors socialism. That assertion can be refuted on a few grounds, including the future financial needs of the Jerusalem congregation and the apparently accepted economic stratification of the church at Ephesus.[34] The communal sharing of property recorded in Acts was voluntary, though commentator Richard Rackham expects a level of moral compulsion likely crept in.[35]

Against this backdrop, the married couple Ananias and Saphira sold property and brought the leadership an offering of part of the proceeds. Choosing the amount of the offering was their prerogative. Unfortunately, Ananias and Saphira misrepresented the percentage given. The Holy Spirit knew of the misrepresentation and provided the information to Peter. Peter confronted each partner. The consequence of lying to the Holy Spirit was sudden death. The mind of the Holy Spirit is indeed life and peace.[36] However, the Holy Spirit is also “the Spirit of Truth.”[37] The love of money and hypocrisy exhibited by Ananias and Saphira had been “sternly denounced in the Pharisees.”[38] When a report of deception, hypocrisy, and greed is given, it should be responded to with contrition and repentance.[39]

Monitoring good behavior

The Book of Job is a story of the suffering and restoration of the title character. The story begins with an incident of monitoring. The monitoring is unique in the sense the Bible records Job as being monitored by both God and Satan. The story includes a conversation where God reports Job’s blameless life and Satan protests by saying God has protected Job from suffering. In effect, Satan argues Job’s behavioral ethic is instrumental. The narrative of the book is God allowing Job to suffer at the hands of Satan. Job lost his donkeys, sheep, oxen, and camels. His servants were killed by a combination of raiders and wildfire. Finally, a windstorm knocked down a building, killing Job’s 10 children. Chapter One closes by reporting Job did not sin by blaming God.

There are two points to be made regarding monitoring and agency behavior. First, Old Testament scholar John Walton writes one of the themes of Job is, “there is such a thing as disinterested righteousness, and it is an ideal to be pursued.”[40] Disinterested righteousness is virtuous action or worship without any expectation of reward.[41] Disinterested righteousness cancels the instrumental ethic charge of Satan against Job. Walton suggests the story of Job is not to rationalize Job's suffering but rather to gain insight into God. Second, it may be God sees an agent's behavior as well-aligned with his interests and yet they still experience suffering. Suffering does not necessarily indicate being out of alignment with the owner. Suffering paired with obedient heart labor could indicate an agent is bonded into the true vine and producing life, peace, and growth in the economy. There is hope for suffering agents in the words of David that "weeping may last for the night, but a shout of joy comes in the morning."[42]

Model response to monitoring

David is the best example of the correct approach to owner monitoring. David's starting position was most often aligned with the interests of the owner. God promoted David to King because he knew David was "a man after My heart, who will do all My will."[43] David actually requested additional monitoring. Agents generally don't like heightened surveillance. David prayed, "Search me, God, and know my heart; put me to the test and know my anxious thoughts; And see if there is any hurtful way in me and lead me in an everlasting way." The request was to close the information gap between David and the owner. At first thought, it is surprising David would want God to search his heart for misalignment. On second thought, it is a rational course. The owner knows how I might be more productive. I should want the owner's information.

David's behavior was not always aligned with the owner's interest. He committed adultery and arranged the death of the offended husband. When Nathan gave his report, David's response was contrition.[44] Of the many elements of David's contrition, four stand out: 1) total surrender for the offense, 2) identification of the owner as the primary offended party, 3) request for grace according to the goodness and mercy of the owner, and 4) a commitment to teaching others what is right and wrong. The model response to misbehavior includes repentance and a commitment to mentor others in owner-aligned behavior.

Bonding to realign with the owner

The first biblical example of agent realignment by bonding is taken from an unusual Old Testament story of Moses. The story of Moses is familiar due in part to the commercial success of Cecil B. DeMille's 1956 movie *The Ten Commandments.* The record of Moses begins well before the crossing of the Red Sea. Moses was a Jew raised in Pharoah's household. As a young man, Moses committed murder in defense of a Jewish slave. As a result, he fled Egypt for Midian. There he married Zipporah, the daughter of Jethro, the pagan priest of Midian. Out of a burning bush, God spoke to Moses, sending him back to Egypt to liberate hundreds of thousands of Jewish people. The nation of Israel had been in Egypt for over 400 years.[45]

Moses was 80 years old when he began the 700-kilometer journey from Midian to Egypt.[46] At the first recorded lodging place, Exodus 4:24 records, "on the way, the Lord met him and sought to put him to death." This is a most unusual action for an all-knowing owner who had spent so much time recruiting and preparing an agent for a huge job. On its face, God's action is hard to understand. Yet, the Bible records that without explanation, God came to kill Moses along the way.

Moses was born an Israelite. Moses knew God. Yet perhaps due to living in Jethro's household, a pagan priest of Midian, Moses had not stayed bonded into the Abrahamic covenant by circumcising his son. Circumcision represented repentance. It represented a turning away from the money-driven ways of the real economy to be obedient to God. Janzen suggests part of the message of the incident is obedience to the law is more important than any special agency assignment.[47] The fact that Zipporah performed the deed rather than Moses is relevant for two reasons. First, it is part of a biblical theme of redemption coming from the woman.[48] Second, it served to bond Zipporah into the Israelite nation as a "marriage-relative of bloodshed."[49] After the incident, Moses' disobedience and Zipporah's outsider status were resolved by bonding through circumcision. Regarding Moses specifically, Janzen writes, "If Moses' relationship to God is set right – through atonement by blood, as we noted – then the way to victory over Pharoah lies open."[50] The application to the model of human agency is success in a new assignment may depend on future bonding rather than qualification by experience.

Bonding by faithfulness

Ruth is an example of an aligned bonded agent. The story of Ruth the Moabite is a modest "vignette of faithfulness among common folks."[51] The story is Ruth had a mother-in-law named Naomi. Naomi's husband and two sons had died. Naomi was left with only two daughters-in-law, Ruth and Orpah. Naomi sent both Ruth and Orpah away to go and try to secure their futures by finding new husbands in their homelands. Orpah left.[52] Ruth did not. Ruth instead committed to being bonded into Naomi's family.

Naomi was from Bethlehem. The God of Bethlehem was YHWH, the God of Israel and the owner in the model of human agency. Walton notes although Ruth was only bonding herself to Naomi it was "enough of a foothold for Yahweh to reveal himself."[53] The short version of the astonishing turn of events for Ruth is she married a man named Boaz. Ruth became the great-grandmother of David and was grafted into the family line of Jesus. Matthew's gospel records, "Salmon was the father of Boaz by Rahab, Boaz was the father of Obed by Ruth, and Obed the father of Jesse. Jesse was the father of David, the king."[54] Faithfulness bonded Ruth into the most important genealogy in the history of humankind. The ultimate outcome of faithfulness and owner-aligned bonding can only be known by the owner himself. The outcome for Ruth could have been an extremely difficult and humiliating life. Instead, Ruth's life was historically consequential.

Bonding by experiencing Jesus

In the New Testament era, the apostle Paul is bonded into the kingdom through his Damascus Road conversion experience,[55] including being filled with the Holy Spirit and time spent with the other disciples, including Peter and James.[56,57,58] The specific note on the work of the Holy Spirit in bonding Paul to his agency role in the kingdom economy corresponds with the messianic era mode of communication listed in Figure 17.1. The second messianic era change in communication is the primacy of the words of Jesus. The book of Hebrews opens by noting God used to speak to spiritual leaders through the Old Testament prophets. Now God speaks through Jesus, the appointed heir of everything and through whom the world was made. In Jesus, God spoke "decisively, finally, and perfectly."[59]

Bonding is for a particular assignment

Paul's salutation in Romans is, "Paul, a bond-servant of Christ Jesus, called as an apostle, set apart for the Gospel of God." The literal definitions include slave and bondservant, implying subjection or subservience.[60] Paul's indication of his position as a bonded agent follows a tradition of individual Israelite leaders such as Moses and Joshua being called bond-servants of God. Paul also refers to himself as an apostle. He was an apostle because of the specific assignment he was given by Jesus on the Damascus Road to preach the *Gospel of God*.[61] Bonding in the real economy is for a specific trade and career. In the kingdom economy bonding is also associated with a particular kingdom economy position or assignment. It is up to me to hear as well as possible, by the Holy Spirit, what that assignment is, and to lay hold of it.[62]

Six applications

A. For a Christ-follower, bonding is the principal method by which behavior stays in alignment with the intentions of the owner. If I feel watched, judged, and condemned, it may be an indication I am not tightly bonded to the true vine. Life in Christ is for freedom and well-bonded behaviors should feel light rather than burdensome.[63]

B. A community of Christ-followers should focus on bonding activities rather than monitoring specific behaviors. Bonding activities include continuing education, spending time together, and apprenticeship-type work.

C. Bonding relationships require maintenance. Heart labor and community involvement keeps kingdom agents bonded to the true vine, Jesus. In a real economy professional association, bonded agents are required to complete continuing education requirements and pay professional dues. In the state of Virginia, for example, a CPA is required to complete 120 hours of continuing education over a rolling three-year period. The requirement works out to about one 46-minute class per week. Staying bonded in the kingdom economy requires ongoing education.

D. It is wise to request heightened monitoring by the Holy Spirit. The owner knows how I might be more productive. I want that information. The correct response to identified misalignment is contrition. Further, I am expected to mentor others in owner-aligned behavior.

E. Bonding is usually associated with a particular job function in the real economy and the kingdom economy. Paul was bonded to be an apostle of the Gospel of God. An accountant obtains a CPA license to perform audits. Each bonded agent has a specific role in the kingdom economy.

F. According to the story of Moses and Zipporah, success with a new assignment may require fresh bonding rather than just prior experience.

Notes

[1] Shapiro, S. P. (2005). Agency theory. *Annual review of sociology*, 263-284. http://dx.doi.org/10.1146/annurev.soc.31.041304.122159.

[2] Francis, J. R., & Wilson, E. R. (1988). Auditor changes: A joint test of theories relating to agency costs and auditor differentiation. *Accounting Review*, 663-682.

[3] Genesis 6:9

[44] Job 1:8

[5] John 1:47-51.

[6] New American Standard Bible, 1971, Acts 5:1-11. The Holy Spirit was monitoring Ananias and Saphira, revealing their lie to Peter.

[7] Genesis 31:34 and subsequent trouble in the camp in Genesis 34 and purification in Genesis 35:1-4..

[8] Job 1:6-12.

[9] Job 1:6-12.

[10] Numan, M., & Young, L. J. (2016). Neural mechanisms of mother–infant bonding and pair bonding: Similarities, differences, and broader implications. *Hormones and behavior, 77*, 98-112. http://dx.doi.org/10.1016/j.yhbeh.2015.05.015.

[11] Tessier, R., Cristo, M., Velez, S., Girón, M., de Calume, S. Z. F., Ruiz-Paláez, J. G., ... & Charpak, N. (1998). Kangaroo mother care and the bonding hypothesis. *Pediatrics, 102*(2), e17-e17. http://dx.doi.org/10.1542/peds.102.2.e17.
[12] Karolyi, G. A. (2012). Corporate governance, agency problems and international cross-listings: A defense of the bonding hypothesis. *Emerging Markets Review, 13*(4), 516-547. http://dx.doi.org/10.1016/j.ememar.2012.08.001.
[13] Lel, U., & Miller, D. P. (2008). International cross-listing, firm performance, and top management turnover: A test of the bonding hypothesis. *The Journal of Finance, 63*(4), 1897-1937. http://dx.doi.org/10.1111/j.1540-6261.2008.01377.x.
[14] Doukas, J. A., & Wang, L. (2014). Does the bonding effect matter in a more integrated capital market world?. *Journal of International Money and Finance, 47*, 162-184. http://dx.doi.org/10.1016/j.jimonfin.2014.05.022.
[15] Galatians 5:1
[16] Romans 8:1
[17] New American Standard Bible, 1971, Hebrews 8:10. New American Standard Bible, 1971, Jeremiah 31:33.
[18] Romans 3:22.
[19] New American Standard Bible, 1971, Colossians 2:13-14.
[20] John 15:1-11.
[21] Bruce, F. F. (1994). *The Gospel of John: Introduction, Exposition, Notes* (p. 310). Wm. B. Eerdmans Publishing.
[22] Elbaum, B., & Singh, N. (1995). The Economic Rationale of Apprenticeship Training: Some Lessons from British and US Experience. *Industrial Relations: A Journal of Economy and Society, 34*(4), 593-622. http://dx.doi.org/10.1111/j.1468-232X.1995.tb00390.x.
[23] Jensen, M. C., & Meckling, W. H. (2019). Theory of the firm: Managerial behavior, agency costs and ownership structure. In *Corporate Governance* (pp. 77-132). Gower.
[24] Shapiro, S. P. (2005). Agency theory. *Annual review of sociology*, 263-284. http://dx.doi.org/10.1146/annurev.soc.31.041304.122159.
[25] Eisenhardt, K. M. (1989). Agency theory: An assessment and review. *Academy of management review, 14*(1), 57-74. http://dx.doi.org/10.2307/258191.
[26] Eisenhardt, K. M. (1989). Agency theory: An assessment and review. *Academy of management review, 14*(1), 57-74. http://dx.doi.org/10.2307/258191.
[27] Matthew 6:33.
[28] Matthew 6:24.
[29] 1 Corinthians 9:24.
[30] Philippians 3:12.
[31] Eisenhardt, K. M. (1989). Agency theory: An assessment and review. *Academy of management review, 14*(1), 57-74. http://dx.doi.org/10.2307/258191.
[32] Levit, D. (2020). Words speak louder without actions. *The Journal of Finance, 75*(1), 91-131. http://dx.doi.org/10.1111/jofi.12834.
[33] Acts 4:32.
[34] Romans 15:25-27. New American Standard Bible, 1971, 1 Corinthians 16:1-3. 1 Timothy 6:17-19.
[35] Rackham, R. B. (1901). *The Acts of the Apostles: An Exposition* (p. 65). Methuen.
[36] Romans 8:6.
[37] John 16:13.
[38] Rackham, R. B. (1901). *The Acts of the Apostles: An Exposition* (pp. 65-66). Methuen.

[39] Psalm chapter 51.
[40] Keener, C. S., & Walton, J. H. (Eds.). (2016). *NIV, Cultural Backgrounds Study Bible: Bringing to Life the Ancient World of Scripture* (p. 847). Zondervan.
[41] Perry, A. (2017). The Suffering Servant of Isaiah and the Suffering of Job. http://www.biblaridion.info/Proverbs/Perry_JOB.pdf.
[42] New American Standard Bible, 1971, Psalm 30:5.
[43] Acts 13:22.
[44] Psalm chapter 51.
[45] New American Standard Bible, 1971, Exodus chapters 1 to 4, a synopsis.
[46] On a modern-day map, the trip began from Western Saudi Arabia, perhaps Tabuk, and ended in the Israeli settlements in Goshen. Ramses II was Pharaoh during Moses time. The storage city of Ramses was in the northeastern part of Nile river delta, a region then including Goshen, and now including the modern Egyptian capital Cairo. The trek across the middle east for Moses was at least seven hundred kilometers.
[47] Janzen, W. (2000). *Exodus: Believers Church Bible Commentary* (p. 85). MennoMedia, Inc.
[48] Consider the cases of Mary the mother of Jesus, Ruth, Rahab the prostitute and Esther.
[49] Osborn, N. D., & Hatton, H. A. (1999). *A handbook on Exodus* (pp. 25-26). United Bible Societies.
[50] Janzen, W. (2000). *Exodus: Believers Church Bible Commentary* (p. 86). MennoMedia, Inc.
[51] Keener, C., & Walton, J. (2006). Cultural Backgrounds Study Bible. p469.
[52] Michael, M. (2011). Orpah and her interpreters: Evaluating the justifications for the traditional-stereotyped readings. *Old Testament Essays, 24*(2), 390-413. Some biblical commentators trace Orpah to "the destroyer, Goliath the Philistine". New American Standard Bible, 1971, 1 Samuel chapter 17. Ruth's grandson David fought Goliath.
[53] Keener, C. S., & Walton, J. H. (Eds.). (2016). *NIV, Cultural Backgrounds Study Bible: Bringing to Life the Ancient World of Scripture* (p. 472). Zondervan.
[54] New American Standard Bible, 1971, Matthew 1:5-6.
[55] Acts 9:1-20.
[56] Galatians 1:18. Paul records 15 days with Peter.
[57] Galatians 2:1. Some commentators believe Galatians 2:1 means Paul spent 14 years in training for 10 years of public ministry, before his death.
[58] Knox, J. (1936). "Fourteen Years Later": A Note on the Pauline Chronology. *The Journal of Religion, 16*(3), 341-349. http://dx.doi.org/10.1086/481845. Knox delineates a different view, which doesn't materially affect any point about bonding into the Body of Christ.
[59] Brown, R. (1982). *The Bible Speaks Today: The Message of Hebrews* (pp. 28). InterVarsity Press.
[60] Strong, J. (2009). *Strong's exhaustive concordance of the Bible* (Greek Dictionary of the New Testament, p. 24). Hendrickson Publishers.
[61] Stott, J. (2014). *The message of Romans: God's good news for the world* (pp. 47-48). InterVarsity Press.
[62] Philippians 3:12.
[63] Matthew 11:28-30.

Chapter 18

Testing

Testing is a procedure to provide information about an object, a person, or a process. An individual test may also be called a trial. Human trials entail physical, emotional, or spiritual challenges. The information gained by testing may indicate if a person is likely to perform as expected. In an educational context, testing provides information to students and instructors about knowledge received in the educational process relative to a standard.

Despite obvious shortcomings, testing is important. Principal-agent models require testing to gather information. This chapter focuses on a scriptural survey and case studies to discern the purpose, procedures, policy, and practical applications of kingdom economy testing. Testing found in the Bible is not generally of the formal educational type. Agents mostly undergo real-life circumstantial trials. Major characters in the Bible experience trials. It is a fact of life in the real economy, particularly for those living first for the kingdom economy. Circumstantial character tests lead to asking a series of *what* questions: 1) what tests did biblical characters experience? 2) what did they say about testing? 3) what actions did they take? 4) what was the result? and 5) what can be learned for real economy life?

Involuntary and voluntary testing is used to gather information

Testing in the real economy may be used to allocate scarce educational or financial resources. Governments pass laws and require many different types of tests. Food safety is tested. New drivers must pass a road test. In many professions, governments require initial and ongoing testing. In the field of investment securities, I was required to pass two Ontario Securities Commission tests and six different U.S. Securities and Exchange Commission ("SEC") exams, including the Series 7, 63, 16, 86, 87, and 24, and various continuing education tests. The series 7 and 24 exams were all-day affairs.

Humans voluntarily put themselves through trials and tests. Runners may enter distance races to achieve a new personal best time. I get blood drawn each year to test my blood chemistry. Some tests are more enjoyable than others. There always seems to be a new personality test people are taking. Myers-Briggs[1] and Enneagram are examples of popular voluntary tests. Testing and information gathering are a fact of life in the real economy.

Real economy testing is imperfect. Students may cheat to pass a test. Students may be exempted from a test based on prior experience or other accommodations. I may not like one test and find a way to exchange it for another. The exchange takes place to reduce the expected difficulty of the trial. Students may even fail a test and be excluded from an elite school through no fault of their own. Tests may be failed due to a lack of money for tutoring, language barriers, malnutrition, dishonest test administrators, or out of the ordinary cognitive and emotional processes.

Real economy test results may not be accurate. The first personality test I took was at a business school orientation. I was married six days prior. In the week leading up to the test, I had been on a honeymoon, moved to a new country, and driven 12 hours overnight. I was not in a normal state of mind. I took the personality test and the results showed I should choose a career as a singer, dancer, or stage actor. I don't sing well and I certainly can't dance.

The disciple James on testing

James, the brother of Jesus, opens the body of his letter with "consider it all joy, my brethren, when you encounter various trials, knowing that the testing of your faith produces endurance".[2] James was executed in AD 62 by Ananus II.[3] James' letter was written and circulated in a period of great difficulty characterized by *Poverty and Revolt in Judea.*[4] The Jewish Diaspora to whom James was most presently writing were impoverished, overtaxed, rural tenant farmers and tenement-dwelling urbanites. Craig Keener's essay notes some of the landowners had "hit squads"[5] to kill uncooperative tenants. Zealots eventually revolted against the empire in AD 66. The Roman army besieged Jerusalem. Jerusalem was taken, the temple destroyed and the last hold at Masada overrun in AD 73. In this setting, James' letter with the opening words, "consider it all joy, my brethren, when you encounter various trials," begins to circulate.[6]

The flow of logic in the first eight verses of James is cyclical. Trials test faith. Testing of faith produces patience. Patience works for spiritual completeness. Spiritual incompleteness includes a lack of wisdom. To obtain wisdom, I ask God for it. Asking for wisdom must be done in faith. Trials test faith. To identify the type of trials and characteristics of faith, consider the three dominant themes of the book of James. The three themes are trials and temptations, wisdom and speech, and poverty and wealth.[7] Evidently, a substantial source of real economy-induced trials come from poverty and wealth.

Jarvis Williams indicates the key message is faith is to "trust in God instead of wealth". Further, faith in God is demonstrated by taking "care of orphans and widows" and avoiding discrimination based on wealth in the community of Christ-followers.[8] To be faithless is to be a rich person engaged in *pursuits*,[9] literally translated as commercial travel and business, without consideration of God and what he requires.

God's time-invariant requirement is to do justice, love mercy and walk humbly.[10] Blomberg put a finer point of James' message of trials and temptations, writing the correct understanding is, "trials in chapter 1 (are) first of all addressed to the socio-economic plight at the forefront of the community's concern."[11] Testing of kingdom agents is inextricably linked to the most basic temptation to love money. Problems associated with real economy wealth disparity affect all four needs in the hierarchy of temptation: physiological, physical security, authority, and identity. The antecedent to right kingdom agent action is to love and serve God only.[12] Trials and temptations test where love is directed.

Job's disinterested righteousness and greater economic justice

The suffering of Job is well-known in popular culture. The person about whom the Book of Job is written is believed to have lived between 2000 BC and 1000 BC,[13] with the timing of the book's writing likely later in the seventh century BC.[14] Regardless of the precise date, God saw fit to address the problem of human suffering very early on. Job raises many uncomfortable questions about the nature of God and the purpose of suffering.[15] An important element of the setup is the taunt Satan directs at God. "Does Job fear God for nothing?"[16] The charge is of the *rational choice theory* sort. It is asserted Job fears God because he is rational. Job is simply a utility maximizer. God gave Job wealth, honor, health, and a large family. Therefore, Job fears God. It was his most rational course. If God were to take away his wealth, honor, health, and family, Job would find another object of worship. Terminology to describe the charge of worshipping God for the benefits include interested righteousness, interested goodness, or extrinsic religion.[17] One of the functions of the Book of Job is to provide Christ-followers with the heart capital to wage war against the mental stronghold of interested righteousness and rational choice. Worshipping God for God alone is the disinterested righteousness of Job.

The last chapter indicates what Job gained from his trials. First, Job gained relational intimacy and revelation about God. "I have heard of You by the hearing of the ear, But now my eye sees You; Therefore I retract, And I repent in dust and ashes." Second, by his service, Job proved disinterested righteousness is attainable. Job served his friends by praying and then he received a future blessing. Disinterested righteousness may be what James meant by "perfect and complete lacking nothing."[18,19] When Job prayed, God restored his fortunes. There is no indication Job prayed first for his restoration or that he knew it was about to happen. Third, Job gained emotional scars. Even though Job's fortunes were restored, the Bible says his brothers and sisters afterward consoled and comforted him for his losses and the scars of the trials.

Job gained virtue and gave an inheritance to his daughters. In ancient culture, it was very unusual for daughters to receive an inheritance.[20] Morrow indicates Job is the only biblical example of a daughter receiving an inheritance while the brother is still alive.[21] Job's daughters are named. The brothers are not named. The honor and shame link was prevalent in ancient culture.[22] Job's revelation of God led to the elevation of his daughters to "relieve repressions responsible for shaming womanhood." Shaming and bias against women still happen in the real economy.[23] Being salt and light, bringing life and peace, requires kingdom agents to elevate women.

Peter is warned

Job did not receive a warning that Satan wanted to test his faith in God. Peter did receive a warning. "Simon, Simon, behold, Satan has demanded permission to sift you like wheat: but I have prayed for you, that your faith may not fail; and you, when once you have turned again, strengthen your brothers."[24] Jesus went on to tell Peter the exact time frame, type and number of repetitions he would face. Job held up much better without a warning than Peter did with a warning.

The scene of Peter's failure and denial of Jesus is well depicted in art. The Denial of Saint Peter by Michelangelo Merisi da Caravaggio was copied an estimated 60 times over 30 years by the *Caravaggisti*. The artists' work captured "the moment in which (Peter) denied being himself."[25] For Christ-followers, the test of public testimony is indeed one of self-affirmation. Once bonded by the Holy Spirit, denying Christ is self-denial and will result in being denied by Jesus in front of God.[26]

On the night of his trial and crucifixion, Jesus told Peter he would be tested and he would fail three times. Peter protested he would not lie about knowing Jesus. Arguing with Jesus suggests Peter was impulsive[27] and lacked humility. Pausing to consider the warning may have allowed Peter to choose faith over fear. The first two instances of denial were to adolescent-aged servants in a courtyard.[28] Peter was very afraid of people. Peter failed the test.

Peter's failure would result in a real economy termination

Measured against the sensibilities of real economy organizations, the failure of Peter was a 10 out of 10. If a close coworker is facing an unjust accusation and, in fear, I lie about them, the relationship would be lost. The more seniority gained, trust and integrity become even more important. Leaders must be able to trust those in their circle. Lying and faltering when conditions are difficult mean termination and a shattered professional reputation. Peter was in the leadership circle. Remarkably, Peter's failure was redeemed. The process of restoration, retest, redemption, and completion is instructive for the testing policy of the kingdom economy.

Restoration by repentance, retest, redemption and completion

The first part of Peter's restoration was his repentance as signified by his immediate bitter weeping.[29] After the resurrection, Jesus appeared to Peter in private and with the other disciples. Jesus restored Peter and forgave him, face to face.[30] Jesus' restoration addressed Peter's deepest motivations and bonded him for a new role of evangelism and apostleship. No longer was Peter a fisherman.[31] After Jesus' ascension, Peter was part of the first group to receive the baptism of the Holy Spirit. Peter preached the first mass evangelism rally.[32] Peter was a leader in the Jerusalem council. Peter was restored and promoted because he was repentant and was now fully bonded for his role in the kingdom of God. When threatened by the Jewish leadership, Peter openly proclaims the truth of the gospel at great personal cost.

Peter's final recorded test on earth was his own imprisonment and execution. Peter knew his martyrdom test was coming. Jesus told Peter in advance about how he would die.[33] Peter no longer denied Jesus to save his own life. Peter had a changed heart. There is an interesting note in one recorded rescue of Peter from prison. In one instance, his angelic rescuer from Herod's jail found him sleeping between two guards.[34] Just before Peter's imprisonment, Herod had killed another disciple, James, by decapitation. Peter was still alive in prison because while Herod wanted to cut off his head, for political reasons he was waiting until after the eight days of unleavened bread.[35] The fact Peter was said to be sleeping in advance of his almost certain execution suggests a man at peace with his bonded kingdom economy role. Peter failed some tests. Yet, it did not disqualify him from fulfilling his agency assignment. James, son of Alphaeus,[36] could have eulogized Peter according to his own letter as *passing into his eternal reward, having allowed testing to do its work in his spirit, meeting Jesus again, perfect and complete, lacking nothing.*

Is it enough that Moses and Isaac survive?

Old Testament temptations, tests, and trials can be difficult to read. Job is one example. Two other difficult stories are God coming to kill Moses and God telling Abraham to sacrifice his son Isaac. I am thankful to live in the messianic era when atonement for sins has come by Jesus and the outward has been transmuted inward. Regardless, the fact the owner's ways are not my way and his thoughts are not my thoughts can make understanding difficult.[37] My preferred action when I lack the wisdom to understand a bible passage or a personal trial is to set it aside and wait for revelation from the Holy Spirit. I compound my problems by rationalizing away the difficulty rather than waiting to receive the truth. My moment of truth regarding the stories of Moses and Zipporah and Abraham and Isaac came in the process of writing this book.

I introduced the story of Moses and Zipporah in the context of bonding (chapter 17). Moses was a Jew raised in Pharoah's household. Moses married Zipporah, the daughter of Jethro, the pagan priest of Midian. God sent Moses back to Egypt to liberate his Jewish people. At the first recorded lodging place, Exodus records, "on the way, the Lord met him and sought to put him to death."[38] The second difficult story involves Abraham and his long-promised son Isaac. When Abraham was 99 years old and his wife Sarah was 90, God made a covenant with Abraham. The promise was Abraham would be the father of nations and Sarah the mother of nations. Sarah thought the promise of bearing a son at 90 was so ridiculous she laughed.[39] The Bible records that Sarah did have a son within the year. Abraham was 100 years old at the time of Isaac's birth.[40] The name of their son would be Isaac, which means laughter.[41] The story then takes a difficult turn. "Now it came about after these things that God tested Abraham." The test was God told Abraham to take a journey with Isaac, the child of promise, to kill him and burn his body as a sacrifice.[42]

Ultimately, God provided a substitute, Isaac grew up, and the promise of Abraham being the father of nations was fulfilled through him. Ultimately, Moses lived because Zipporah circumcised their son and was thereby bonded to Moses and the people of Israel. Regardless, the setup of both situations still seemed to me to be mean and capricious.

Beginning of monotheism

The situation of Abraham is perhaps more straightforward to understand. The substitution of an animal for Isaac indicated to Abraham that the service of God alone meant the rejection of human sacrifice.[43] In the context of an agency model, the experience also served to bond Abraham to God by faith credited to him as righteousness. Abraham says to Isaac before the substitution is known, "God will provide", and then after the substitution was provided, labeled the site where they were with the same phrase.[44] The site name was confirmation that God watches over his agents in the short term, and not just the long term. The polytheism of antiquity often split gods into categories by the timing and type of needs they helped with. Abraham was learning to serve the one true God by discovering he watches over his followers at all times.[45]

Testing when the owners knows the future

Before finishing the analysis on the testing of Abraham and Moses, consider a story about the testing of new investment research professionals at Wall Street brokerages. As I gained investment research experience and responsibilities, I was able to hire additional team members. Industry rules required all new team members to pass the Series 7 exam. This requirement yields an important clue regarding the kingdom economy agency testing policy.

In the early 2000s, I took over coverage of the U.S. Semiconductor industry. Shortly after taking over coverage, I had an opportunity to hire an outstanding young electrical engineer named Jasmine.[46] She was working in the semiconductor industry and was a graduate of an exceptional university. Jasmine was a person of high integrity. I was most pleased when Jasmine accepted the job offer.

On her first day, I informed Jasmine she needed to take the Series 7 exam. As expected, she asked about the consequences of failing the Series 7. "Termination" was my reply. All investment research professionals must pass the Series 7 exam and be licensed. This dire news caused Jasmine great consternation. She had just left a promising and well-paying technology job to join my team. During the recruiting period, I had not told her about taking the Series 7 exam. Now, on her first day, she was faced with the prospect of termination. Jasmine was very unhappy with me. I was not worried. I tried to assuage Jasmine's fears, fully confident in her abilities. Jasmine set about studying for the Series 7. At the time, a passing grade on the exam was 80%.[47] As required, Jasmine took the Series 7 exam. Jasmine scored 100%.

Real economy organizations spend a tremendous amount of time and money recruiting the best and brightest people. There is a great celebration when an exceptional new individual joins the team. At the same moment, it is entirely reasonable to expect all new hires to be subjected to required training and testing. An experienced business owner, adept at hiring and integrating new talent, has no fear of placing hurdles in front of new hires. A good hire will pass the required tests. Based on several interviews and industry experience, I knew there was *zero* chance Jasmine would fail the Series 7 exam. My almost perfect foreknowledge did not alleviate her anxiety, nor did her anxiety make it any less likely she would pass. It is also true Jasmine could not be exempted from the test. She would learn important lessons about financial analysis and brokerage industry compliance. If a new hire were not required to take the Series 7, they would be in personal legal jeopardy. Investment banks, money managers, and brokers are not permitted to serve clients without properly trained, tested, and licensed agents.

God knew there was zero chance Abraham would fail the test. There was zero chance Moses and Zipporah would fail the test. Given God is all-knowing, was the peril real? That is a question for philosophers and theologians. I say absolutely, yes. The trials and temptations I encounter are difficult and real. Yet the owner is faithful.[48] Any temptation will have a way of escape and any test or trial will be accompanied by the owner's grace sufficient to endure it.[49]

Testing promotes and empowers agents for service

Summarizing the cases, I propose several essential[50] propositions regarding the testing of agents. Kingdom economy testing is associated with promotion, power, and service. Abraham, Sarah, Moses, and Zipporah all had tremendous assignments. The severe tests and trials were not mean or capricious. The tests were necessary for each to bond with the owner and gain the strength and experience to be obedient in the face of extreme future difficulties. Following a period of temptation, Jesus returned in the power of the Spirit to begin his public ministry[51] and service to all.[52] Peter was told after his period of testing to "strengthen your brothers."[53]

Passing the Series 7 test gives brokerage employees the power to sell securities. The Series 7 test is also administered in part because the regulator and employer each want to verify the research analyst is qualified. The research analyst passing the test receives the commercial benefit of qualification and confidence of verification. God does not have a verification motive.

In the kingdom economy, trials and testing are for the benefit of the agent, for qualification to perform in the kingdom economy. Having been qualified through a trial, the agent is often promoted to a new level of authority. With each trial, God's grace is sufficient and "Christ's power"[54] rests on them. Peter, Paul, Moses, Zipporah, Sarah, and Abraham were able to perform well because they were tested, qualified, verified, and received the grace of the owner. Kingdom economy testing is for promotion, power and service.

Kingdom economy testing is for promotion, power and service.

Testing is a sign of productivity

Kingdom economy testing is common and desirable. James speaks of many and various trials.[55] Testing is also a fact of life in the real economy. In the real economy, lack of testing is a sign of a lack of progress. After completing a bachelor's degree, I sat for four different graduate entrance exams. The best result was on the graduate management admissions test ("GMAT") and so I went to business school. The standardized tests were the beginning of an unending string of academic and professional tests in the decades to come. The parade of tests includes regulatory exams, new degrees, continuing professional education, and research peer review. Testing never stops. Temptation never stops, either. Some temptation is of my own doing and some is from the fact Satan is an active opponent who leaves only until a future "opportune time."[56] Testing, trials, and temptation are signs of productivity. It is a sign I am making progress in the real economy. It is also a sign of productivity and a blessing in the kingdom economy. Kingdom agents do well to consider it all pure joy, as testing is a sign of productivity and movement toward spiritual completeness.

No exemptions and unlimited attempts

Tests must be completed. If a test is not completed, it will be administered again. There are no exemptions or substitutions. In Star Wars Episode V: The Empire Strikes Back, Master Jedi Yoda says to Luke Skywalker, "There is no try". In the book of Jonah, the title character receives the same command from God in chapter 1 and chapter 3. Jonah was required to do what God commanded. Peter had to overcome his fear of people to perform his agency role in the kingdom economy. Peter took "his stand with the eleven, raised his voice, and" preached the first message of the new Christian church.[57]

Jonah is an Old Testament example of multiple test attempts. The command to go to Nineveh came twice[58] because in the first instance Jonah chose to avoid the assignment. Nineveh was one of the urban centers of the Assyrian empire,[59] located on the site of Mosul, Iraq. According to most commentaries, it was a large city and it was guarded by a ruthless military. The culture of murder and death is depicted in French painter Eugene Delacroix's *Death of Sardanapalus.* Jonah may have been afraid for himself, or perhaps he didn't consider the Ninevites worthy of forgiveness. Regardless, Jonah was given an assignment and failed the test of obedience.

Spurgeon suggests that Jonah may have mistakenly followed providence rather than precepts. Jonah may have believed providence gave him a ship to get away from Nineveh to Tarshish, and that God may overlook his shirking. Spurgeon wrote, "Your guide in life is not so-called providence, but an unquestionable precept of the Lord. Do as God bids you and do it at once."[60] Jonah failed his first attempt at the Nineveh test of obedience. After his ordeal at sea, Jonah received the same command from God. On the second attempt, Jonah passed, and the owner's plan of redemption moved forward.

The cumulative kingdom economy grade may generally be an "I", for incomplete. *The Theory of the Kingdom* addresses how to live in the real economy as an agent of the kingdom economy. As long as kingdom agent is alive, the grade book indicates incomplete. The purpose of trials is to move me along toward completion, ultimately realized in the kingdom fully come. It is true I can disqualify myself from kingdom agency either by an act of deception like Ananias and Saphira[61] or, in certain circumstances, an act of betrayal and ultimate self-harm like Judas Iscariot.[62]

However, the owner has most often shown himself willing to offer many attempts to pass a test and many opportunities to be salt and light, producing life and peace in the real economy. God can be patient and generous with my progress because of his character. God is holy, loving, sovereign, and unlimited. God is holy. My faith will be tested as part of being transformed in my mind to prove the good, acceptable, and perfect will of God.[63] It is because of the owner's love I am not fired for my failures.[64] The owner's "acts of mercy indeed do not end, for His compassions do not fail. They are new every morning."[65] God's ways are not my ways and his process of refining and completing each agent is his alone.[66] It is highly motivating that God is unlimited. He can make up any losses I incur and offer a new attempt.[67]

Application. The missing servants

I previously discussed two variations of the parable of the talents. I will not repeat the analysis here. However, I note here real economy investing and entrepreneurship often comes with wins and losses. Both the Matthew and Luke versions of the parable omit the most common type of loser, the one that tries hard and fails. God is unlimited and can make up losses while I am still invested in the kingdom economy.

Several of the biblical trials outlined in this chapter do not indicate fault. In the case of Abraham, there is no specific sin for which the assignment of sacrificing Isaac was given. The charge in Job's case was made by Satan against God rather than due to a dishonorable act by Job. Whether I fail a trial of my own making, one of unfortunate real-economy circumstances, or one that is God-given, God is still unlimited. Nothing of value is ever lost in the kingdom economy. No contrite agent is turned away from another attempt. The owner "gives most people many second chances."[68] The owner of the kingdom economy can be more gracious than real economy owners because his resources are unlimited.

Restoration after all is lost

Biblical resource restoration is a regular occurrence. Resource restoration often comes when all has been lost. First, David's army returned to a town called Ziklag to find every person gone, every animal gone and the town burned to the ground. His own men wanted David dead. With God's help, David went on to recover all without any loss of life.[69] Second, the book of Joel speaks of an early rain for vindication and that God will take away the shame and "make up to you for the years that the swarming locust has eaten."[70] Third, it was the owner that restored Job's fortunes.[71] Fourth, the owner provided Isaac with space for a well after he had been pushed off two other well sites, including being pushed off the well of his father, Abraham.[72]

Application. Trust the owner and keep investing

In the real economy, I may lose title to a valuable plot of land, or I may make a bad losing investment. The owner is unlimited. He loves me and has the ways and means to set me free to begin all over again.[73] There is no interim accounting in the kingdom economy. Agency accounts are not closed until the owner finally calls them in. Investment in the kingdom economy is resourced by the king, not by the retained earnings of real economy business ventures. For as long as an agent is alive on the earth, the objective is to invest time and money as earnestly and aggressively as possible for life, peace, and growth. The owner fills in the potholes, including many of my own doing, according to his love and unlimited resources.

Notes

[1] Pittenger, D. J. (1993). The utility of the Myers-Briggs type indicator. *Review of educational research, 63*(4), 467-488. http://dx.doi.org/10.3102/00346543063004467.

[2] James 1:2-3.

[3] Keener, C. S., & Walton, J. H. (Eds.). (2016). *NIV, Cultural Backgrounds Study Bible: Bringing to Life the Ancient World of Scripture* (p. 2241). Zondervan.

[4] Keener, C. S., & Walton, J. H. (Eds.). (2016). *NIV, Cultural Backgrounds Study Bible: Bringing to Life the Ancient World of Scripture* (p. 2243, "Poverty and Revolt in Judea"). Zondervan.

[5] Keener, C. S., & Walton, J. H. (Eds.). (2016). *NIV, Cultural Backgrounds Study Bible: Bringing to Life the Ancient World of Scripture* (p. 2243, "Poverty and Revolt in Judea"). Zondervan.

[6] James 1:2.

[7] Blomberg, C. L. (1999). *Neither Poverty Nor Riches. New Studies in Biblical Theology* (p. 148). Grand Rapids/Cambridge: William B. Eerdman's Publishing Co.

[8] Williams, J. J. (2021). *Redemptive Kingdom Diversity: A Biblical Theology of the People of God* (pp. 136-137). Baker Academic.

[9] James 1:11.

[10] Micah 6:8.

[11] Blomberg, C. L. (1999). *Neither Poverty Nor Riches. New Studies in Biblical Theology* (pp. 148-149). Grand Rapids/Cambridge: William B. Eerdman's Publishing Co.

[12] Matthew 6:24.

[13] Carson, D. A. (Ed.). (2017). *NIV Zondervan Study Bible* (p. 731). Hodder & Stoughton.

[14] Hartley, J. E. (1988). *The book of Job* (p. 20). Wm. B. Eerdmans Publishing.
[15] Atkinson, D. J. (2022). *The message of Job.* InterVarsity Press.
[16] Job 1:9.
[17] Carson, D. A. (Ed.). (2017). *NIV Zondervan Study Bible* (p. 731). Hodder & Stoughton.; Keener, C. S., & Walton, J. H. (Eds.). (2016). *NIV, Cultural Backgrounds Study Bible: Bringing to Life the Ancient World of Scripture* (p. 847). Zondervan.
[18] James 1:3-4.
[19] Matthew chapter 26. Mark chapter 14. Luke chapter 7. New American Standard Bible, 1971, John 11:2. It may be the act of the anointing of Jesus with the extremely expensive perfume is another act of disinterested righteousness, like the worship of Job. The story the woman with the perfume appears in all four gospels:
[20] Keener, C. S., & Walton, J. H. (Eds.). (2016). *NIV, Cultural Backgrounds Study Bible: Bringing to Life the Ancient World of Scripture* (p. 907). Zondervan.
[21] Morrow, W. S. (1998). Toxic religion and the daughters of Job. *Studies in Religion/Sciences Religieuses, 27*(3), 263-276. http://dx.doi.org/10.1177/000842989802700302.
[22] Keener, C. S., & Walton, J. H. (Eds.). (2016). *NIV, Cultural Backgrounds Study Bible: Bringing to Life the Ancient World of Scripture* (p. 906). Zondervan.
[23] Madden, J. F. (2012). Performance-support bias and the gender pay gap among stockbrokers. *Gender & Society, 26*(3), 488-518. http://dx.doi.org/10.1177/0891243212438546.; Ruffle, B. J., & Shtudiner, Z. E. (2015). Are good-looking people more employable?. *Management Science, 61*(8), 1760-1776. http://dx.doi.org/10.1287/mnsc.2014.1927.
[24] Luke 22:31-32.
[25] Marinelli, A. (2020). Truth and Denial: Intertextual Compositions and Visual Transformations in the 'Caravaggisti' Gallery Paintings. *Object, 22*(1).
[26] Matthew 10:33.
[27] Blomberg, C. L. (1992). *Matthew: An exegetical and theological exposition of Holy Scripture* (Vol. 22, p. 393). B&H Publishing Group.
[28] Matthew 26:67-75.
[29] Matthew 26:75.
[30] Luke 24:34. 1 Corinthians 15:5. New American Standard Bible, 1971, John 21:15-17.
[31] Tenney, M. C. (1997). *John: the gospel of belief* (pp. 290-291). Wm. B. Eerdmans Publishing.
[32] Acts 2:14-39.
[33] John 21:18.
[34] New American Standard Bible, 1971, Acts 12:6-17.
[35] Rackham, R. B. (1901). *The Acts of the Apostles: An Exposition* (p. 177). Methuen.
[36] Luke 6:12-16. James son of Alphaeus was the 'other' James. The James that was killed was the brother of John.
[37] Isaiah 55:8-9.
[38] Exodus 4:24.
[39] New American Standard Bible, 1971, Genesis 18:10-15.
[40] New American Standard Bible, 1971, Genesis 21:1-7.
[41] Genesis 17:1-22.
[42] Genesis 22:1-2.

[43] Daly, R. J. (1977). The soteriological significance of the sacrifice of Isaac. *The Catholic Biblical Quarterly*, 45-75.
[44] Genesis 22:14.
[45] Keener, C. S., & Walton, J. H. (Eds.). (2016). *NIV, Cultural Backgrounds Study Bible: Bringing to Life the Ancient World of Scripture* (p. 56, "The Lord Will Provide"). Zondervan.
[46] The name has been changed for anonymity.
[47] My unverifiable recollection is I scored around eighty-five percent.
[48] New American Standard Bible, 1971, 1 Corinthians 10:13.
[49] New American Standard Bible, 1971, 2 Corinthians 12:9.
[50] Essentials means the propositions most important for agent life. Less essential but still important items include the inability to cheat due to an all-knowing proctor, the perfection of test content and timing and justice, mercy and covering of the test administrator.
[51] Luke 4:14.
[52] Mark 9:35. Mark 10:41-45.
[53] Luke 22:32.
[54] 2 Corinthians 12:9.
[55] James 1:2 Literal translation of the Greek word for divers in the King James version is *manifold* which is many and various. The New American Standard Bible uses the word *various.*
[56] Luke 4:13.
[57] Acts 2:14.
[58] New American Standard Bible, 1971, Jonah 1:2. New American Standard Bible, 1971, Jonah 3:2.
[59] Keener, C. S., & Walton, J. H. (Eds.). (2016). *NIV, Cultural Backgrounds Study Bible: Bringing to Life the Ancient World of Scripture* (p. 1558). Zondervan.
[60] Spurgeon, C. (1894). THE METROPOLITAN TABERNACLE PULPIT VOL. 36.
[61] Acts 5:1-11.
[62] Matthew 27:5.
[63] Romans 12:2.
[64] John 3:16.
[65] New American Standard Bible, 1971, Lamentations 3:22-23.
[66] Isaiah 55:8-9.
[67] Joel 2:25. Job 42:10. 1 Samuel 30:18-19.
[68] Blomberg, C. L. (1992). *Matthew: An exegetical and theological exposition of Holy Scripture* (Vol. 22, p. 374). B&H Publishing Group.
[69] 1 Samuel chapter 30.
[70] Joel 2:21-27.
[71] Job 42:10.
[72] Genesis 26:18-25.
[73] The Passion Translation Bible, 2017, Psalm 130:7. "O Israel, keep hoping, keep trusting and keep waiting on the Lord, for he is tenderhearted, kind and forgiving. He has a thousand ways to set you free!"

Conclusion

This original monograph presented a theory of the economy of the kingdom of God. The conclusion of the study is focused on practical application. Most chapters ended with applications of the model of human agency. In this chapter, I present a condensed list of potential applications, organized on three dimensions. First, individual agents are to be salt and light in the real economy. There are *tangible individual actions* that will reveal the truth and arrest corruption in the real economy. Second, some of the most important actions are less tangible in terms of the immediate outcome in the real economy. The second category is intangible ways individuals transport the resources of the kingdom economy across the messianic membrane into the real economy. Third, my research showed how organizations can yield kingdom products in the real economy now. Large organizations control large amounts of resources. The third dimension suggests practical ways kingdom agents can influence organizations to govern resources for life, peace and growth.

Tangible individual actions

A. Individual action can be oriented to the kingdom objectives of life, peace and growth. Marriage, parenting, coaching, neighboring, teaching, or working can produce life, peace and growth. Coaching Little League baseball to maximize peace looks very different than coaching to maximize wins. Parenting for peace differs from parenting to maximize a child's future income potential.

B. The final report of kingdom investment success is not due until the owner calls for a final accounting. Until then, agents may continue to invest, knowing the owner is unlimited. The moment investing stops, an agent becomes useless. I continue to take risks, regardless of the real economy tally at any moment in time. Nothing is ever lost for the owner of the kingdom economy.

C. Use all land and buildings as intensively as possible to bring even a small measure of life and peace into the real economy. Something as simple as letting young families use an outdoor shower or a bathroom brings a measure of peace to a community.

D. Spiritual credence goods are promoted through word-of-mouth customer testimonials. The strategy given by Peter in his letters is, "always being ready to make a defense to everyone who asks you to give an account for the hope that is in you, yet with gentleness and reverence."[1] Agents can always be ready and willing to answer questions about the kingdom economy.

E. Agency bonding requires maintenance. Heart labor and community involvement keep kingdom agents bonded to the true vine, Jesus. In a real economy professional association, bonded agents are required to complete continuing education requirements and pay professional dues. Minimally, staying bonded in the kingdom economy should include going to bible study and donating to a local church.

Intangible individual actions

A. It is up to each agent to take advantage of the opportunity to communicate with the owner.[2] Communication doesn't require a priest or anyone else to speak with God.[3] Jesus experienced all types of suffering and empathizes with real economy problems.[4] There is no problem or pain Jesus cannot relate to. God invites praying with boldness and to shovel each problem onto him.[5]

B. A kingdom economy resource-based analysis may reveal the cause and cure of misbehavior. Self-evaluation may reveal if dysfunction is due to a deficit of heart capital, heart labor, or is a problem with a spiritual stronghold. If the issue is heart capital, more bible study, nature walks, or time waiting on God may help. For a deficit of heart labor, time in prayer will help. If it is a spiritual stronghold, particularly if it is a generational issue, take up the weapons of warfare to take back the territory surrendered to the enemy.

C. Work continuously to increase the proportional offering of time, effort and money. The supply of kingdom spiritual goods is unlimited. The owner has already set aside the resources each agent could ever need. Goods are supplied according to proportional sacrifice and diligence in faith.[6]

D. Obtain heart capital by memorizing scripture. William Wilberforce became a social reformer in part by memorizing bible passages, including Psalm 119. God's word is perfect. It is a source of good heart capital, enabling an agent to do good.

E. Don't be satisfied with current spiritual awareness. Seek to know as much about your heart as the owner will reveal. Heart revelation comes by asking God. Being engaged in a local Christian community gives an agent additional revelation about God's character and what he is doing in the real economy.

F. Priscilla and C.T. Studd demonstrated long periods of prayer and fasting and being full of the Holy Spirit increases the willingness to take risks.[7] They exhibited a high level of love, trust, obedience and unity. The Studds extensively collaborated with a diverse group of kingdom agents.[8] Heart labor applied to heart capital can produce a lifetime of risk-taking.

Tangible organizational actions

A. Hire and promote following God's instruction to Samuel to focus on heart qualities. Do not hire according to visible qualities. Ask the Holy Spirit for guidance to see what the owner sees in the heart of each person. A candidate's appearance and resume will be deceiving. When asked in faith, the Holy Spirit will help make the right human resource decision, producing more life and peace in the real economy.

B. In modern businesses, agents make both mandatory and voluntary disclosures to owners. Chief Executive Officers and Chief Financial Officers tend to disclose only what is mandatory. Any additional information is selected to put them in the most positive light. The kingdom model is visibility. Disclosures intended to hide or manipulate truth are unacceptable. The kingdom agency approach is to voluntarily disclose as much data as possible.

C. Act quickly to resolve organizational inequities. Agents may be biased without knowing it.[9] Kingdom oriented servant leaders act quickly. The model demonstrated in the early New Testament church was to delegate management of a disputed resource to mature individuals in the aggrieved party raising the issue.

D. Kingdom economy organizational investment is group-level work undertaken to increase the government of peace, making disciples, revealing truth, arresting corruption, and producing life.[10] The guidelines of how organizations should invest include remaining active, praying for wisdom, listening to the Holy Spirit and working in unity. Kingdom-oriented organization investment requires looking past real economy cycles. Kingdom investment projects are best led by zealous finishers and funded with freewill offerings.

E. A first order heart labor for kingdom-oriented organizations is to pray together for good government. According to Paul in 1 Timothy, agents are obligated to pray for good government. The purpose of the prayer is to bring a measure of peace so that the gospel can be preached and every person has a chance to hear about Jesus.

F. Kingdom-oriented organizations should focus on lowering agency costs through bonding activities rather than monitoring. Bonding activities include continuing education, spending time together and apprenticeship.

G. Stay in the game! In the real economy, a group may lose title to a valuable plot of land, or may make a bad investment. As long as the real economy is in force, the objective is to invest time and money as earnestly and aggressively as possible. The owner is unlimited and is able to fill in any potholes, including many of an organization's own making, according to his love and unlimited resources.

Notes

[1] 1 Peter 3:15.
[2] 1 John 4:19-21.
[3] Ephesians 3:11-13.
[4] Hebrews 4:14-16.
[5] 1 Peter 5:7.
[6] 2 Peter 1:5, James 2:18, Ephesians 2:8.
[7] Grubb, N. (2014). *CT Studd: cricketer and pioneer* (p. 86). The Lutterworth Press., "after eight days spent alone in prayer and fasting."
[8] Grubb, N. (2014). *CT Studd: cricketer and pioneer* (p. 127). The Lutterworth Press. "I observe in the New Testament, is not apparent politeness and manifest disobedience, but filial or childlike obedience, trust and love."
[9] Psalm 19:12.
[10] Isaiah 9:6-7. Matthew 28:18-20. Matthew 5:13-16. John 10:10.

Epilogue

I am an unlikely candidate to write an academic book about the invisible agency-oriented economy of the kingdom of God. I spent 22 years working at various investment banks and hedge funds. For 20 of those years, my wife and I lived in Westchester County, just to the north of New York City. Over the years, I gained experience in capital markets, equity research, leadership, compliance, and corporate governance. By some measures, I was successful in my career. I had some successes and some failures. I always enjoyed my colleagues and capital markets tremendously. The people I worked with made every day a pleasure and a challenge.

As our children grew, my wife and I began to feel a career change was coming. I was offered an opportunity to teach Finance at Regent University in Virginia Beach. After a year of adjunct teaching, I took a full-time offer and moved from Bedford, New York, to Norfolk, Virginia.

The story is relevant because my wife and I were acting on what we thought God was telling us to do. It was not an audible telling. Rather, it was God speaking to our hearts. It was a steady push in a new direction. Steps were revealed one at a time. To feel the push, we engaged in the heart labors of prayer, worship, bible study, and fasting. We were simply attempting to listen closely and live for God's purposes in our family.

Fortunately, there is an excellent Finance Ph.D. program at Old Dominion University in Norfolk, Virginia. I graduated with a Ph.D. in Business Administration, with a concentration in Finance and International Business. Before the program, I thought I knew how to conduct research. I have been employed as a Wall Street analyst and research director for over 20 years. I have been a managing director at two global investment banks. Yet, the ODU program gave me an entirely new set of research tools. I assumed a Ph.D. would help with tenure, pay, promotion, and consulting opportunities. It does do that, but God's main purpose in leading me out of capital markets was to give me two specific insights. Out of the two insights, I received a research assignment. The assignment is to bring light to the agency-oriented model of the kingdom of God.

The first insight came out of studying agency theory, including the seminal paper by Jensen & Meckling.[1] The paper defines agency theory for businesses and academics. Owners of modern businesses use agents to manage day-to-day operations. Using agents enables a firm to grow very large and simultaneously maximize the value of the firm. The owner-agent setup is familiar as it is the reality of almost any employee or business owner. Agency theory, according to Jensen & Meckling, served as motivation for this study for the purpose of developing a detailed point of social science comparison. There are several well-entrenched alternative theories and updates to agency theory as well. Alternatives include the Upper Echelon theory,[2] stakeholder theory,[3] transaction cost theories,[4] and the behavioral finance stream.[5] Within agency theory, Jensen & Meckling is not the last word. The research of sociologist Kathleen Eisenhardt[6] has provided important updates to the theory and new propositions. There are future research opportunities in evaluating the kingdom economy with regard to multiple theories and multiple methods.

The methodology of this study is best described as a bibliology rather than a full systematic theology. There are additional elements of a systematic theology, including the eschatology and pneumatology embedded in the model of human agency. However, those are outcomes of the bibliology. I read through the bible twice, taking extensive notes, with a specific purpose of looking for elements of an economic system. The first read-through was with a New Living Translation. The second read-through was with a New American Standard version.[7] Chapter endnotes include a sample of the bible passages that inform the Theory of the Kingdom. The internal consistency of the bible, from the first book to the last, in terms of human agency and economic principles, is striking.

Once the bibliology was complete, I organized the chapters according to prior literature on agency. The general pattern of each chapter was to introduce the topic, present relevant bible passages and case studies, compare and inform the study with prior academic literature and then offer individual and organization level practical applications.

What began as a Ph.D. journey ended with a research mission to shed light on the model of human agency described in the Bible. I am hopeful this study is the first in a series of articles and books. I expect the next book project to focus on the anthropological part of the kingdom economy. As this first study was a bibliology, with some additional elements of systematic theology, there is a remaining gap for a detailed study of topics including the anthropology of the kingdom economy. The Bible has much to say about economic and finance issues concerning humanity, including equity and the environment.

I welcome your feedback. I can be contacted at linkedin.com/in/Andrewroot1 or at my Regent University faculty email.

Notes

[1] Jensen, M. C., & Meckling, W. H. (1976). Theory of the Firm: Managerial Behavior, Agency Costs and Ownership Structure. *Journal of Financial Economics, 3*(4), 305-360. http://dx.doi.org/10.1016/0304-405X(76)90026-X.

[2] Hambrick, D. C., & Mason, P. A. (1984). Upper echelons: The organization as a reflection of its top managers. *Academy of management review, 9*(2), 193-206. http://dx.doi.org/10.2307/258434.

[3] Freeman, R. E. (2010). *Strategic management: A stakeholder approach.* Cambridge university press. http://dx.doi.org/10.1017/CBO9781139192675.

[4] Coase, R. H. (1937). The nature of the firm. *Economica, 4*(16), 386-405. http://dx.doi.org/10.1111/j.1468-0335.1937.tb00002.x.; Williamson, O. E. (1981). The economics of organization: The transaction cost approach. *American journal of sociology, 87*(3), 548-577. http://dx.doi.org/10.1086/227496.

[5] Barberis, N., & Thaler, R. (2003). A survey of behavioral finance. In G. Constantinides, M. Harris, & R. Stulz (Eds.), *Handbook of the Economics of Finance* (Vol. 1., pp. 1053-1128). Elsevier. http://dx.doi.org/10.2139/ssrn.327880.

[6] Eisenhardt, K. M. (1989). Agency theory: An assessment and review. *Academy of management review, 14*(1), 57-74. http://dx.doi.org/10.2307/258191.

[7] Credit for my hardcover copy, on long term borrow, goes to the Gideons and my friend Jack.

Bibliography

Abel, J. R., & Deitz, R. (2014). Do the benefits of college still outweigh the costs?. *Current issues in economics and finance, 20*(3).

Akerlof, G. A. (1978). The market for "lemons": Quality uncertainty and the market mechanism. In *Uncertainty in economics* (pp. 235-251). Academic Press. http://dx.doi.org/10.1017/CBO9780511528248.007.

Akerlof, G. A., & Shiller, R. J. (2010). *Animal spirits: How human psychology drives the economy, and why it matters for global capitalism.* Princeton university press. http://dx.doi.org/10.2307/j.ctv36mk90z.

Alcorn, R. (2003). *The Law of Rewards: Giving What You Can't Keep to Gain What You Can't Lose.* Tyndale House Publishers, Inc.

Alonso, W. (2013). Location and land use. In *Location and land use.* Harvard university press. http://dx.doi.org/10.4159/harvard.9780674730854.

Anderson, J. E. (2005). A biblical and economic analysis of jubilee property provisions. *Faith and Economics, 46,* 25-41.

Apple Inc., (2021, October 29). SEC Form 10-K (p. 40). *Apple Inc.* chrome-extension://efaidnbmnnnibpcajpcglclefindmkaj/https://d18rn0p25nwr6d.cloudfront.net/CIK-0000320193/42ede86f-6518-450f-bc88-60211bf39c6d.pdf

Archdiocese of New Orleans. (2022). *The Three Pillars of Lent: Prayer, Fasting and Almsgiving* (Spring). https://nolacatholic.org/prayer-fasting-and-almsgiving.

Atkinson, D. J. (2022). *The message of Job.* InterVarsity Press.

Augustin, P., Brenner, M., & Subrahmanyam, M. G. (2019). Informed options trading prior to takeover announcements: Insider trading?. *Management Science, 65*(12), 5697-5720. http://dx.doi.org/10.1287/mnsc.2018.3122.

Azzi, C., & Ehrenberg, R. (1975). Household allocation of time and church attendance. *Journal of political Economy, 83*(1), 27-56. http://dx.doi.org/10.1086/260305.

Balafoutas, L., & Kerschbamer, R. (2020). Credence goods in the literature: What the past fifteen years have taught us about fraud, incentives, and the role of institutions. *Journal of Behavioral and Experimental Finance, 26,* 100285. http://dx.doi.org/10.1016/j.jbef.2020.100285.

Ballantine, H. W. (1946). *Corporations.* Callagham.

Bank of Japan. (2022) *About the Bank.* https://www.boj.or.jp/en/about/outline/index.htm/.

Banks, J., Blundell, R., & Tanner, S. (1998). Is there a retirement-savings puzzle?. *American Economic Review,* 769-788.

Barberis, N., & Thaler, R. (2003). A survey of behavioral finance. In G. Constantinides, M. Harris, & R. Stulz (Eds.), *Handbook of the Economics of Finance* (Vol. 1., pp. 1053-1128). Elsevier. http://dx.doi.org/10.2139/ssrn.327880.

Barna, G. (1993). *Turn Around Churches.* Regal Books.

Barrett, C. K. (1978). *The Gospel according to St. John: An introduction with commentary and notes on the Greek Text.* Westminster John Knox Press.

Barro, R. J., Mankiw, N. G., & Sala-i-Martin, X. (1992). *Capital mobility in neoclassical models of growth* (No. w4206). National Bureau of Economic Research.

Baugus, B. (2019). *A Biblical Path for a Prosperous Society.* Rowman & Littlefield.

BBC News. (2013, March 14). How many Roman Catholics are there in the world? *British Broadcasting Corporation.* https://www.bbc.com/news/world-21443313.

Bebchuk, L. A., & Tallarita, R. (2022). Will Corporations Deliver Value to All Stakeholders?. *Forthcoming, Vanderbilt Law Review, 75.* http://dx.doi.org/10.2139/ssrn.3899421.

Becker, G. S. (1992, October 13) Nobel Prize Outreach AB 2023. *NobelPrize.org.* https://www.nobelprize.org/prizes/economic-sciences/1992/becker/facts/

Becker, G. S. (2009). *Human capital: A theoretical and empirical analysis, with special reference to education* (p. 17). University of Chicago Press. http://dx.doi.org/10.7208/chicago/9780226041223.001.0001.

Benartzi, S., & Thaler, R. H. (1995). Myopic loss aversion and the equity premium puzzle. *The quarterly journal of Economics, 110*(1), 73-92. http://dx.doi.org/10.2307/2118511.

Bennett, J. C. (1954). *Christian values and economic life* (p. 210). Harper.

Berenskoetter, F., & Williams, M. J. (Eds.). (2007). *Power in world politics (p. 83).* Routledge. http://dx.doi.org/10.4324/9780203944691.

Bernanke, B. S. (1983). Irreversibility, uncertainty, and cyclical investment. *The quarterly journal of economics, 98*(1), 85-106. http://dx.doi.org/10.2307/1885568.

Bertrand, M., & Mullainathan, S. (2003). Enjoying the quiet life? Corporate governance and managerial preferences. *Journal of political Economy, 111*(5), 1043-1075. http://dx.doi.org/10.1086/376950.

Bible, H. New American Standard Bible. 1971. *LaHabra, California: The Lockman Foundation.*

Bible, H. (1996). New living translation. *Tyndale House Foundation: Carol Stream, Illinois, USA, 2004,* 2015.

Blank, R. M., & McGurn, W. (2003). *Is the market moral?: a dialogue on religion, economics and justice.* Rowman & Littlefield.

Block, W. E. (2011). Review of Ostrom's governing the commons. *Libertarian papers, 3,* 1.

Blomberg, C. L. (1992). *Matthew: An exegetical and theological exposition of Holy Scripture* (Vol. 22). B&H Publishing Group.

Blomberg, C. L. (1999). *Neither Poverty Nor Riches. New Studies in Biblical Theology.* Grand Rapids/Cambridge: William B. Eerdman's Publishing Co.

Blomberg, C. L. (2001). Neither poverty nor riches: A biblical theology of material possessions. *Pro Ecclesia, 10*(2), 235-237. http://dx.doi.org/10.1177/106385120101000209.

Blomberg, C. L. (2020). *Can We Still Believe in God?: Answering Ten Contemporary Challenges to Christianity* (p. 87). Brazos Press.

Blumhofer, E. (2006). Azusa Street revival. *Christian Century, 123*(5), 20-22.

Board of Governors of the Federal Reserve. (2022). *Monetary policy objectives. Section 2A.* https://www.federalreserve.gov/aboutthefed/section2a.htm.

Board of Governors of the Federal Reserve. (2022). *Monetary Policy: What Are Its Goals? How Does It Work?* https://www.federalreserve.gov/monetarypolicy/monetary-policy-what-are-its-goals-how-does-it-work.htm.

Böckerman, P., & Vainiomäki, J. (2013). Stature and life-time labor market outcomes: Accounting for unobserved differences. *Labour Economics, 24,* 86-96. http://dx.doi.org/10.1016/j.labeco.2013.06.003.

Bond, P., Edmans, A., & Goldstein, I. (2012). The real effects of financial markets. *Annu. Rev. Financ. Econ., 4*(1), 339-360. http://dx.doi.org/10.1146/annurev-financial-110311-101826.

Bóo, F. L., Rossi, M. A., & Urzúa, S. S. (2013). The labor market return to an attractive face: Evidence from a field experiment. *Economics Letters, 118*(1), 170-172.

Boubakri, N., Dionne, G., & Triki, T. (2008). Consolidation and value creation in the insurance industry: The role of governance. *Journal of Banking & Finance, 32*(1), 56-68. http://dx.doi.org/10.1016/j.jbankfin.2007.09.004.

Brannan, R. (2017). *The Apostolic Fathers: A New Translation* (pp. 263-276). Lexham Press.

Brighenti, A. (2006). On territory as relationship and law as territory. *Canadian Journal of Law and Society/La Revue Canadienne Droit et Société, 21*(2), 65-86. http://dx.doi.org/10.1017/S0829320100008954.

Brooks, R. (2013). *Financial management: core concepts* (p. 220). Pearson.

Brown, R. (1982). *The Bible Speaks Today: The Message of Hebrews.* InterVarsity Press.

Bruce, F. F. (1973). The Holy Spirit in the Acts of the Apostles. *Interpretation, 27*(2), 166-183. http://dx.doi.org/10.1177/002096437302700203.

Bruce, F. F. (1994). *The Gospel of John: Introduction, Exposition, Notes.* Wm. B. Eerdmans Publishing.

Brune, C., & Files, J. (2019). Biblical screens and the stock selection process: applications for a student-managed fund. *Christian Business Academy Review, 14.*

Brunner, E. (1934). *The mediator: A study of the central doctrine of the Christian faith* (Vol. 3, Chapter 18, paragraph 2), James Clarke & Co.

Bubola, E. (2022, June 14). The Grenfell Fire, 5 Years Later. *The New York Times.* https://www.nytimes.com/2022/06/14/world/europe/grenfell-fire-london-explainer.html.

Burge, G. M., Cohick, L. H., & Green, G. L. (2010). *The New Testament in Antiquity: A Survey of the New Testament within Its Cultural Context.* Zondervan Academic.

Burge, G. M., & Green, G. L. (2020). *The New Testament in Antiquity: A Survey of the New Testament Within Its Cultural Contexts Second Edition.* Zondervan Academic.

Butter, M., & Knight, P. (Eds.). (2020). *Routledge handbook of conspiracy theories*. Routledge. http://dx.doi.org/10.4324/9780429452734.

Caglio, A., Dossi, A., & Van der Stede, W. A. (2018). CFO role and CFO compensation: An empirical analysis of their implications. *Journal of Accounting and Public Policy, 37*(4), 265-281. http://dx.doi.org/10.1016/j.jaccpubpol.2018.07.002.

Cardarelli, F. (2003). *Encyclopedia of Scientific units, weights and measures: their SI equivalences and origins*. Springer Science & Business Media.

Carhart, M. M. (1997). On persistence in mutual fund performance. *The Journal of finance, 52*(1), 57-82. http://dx.doi.org/10.1111/j.1540-6261.1997.tb03808.x.

Carson, D. A. (1999). God Is Love. *Bibliotheca Sacra-Dallas-, 156*, 131-142.

Carson, D. (2019, July 29). What Does 'Born of Water and the Spirit' Mean in John 3:5? *The Gospel Coalition*. https://www.thegospelcoalition.org/article/born-water-spirit-mean/

Carson, D. A. (Ed.). (2017). *NIV Zondervan Study Bible* (p. 731). Hodder & Stoughton.

Cartwright, M. (2013, November 1) Slavery in the Roman World. *World History Encyclopedia*. https://www.worldhistory.org/article/629/slavery-in-the-roman-world/

Chava, S., & Purnanandam, A. (2010). CEOs versus CFOs: Incentives and corporate policies. *Journal of financial Economics, 97*(2), 263-278. http://dx.doi.org/10.1016/j.jfineco.2010.03.018.

Chen, J., Kanjilal-Bhaduri, S., & Pastore, F. (2022). *Updates on Returns to Education in India: Analysis using PLFS 2018-19 Data* (No. 1016). GLO Discussion Paper. http://dx.doi.org/10.2139/ssrn.4114527.

Claar, V. V., & Klay, R. J. (2015). *Economics in Christian Perspective: Theory, Policy and Life Choices*. InterVarsity Press

Coase, R. H. (1937). The nature of the firm. *Economica, 4*(16), 386-405. http://dx.doi.org/10.1111/j.1468-0335.1937.tb00002.x.

Coffey, D. (1990). The Holy Spirit as the mutual love of the Father and the Son. *Theological Studies, 51*(2), 193-229. http://dx.doi.org/10.1177/004056399005100202.

Coibion, O., Gorodnichenko, Y., & Wieland, J. (2012). The optimal inflation rate in New Keynesian models: should central banks raise their inflation targets in light of the zero lower bound?. *Review of Economic Studies, 79*(4), 1371-1406. http://dx.doi.org/10.1093/restud/rds013.

Collins, F. S. (2006). *The language of God: A scientist presents evidence for belief* (No. 111). Simon and Schuster.

Compassion International. (2022, October). Releasing Children from Poverty in Jesus' Name. *Compassion International*. https://www.compassion.com/about/about-us.htm

Daly, R. J. (1977). The soteriological significance of the sacrifice of Isaac. *The Catholic Biblical Quarterly*, 45-75.

Damodaran, A. (2022, January). Historic Returns on Stocks, Bonds and Bills: 1928-2021. NYU Stern School of Business. https://pages.stern.nyu.edu/~adamodar/New_Home_Page/datafile/histretSP.html

De Lacey, D. R. (1987). Jesus as mediator. *Journal for the Study of the New Testament, 9*(29), 101-121. http://dx.doi.org/10.1177/0142064X8700902906.

Dein, S. (2021). Covid-19 and the apocalypse: Religious and secular perspectives. *Journal of religion and health, 60*(1), 5-15. http://dx.doi.org/10.1007/s10943-020-01100-w.

Dion, K., Berscheid, E., & Walster, E. (1972). What is beautiful is good. *Journal of personality and social psychology, 24*(3), 285. http://dx.doi.org/10.1037/h0033731.

Docherty, S. (2015). *The Jewish Pseudepigrapha: An Introduction to the Literature of the Second Temple Period* (p. 5). Fortress Press.

Donnelly, J. (1970, July). Creation ex nihilo. In *Proceedings of the American Catholic Philosophical Association* (Vol. 44, pp. 172-184).

Doukas, J. A., & Wang, L. (2014). Does the bonding effect matter in a more integrated capital market world?. *Journal of International Money and Finance, 47*, 162-184. http://dx.doi.org/10.1016/j.jimonfin.2014.05.022.

Dow, D., Cuypers, I. R., & Ertug, G. (2016). The effects of within-country linguistic and religious diversity on foreign acquisitions. *Journal of International Business Studies, 47*(3), 319-346. http://dx.doi.org/10.1057/jibs.2016.7.

Dworkin, R. (2002). *Sovereign virtue: The theory and practice of equality.* Harvard university press. http://dx.doi.org/10.2307/j.ctv1c3pd0r.

Edin, M. H. (1998). Learning what righteousness means. Hosea 6: 6 and the ethic of mercy in Matthew's gospel. *Word & world, 18*(4), 355-363.

Edmans, A. (2020). *Grow the Pie: How Great Companies Deliver Both Purpose and Profit–Updated and Revised.* Cambridge University Press. http://dx.doi.org/10.1017/9781108860093.

Eisenhardt, K. M. (1989). Agency theory: An assessment and review. *Academy of management review, 14*(1), 57-74. http://dx.doi.org/10.2307/258191.

Ekelund, R. B., Tollison, R. D., Anderson, G. M., Hébert, R. F., & Davidson, A. B. (1996). *Sacred trust: the medieval church as an economic firm* (p. 6). Oxford University Press.

Elbaum, B., & Singh, N. (1995). The Economic Rationale of Apprenticeship Training: Some Lessons from British and US Experience. *Industrial Relations: A Journal of Economy and Society, 34*(4), 593-622. http://dx.doi.org/10.1111/j.1468-232X.1995.tb00390.x.

Elden, S. (2010). Thinking territory historically. *Geopolitics, 15*(4), 757-761. http://dx.doi.org/10.1080/14650041003717517.

Elvidge, C. D., Baugh, K. E., Kihn, E. A., Kroehl, H. W., Davis, E. R., & Davis, C. W. (1997). Relation between satellite observed visible-near infrared emissions, population, economic activity and electric power consumption. *International Journal of Remote Sensing, 18*(6), 1373-1379. http://dx.doi.org/10.1080/014311697218485.

Emons, W. (2001). Credence goods monopolists. *International Journal of Industrial Organization, 19*(3-4), 375-389. http://dx.doi.org/10.1016/S0167-7187(99)00023-5.

Erickson, M. J. (1998). *Christian theology* (pp. 21-23) Baker Academic.

Eskola, T. (2015). *A narrative theology of the New Testament: exploring the metanarrative of exile and restoration* (Vol. 350). Mohr Siebeck.

European Central Bank. (2022). *Introduction.* https://www.ecb.europa.eu/mopo/intro/html/index.en.html.

Evans, J. L., & Archer, S. H. (1968). Diversification and the reduction of dispersion: an empirical analysis. *The Journal of Finance, 23*(5), 761-767. http://dx.doi.org/10.2307/2325905.

Fama, E. F. (1970). Efficient capital markets: A review of theory and empirical work. *The journal of Finance, 25*(2), 383-417. http://dx.doi.org/10.2307/2325486.

Fama, E. F., & French, K. R. (2015). A five-factor asset pricing model. *Journal of financial economics, 116*(1), 1-22. http://dx.doi.org/10.1016/j.jfineco.2014.10.010.

Federal Reserve Bank of St. Louis. (2022, May 10). *Economic Lowdown Video Series* (Episode 6). The Federal Reserve, Federal Reserve Bank of St. Louis. https://www.stlouisfed.org/education/economic-lowdown-video-series/episode-6-circular-flow

Federal Reserve Bank of St. Louis. (2022, September 15). *Personal Saving Rate.* The Federal Reserve, Federal Reserve Bank of St. Louis. https://fred.stlouisfed.org/series/PSAVERT

Feingold, A. (1992). Good-looking people are not what we think. *Psychological bulletin, 111*(2), 304. http://dx.doi.org/10.1037/0033-2909.111.2.304.

Feldman, L. H. (1994). Josephus' portrayal of the Hasmoneans compared with 1 Maccabees (pp 41-68. In *Josephus and the History of the Greco-Roman Period.* http://dx.doi.org/10.1163/9789004509122_006.

Filmer, W. E. (1966). The Chronology of the Reign of Herod the Great. *The Journal of Theological Studies,* 283-298. http://dx.doi.org/10.1093/jts/XVII.2.283.

Finke, R. (2003). Spiritual capital: Definitions, applications, and new frontiers. *Retrieved April, 24,* 2005. http://www.metanexus.net/archive/spiritualcapitalresearchprogram/pdf/finke.pdf.

Fisher, I. (1906). *The nature of capital and income.* Macmillan and Cie. http://dx.doi.org/10.1515/9783112351369.

Fisher, I. (1930). *Theory of interest: as determined by impatience to spend income and opportunity to invest it.* Augustusm Kelly Publishers, Clifton.

Francis, J. R., & Wilson, E. R. (1988). Auditor changes: A joint test of theories relating to agency costs and auditor differentiation. *Accounting Review,* 663-682.

Franklin, J. (2014). *Fasting: Opening the Door to a Deeper, More Intimate, More Powerful Relationship with God.* Charisma Media.

Freeman, R. B. (1999). The economics of crime. *Handbook of labor economics, 3,* 3529-3571.

Freeman, R. E. (2010). *Strategic management: A stakeholder approach.* Cambridge university press. http://dx.doi.org/10.1017/CBO9781139192675.

Friedman, M. (1975). *There's no such thing as a free lunch* (pp. 113-15). LaSalle, IL: Open Court.

Gadinis, S. (2012). The SEC and the financial industry: Evidence from enforcement against broker-dealers. *The Business Lawyer*, 679-728. http://dx.doi.org/10.2139/ssrn.1333717.

Garcia, M. (2023, January 4). *International Space Station Facts and Figures*. National Aeronautics and Space Administration. https://www.nasa.gov/feature/facts-and-figures.

Garvey, R., & Murphy, A. (2004). Are professional traders too slow to realize their losses?. *Financial Analysts Journal*, *60*(4), 35-43. http://dx.doi.org/10.2469/faj.v60.n4.2635.

Gasiorowski, M. J. (1995). Economic crisis and political regime change: An event history analysis. *American political science review*, *89*(4), 882-897. http://dx.doi.org/10.2307/2082515.

Gay, D. (1996). Book Review: Divine Discourse: Philosophical Reflections on the Claim That God Speaks. *Christianity & literature*, *45*(3/4), 401-403. http://dx.doi.org/10.1177/014833319604500314.

Gaynor, M., & Pauly, M. (1987). *Alternative compensation arrangements and productive efficiency in partnerships: evidence from medical group practice [Working paper]*. National Bureau of Economic Research. https://www.nber.org/papers/w2170.

Glasson, T. F. (1965). *The Revelation of John* (Vol. 63, p. 29). CUP Archive.

Goldstein, I., & Yang, L. (2022). Commodity financialization and information transmission. *The Journal of Finance*, *77*(5), 2613-2667. http://dx.doi.org/10.1111/jofi.13165.

Graham, L. (2017). *Investing with integrity*. Kingdom Life Publishing.

Grant, F. C. (1926). *The Economic background of the Gospels*. Oxford University Press, H. Milford.

Grenz, S. J. (2001). *The social God and the relational self: A Trinitarian theology of the imago Dei* (Vol. 1, pp 165-166.). Westminster John Knox Press.

Greshko, M. (2021, December 17). *The Universe is expanding faster than it should be*. https://www.nationalgeographic.com/science/article/the-universe-is-expanding-faster-than-it-should-be.

Groh, A. Liechtenstein, H. Lieser, K. & Biesinger, M. (2022, September 15). The Venture Capital and Private Equity Country Attractiveness Index. *IESE Business School*. https://blog.iese.edu/vcpeindex/.

Grossman, S. J., & Stiglitz, J. E. (1980). On the impossibility of informationally efficient markets. *The American economic review*, *70*(3), 393-408.

Grubb, N. (2014). *CT Studd: cricketer and pioneer*. The Lutterworth Press.

Grubb, N. (2014). *Rees Howells, Intercessor*. The Lutterworth Press.

Gruber, J., & Owings, M. (1996). Physician Financial Incentives and Cesarean Section Delivery. *The RAND Journal of Economics*, *27*(1), 99. http://dx.doi.org/10.2307/2555794.

Grudem, W. A. (2009). *Systematic theology: An introduction to biblical doctrine*. Zondervan Academic.

Gryta, T., Lublin, J. S. & Maremont, M. (2017, October 29). GE Board Kept in the Dark About CEO's Extra Plane. *The Wall Street Journal*. https://www.wsj.

com/articles/ge-board-was-kept-in-the-dark-about-ceos-extra-plane-1509 274805.

Guiso, L., Sapienza, P., & Zingales, L. (2015). The value of corporate culture. *Journal of Financial Economics, 117*(1), 60-76. http://dx.doi.org/10.1016/j.jfineco.2014.05.010.

Gupta, A., Briscoe, F., & Hambrick, D. C. (2018). Evenhandedness in resource allocation: Its relationship with CEO ideology, organizational discretion, and firm performance. *Academy of Management Journal, 61*(5), 1848-1868. http://dx.doi.org/10.5465/amj.2016.1155.

Guthrie, K., Sokolowsky, J., & Wan, K. M. (2012). CEO compensation and board structure revisited. *The Journal of Finance, 67*(3), 1149-1168. http://dx.doi.org/10.1111/j.1540-6261.2012.01744.x.

Guzik, D. (2021). Isaiah 55: An Invitation to Receive the Glory of the Lord's Restoration. *Enduring Word.* https://enduringword.com/bible-commentary/isaiah-55/

Habig, M. A. (1973). St. Francis of Assisi: Omnibus of Sources (Rule of 1221, pp. 44-45). *London, SPCK.*

Hambrick, D. C., & Mason, P. A. (1984). Upper echelons: The organization as a reflection of its top managers. *Academy of management review, 9*(2), 193-206. http://dx.doi.org/10.2307/258434.

Hansson, M. G. (2007). *The private sphere: an emotional territory and its agent* (Vol. 15, p. 3). Springer Science & Business Media.

Haroutunian, J. (1958). *Calvin: Commentaries* (p. 155). L. P. Smith (Ed.). London: SCM Press.

Harris, D. M. (2009). *The eternal inheritance in Hebrews: The appropriation of the Old Testament inheritance motif by the author of Hebrews.* Trinity International University.

Harris, D. M. (2019). *Hebrews.* B&H Publishing Group.

Hartley, J. E. (1988). *The book of Job* (p. 20). Wm. B. Eerdmans Publishing.

Hawking, S. (1996). *The illustrated a brief history of time* (p. 11, figure 1.4). Bantam.

Hayek, F. A. (2009). The use of knowledge in society. In *Knowledge management and organizational design* (pp. 7-15). Routledge. http://dx.doi.org/10.1017/CBO9780511817410.007.

He, L., & Luo, Q. (2021, January). The development and research of Chinese Artistic Swimming under the background of big data--compared with the world's top three teams. In *2021 International Conference on Information Technology and Contemporary Sports (TCS)* (pp. 318-321). IEEE. http://dx.doi.org/10.1109/TCS52929.2021.00071.

Healy, P. M., & Palepu, K. G. (2001). Information asymmetry, corporate disclosure, and the capital markets: A review of the empirical disclosure literature. *Journal of accounting and economics, 31*(1-3), 405-440. http://dx.doi.org/10.1016/S0165-4101(01)00018-0.

Helander, K. (2020, September 22). Wells Fargo's CEO comments about diverse talent anger some employees. *CNBC.* https://www.cnbc.com/2020/09/22/wells-fargo-ceo-ruffles-feathers-with-comments-about-diverse-talent.html.

Heller, W. P., & Starr, R. M. (1976). Equilibrium with non-convex transactions costs: monetary and non-monetary economies. *The Review of Economic Studies, 43*(2), 195-215. 176-185. http://dx.doi.org/10.2307/2297318.

Henderson, J. W., Pisciotta, J. O., & Pisciotta, J. L. (Eds.). (2005). *Faithful economics: the moral worlds of a neutral science.* Baylor University Press.

Henry, M. (1991). *Matthew Henry's commentary on the whole Bible* (Vol. 5, Acts 17). Peabody^ eMA MA: Hendrickson Publishers.

Herford, R. T. (2006). *Christianity in Talmud and Midrash.* KTAV Publishing House, Inc.

Hertzke, A. D. (2008). International religious freedom policy: Taking stock. *The Review of Faith & International Affairs, 6*(2), 17-23. http://dx.doi.org/10.1080/15570274.2008.9523333.

Hilary, G., & Hui, K. W. (2009). Does religion matter in corporate decision making in America?. *Journal of financial economics, 93*(3), 455-473. http://dx.doi.org/10.1016/j.jfineco.2008.10.001.

Hirshleifer, D., Low, A., & Teoh, S. H. (2012). Are overconfident CEOs better innovators?. *The journal of finance, 67*(4), 1457-1498. http://dx.doi.org/10.1111/j.1540-6261.2012.01753.x.

Hoge, D. R. (Ed.). (1996). *Money matters: Personal giving in American churches* (p. 60). Westminster John Knox Press.

Hou, K., Xue, C., & Zhang, L. (2015). Digesting anomalies: An investment approach. *The Review of Financial Studies, 28*(3), 650-705. http://dx.doi.org/10.1093/rfs/hhu068.

Howard, K., & Sharp, J. A. (1985). Social indicators and policy selection: An experiment in constructing a social objective function. *European Journal of Operational Research, 19*(2). http://dx.doi.org/10.1016/0377-2217(85)90170-5.

Hull, B. B., & Bold, F. (1989). Towards an economic theory of the church. *International Journal of Social Economics.* http://dx.doi.org/10.1108/EUM0000000000444.

Hurd, E. S. (2015). Beyond religious freedom. In *Beyond Religious Freedom.* Princeton University Press. http://dx.doi.org/10.1515/9781400873814.

Iannaccone, L. R. (1984). *Consumption Capital and Habit Formation with an Application to Religious Participation* (Publication No. T29220) [Doctoral dissertation, The University of Chicago]. ProQuest Dissertations & Theses Global.

Iannaccone, L. R. (1988). A formal model of church and sect. *American journal of sociology, 94,* S241-S268. http://dx.doi.org/10.1086/228948.

Iannaccone, L. R. (1992). Religious markets and the economics of religion. *Social compass, 39*(1), 123-131. http://dx.doi.org/10.1177/003776892039001012.

Iannaccone, L. R. (1998). Introduction to the Economics of Religion. *Journal of economic literature, 36*(3), 1465-1495.

Işgın, E., & Sopher, B. (2015). Information transparency, fairness and labor market efficiency. *Journal of Behavioral and Experimental Economics, 58,* 33-39. http://dx.doi.org/10.1016/j.socec.2015.06.005.

James III, R. N., & Jones, K. S. (2011). Tithing and religious charitable giving in America. *Applied Economics, 43*(19), 2441-2450. http://dx.doi.org/10.1080/00036840903213384.

Janzen, W. (2000). *Exodus: Believers Church Bible Commentary* (p. 85). MennoMedia, Inc.

Jegadeesh, N. (1990). Evidence of predictable behavior of security returns. *The Journal of finance, 45*(3), 881-898. http://dx.doi.org/10.1111/j.1540-6261.1990.tb05110.x.

Jensen, M. C., & Meckling, W. H. (1976). Theory of the Firm: Managerial Behavior, Agency Costs and Ownership Structure. *Journal of Financial Economics, 3*(4), 305-360. http://dx.doi.org/10.1016/0304-405X(76)90026-X.

Jensen, M. C., & Meckling, W. H. (2019). Theory of the firm: Managerial behavior, agency costs and ownership structure. In *Corporate Governance* (pp. 77-132). Gower.

Joseph, S. (2020). Isolation and Mental Health: The Psychological Impact of COVID-19 Lockdown on Children. *Mukt Shabd Journal, 9*(8), 399-405.

Judge, W. Q., & Douglas, T. J. (2013). Entrepreneurship as a leap of faith. *Journal of management, spirituality & religion, 10*(1), 37-65. http://dx.doi.org/10.1080/14766086.2012.758047.

Kabel, A., & Chmidling, C. (2014). Disaster prepper: Health, identity, and American survivalist culture. *Human organization, 73*(3), 258-266. http://dx.doi.org/10.17730/humo.73.3.l34252tg03428527.

Kahneman, D., & Tversky, A. (2013). Prospect theory: An analysis of decision under risk. In *Handbook of the fundamentals of financial decision making: Part I* (pp. 99-127). http://dx.doi.org/10.1142/9789814417358_0006.

Kane, T. J., & Rouse, C. E. (1995). Labor-Market Returns to Two-and Four-Year College. *The American Economic Review, 85*(3), 600.

Kantrowitz, M. (2007). The financial value of a higher education. *Journal of Student Financial Aid, 37*(1), 5. http://dx.doi.org/10.55504/0884-9153.1075.

Kaplan, S. N. (2008). Are US CEOs Overpaid?. *Academy of Management Perspectives, 22*(2), 5-20.

Karolyi, G. A. (2012). Corporate governance, agency problems and international cross-listings: A defense of the bonding hypothesis. *Emerging Markets Review, 13*(4), 516-547. http://dx.doi.org/10.1016/j.ememar.2012.08.001.

Kay, G. (2022, April 19). Elon Musk said life on Mars won't be luxurious – it will be 'cramped, difficult, hard work'. *Insider*. https://www.businessinsider.com/elon-musk-mars-trip-cramped-difficult-hard-work-2022-4.

Keener, C. (2022, October 1). *Mark in 51 Minutes*. https://craigkeener.com/mark-in-51-minutes/

Keener, C. S., & Walton, J. H. (Eds.). (2016). *NIV, Cultural Backgrounds Study Bible: Bringing to Life the Ancient World of Scripture*. Zondervan.

Keister, L. A. (2011). *Faith and money: How religion contributes to wealth and poverty* (pp. 26-29). Cambridge University Press. http://dx.doi.org/10.1017/CBO9781139028547.

Keller, T. (2023, June 21). Vocation: Discerning Your Calling. *Redeemer City to City*. http://storage.cloversites.com/highpeakfellowship/documents/Vocation-Discerning_Your_Calling.pdf

Kelly, C. (2006). *The Roman Empire: a very short introduction*. OUP Oxford. http://dx.doi.org/10.1093/actrade/9780192803917.001.0001.

Kidner, D. (1982). Sacrifice—Metaphors and Meaning. *Tyndale Bulletin, 33*, 119-136. http://dx.doi.org/10.53751/001c.30604.

Knobbe, A., Orie, J., Hofman, N., Van der Burgh, B., & Cachucho, R. (2017). Sports analytics for professional speed skating. *Data Mining and Knowledge Discovery, 31*(6), 1872-1902. http://dx.doi.org/10.1007/s10618-017-0512-3.

Knox, J. (1936). "Fourteen Years Later": A Note on the Pauline Chronology. *The Journal of Religion, 16*(3), 341-349. http://dx.doi.org/10.1086/481845.

Krugman, P. R. (1979). Increasing returns, monopolistic competition, and international trade. *Journal of international Economics, 9*(4), 469-479. http://dx.doi.org/10.1016/0022-1996(79)90017-5.

Lee, W. (1986). *God's New Testament Economy*. Living Stream Ministry.

Lel, U., & Miller, D. P. (2008). International cross-listing, firm performance, and top management turnover: A test of the bonding hypothesis. *The Journal of Finance, 63*(4), 1897-1937. http://dx.doi.org/10.1111/j.1540-6261.2008.01377.x.

León, A. K., & Pfeifer, C. (2013). *Religious activity, risk taking preferences, and financial behaviour: Empirical evidence from German survey data*. Inst. für Volkswirtschaftslehre. http://dx.doi.org/10.1016/j.socec.2017.05.005

Lerner, J. S., & Keltner, D. (2001). Fear, anger, and risk. *Journal of personality and social psychology, 81*(1), 146. http://dx.doi.org/10.1037/0022-3514.81.1.146.

Lev, B., & Radhakrishnan, S. (2005). The valuation of organization capital. In *Measuring capital in the new economy* (pp. 73-110). University of Chicago Press. http://dx.doi.org/10.7208/chicago/9780226116174.003.0004.

Levit, D. (2020). Words speak louder without actions. *The Journal of Finance, 75*(1), 91-131. http://dx.doi.org/10.1111/jofi.12834.

Lewis, C. S. (1939). Learning in War-time. *The Weight of Glory and Other Addresses*, 47-63. http://www.orcuttchristian.org/Lewis_Learning%20in%20War-Time.pdf

Lewis, C. S. (2001). *The problem of pain*. Zondervan.

Lewis, M. (2004). *Moneyball: The art of winning an unfair game*. WW Norton & Company.

Lincoln, A. T. (2004). *Paradise now and not yet: studies in the role of the heavenly dimension in Paul's thought with special reference to his eschatology* (Vol. 43). Cambridge University Press. http://dx.doi.org/10.1017/CBO9780511555008.

Lintner, J. (1965). Security prices, risk, and maximal gains from diversification. *The journal of finance, 20*(4), 587-615. http://dx.doi.org/10.2307/2977249.

Liu, T. (2011). Credence goods markets with conscientious and selfish experts. *International Economic Review, 52*(1), 227-244. http://dx.doi.org/10.1111/j.1468-2354.2010.00626.x.

Long, G. *The Discourses of Epictetus: With the Encheiridion and Fragments*. G. Bell and sons, 1890.

Loughran, T., & Ritter, J. R. (1996). Long-term market overreaction: The effect of low-priced stocks. *The Journal of Finance, 51*(5), 1959-1970. http://dx.doi.org/10.1111/j.1540-6261.1996.tb05234.x.

Lovett, M. J., Peres, R., & Shachar, R. (2013). On brands and word of mouth. *Journal of marketing research, 50*(4), 427-444. http://dx.doi.org/10.1509/jmr.11.0458.

Lowenstein, R. (2001). *When genius failed: The rise and fall of Long-Term Capital Management.* Random House trade paperbacks.

Mackay, C. (2012). *Extraordinary popular delusions and the madness of crowds.* Simon and Schuster. http://dx.doi.org/10.1037/14716-000.

Macrotrends. (2023, August 20). Warsaw, Poland Metro Area Population 1950-2022. *Macrotrends.* https://www.macrotrends.net/cities/22161/warsaw/population

Madden, J. F. (2012). Performance-support bias and the gender pay gap among stockbrokers. *Gender & Society, 26*(3), 488-518. http://dx.doi.org/10.1177/0891243212438546.

Malkiel, B. G. (1999). *A random walk down Wall Street: including a life-cycle guide to personal investing.* WW Norton & Company.

Malloch, T. R. (2011). *Doing virtuous business: The remarkable success of spiritual enterprise.* Thomas Nelson.

Mandela, N. (2008). *Long walk to freedom: The autobiography of Nelson Mandela* (pp. 364-365). Hachette UK.

Marinelli, A. (2020). Truth and Denial: Intertextual Compositions and Visual Transformations in the 'Caravaggisti' Gallery Paintings. *Object, 22*(1).

Marshak, A. K. (2015). *The many faces of Herod the Great* (p. xiii), Wm. B. Eerdmans Publishing.

Marshall, A. (2009). *Principles of economics: unabridged eighth edition.* Cosimo, Inc. http://dx.doi.org/10.1057/9781137375261.

Maslow, A. H. (1958). A Dynamic Theory of Human Motivation. http://dx.doi.org/10.1037/11305-004.

McGuire, S. T., Omer, T. C., & Sharp, N. Y. (2012). The impact of religion on financial reporting irregularities. *The Accounting Review, 87*(2), 645-673. http://dx.doi.org/10.2308/accr-10206.

McGuire, T. (2010). From emotions to spirituality: "Spiritual labor" as the commodification, codification, and regulation of organizational members' spirituality. *Management Communication Quarterly, 24*(1), 74-103. http://dx.doi.org/10.1177/0893318909351432.

McNeal, R. (2011). *A work of heart: Understanding how God shapes spiritual leaders* (Vol. 60, p. xix.). John Wiley & Sons.

Meta. (2021, October 28). *Introducing Meta: A Social Technology Company.* https://about.fb.com/news/2021/10/facebook-company-is-now-meta/.

Michael, M. (2011). Orpah and her interpreters: Evaluating the justifications for the traditional-stereotyped readings. *Old Testament Essays, 24*(2), 390-413.

Mintzberg, H. (2017). Developing theory about the development of theory. In S.W. Floyd & B. Wooldridge (Eds.), *Handbook of middle management strategy* process research (pp. 177-196). Edward Elgar Publishing. http://dx.doi.org/10.4337/9781783473250.

Mischel, W. (2015). *The marshmallow test: Why self-control is the engine of success.* New York: Little, Brown.

Mishler, C. J. (1983). Adults' perceptions of the benefits of a college degree. *Research in Higher Education, 19*(2), 213-230. http://dx.doi.org/10.1007/BF00974760.

Modigliani, F., & Miller, M. H. (1958). The cost of capital, corporation finance and the theory of investment. *The American economic review, 48*(3), 261-297.

Morgan, T. (2015). *Roman faith and Christian faith: Pistis and fides in the early roman empire and early Churches.* OUP Oxford. http://dx.doi.org/10.1093/acprof:oso/9780198724148.001.0001.

Morris, R. (2016). *The Blessed Life: Unlocking the Rewards of Generous Living.* Baker Books.

Morrow, W. S. (1998). Toxic religion and the daughters of Job. *Studies in Religion/Sciences Religieuses, 27*(3), 263-276. http://dx.doi.org/10.1177/000842989802700302.

Moxnes, H. (2004). *The economy of the kingdom: Social conflict and economic relations in Luke's Gospel* (Vol. 23). Wipf and Stock Publishers.

Munroe, M. (2011). *Understanding Your Place in God's Kingdom: Your Original Purpose for Existence* (p. 115). Destiny Image Publishers.

Murray, A. (2017). *Humility.* B&H Publishing Group.

Nekoei, A., & Seim, D. (2023). How do inheritances shape wealth inequality? Theory and evidence from Sweden. *The Review of Economic Studies, 90*(1), 463-498. http://dx.doi.org/10.1093/restud/rdac016.

Nelson, R. H. (2015). *Economics as religion: From Samuelson to Chicago and beyond.* Penn State Press. http://dx.doi.org/10.5325/j.ctv1rnpjqb.

Norman, E., Sirmans, S., & Benjamin, J. (1995). The historical environment of real estate returns. *Journal of Real Estate Portfolio Management, 1*(1), 1-24. http://dx.doi.org/10.1080/10835547.1995.12089516.

North, D. C. (1990). *Institutions, institutional change and economic performance.* Cambridge university press. http://dx.doi.org/10.1017/CBO9780511808678.

Nowalk, N. (2011, May). Pascal's God-Shaped Hole. *Harvard Ichthus.* https://harvardichthus.org/2011/05/pascal_hole/

Numan, M., & Young, L. J. (2016). Neural mechanisms of mother–infant bonding and pair bonding: Similarities, differences, and broader implications. *Hormones and behavior, 77,* 98-112. http://dx.doi.org/10.1016/j.yhbeh.2015.05.015.

Omartian, S. (2007). *The Power of a Praying® Wife.* Harvest House Publishers.

Online Library Learning Center. (2022). *A Network of Networks.* Board of Regents of the University System of Georgia. https://www.usg.edu/galileo/skills/unit07/internet07_02.phtml.

Operation Blessing. (2022, October). What We Do. *Operation Blessing.* https://www.ob.org/what-we-do/.

Osborn, N. D., & Hatton, H. A. (1999). *A handbook on Exodus* (pp. 25-26). United Bible Societies.

Osella, F., & Rudnyckyj, D. (2017). Introduction: Assembling market and religious moralities. *Religion and the Morality of the Market*, 1-28. http://dx.doi.org/10.1017/9781316888704.001.

Ostrom, E. (1990). *Governing the commons: The evolution of institutions for collective action.* Cambridge university press. http://dx.doi.org/10.1017/CBO9780511807763.

Oxley, Michael et al. (2002, July 30). H.R. 3763 - Sarbanes-Oxley Act of 2002. *Congress.gov.* https://www.congress.gov/bill/107th-congress/house-bill/3763.

Pamment, M. (1983). John 3: 5:'Unless one is born of water and the Spirit, he cannot enter the kingdom of God.'. *Novum Testamentum, 25*(2), 189-190.

Parboteeah, K. P., Walter, S. G., & Block, J. H. (2015). When does Christian religion matter for entrepreneurial activity? The contingent effect of a country's investments into knowledge. *Journal of Business Ethics, 130*(2), 447-465. http://dx.doi.org/10.1007/s10551-014-2239-z

Paul, John II, His Holiness. (1979, June 2). Apostolic Journey to Poland, Welcoming Ceremony in Warsaw. *The Holy See.* https://www.vatican.va/content/john-paul-ii/en/speeches/1979/june/documents/hf_jp-ii_spe_19790602_polonia-varsavia-okecie-arrival.html

People's Bank of China. (2003). *Law of the People's Republic of China on The People's Bank of China.* http://www.pbc.gov.cn/english/130733/2941519/2015082610501049304.pdf.

Perry, A. (2017). The Suffering Servant of Isaiah and the Suffering of Job. http://www.biblaridion.info/Proverbs/Perry_JOB.pdf.

Pew Research Center. (2011, December 19). *Global Christianity – A Report on the Size and Distribution of the World's Christian Population.* https://www.pewresearch.org/religion/2011/12/19/global-christianity-exec/.

Pfeiffer, C., & Harrison, E. (Eds.). (1962). *The Wycliffe Bible Commentary.* Moody Publishers.

Phelps, E. S. (1962). The accumulation of risky capital: A sequential utility analysis. *Econometrica: Journal of the Econometric Society*, 729-743. http://dx.doi.org/10.2307/1909322.

Piketty, T. (2014). *Capital in the twenty-first century.* Harvard University Press. http://dx.doi.org/10.4159/9780674369542.

Piketty, T. (2020). *Capital and ideology.* Harvard University Press. http://dx.doi.org/10.4159/9780674245075.

Pittenger, D. J. (1993). The utility of the Myers-Briggs type indicator. *Review of educational research, 63*(4), 467-488. http://dx.doi.org/10.3102/00346543063004467.

Prescott, E. C., & Visscher, M. (1980). Organization capital. *Journal of political Economy, 88*(3), 446-461. http://dx.doi.org/10.1086/260879.

Prince, D. (2002). *Shaping history through prayer and fasting* (p. 42). Whitaker House.

Qin, D. (2020). Samuel Lamb's Exhortation Regarding Eternal Rewards: A Socio-Political Perspective. *Studies in World Christianity, 26*(1), 63-83. http://dx.doi.org/10.3366/swc.2020.0282.

Rackham, R. B. (1901). *The Acts of the Apostles: An Exposition* (p. 65). Methuen.

Rackham, R. B. (1901). *Westminster Commentaries* (Vol. 44, 1.1, p. 5). Methuen.

Radelet, S. (2015). *The great surge: The ascent of the developing world.* Simon and Schuster.

Rainer, T. S. (2014). *Autopsy of a deceased church: 12 ways to keep yours alive.* B&H Publishing Group.

Ramsey, D., & Ramsey, S. (1997). *Financial peace.* Viking.

Remler, Dahlia (2014, April 14). Are 90% of academic papers really never cited? Reviewing the literature on academic citations. *The London School of Economics and Political Science.* https://blogs.lse.ac.uk/impactofsocialsciences/2014/04/23/academic-papers-citation-rates-remler/.

Reuschling, W. C. (2014). The Means and End in 2 Peter 1: 3—11: The Theological and Moral Significance of" Theōsis". *Journal of Theological Interpretation, 8*(2), 275-286. http://dx.doi.org/10.2307/26373929.

Rhodes, M., Holt, R., & Fikkert, B. (2018). *Practicing the King's Economy: Honoring Jesus in how We Work, Earn, Spend, Save, and Give.* Baker Books.

Richard, E. (2000). *Reading 1 Peter, Jude, and 2 Peter: A literary and theological commentary* (pp. 65-66). Smyth & Helwys Publishing, Inc.

Robertson, P., & Slosser, B. (1982). *The Secret Kingdom: A Promise of Hope and Freedom in a World of Turmoil.* T. Nelson.

Roller, B. (2021). The Treasure Principle Reconsidered: Storing Up True Treasures in Heaven. *Journal of Biblical Integration in Business, 24*(1).

Root, A. (2022, September). *LeBron gets it more than Jamie does.* LinkedIn. https://www.linkedin.com/pulse/lebron-gets-more-than-jamie-does-andrew-root/?trackingId=fM3ICdlZ0TZpic38pMADVA%3D%3D.

Root, A., & Yung, K. (2022). Resolving agency and product market views of cash holdings. *Research in International Business and Finance, 59,* 101518. http://dx.doi.org/10.1016/j.ribaf.2021.101518.

Rothbard, M. N. (1990). Karl Marx: Communist as religious eschatologist. In *The Review of Austrian Economics* (pp. 123-179). Springer, Dordrecht. http://dx.doi.org/10.1007/BF02426366.

Ruffle, B. J., & Shtudiner, Z. E. (2015). Are good-looking people more employable?. *Management Science, 61*(8), 1760-1776. http://dx.doi.org/10.1287/mnsc.2014.1927.

Salzman, D., & Zwinkels, R. C. (2017). Behavioral real estate. *Journal of Real Estate Literature, 25*(1), 77-106. http://dx.doi.org/10.1080/10835547.2017.12090455.

Sanchez-Munoz et al. (2021, December 16). The World's Top Recipients of Foreign Direct Investments. *International Monetary Fund.* https://blogs.imf.org/2021/12/16/the-worlds-top-recipients-of-foreign-direct-investment/.

Schnabel, E. J. (2010). *Acts* (p. 334). Zondervan Academic. http://dx.doi.org/10.2307/26424315.

Schürer, E. (1891). *A history of the Jewish people in the time of Jesus Christ* (Vol. 5, pp. 409-410). Scribner.

Schweizer, E. (1975). *The good news according to Matthew* (pp. 252-254). Westminster John Knox Press.

Scott, W. R. (2008). *Institutions and organizations: Ideas and interests.* Sage.

Segal, A. F. (1986). *Rebecca's children: Judaism and Christianity in the Roman world* (pp. 93-94), Harvard University Press.

Seuss. (2015). *How the Grinch Stole Christmas!.* Random House Books for Young Readers.

Shapiro, S. P. (2005). Agency theory. *Annual review of sociology,* 263-284. http://dx.doi.org/10.1146/annurev.soc.31.041304.122159.

Sharfman, K. (2006). The Law and Economics of Hoarding. *Loyola Consumer Law Review, 19*(2), 179.

Sharma, A., Pillai, D. R., Lu, M., Doolan, C., Leal, J., Kim, J., & Hollis, A. (2020). Impact of isolation precautions on quality of life: a meta-analysis. *Journal of Hospital Infection, 105*(1), 35-42. http://dx.doi.org/10.1016/j.jhin.2020.02.004.

Sharpe, W. F. (1977). The capital asset pricing model: a "multi-beta" interpretation. In *Financial Dec Making Under Uncertainty* (pp. 127-135). Academic Press. http://dx.doi.org/10.1016/B978-0-12-445850-5.50011-8.

Shaw, M. R. (2010). *Global awakening: How 20th-century revivals triggered a Christian revolution.* InterVarsity Press.

Shefrin, H., & Statman, M. (1985). The disposition to sell winners too early and ride losers too long: Theory and evidence. *The Journal of finance, 40*(3), 777-790. http://dx.doi.org/10.1111/j.1540-6261.1985.tb05002.x.

Shu, T., Sulaeman, J., & Yeung, P. E. (2012). Local religious beliefs and mutual fund risk-taking behaviors. *Management Science, 58*(10), 1779-1796. http://dx.doi.org/10.1287/mnsc.1120.1525.

Smith, A. (1869). *An Inquiry into the Nature and Causes of the Wealth of Nations, volume 1* (Vol. 1). Oxford: Clarendon Press. http://dx.doi.org/10.1093/oseo/instance.00043218.

Snyder, C. R. (2002). Hope theory: Rainbows in the mind. *Psychological inquiry, 13*(4), 249-275.

Soelle, D. (1989). *Suffering* (p. 1). Fortress Press.

Soller, M. (2019). Joseph and the enslavement of the Egyptians. *The Jewish Bible quarterly, 47*(1), 39-44.

Solow, R. M. (1963). *Capital theory and the rate of return* (p. 14). Amsterdam: North-Holland Publishing Company.

Solow, R. M. (1987, December 8). Growth Theory and After. *NobelPrize.org.* https://www.nobelprize.org/prizes/economic-sciences/1987/solow/lecture/

Sproul, R. C. (2013). *The holiness of God.* Tyndale House Publishers, Inc.

Sproul, R.C. (2014, August 15). What's the Difference between the Ontological and Economic Trinity. *Ligonier.* https://www.ligonier.org/learn/articles/whats-difference-between-ontological-and-economic-trinity.

Spurgeon, C. (1894). THE METROPOLITAN TABERNACLE PULPIT VOL. 36.

Stapleford, J. E. (2015). *Bulls, bears and golden calves: Applying Christian ethics in economics.* InterVarsity Press.

Stark, R., & Bainbridge, W. S. (1985). *The future of religion: Secularization, revival, and cult formation.* Univ of California Press. http://dx.doi.org/10.1525/9780520341340.

Stark, T., & Van Deventer, H. J. (2009). The 'Jezebel spirit': A scholarly inquiry. *Verbum et Ecclesia, 30*(2), 68-76. http://dx.doi.org/10.4102/ve.v30i2.301.

Starr, R. M. (1989). The structure of exchange in barter and monetary economies. In *General Equilibrium Models of Monetary Economies* (pp. 129-143). Academic Press. http://dx.doi.org/10.1016/B978-0-12-663970-4.50014-1.

Statista Research Department. (2022, October 9). Largest stock exchange operators worldwide as of August 2022, by market capitalization of listed companies. *Statista.* https://www.statista.com/statistics/270126/largest-stock-exchange-operators-by-market-capitalization-of-listed-companies/.

Statman, M. (1995). A Behavioral Framework for Dollar-Cost Averaging. *The Journal of Portfolio Management, 22*(1), 70-78. http://dx.doi.org/10.3905/jpm.1995.409537.

Stegemann, E., & Stegemann, W. (1999). *Jesus movement: A social history of its first century.* A&C Black.

Stewart, E. C. (2012). New Testament space/spatiality. *Biblical Theology Bulletin, 42*(3), 139-150. http://dx.doi.org/10.1177/0146107912452245.

Stott, J. (2014). *The Message of the Sermon on the Mount.* InterVarsity Press.

Stott, J. (2014). *The message of Romans: God's good news for the world.* InterVarsity Press.

Strong, J. (2009). *Strong's exhaustive concordance of the Bible.* Hendrickson Publishers.

Subrahmanyam, A. (2010). The cross-section of expected stock returns: what have we learnt from the past twenty-five years of research?. *European Financial Management, 16*(1), 27-42. http://dx.doi.org/10.1111/j.1468-036X.2009.00520.x.

Summers, L. H. (1982). *The Nonadjustment of Nominal Interest Rates: A Study of the Fisher Effect* (No. 0836). National Bureau of Economic Research, Inc.

Sumney, Jerry L. (2007) *The Book of Tobit. In Saint Mary's Press College Study Bible,* 587-88. Winona, MN: Saint Mary's Press.

Tanzi, V. (1980). Inflationary expectations, economic activity, taxes, and interest rates. *The American Economic Review, 70*(1), 12-21.

Ten Boom, C., Sherrill, E., & Sherrill, J. (2006). *The hiding place.* Chosen Books.

Tenney, M. C. (1997). *John: the gospel of belief.* Wm. B. Eerdmans Publishing.

Tessier, R., Cristo, M., Velez, S., Girón, M., de Calume, S. Z. F., Ruiz-Paláez, J. G., ... & Charpak, N. (1998). Kangaroo mother care and the bonding hypothesis. *Pediatrics, 102*(2), e17-e17. http://dx.doi.org/10.1542/peds.102.2.e17.

The Genome Sequencing Consortium. (2001). Initial sequencing and analysis of the human genome. *Nature.409 (6822),* 860-921. https://doi.org/10.1073/pnas.90.10.4338.

The Holy Father, Francis. (2015, May 24). On Care For Our Common Home. *The Holy See.* https://www.vatican.va/content/dam/francesco/pdf/encyclicals/documents/papa-francesco_20150524_enciclica-laudato-si_en.pdf

Thompson, M. M. (2001). *The God of the gospel of John.* Wm. B. Eerdmans Publishing.

Thornton, J. (2001). Age Structure and the Personal Savings Rate in the United States, 1956-1995. *Southern Economic Journal, 68*(1), 166-170.

Tomasi, J. (2012). Free market fairness. In *Free Market Fairness.* Princeton University Press. http://dx.doi.org/10.23943/princeton/9780691144467.001.0001.

Tozer, A. W. (2015). *Born after midnight.* Moody Publishers.

Turvey, R. (1964). Review of Location and land use by William Alonso. *American Economic Review, 54,* 844-845.

Tyndale, & Tyndale House Publishers. (2004). *Life Application Study Bible: New Living Translation* (p. 160). Tyndale House Publishers, Inc.

US Patent and Trademark Office. (2021, May 31) U.S. Patent Statistics Chart Calendar Years 1963-220. U.S. *Patent and Trademark Office, Patent Technology Monitoring Team (PTMT).* https://www.uspto.gov/web/offices/ac/ido/oeip/taf/us_stat.htm

US Securities and Exchange Commission. (2021). *SEC Announces Enforcement Results for FY 2021.* https://www.sec.gov/news/press-release/2021-238.

Van Essen, M., Otten, J., & Carberry, E. J. (2015). Assessing managerial power theory: A meta-analytic approach to understanding the determinants of CEO compensation. *Journal of management, 41*(1), 164-202. http://dx.doi.org/10.1177/0149206311429378.

Vine, W. E., & Unger, M. (1996). *Vine's complete expository dictionary of Old and New Testament words: with topical index.* Thomas Nelson. p140.

Viola, F., & Barna, G. (2010). *Pagan Christianity?: Exploring the roots of our church practices.* Tyndale House Publishers, Inc.

Votaw, C. W. (1905). The Chronology of Jesus' Public Ministry. *The Biblical World, 26*(6), 425-430. http://dx.doi.org/10.1086/473674.

Wagner, W. H., & Lau, S. C. (1971). The effect of diversification on risk. *Financial Analysts Journal, 27*(6), 48-53. http://dx.doi.org/10.2469/faj.v27.n5.48.

Walljasper, J. (2011). Elinor Ostrom's 8 Principles for Managing A Commons. *On the Commons, 446.*

Walls, D., & Anders, M. E. (1999). *Holman New Testament Commentary-1 and 2 Peter, 1 2 and 3 John and Jude* (Vol. 11, pp. 108-109). B&H Publishing Group.

Weber, M., Parsons, T., & Tawney, R. H. (1930). *The Protestant Ethic and the Spirit of Capitalism. Translated by Talcott Parsons... With a Foreword by RH Tawney.* G. Allen & Unwin. http://dx.doi.org/10.4324/9780203995808.

Wendt, A. (1999). *Social theory of international politics* (Vol. 67, p. 211). Cambridge University Press. http://dx.doi.org/10.1017/CBO9780511612183.

Westphal, J. D. (1999). Collaboration in the boardroom: Behavioral and performance consequences of CEO-board social ties. *Academy of management Journal, 42*(1), 7-24. http://dx.doi.org/10.2307/256871.

Whitwell, C. (2009). The variation of nature in Ecclesiastes 11. *Journal for the Study of the Old Testament, 34*(1), 81-97. http://dx.doi.org/10.1177/0309089209346354.

Wilberforce, W. (2011). *The Correspondence of William Wilberforce* (Vol. 2, p. 273). Cambridge University Press. http://dx.doi.org/10.1017/CBO9780511792052.

Wilberforce, W. (2021, June). William Wilberforce papers, 1782-1837 and undated (1819 Journal, pp. 45). *Duke University Libraries, Archives & Manuscripts Collection Guides.* https://archives.lib.duke.edu/catalog/wilberf.

Wilkinson, B. (2010). *The prayer of Jabez: Breaking through to the blessed life.* Multnomah.

Williams, C. C. (1996). The new barter economy: an appraisal of Local Exchange and Trading Systems (LETS). *Journal of Public Policy, 16*(1), 85-101. http://dx.doi.org/10.1017/S0143814X0000787X.

Williams, J. J. (2021). *Redemptive Kingdom Diversity: A Biblical Theology of the People of God.* Baker Academic.

Williamson, O. E. (1981). The economics of organization: The transaction cost approach. *American journal of sociology, 87*(3), 548-577. http://dx.doi.org/10.1086/227496.

Wittmann, M., & Lehnhoff, S. (2005). Age effects in perception of time. *Psychological reports, 97*(3), 921-935. http://dx.doi.org/10.2466/pr0.97.3.921-935.

Wolterstorff, N. (1998). Divine discourse: Philosophical reflections on the claim that God speaks. *Pro Ecclesia, 7*(2), 242-244. p8. http://dx.doi.org/10.1177/106385129800700210.

Woods, R. (2004). Exploring the emotional territory for brands. *Journal of Consumer Behaviour: An International Research Review, 3*(4), 388-403. http://dx.doi.org/10.1002/cb.150.

Wright, A. G. (1982). The Widow's Mites: Praise or Lament?—A Matter of Context. *The Catholic Biblical Quarterly, 44*(2), 256-265.

Yancey, P., & Stafford, T. (2011). *NIV, Student Bible* (p. 1167). Zondervan.

Young, L. A. (2016). *Rational choice theory and religion: Summary and assessment* (p. 26). Routledge.

Zohar, D., & Marshall, I. (2004). *Spiritual capital: Wealth we can live by.* Berrett-Koehler Publishers.

Subject index

A

B

C

I

J

K

L

M

O

P

R

S

T

V

W

Bible chapter index

1

2

A

H

I

J

L

M

N

P

R

T

Z

www.ingramcontent.com/pod-product-compliance
Lightning Source LLC
LaVergne TN
LVHW010722210926
848485LV00007B/1418/J

* 9 7 8 1 6 4 8 8 9 7 5 7 3 *